Economic Commission for Europe
Geneva

ECONOMIC SURVEY
OF EUROPE

2005 No. 1

Prepared by the
SECRETARIAT OF THE
ECONOMIC COMMISSION FOR EUROPE
GENEVA

UNITED NATIONS
New York and Geneva, 2005

PER
UNI
E/ECE
E IS7

ungov
HC
240
.A1
UN5

NOTE

The present *Survey* is the fifty-eighth in a series of annual reports prepared by the secretariat of the United Nations Economic Commission for Europe to serve the needs of the Commission and of the United Nations in reporting on and analysing world economic conditions.

The Survey is published on the sole responsibility of the Executive Secretary of the ECE and the views expressed in it should not be attributed to the Commission or to its participating governments.

The designations employed and the presentation of the material in this publication do not imply the expression of any opinion whatsoever on the part of the Secretariat of the United Nations concerning the legal status of any country, territory, city or area, or of its authorities, or concerning the delimitation of its frontiers or boundaries.

The analysis in this issue is based on data and information available to the secretariat in mid-December 2004.

UNITED NATIONS PUBLICATION
Sales No. E.05.II.E.7
ISBN 92-1-116922-4 ISSN 0070-8712

CONTENTS

LIST OF TABLES

LIST OF CHARTS

LIST OF BOXES

EXPLANATORY NOTES

The following symbols have been used throughout this *Survey*:

    .. = not available or not pertinent

    – = nil or negligible

    * = estimate by the secretariat of the Economic Commission for Europe

    | = break in series

In referring to a combination of years, the use of an oblique stroke (e.g. 1998/99) signifies a 12-month period (say, from 1 July 1998 to 30 June 1999). The use of a hyphen (e.g. 1999-2001) normally signifies either an average of, or a total for, the full period of calendar years covered (including the end-years indicated).

Unless the contrary is stated, the standard unit of weight used throughout is the metric ton. The definition of "billion" used throughout is a thousand million. The definition of "trillion" used throughout is a thousand billion. Minor discrepancies in totals and percentages are due to rounding.

References to dollars ($) are to United States dollars unless otherwise specified.

The membership of the United Nations Economic Commission for Europe (UNECE) consists of all the states of western Europe, eastern Europe, the Commonwealth of Independent States (CIS), North America and Israel.

The term EU-15 refers to the aggregate of the following 15 member states of the European Union: Austria, Belgium, Denmark, Finland, France, Germany, Greece, Ireland, Italy, Luxembourg, Netherlands, Portugal, Spain, Sweden and the United Kingdom.

EU-25 refers to the 15 above-mentioned member states plus the 10 countries that joined the European Union in May 2004: Cyprus, Czech Republic, Estonia, Hungary, Latvia, Lithuania, Malta, Poland, Slovakia and Slovenia.

WECEE comprises the EU-25 plus the countries of Iceland, Norway and Switzerland.

EU-8 (central Europe and Baltic states) includes the new member states listed above excluding Cyprus and Malta.

For the convenience in presentation, countries are sometimes grouped into the following subregions, based on geographical proximity:

- Baltic states: Estonia, Latvia and Lithuania;

- Central Europe: Czech Republic, Hungary, Poland, Slovakia and Slovenia;

- South-east Europe: Albania, Bosnia and Herzegovina, Bulgaria, Croatia, Romania, Serbia and Montenegro, The former Yugoslav Republic of Macedonia and Turkey;

- Caucasian CIS: Armenia, Azerbaijan and Georgia;

- Central Asian CIS: Kazakhstan, Kyrgyzstan, Tajikistan, Turkmenistan and Uzbekistan;

- European CIS (excluding Russia): Belarus, Republic of Moldova and Ukraine.

ABBREVIATIONS

BBC	British Broadcasting Corporation
BEC	broad economic category
BIS	Bank for International Settlements
CEFTA	Central European Free Trade Agreement
CEPR	Center for Economic Policy Research
c.i.f.	cost, insurance, freight
CIS	Commonwealth of Independent States
CMEA	(former) Council for Mutual Economic Assistance
CPI	consumer price index
ECB	European Central Bank
ECE	Economic Commission for Europe
ECLAC	Economic Commission for Latin America and the Caribbean
EITO	European Information Technology Observatory
EME	ECE emerging market economies
EMU	Economic and Monetary Union
ERM-2	Exchange Rate Mechanism-2 (of the EU)
EU	European Union
EURIBOR	euro interbank offered rate
FDI	foreign direct investment
FTA	Free Trade Agreement
G7	Group of Seven
G-20	Group of Twenty
GATT	General Agreement on Tariffs and Trade
GDP	gross domestic product
HICP	Harmonized Index of Consumer Prices
HWWA	Hamburgisches Welt-Wirtschafts-Archiv (Hamburg Institute of International Economics)
ICT	information and communication technologies
IDA	International Development Association (of the World Bank)
IEA	International Energy Agency
IFI	international financial institution
IIF	Institute of International Finance
ILO	International Labour Office

IMD	International Institute of Management Development
IMF	International Monetary Fund
ISM	Institute for Supply Management
LFS	labour force survey
NBER	National Bureau of Economic Research
OECD	Organisation for Economic Co-operation and Development
OPT	outward processing trade
PMI	Purchasing Managers' Index
PPI	producer price index
PPP	purchasing power parity
R&D	research and development
SITC	Standard International Trade Classification
SME	small and medium enterprises
TACIS	Technical Assistance for the Commonwealth of Independent States (of the EU)
ULC	unit labour costs
UNCTAD	United Nations Conference on Trade and Development
UNECE	United Nations Economic Commission for Europe
VAT	value added tax
WEF	World Economic Forum
WIFO	Österreichisches Institut für Wirtschaftsforschung (Austrian Institute of Economic Research)
WTO	World Trade Organization

ACKNOWLEDGEMENTS

This *Survey* was prepared, under the general direction and on the responsibility of the Executive Secretary, Brigita Schmögnerová, by a team led by Rumen Dobrinsky, Dieter Hesse and Robert Shelburne. Abdur Chowdhury, Director, Economic Analysis Division (EAD), was responsible for overall production.

The other members of the team included Laura Altinger, Fabrizio Carmignani, Jaromir Cekota, Handan Del Pozzo, Nikolai Dmitrevsky, Vitalija Gaucaite-Wittich, Ralph Heinrich, Robert Nowak, José Palacín and Rolf Traeger. Chapter 7 is the revised version of a paper presented by Karl Aiginger at the UNECE Spring Seminar on *Competitiveness and Economic Growth in the ECE Region*, held in Geneva in February 2004.

The statistical data were prepared by the Statistics Division of the ECE under the general supervision of Darryl Rhoades, Daniel Bachmann and Serguei Malanitchev. Victoria Goudeva and Laurence Mancini provided research assistance. Parts of the manuscript were edited by Praveen Bhalla. Felirose Gutierrez, Kris Miller and Jelena Torbica, EAD's Publication Production Team, were responsible for table production, copy-editing, and electronic formatting of the report. The support, comments and contributions from members of other Divisions in the ECE are noted with appreciation.

FOREWORD

The global economy performed quite favourably in 2004. The recovery spread to all major regions and the average rate of economic growth was the highest in three decades. That such a performance was possible despite the large increase in crude oil prices is testimony to the much greater resilience of economic activity in most of the major economies to oil price shocks than in the 1970s and 1980s.

A striking feature of Europe is the contrast between the persistence of moderate growth in the euro area and the economic dynamism in most of the rest of the region. In the euro area, the recovery, which had relied largely on exports, weakened significantly in the second half of 2004. Current forecasts, however, assume that this is only a pause before growth resumes, albeit at a moderate rate, in the course of 2005. In the new EU member states and in south-east Europe, economic growth has continued at much higher rates than in the "old" EU member countries. Their relatively high rates of growth have been broadly based on robust domestic demand and rapid export growth, and the outlook for 2005 is that this relatively strong performance will be maintained.

The CIS, together with developing Asia, was one of the two fastest growing regions of the world economy in 2004 (as in 2003). Rapid growth was propelled by the surge in international demand and prices for primary commodities and associated spillover effects on domestic demand. CIS growth is also expected to be maintained at a high rate in 2005.

The global economic outlook, however, remains subject to a number of major downside risks. A major challenge is how to achieve a gradual reversal of the United States huge current account deficit without triggering disruptive capital flows and a possible financial crisis with the risk of a serious setback for global economic growth. This is not only a task for the United States but one that will require a high degree of collaboration and policy coordination among the major economies. A stronger rate of growth of domestic demand in Europe, especially in the euro area, would be an important element in supporting a gradual adjustment in the United States external balance.

Despite their moderate impact in 2004, if oil prices remain at a high level they could eventually dampen global economic activity, at least in the short and medium term. The short-term outlook for Europe, moreover, is sensitive to developments in the foreign exchange markets: a further sharp depreciation of the dollar would most likely put a brake on the recovery. Disruptions to and increased instability of international capital flows, with consequent pressures for higher interest rates, would also adversely effect the ECE emerging market economies, given their reliance on foreign capital to finance their current account deficits. The fortunes of the CIS region are closely linked to developments in the international markets for oil and other raw materials.

Benchmarks for gauging relative economic performance differ across individual countries and regions. For the more advanced west European countries, a major target is to strengthen their competitiveness in order to catch up with the level of real income in the United States. The European Union's Lisbon Agenda is designed to promote this process, but so far has been falling short of its ambitious targets. The recent review and proposed streamlining of the strategy is perhaps a first step towards closing the gap between the rhetoric and actual implementation of the required policies.

In fact, the large gap in real income between the United States and the European Union reflects not so much differences in productivity (in terms of output per hour worked) but rather the lower proportion of persons of working age actually in work and, to a lesser extent, the smaller number of total hours worked per worker in Europe. This explains why increasing the employment rate is a major objective of the EU. But raising competitiveness, growth and employment will not be possible without much higher rates of investment in major growth factors such as education and training, research and innovation, and in ways to accelerate the diffusion of advanced technologies. Such investment may need to be complemented by further reforms of product and labour markets, but it will especially require a more flexible macroeconomic policy framework that will underpin business confidence that GDP growth will be sustained at rates above those of recent years. A reform of the EU's fiscal policy framework is therefore urgently needed. Moreover, monetary policy in the euro area is too narrowly focused on price stability to the exclusion of other objectives, namely the achievement of a high level of employment and sustained economic growth, that are accepted by central banks elsewhere.

In the new EU member states and south-east Europe, the challenge is to sustain sufficiently high rates of growth that will allow them to continue catching up with the real income levels of western Europe. The *acquis communautaire* as well as the Copenhagen criteria provide them with anchors for the necessary deepening of institutional reforms; this is also the case for the prospective member states for which the prospect of membership is a major incentive for reform. A key requirement is to improve the quality of education systems in order to meet the skill requirements of increasingly knowledge-based economies. These countries have been drawing extensively on the excess savings of the rest of the world to promote the renewal of their productive capacity, a normal feature for their stage of development. But in several of them the associated cumulative current account deficits are now quite large and, in some cases, also appear to be increasingly driven by consumption rather than fixed investment. Such a pattern is not sustainable in the medium term. There is therefore a need for domestic policies to reduce these deficits to more sustainable levels. This will reduce their vulnerability to sudden changes in investor sentiment, which can trigger capital outflows and the risk of a currency crisis. The need for more prudent policies could become more acute in 2005 if international interest rates rise significantly more than currently expected.

Despite the current economic boom in the CIS, there is a real need to broaden the basis of economic activity and thereby reduce the vulnerability of the member states to adverse developments in the international commodity markets. This is evidently a longer-term agenda, which will not only require structural and institutional reforms on a broad front but also the design of a strategic industrial policy. The European Union's "New Neighbourhood" Policy may be helpful in this context, especially if it includes the promotion of institutional development geared to the specific socio-economic circumstances in these countries, greater access to the EU market, facilitation of labour mobility and effectual levels of technical assistance.

The search for sustained and rapid rates of growth in much of the ECE region is taking place under conditions of intensified competitive pressures arising especially, but not only, from the emergence of China and India as important suppliers of manufactured products and, to a lesser extent, certain services. Each country has to find its own niche in the evolving international division of labour, but doing so is becoming more difficult for middle-income countries, including many of those in central and eastern Europe. On the one hand they are subject to intense competitive pressures from low-wage, developing countries, but, on the other, they are not yet in a position to compete effectively in the markets for high-tech, knowledge-intensive products. At the same time there are also increasing concerns in some of the more advanced economies at the alleged adverse labour market implications of "outsourcing" higher-skilled activities. More generally, there is a need to develop appropriate institutions and effective economic policies to deal with the adjustment costs originating in the process of globalization; if these costs are ignored – and they can affect both labour and capital – the consequence is likely to be a resurgence of protectionist pressures.

Brigita Schmögnerová
Executive Secretary
Economic Commission for Europe

CHAPTER 1

THE ECONOMIC SITUATION IN THE ECE REGION AND SELECTED POLICY ISSUES

1.1 Europe and the CIS in 2004-2005

(i) Major developments

A favourable global context for Europe and the CIS

Overall, 2004 was a very good year for the world economy. The recovery continued at a robust rate, although the sharp rise in oil prices dampened the cyclical momentum in the course of the year. The United States and China remained the principal engines of global growth. In the United States, the recovery continued to be driven by strong domestic demand and accommodative economic policies. In China, the long economic boom abated slightly due to headwinds from the rise in energy prices and measures to check overheating and achieve a soft landing. Hopes that in Japan the economy would finally achieve a sustained recovery were frustrated. Global inflation remained moderate despite the upward pressures on energy prices. Emerging markets continued to benefit from favourable financing conditions in the international capital markets, with risk premia remaining at very low levels.   In the foreign exchange markets, the dollar came under renewed selling pressure in the second half of 2004, reflecting concerns over the widening United States current account deficit and persistently high fiscal deficits.

The increase in the external imbalances between the major economies, however, poses a major threat to the stability of the world economy. A major policy challenge is to achieve an orderly realignment of the exchange rates of major currencies. Redressing these global imbalances without disruptive exchange rate movements will require appropriate national and international economic policy responses (section 1.2(i)).

A permanent upward shift of oil prices?

In mid-December 2004, oil prices had fallen by some $10 per barrel from their record level (in nominal terms) of more than $50 per barrel in October 2004. To some extent this fall may reflect the lingering volatility of assessments concerning the short-term balance of supply and demand, and also a reduced presence of speculators in the oil markets. But there appears to be a broad consensus that high oil prices are likely to be a feature of the world economy for many years to come. This is based on the projected strong rise in demand for oil and

other energy products in rapidly growing (and industrializing) emerging market economies such as China and India. These countries, moreover, are still characterized by relatively low levels of energy efficiency. The recent surge in global demand for oil has also coincided with relatively tight supply capacities, given a lack of sufficient investment in the development of new oil fields in recent years. Enhancing oil supply capacity will not only take time but is also subject to large risks and constraints, including those imposed by environmental concerns. This situation makes oil prices vulnerable to interruptions of supply due to unforeseen developments, including geopolitical uncertainties.   A significant and permanent increase in oil prices will inevitably have negative effects on levels of output in the oil importing countries in the short and medium run. But in the long run, higher oil prices should stimulate investment to improve energy efficiency and accelerate the process of substitution away from oil to other forms of energy (including renewable energy sources such as wind, sun and hydroelectric power), thereby reducing the vulnerability of the global economy to new oil price shocks. An appropriate orientation of energy policies can foster this process, also taking into account the need to ensure security of energy supplies and to curb carbon emissions from the burning of fossil fuels.

Rising oil prices moderately dampen the cyclical momentum in 2004

The sharp rise in oil prices in 2004, so far, appears to have had only a relatively moderate negative impact on global economic activity. This is reflected in the fact that demand for crude oil (in volume) rose at its fastest rate in nearly 30 years. The growth of global output and incomes has thus clearly dominated the dampening effects on oil demand resulting from higher prices. About half of the rise in oil demand in 2004 was due to China and the United States.

The impact of a given rise in oil prices on economic growth and inflation in western Europe and North America is now much smaller compared with the 1970s or 1980s because of the substantial decline in the oil intensity of output.[1] The resilience of the advanced industrialized

---

[1] Oil intensity of output is defined as oil consumption (in physical units) per unit of real GDP.

countries to oil price shocks has also been strengthened by more flexible product and labour markets. In Europe, the appreciation of the euro and other currencies against the dollar also mitigated the adverse impact. In several major Asian economies final energy users were shielded by retail and wholesale price controls (and associated oil subsidies) from the full impact of rising world market prices.[2]

It is noteworthy that so-called second-round effects of higher oil prices were largely absent in 2004. The oil price shock therefore had little, if any, impact on the stance of monetary policy in the major economies, given the persistently low rates of core inflation. Although the subject of extensive research, the impact of oil prices on economic activity remains difficult to assess, and estimates are surrounded by a large margin of uncertainty.[3] The impact will vary across regions depending, *inter alia*, on the oil intensity of economic activity, the share of oil imports in total energy consumption and on economic policy responses. (It goes without saying that rising oil prices tend to boost economic activity in the oil exporting countries.) What is also difficult to gauge is the extent to which rising energy prices affect business and consumer confidence, with attendant negative effects on spending propensities. The reason is that, apart from raising energy input costs and reducing real disposable incomes, a surge in oil prices increases uncertainty about future price developments and the economic outlook in general.

Western Europe's recovery lost momentum

In western Europe, the cyclical recovery lost significant momentum in the second half of 2004. Export growth, which had been leading the recovery, weakened against the background of a moderate slowdown in the global economy. Domestic demand was sluggish and consequently lacked the vigour to offset the weakening of external demand. Business confidence was dampened by the sharp appreciation of the euro in the final weeks of 2004. Real GDP in western Europe rose by 2.2 per cent in 2004. In the euro area, the increase was slightly lower at 1.9 per cent (table 1.1.1). Economic activity continued to be supported by low interest rates, but the accelerating apreciation of the euro in the second half of 2004 led to a further tightening of monetary conditions. Fiscal policy in the euro area was slightly expansionary in 2004.

...but growth was robust in central and eastern Europe and the CIS

Economic activity in the eight new EU member states from central and eastern Europe (EU-8) picked up

---

[2] IEA, *Oil Market Report* (Paris), 10 December 2004, p. 12 [www.oilmarketreport.org]. To the extent that these energy subsidies are not sustainable, the adjustment costs to higher world market prices are, of course, only postponed.

[3] R. Barrel and O. Pomerantz, "Oil prices and the world economy", Austrian National Bank, *Focus on European Economic Integration*, 1/2004 (Vienna), pp. 152-177. See also UNECE, *Economic Survey of Europe, 2004 No. 2*, p. 5, box 1.1.1.

TABLE 1.1.1

Annual changes in real GDP in Europe, North America and Japan, 2002-2005

(Percentage change over the previous year)

	2002	2003	2004 [a]	2005 [a]
France	1.2	0.5	2.2	1.9
Germany	0.1	-0.1	1.7	1.3
Italy	0.4	0.3	1.2	1.6
Austria	1.2	0.8	1.8	2.3
Belgium	0.9	1.3	2.6	2.4
Finland	2.3	1.9	2.9	2.9
Greece	3.6	4.5	3.8	2.7
Ireland	6.1	3.7	4.3	4.6
Luxembourg	2.5	2.9	4.0	3.5
Netherlands	0.6	-0.9	1.2	1.6
Portugal	0.4	-1.2	1.2	1.9
Spain	2.2	2.5	2.6	2.5
Euro area	0.9	0.6	1.9	1.8
United Kingdom	1.8	2.2	3.2	2.5
Denmark	1.0	0.5	2.2	2.3
Sweden	2.0	1.5	3.4	2.9
EU-15	1.1	0.9	2.2	2.0
Cyprus	2.1	1.9	3.2	3.6
Czech Republic	1.5	3.7	3.8	3.9
Estonia	7.2	5.1	5.9	5.6
Hungary	3.5	3.0	3.8	3.8
Latvia	6.4	7.5	7.0	6.0
Lithuania	6.8	9.7	6.7	5.8
Malta	2.6	-0.3	1.0	1.5
Poland	1.4	3.8	5.7	4.9
Slovakia	4.6	4.5	5.1	5.0
Slovenia	3.3	2.5	3.8	3.9
New EU members-10	2.4	4.0	4.9	4.5
EU-25	1.2	1.1	2.4	2.2
Iceland	-0.5	4.0	4.3	4.7
Israel	-0.7	1.3	3.5	3.7
Norway	1.4	0.4	3.4	2.9
Switzerland	0.3	-0.4	1.8	1.7
WECEE	1.2	1.1	2.4	2.2
Canada	3.4	2.0	2.7	3.0
United States	1.9	3.0	4.4	3.5
North America	2.0	3.0	4.3	3.5
Japan	-0.3	1.3	3.9	1.5
Europe, North America and Japan	1.3	1.9	3.4	2.7
Memorandum items:				
EU-8	2.4	4.0	5.0	4.6
Western Europe-20	1.1	0.9	2.2	2.0
Western Europe and North America	1.6	2.0	3.3	2.8

Source: Eurostat; OECD national accounts and national statistics; UNECE secretariat estimates; Consensus Economics, *Consensus Forecasts*, 6 December 2004 and *Eastern Europe Consensus Forecasts*, 15 November 2004.

Note: All aggregates exclude Israel. WECEE (western Europe, central and eastern Europe) comprises the EU-25 plus Iceland, Norway and Switzerland. EU-8 (central Europe and the Baltic states) includes the new EU members less Cyprus and Malta. Western Europe-20 comprises the EU-15 plus Cyprus, Iceland, Malta, Norway and Switzerland. For data on south-east European and European CIS countries, see table 1.1.2.

[a] Forecasts.

noticeably in 2004. Preliminary estimates suggest that their aggregate GDP grew by some 5 per cent led by a strengthening recovery in Poland. In 2004, growth in the

TABLE 1.1.2

Annual changes in real GDP in south-east Europe and the CIS, 2002-2005

(Percentage change over the previous year)

	2002	2003	2004 [a]	2005 [e]
South-east Europe	6.5	5.1	7.9	5.2
Albania	3.4	6.0	6.0	6.0
Bosnia and Herzegovina	3.7	3.2	4.0	4.3
Bulgaria	4.9	4.3	5.5	5.3
Croatia	5.2	4.3	4.0	4.4
Romania	5.0	4.9	7.5	5.2
Serbia and Montenegro [b]	3.8	1.5	7.0	4.5
The former Yugoslav Republic of Macedonia	0.9	3.4	2.5	3.5
Turkey	7.9	5.8	9.0	5.3
CIS	5.2	7.7	7.9	6.4
Armenia	15.1	13.9	10.0	8.0
Azerbaijan	10.6	11.2	9.5	14.0
Belarus	5.0	6.8	10.0	9.0
Georgia	5.5	11.1	6.0	5.0
Kazakhstan	9.8	9.3	9.3	7.9
Kyrgyzstan	0.0	6.7	6.5	7.0
Republic of Moldova [c]	7.8	6.3	8.0	6.0
Russian Federation	4.7	7.3	6.8	5.8
Tajikistan	9.5	10.2	11.0	8.3
Turkmenistan [d]	1.8	6.8	6.0	7.0
Ukraine	5.2	9.4	12.4	6.5
Uzbekistan	4.2	4.4	7.6	6.4
Total above	5.6	6.9	7.9	6.0
Memorandum items:				
South-east Europe without Turkey	4.6	4.2	6.4	5.0
CIS without Russian Federation	6.2	8.5	10.1	7.5
Caucasian CIS countries	9.9	11.7	8.6	10.0
Central Asian CIS countries	6.6	7.5	8.4	7.3
Three European CIS countries	5.3	8.6	11.6	7.2
Low-income CIS economies	6.3	7.7	8.1	7.9

Source: National statistics, CIS Statistical Committee; reports by official forecasting agencies.

Note: The aggregation was performed using weights based on purchasing power parities. Aggregates shown are: south-east Europe (the 8 countries below that line); CIS (the 12 member countries of the Commonwealth of Independent States). Sub-aggregates are: Caucasian CIS countries: Armenia, Azerbaijan, Georgia; central Asian CIS countries: Kazakhstan, Kyrgyzstan, Tajikistan, Turkmenistan, Uzbekistan; three European CIS countries: Belarus, Republic of Moldova, Ukraine; low-income CIS economies: Armenia, Azerbaijan, Georgia, Republic of Moldova, Kyrgyzstan, Tajikistan and Uzbekistan. Unless otherwise noted, country forecasts shown are those reported by official forecasting agencies.

[a] Forecasts.

[b] Excluding Kosovo and Metohia.

[c] Excluding Transdniestria.

[d] UNECE secretariat estimates. On the methodology used, see box 5.2.1.

EU-8 economies became more broadly based, driven by robust consumption and investment expenditures and strong external demand. Macroeconomic policies were broadly supportive of growth. Good fiscal outcomes allowed the central banks to maintain accommodating monetary conditions.

Economic growth in south-east Europe also accelerated considerably, underpinned by strong domestic demand and exports. According to preliminary estimates, aggregate GDP rose by some 8 per cent (table 1.1.2) on the strength of the recovery in the region's largest economies, Romania and Turkey.

The CIS economies continued to grow strongly for a second consecutive year, with GDP increasing by almost 8 per cent. The whole CIS region, including the largest economy, Russia, continued to benefit from the surge in world commodity prices. In most resource-rich CIS economies, the main factor behind their output growth was the rapid growth of commodity exports (particularly oil and natural gas). At the same time, several years of strong output growth have been associated with a surge in domestic demand, especially private consumption. In many countries, fixed investment has also recovered, most of it in extractive industries. Total employment in the CIS has continued to increase since the last quarter of 2003; however, this mainly reflects developments in some of the largest economies (foremost Russia). Macroeconomic policy in many CIS economies was expansionary, which gave a further boost to economic activity. One consequence, however, was that rates of inflation began to fall more slowly, and in some cases there was also a deterioration of fiscal balances. The currencies of most commodity exporting economies were under growing pressure to appreciate as a result of their surging export revenues. The symptoms of the "Dutch Disease" are increasingly evident in some economies, particularly Russia, putting monetary management under considerable strain.

(ii) The short-term outlook

A still favourable but somewhat less supportive international economic environment

Global economic growth is expected to slow down in 2005, but it should still average close to 4 per cent, more than 1 percentage point less than in 2004.[4] The continued robust expansion of the world economy is also mirrored in world trade, which is projected to increase by some 8 per cent in 2005, down from nearly 10 per cent in 2004. The global business cycle will continue to rely on China and the United States as the main locomotives of growth. Rapid growth rates are also expected to continue in Asia and Latin America. The moderate slowdown in the global economy mainly reflects the lagged effects of the sharp rise in oil prices on economic activity in combination with a gradual tightening of economic policies in China, Japan and the United States.

In the United States, real GDP is forecast to increase by some 3.5 per cent in 2005, down from 4.4. per cent in 2004 (table 1.1.1). The rate of growth will still remain slightly above potential in 2005. Overall, activity will be supported by the continued, albeit moderating, strength of domestic demand. Exports should be stimulated by the

---

[4] Calculated on the basis of GDP weights based on PPPs. On the basis of weights at market exchange rate, world output is expected to increase by 3.1 per cent in 2005, down from 4.1 per cent in 2004.

depreciation of the dollar and by strong external demand in the United States major markets in Asia[5] and Latin America. But imports will also rise and so the change in real net exports will continue to act as a drag on economic activity. The Federal Reserve is expected to continue gradually raising short-term interest rates[6] to move monetary policy closer to a neutral stance during 2005. Fiscal policy will be slightly restrictive in 2005.

In Japan, forecasts for economic growth were lowered significantly in late 2004, reflecting the stalling of the recovery in the second and third quarters of 2004. Real GDP is now expected to increase by only 1.5 per cent in 2005, reflecting the combined impact of slower growth of both domestic demand and exports.

Continued growth in Europe and the CIS but at different rates

The short-term outlook for Europe and the CIS is for economic growth to continue in 2005, albeit at significantly different rates in the major subregions. The euro area will continue to lag behind the other major regions of the world economy. Central and eastern Europe will continue to perform significantly better than the euro area. Economic growth will weaken somewhat in the CIS, but average rates will remain well above the European average.

A moderate rate of recovery in the euro area

For the euro area, real GDP is forecast to increase on average by 1.8 per cent in 2005 (table 1.1.1). For western Europe as a whole, the growth rate will be marginally higher at 2 per cent, reflecting the slightly stronger growth momentum in countries outside the euro area. These growth rates for 2005 are slightly lower than in 2004, partly because of a smaller number of working days.[7] Positive growth in the rest of the world will continue to support exports, which remain the mainstay of growth. For the recovery to accelerate, domestic demand would have to pick up more strongly than is currently expected. Among the four major west European economies, economic growth will remain relatively sluggish in Germany and Italy; only in the United Kingdom is real GPD forecast to increase by more than 2 per cent in 2005. The stance of fiscal policy is expected to be broadly neutral (possibly even slightly restrictive) for the euro area and western Europe in aggregate in 2005. In view of the fragility of factors of

domestic growth and the dampening effects of the stronger euro on domestic economic activity and inflation, monetary policy in the euro area is likely to continue to "wait-and-see". The European Central Bank (ECB) is expected to leave interest rates unchanged in 2005, but there is scope for countering any weakening of the recovery by lowering interest rates, particularly as the stronger euro will dampen imported inflation.

Economic growth should remain strong in central and eastern Europe and the CIS

Although GDP growth has started to decelerate in the EU-8 countries, recent economic sentiment indicators suggest a favourable short-term outlook. In 2005, the average rate of growth in the EU-8 may slow down somewhat compared with 2004 but, at some 4½ per cent, will remain considerably above the average of western Europe. A noticeable surge in greenfield FDI projects should accelerate the ongoing process of restructuring and boost exports. Further fiscal consolidation is envisaged in some countries in 2005 but its dampening effect on domestic demand should be marginal. Most of the southeast European economies are also set to maintain strong rates of growth in 2005 but the unusually high rates in some countries in 2004 will be difficult to sustain. Overall, domestic demand is set to remain buoyant, and should provide solid support to economic activity in these countries. Better financial intermediation and rapid credit expansion will continue to fuel output growth throughout central and eastern Europe. However, despite the relatively strong rates of output growth in 2005 the increases in employment are likely to be small.

Economic activity in the CIS as a whole may lose some steam in 2005, but aggregate GDP is nevertheless expected to expand by some 6½ per cent. Decelerating growth rates will prevail in all the large CIS economies – Belarus, Kazakhstan, Russia and Ukraine – following the evolution of external factors such as commodity prices and demand in the region's main markets. Domestic demand in the CIS should generally remain buoyant but its effect on domestic economic activity will depend on the responsiveness of domestic supply. The macroeconomic policy stance should remain broadly neutral in the large economies, with the possible exception of Ukraine where some fiscal tightening can be expected. While in the short run there may be some further improvement in the labour markets, many CIS economies still have to address the challenge of restructuring as labour adjustment has in general been lagging behind that in output.

Downside risks are dominating

The baseline short-term outlook is relatively favourable for the global economy, although this masks disappointingly weak growth in the euro area. But the outlook is surrounded by risks, which continue to be predominantly on the downside. A major uncertainty is the likely development of the international oil markets.

---

[5] The overall economic impact of the devastating tidal waves ("tsunamis") in several countries caused by an earthquake in the Pacific on 26 December 2004 is currently estimated to be relatively small.

[6] In mid-December 2004, the Federal Reserve raised its target for the federal funds rate by a further 25 basis points to 2¼ per cent.

[7] It should be noted that annual changes in real GDP are not adjusted for the number of working days. In contrast, seasonally adjusted quarterly GDP data typically take into account calendar effects.

On the one hand, oil prices remain subject to potential upward pressure from actual or threats of supply disruptions and the continued robust growth of the world economy. On the other hand, a return of oil inventories to more comfortable levels and reduced speculation could introduce some downward pressure on prices. The latter, however, is expected to remain relatively moderate.

The fact that the global economy continues to rely so much on the United States as a major engine of growth evidently makes the outlook very vulnerable to a more pronounced slowdown of the United States economy. This is all the more so, because the necessary correction of the large domestic and external imbalances that have developed in the United States economy will hardly be possible without a more or less pronounced slowdown of domestic demand and output growth. Downside risks are also related to uncertainty about the strength of personal consumption spending, given that the savings rate fell to a very low level in 2004 and that the wealth effects from rising house prices may start to wane in 2005. Consumer spending could also be restrained by a weaker than expected improvement in the labour markets. In any case, a sharp fall in house prices would be likely to have a considerable dampening effect on private household spending and overall economic growth. This could create a dilemma for the United States monetary authorities because a lowering of interest rates in response to such a development would risk a further decline in the value of the dollar with the attendant risk of higher inflation. Long-term interest rates have remained at unusually low levels in the recovery so far, reflecting, *inter alia*, the persistence of moderate inflationary expectations, a weak supply of corporate bonds (a reflection of balance sheet consolidation) and the massive purchase of United States treasury bills by Asian central banks. A stronger than expected rise in long-term interest rates could be caused by the fading of these factors but also by increasing concerns in financial markets about the persistently large fiscal deficit, with a consequent dampening effect on economic growth.

Other risks to the outlook include a possible hard landing in China, which has become an important source of demand for goods and services produced in the rest of Asia and other regions of the world economy.

In western Europe, given its present strong reliance on export growth, the recovery is very vulnerable to a more pronounced weakening of global growth than is currently forecast. A further sharp appreciation of the euro could considerably dampen growth prospects with even the risk of economic growth stalling in 2005. In some countries (France, Ireland, Spain, United Kingdom), the downside risks also include a possible sudden and pronounced reversal of the rise in house prices, with consequent negative wealth effects and, in turn, severe repercussions on private household consumption and the overall rate of economic growth. A potential upside risk is that business investment may respond more favourably than anticipated to the continuation of favourable financing conditions and

improved profitability. But the probability of the latter occurring is not very high given the expected deceleration in economic growth.

The main external risks to the outlook for central and eastern Europe include a possible sharp deceleration of economic growth in the euro zone and significantly higher than expected energy prices. If imported inflation continues to rise, this may prompt a more restrictive policy stance, with negative implications for economic activity. A number of economies in this region still face important macroeconomic policy challenges such as large fiscal and current account deficits. Forthcoming elections in several countries carry the risk of pre-election increases in public spending, which could undermine policy credibility and probably result in monetary tightening, lower inflows of FDI and reduced competitiveness. The most pressing policy challenges facing the new EU member states are to achieve sustainable fiscal consolidation and implement structural reforms for job-rich growth.

The main structural weakness of the CIS economies remains their high dependence on exports of natural resources and low value added products, implying a high degree of vulnerability to external shocks. In addition, there are already signs, especially in Russia, that the loss of competitiveness associated with real exchange rate appreciation (the "Dutch Disease") is becoming a burden on local producers and is choking off aggregate domestic economic activity. The capacity of macroeconomic policy to address these negative developments is fairly limited. Unless local producers manage to counteract them at the micro level through further restructuring, there are likely to be negative repercussions on output growth in the affected countries, especially in their manufacturing industries. The long-term growth prospects of the CIS economies thus hinge on their success in diversifying their economies and implementing key reforms in product and financial markets.

1.2 Selected policy issues

(i) Reducing global imbalances

The large and rising current account deficit of the United States has been an important potential downside risk for the global economy for some time.[8] It rose to $670 billion or 5.7 per cent of GDP in 2004 and on current economic trends is projected to reach $760 billion or 6.2 per cent of GDP in 2005. The external deficit has now passed the threshold (some 5 per cent of GDP), which in the past has tended to trigger current account reversals in industrialized countries.[9] But the reversal of the United States deficit seems to have been postponed by

---

[8] UNECE, *Economic Survey of Europe, 2004 No. 1*, chap. 1, pp. 5-6 and *Economic Survey of Europe, 2003 No. 1*, chap. 1, p. 12.

[9] C. Freund, *Current Account Adjustment in Industrialized Countries*, Board of Governors of the Federal Reserve System, International Finance Discussion Papers, No. 692 (Washington, D.C.), December 2000.

the country's unique position in the international economy. The cumulative deficits have led to a progressive deterioration of the United States net investment position, i.e. the balance of United States-owned assets abroad and foreign-owned assets in the United States. The United States net foreign liabilities corresponded to some 25 per cent of GDP in 2004. Whereas in 1980 the United States was the world's largest creditor, it has now become the world's largest debtor. The point has been reached, where these imbalances have to be corrected for the sake of the stability of the United States economy and the world economy at large. The orderly reversal of the United States current account deficit is therefore a major challenge for policy makers both in the United States and other major economies.

The current account deficit is largely the consequence of the unbalanced growth of the United States economy since the second half of the 1990s, with buoyant domestic demand leading to a surge in imports from the rest of the world. At the same time, exports were restrained by the pronounced real appreciation of the dollar (until early 2002) and the uneven distribution of economic growth rates in the global economy. Domestic demand growth in the other major trading economies has been weaker than in the United States, with a correspondingly reduced demand for United States products abroad.

A current account deficit reflects, by definition, an excess of domestic investment over national saving.[10] Accordingly, domestic absorption of goods and service is larger than national output and income. This gap is financed by borrowing abroad, i.e. by attracting the excess savings of the rest of the world. From this perspective, the root cause of the widening current account imbalance is the decline, to a very low level, of the United States national saving rate, both private and public. The former reflects mainly the declining trend in personal savings since the early 1990s, which had fallen to only 0.2 per cent of disposable incomes by the autumn of 2004. A major concern is that the external deficit has been used not only to finance investment in productive capacity but also private consumption, which has been supported by the real estate boom. The main counterpart to the current account deficit since 2002, however, has been the swing in the government financial balance from a comfortable surplus in 2000 to a large deficit of more than 4 per cent of GDP in 2004.

The financing of the current account deficit, moreover, now relies to a large extent on massive purchases of United States government bonds by foreign, mainly Asian, central banks (especially China and Japan) whose motive has been to defend existing exchange rate parities or, at least, to limit the appreciation of their currencies against the dollar. It can be assumed that eventually the financing of the current account deficit will face ever greater problems in view of an increasingly "unacceptable amount of concentration risk",[11] which will affect the willingness of private investors and foreign central banks to hold more dollar-denominated financial assets at current exchange rates and interest rates. This exposes the United States to the risk of sudden and sharp portfolio adjustments with associated downward pressure on the dollar and risks for overall economic stability. Viewed from the perspective of China and Japan, the question is at what point will they consider the costs of accumulating more dollars to outweigh the benefits of stabilizing their exchange rates and maintaining their export competitiveness. The possibility of sudden massive reserve sales by foreign central banks evidently has also a geopolitical dimension.[12] It could, of course, be argued that the reserve holdings of the central banks of China and Japan are now so huge that they will likely not easily risk the losses associated with "sudden massive reserve sales" of the dollar. (Central banks were also very careful about the effects on the gold price in reducing their gold holdings.) In any case, there are fears of strong selling pressure on the dollar, feeding on itself and becoming unstoppable, leading to a "hard landing" (or even a crash) rather than the desired gradual decline or "soft landing" of the currency. The risk of a hard landing could be accentuated by portfolio shifts of United States investors towards foreign currency-denominated financial assets.

While there exists a broad consensus that the United States current account deficit is not sustainable, what is uncertain is the timing and extent of the necessary adjustment of the deficit to a level that is likely to be sustainable over the medium term. The latter is estimated by the IMF to be around 2-3 per cent of GDP.[13]

The current account adjustment will involve a combination of reduced domestic absorption (i.e lower domestic demand for goods and services) and a depreciation of the real effective exchange rate. The latter is likely to be brought about by a decline of the nominal

---

[10] The latter can be further disaggregated into the private sector saving-investment balance and the government net saving, i.e. the government budget deficit or surplus. If private sector savings are equal to private sector investments then any current account deficit (surplus) is matched by a corresponding government budget deficit (surplus). In such a case, current account deficits and budget deficits will move together, a constellation which has been labeled the "twin deficits" problem.

[11] Remarks made by Chairman Greenspan at the European Banking Congress 2004 (Frankfurt), 19 November 2004, [www.federalreserve.gov/boarddocs/speeches].

[12] It "cannot be prudent for [the United States] to rely on a kind of balance of financial terror to hold back reserve sales that would threaten our stability". L. Summers, *The United States and the Global Adjustment Process*, Third Annual Stavros S. Niarchos Lecture, Institute for International Economics (Washington, D.C.), 23 March 2004 [www.iie.com/publications/papers].

[13] R. Rajan, "Credible policies will break the dollar's fall", *Financial Times*, 15 December 2004.

effective exchange rate. This has been the case in previous episodes of current account adjustment in the United States and other industrialized countries.[14] The adjustment would, of course, be facilitated by the strong growth of domestic demand in the rest of the world, which would provide an additional stimulus to United States exports.

It is not possible, however, to say how large an exchange rate depreciation will be required to achieve a given reduction of the deficit. This is so because the dollar exchange rate is not exogenously determined but is rather endogenous to the global economic system. In any case, depreciation will stimulate United States exports, while at the same time dampening the demand for imports from the rest of the world.

The effectiveness of the exchange rate as an adjustment instrument will depend on the flexibility of the exchange rate policies pursued by the United States major trading partners. So far the major adjustment burden of the declining dollar has been borne by the euro,[15] given the policies pursued in Asia, especially China and Japan.[16] This raises the issue of an appropriate burden sharing of these inevitable exchange rate adjustments across the major regions of the world economy.

Given the size of the United States current account deficit, it can nevertheless be assumed that a substantial depreciation of the real effective exchange rate of the dollar will be needed to achieve better internal and external balance. The dollar has declined so far in a relatively orderly fashion and both the nominal and real effective exchange rates have fallen significantly compared with their recent peak in February 2002. But a further sharp decline is likely and the risks of disruptions in the international financial markets cannot be ignored. How smooth this adjustment process will be depends also on credible policy responses designed to redress the global imbalances, which, in turn, will shape the expectations and behaviour of investors in the financial markets.

The main role of a depreciation of the dollar is to help reduce the United States excess demand for foreign goods. This will occur not only via the impact on the prices of tradeables (relative to non-tradeables) but also because the sales of dollar-denominated financial assets (which bring about the depreciation) will tend to put upward pressure on United States interest rates which, in

turn, will lead to lower domestic expenditure. The exchange rate adjustment is thus complementary to policies aimed directly at reducing domestic absorption, or, conversely, at raising the level of domestic savings relative to investment. Domestic savings can notably be raised by a reduction of the United States fiscal deficit, which can be expected to lead to a lower current account deficit.[17] In the private sector, corporate net saving (i.e. undistributed profits) rose to very high levels in 2004 both in comparison with their recent low in 2000 and also in a longer-term perspective. Any rise in the private sector's overall saving rate will therefore most likely depend on an increase in the personal savings rate from its present unsustainably low level. An open question is to what extent this can be fostered by appropriate policy measures.

The upshot is that the adjustment of global financial imbalances will inevitably involve a – possibly quite significant – weakening of United States domestic demand with adverse consequences for economic growth in the rest of the world economy. The risk of a recession in the United States cannot be excluded. To some extent the current account adjustment could be facilitated by stronger demand in the rest of the world, although United States exports respond less strongly to changes in foreign economic activity than United States imports to changes in United States real incomes.[18] In the absence of such a conducive external environment a greater burden will have to be carried by exchange rate adjustments with a concomitantly larger risk of disruptive capital flows. To the extent that exchange rate adjustments are successfully resisted, a larger share of the adjustment burden will fall on domestic absorption, with possibly even worse consequences for the world economy.

It is against this background that the recent G-20 Meeting of Finance Ministers and Central Bank Governors underscored "the importance of medium-term fiscal consolidation in the United States, continued structural reforms to boost growth in Europe and Japan, and, in emerging Asia, steps towards greater exchange rate flexibility, supported by continued financial sector reform, as appropriate".[19]

Given the formidable adjustment challenge that lies ahead, there is an important role to be played by policy

---

[14] C. Freund, op. cit.

[15] An open issue is to what extent a more accommodative monetary policy and a more flexible Stability and Growth Pact in the euro area would have reduced this adjustment burden.

[16] To illustrate: compared with its recent peak in February 2002, the broad nominal effective exchange rate of the dollar had declined by 14.4 per cent by November 2004. Over the same period, the narrower effective exchange rate against major currencies (which excludes the Chinese yuan and the currencies of other emerging Asian economies) fell by 27.6 per cent.

[17] Although the actual fiscal and current account deficits are often characterized as "twin deficits" this is *stricto sensu* only true in the definitional sense of national income accounting. A reduction of the fiscal deficit need not necessarily lead to a proportionate decline of the current account deficit. This will also depend on the private sector's spending (and saving) behaviour.

[18] Liberalization of trade in services should also tend to improve the United States structural trade balance, given its comparative advantages in this sector, reflected in the long-standing surplus in services. C. Mann, *Is the U.S. Trade Deficit Sustainable?* (Washington, D.C., Institute for International Economics, 1999), pp. 88-89.

[19] "Communiqué. Meeting of Finance Ministers and Central Bank Governors" (Berlin), 20-21 November 2004 [www.g7.utoronto.ca/g20].

coordination, be it in the form of exchanges of information, shared analysis or cooperation over exchange rate policies.[20] The latter would notably involve cooperation between the Federal Reserve, the ECB and the Bank of Japan,[21] but also the central banks of other countries, especially China.

In a more general way, the gyrations in the dollar exchange rate not only confirm the tendency for significant overshooting but also the risk of speculative bubbles in the foreign exchange markets as in other asset markets. This instability has damaging effects on the real economy and points to broader issues of international economic governance.

(ii) Finding the balance: structural reforms and the macroeconomic policy framework in Europe

In Europe, the short-term prospects for weak domestic demand growth being offset by a strengthening of exports to the rest of the world do not look very favourable. The recovery in the European economy virtually came to a halt in the third quarter of 2004 and current forecasts are for only a moderate rise in economic activity in 2005.

The main policy challenge is to bridge the gap between the rhetoric of the ambitious Lisbon agenda, which aims at creating a competitive and dynamic economy at par with the United States, and the disappointing reality of progress falling significantly short of the intermediate targets. A major problem with the Lisbon agenda is its almost exclusive focus on supply-side reforms as a basis for creating a dynamic economy that combines both strong employment and productivity growth. But market outcomes are not determined solely by supply but by the interaction of the forces of supply and demand. It will be difficult to meet the targets of the Lisbon agenda in a context of weak growth of domestic demand.

Sustaining higher rates of growth is also a *conditio sine qua non* for preserving the European model, with its strong concern for social cohesion. The adjustment pressures arising from the intensification of international competitive pressures, rapid rates of technical change (with a clear bias against low-skilled labour), as well as population ageing, all make this challenge even more difficult.

A recent review of the Lisbon strategy[22] – the so-called Kok report – has concluded that the agenda is far

too broad and has partly conflicting objectives. It therefore proposed that the strategy should focus on five, although still quite broad, priority areas where progress is to be pursued within the framework of national action programmes. These areas are the formation of a knowledge society with a strong emphasis on innovation and research; the completion of the internal market, which requires a closer integration of services markets and network industries; the fostering of a more conducive business climate, *inter alia*, by facilitating market entry and the development of venture capital markets; further reforms of labour markets designed to improve intra-EU labour mobility; and the promotion of environmental sustainability.

Raising Europe's growth potential, however, requires not only supply-side reforms but also a sufficiently flexible macroeconomic policy framework (i.e. mainly monetary and fiscal policy) that is "as supportive of growth as possible",[23] while paying adequate attention to preserving macroeconomic stability.[24] In a similar vein, the Sapir Report[25] has emphasized the need for combining microeconomic reforms with a revision of the EMU's macroeconomic policy framework, taking especially into account the increased heterogeneity of the EU after enlargement, which calls for more flexible rules to limit the potentially adverse implications of "one-size-fits-all" policies. The challenge is to find the proper balance between discipline and flexibility.[26]

Against this background, it is important that a sensible reform of the Stability and Growth Pact be achieved as soon as possible.[27] It would strengthen private sector confidence that the overriding priority of fiscal policy is to ensure the sustainability of the public finances while at the same time allowing sufficient flexibility for anti-cyclical fiscal policy responses.[28] The recent proposals made by the European Commission[29] therefore go in the right direction, but it may not be easy to achieve a consensus on these matters.

A sensible reform of the Stability and Growth Pact, combined with realistic and firm objectives for medium-

---

[20] E. Truman, "The US current account deficit and the euro area", speech prepared for the conference, *The ECB and its Watchers VI* (Frankfurt), 2 July 2004 [www.iie.com/publications].

[21] "ECB considers joint currency move", *Financial Times*, 2 December 2004.

[22] "Facing the challenge", report from the High Level Group chaired by Wim Kok (Brussels), November 2004 [europa.eu.int/comm/lisbon_strategy/index_en.html].

[23] Ibid., p. 6

[24] UNECE, *Economic Survey of Europe, 2004 No. 2*, pp. 49-50.

[25] "An agenda for a growing Europe – making the EU economic system deliver", report of an Independent High-Level Study Group established on the initiative of the President of the European Commission (Brussels), July 2003 [www.euractiv.com/ndbtext/innovation/sapirreport.pdf].

[26] Ibid., p. 135.

[27] This is also proposed in the Kok report.

[28] UNECE, *Economic Survey of Europe, 2004 No. 1*, pp. 10-15.

[29] Communication by the Commission on, *Strengthening Economic Governance and Clarifying the Implementation of the Stability and Growth Pact*, COM (2004) 581 (Brussels), 3 September 2004.

term fiscal consolidation, could also create a new basis for a kind of European "policy mix", that is, for cooperation between the European Central Bank and the European Council (or the so-called euro group).[30] Monetary policy should be symmetric over the business cycle, giving equal weight to upside and downside risks to both price stability and economic growth. This becomes even more important given the general orientation of fiscal policy towards ambitious consolidation targets, which will be achieved much more easily in a context of sustained economic growth.

(iii) The policy challenge of economic diversification in the CIS

While rates of GDP growth in most CIS economies have been impressive in recent years, there are nevertheless concerns about their sustainability. The key factor behind the economic boom in the resource-rich CIS economies has been the expansion of their extractive industries (especially, the crude oil and natural gas sectors) coupled with a surge in world commodity prices in the last few years. The narrow base of the recovery exposes these economies to fluctuations in the highly volatile global commodity markets, making them vulnerable to external shocks. Besides, mineral extraction is a capital-intensive activity generating little employment and is likely to result in geographically unbalanced development and greater income inequality.

The key policy issue is whether and how public policy can help to broaden the growth base and reduce the excessive reliance on natural resources in the medium and longer term. The recent policy debate in some CIS economies has focused on the need for economic diversification as a key factor of economic development as well as the basis of high and sustainable rates of growth. Despite the differences in national circumstances, diversification has figured prominently in the development strategies recently elaborated in some countries.[31] However, there is still much ambiguity as regards the ways and means to achieve this objective.

The disintegration of the CMEA and then of the Soviet Union triggered a collapse of much of the manufacturing industry in the CIS. As a result, the production and export structures in most CIS economies have become more specialized and concentrated, especially in the resource-rich economies. For example, in Russia the share of the top five export products in total exports increased from 62 per cent in 1996 to 68 per cent in 2003 (four of these five products were primary commodities and fuels) and the share of the top 10 products increased from 72 per cent to 77 per cent.[32] A similar process of concentration towards commodity exports is observable in many CIS economies.[33] Such a narrow specialization pattern may be counterproductive for a balanced development path, especially for the low-income CIS countries.[34]

Economic diversification has, of course, different aspects and dimensions across the CIS countries. There is a clear distinction between economies with abundant resources of crude oil and natural gas, and the less richly endowed countries, where the increased shares of commodity exports mostly reflect the outcomes of post-Soviet deindustrialization. At the same time, resource-rich economies face specific problems that may even risk becoming impediments to their economic development.

While natural resource abundance can in principle be an important source of development finance, the relationship between natural resource endowments and economic performance cannot be considered as deterministic. In fact, past experience provides ample evidence of a negative relationship, sometimes referred to as the "resource curse".[35] The channels through which

---

[30] *Le sursaut. Vers une nouvelle croissance pour la France,* Rapport officiel, Groupe de travail présidé par Michel Camdessus, La documentation Française (Paris), 2004, pp. 142-143 [www.ladocumentationfrancaise.fr].

[31] In Russia, the policy debates on the need for economic diversification have been underway for several years. The recently announced draft medium-term economic programme sets the target of shifting from a resource-based to a technology-driven growth pattern. "Programma sotsial'no-ekonomicheskogo razvitiya Rossiiskoi Federatsii na srednesrochnuyu perspektivu (2005-2008 gody) (proekt)" [www.economy.gov.ru/wps/portal]. The government of Kazakhstan has adopted an "Innovative Industrial Development Strategy of the Republic of Kazakhstan for 2003-2015 [www.undp.kz/library_of_publications/files/2846-13355.pdf]. In Azerbaijan, the authorities also address the issue of economic diversification in the recent policy document "Republic of Azerbaijan State Programme on Poverty Reduction and Economic Development 2003-2005" [www.economy.gov.az]. The authorities in Turkmenistan have also recently announced plans to reduce the dependence of the economy on the exports of unprocessed primary commodities.

[32] The products are identified at the three-digit level of the SITC, Rev.3 classification. UNECE secretariat calculations on the basis of data from the United Nations COMTRADE Database.

[33] Thus in 2003, the top five products accounted for 90 per cent of total exports in Azerbaijan; for 72 per cent in the case of Kazakhstan; 68 per cent in Armenia and 66 per cent in Kyrgyzstan. In almost all these cases the top export products were dominated by commodities. The trend towards this type of export specialization is also evident in the recent dynamics of other export concentration indices for the CIS economies. UNCTAD, *Handbook of Statistics 2004 on CD-Rom* (New York), 2004. For comparison, the average share of the top five export products in the central European and Baltic countries (EU-8) in 2003 was 32.5 per cent.

[34] A recent cross-country study based on a large sample of more than 90 countries comes up with the robust finding that economic diversification has been the typical evolutionary pattern over the development path of most countries, until they reach a certain (fairly high) level of per capita income; above that threshold the prevailing pattern is that of specialization. J. Imbs and R. Wacziarg, "Stages of diversification", *American Economic Review*, Vol. 93, No. 1, March 2003, pp. 63-86. This analysis supports the view that for less advanced economies development goes along with diversification and vice versa; these are indeed the two sides of one and the same coin.

[35] P. Stevens, "Resource impact: curse or blessing? A literature survey", *Journal of Energy Literature*, Vol. 9, No. 1, June 2003, pp. 3-42; D. Lederman and W. Maloney, *Open Questions about the Link between Natural Resources and Economic Growth: Sachs and Warner Revisited,* Central Bank of Chile Working Papers, No. 141 (Santiago), February 2002.

the "resource curse" can emerge and escalate include, *inter alia*, a weak institutional environment and poor public governance (notably, resource riches tend to be associated with higher degrees of corruption and rent-seeking activities). The real exchange rate appreciation associated with large and rising exports of natural resources can become an impediment to other economic activities (the so-called Dutch Disease). Another problem is the general economic volatility and vulnerability of the economy to external shocks.[36] However, there have also been a number of cases where natural resources have served as a basis for successful economic diversification and development of a country.[37] Prudent financial management and an appropriate institutional environment (Norway being a good example) can prevent or minimize the potential negative side effects. Whether a resource-rich country falls into the trap of the "resource curse" or manages to use the resource endowment to jump-start economic diversification largely depends on the country-specific institutional context and the policy framework designed to foster economic development.[38] In any case, a carefully designed, and duly implemented, policy agenda can greatly reduce the risks of the "resource curse" in the resource-rich CIS countries and can facilitate the process of their economic diversification.

The policy challenge of economic diversification is even more daunting in the CIS countries that are not so rich in natural resources. These are also the countries with lower levels of per capita income and a higher incidence of poverty. While policy makers in these economies face some basic development problems, they do not have at their disposal the financial cushion created by resource windfalls. Nevertheless, the main principles of addressing the goal of economic diversification should be broadly similar across the CIS.

---

[36] It has also been argued that the transmission channels from natural resource abundance to slow economic growth can be described in terms of crowding out: a heavy dependence on natural capital tends to crowd out other types of capital, with negative implications on economic growth. T. Gylfason, *Natural Resources and Economic Growth: From Dependence to Diversification*, CEPR Discussion Paper, No. 4804 (London), December 2004.

[37] Thus, the transformation of Finland and Sweden, two of Europe's poorest countries until the middle of the nineteenth century, into leading industrialized economies is an example of successful diversification initially drawing on domestic natural resources. M. Blomström and A. Kokko, *From Natural Resources to High-tech Production: The Evolution of Industrial Competitiveness in Sweden and Finland*, CEPR Discussion Paper, No. 3804 (London), February 2003. The experience of some newly industrialized economies in south-east Asia also provides examples of how natural riches can be used as part of an overall development strategy to diversify the economy away from primary commodities. K. Jomo and M. Rock, *Economic Diversification And Primary Commodity Processing In The Second-tier South-east Asian Newly Industrializing Countries*, UNCTAD Discussion Paper, No. 136 (Geneva), June 1998.

[38] For a discussion of the potential dangers of resource-led development in Russia and other CIS countries see Y. Kim, *The Resource Curse in a Post-communist Regime: Russia in Comparative Perspective* (Aldershot, Ashgate, 2003).

The economic argument underlying diversification policies is that a comparative advantage in the international division of labour should not be regarded as something given once and for all. Comparative advantage (as revealed in the structure of net exports) changes over time as a result of shifts in the pattern of physical and human capital accumulation. But new areas of comparative advantage will only be cultivated if properly developed by venturing entrepreneurs. The CIS economies are by no means doomed to be locked into their current, highly skewed production and export structures; they need, however, to undertake a dedicated long-term effort to cultivate their potential and develop new areas of comparative advantage.

The potential existence of comparative advantage (of the type discussed above) that is not cultivated under market conditions may be regarded as a case of market failure. Both economic theory and experience indicate that one of the efficient ways to deal with this type of market failure is through appropriate policy intervention.[39] In a global perspective, successful industrialization or economic diversification (including west European industrialization in the nineteenth century but also the post-war rise of the south-east Asian economies and, more recently, the experience of Ireland), has almost always been driven by an active government policy stance.[40] However, experience has also shown that while markets alone may not be sufficient to steer economic restructuring, governments alone cannot deliver satisfactory results either, as illustrated by the disastrous welfare outcome of central planning (of which the CIS economies still bear the cost). Also some traditional approaches to industrial policy (such as "picking winners", or import substitution policies) are notorious for negative side effects such as market distortions, inefficient resource allocation and corruption.

In the absence of well functioning markets there may be other factors impeding the cultivation of potential comparative advantage (for example, poor protection of property rights, weak contract enforcement, etc.). This argument applies to many of the CIS economies, especially those that are less advanced in their economic transformation. The establishment of well functioning markets is thus not only a necessary condition for the successful implementation of diversification policies but can be expected to provide a further boost to this process.

---

[39] D. Rodrik, *Industrial Policy for the Twenty-first Century*, CEPR Discussion Paper, No. 4767 (London), November 2004. Rodrik points to two fundamental economic factors that explain why market forces alone are not sufficient to drive economic diversification: 1) the existence of information externalities (the markets cannot provide information of the cost structure/profitability of products that do not yet exist); 2) the existence of coordination externalities (many projects require simultaneous, large-scale investments to be made in order to become profitable).

[40] K. Jomo and M. Rock, op. cit.; D. Rodrik, op. cit.

Based on the experiences of other countries, the broad paradigm of a policy framework targeting economic diversification in the CIS economies should incorporate key ingredients such as:

- A coherent long-term strategy outlining the main goals to be achieved. Importantly, the formulation of long-term goals should involve a broad public debate. It is essential that the strategy reflect national goals that enjoy broad public support and popular legitimacy and will not be subject to revisions over the political cycles;

- An incentive structure that will stimulate economic agents to act in a direction consistent with the policy goals as well as the mechanisms of coordination and management of conflicting interests (for example, between the public and private sectors). Incentives should include both "carrots" (motivating agents to undertake specific actions) and "sticks" (including early identification of failure and exit strategies);

- An appropriate framework of public institutions with delegated authority to implement the related policies. Clear rules of practical implementation of policy conventions coupled with transparency and accountability in the operation of these institutions are essential to avoid the capture of policy by vested interests and to prevent corrupt practices;

- Adequate funding. Policy actions targeting diversification inevitably involve public funding. Resource-rich economies can in principle draw on the rents associated with natural resources to fund the strategies targeting new areas of comparative advantage. When natural wealth is not abundant, the channelling of public funds towards diversification policies should not endanger long-term fiscal sustainability.

There is no unique policy model of economic diversification (and for that matter, no unique diversification pattern); success (as well as failure) can take many different forms, and this applies with full force to the related policy agenda in the CIS. But experience of other countries unambiguously suggests that the adequacy and quality of the institutional arrangement is probably the key factor of success in implementing diversification policies. In other words, the normative policy rules and objectives must be matched by an appropriate institutional framework in the broader sense of formal and informal "rules of the game".[41] Many negative side effects of industrial policy in the traditional sense can be directly linked to the deficiency or inadequacy of the institutional framework within which it was being implemented. In this regard, the establishment of adequate institutions should be regarded as part and parcel of the diversification

strategy. Strong and dependable institutions are also required for high rates of GDP growth to be sustained in the context of adverse shocks. The actual institutional changes will depend on the specific socio-economic and political context in the country where such a strategy is being implemented.

In countries that are still undergoing a profound economic transformation, such as the CIS economies, the policy challenges of economic diversification are compounded by their unfinished systemic and structural reforms required to establish a fully functioning market economy. At the same time, the existing gaps in some areas of market development can also be regarded as an opportunity for policy makers. Indeed, it may be easier to establish a new, well-functioning institution starting from scratch (provided it is well designed and properly assembled) than by trying to change or amend an already existing (but malfunctioning) institution.

Recent experience suggests that the most effective institutional arrangements targeting economic diversification are those that engage all the relevant stakeholders (both from the public and from the private sector) in the process of policy design and in its implementation, and steer them towards the common goal.[42] Instead of "picking winners" in the sense of traditional industrial policy, this approach involves a more flexible strategic alliance (that can be of a long-term nature) in which the government and the private sector exchange information and ideas, and coordinate their actions in the development of new activities, products or technologies.[43] Through strategic collaboration between

---

[41] D. North, *Institutions, Institutional Change and Economic Performance* (Cambridge, Cambridge University Press, 1990).

[42] There can be a wide variety of efficient institutional arrangements that involve the private and the public sectors in the pursuit of goals of common interest related to economic diversification. For a comparative cross-country overview of relevant practices see D. Rodrik, op. cit. Specific cases of successful implementation of this approach are described in F. Bonaglia and K. Fukasaku, *Export Diversification In Low-Income Countries: An International Challenge After Doha*, OECD Development Centre, Technical Paper No. 209 (Paris), June 2003.

[43] UNECE has been promoting the development of some forms of public-private partnerships in the ECE region (especially in the countries undertaking transition from plan to market) as an institutional framework for sharing the risks between, as well as for coordinating the interests of, the private and public sectors (in particular, in large-scale public investment projects). Within the ECE emerging market economies, the greatest number of functioning public-private partnerships have been established in infrastructure development (in the sectors of energy, transport and telecommunications). More recently, public-private partnerships have gained entry into urban development, municipal and social services. UNECE has also been instrumental in steering intergovernmental policy discussions on various issues related to the institutional building of efficient public-private partnerships, including the issue of good governance. UNECE Committee for Trade, Industry and Enterprise Development, *Report of the Third PPP Alliance Meeting*, TRADE/WP.5/AG.1/2004/3 (Barcelona), 14-17 September 2004. A recent UNECE intergovernmental forum advanced the idea of promoting public-private partnerships as an institutional framework for industrial restructuring in the CIS region. Forum on "Public-Private Co-operation in Industrial Restructuring", co-organized by UNECE and the Organization for Security and Co-operation in Europe (OSCE) (Almaty, Kazakhstan), 3-4 November 2004 [www.unece.org/ie/wp8/almt.html].

the parties involved, this policy model seeks to identify the causes of market failures that result in the underprovision of entrepreneurship in the pursuit of economic restructuring.[44] If properly designed and instituted, the rules of interaction, the shared commitments and responsibilities, the transparency in operation and accountability in the use of public funds within such alliances should help to minimize the market distortions and corrupt practices that sometimes taint conventional industrial policy.

Obviously, the appropriate institutional framework is only one component of the broad policy agenda targeting economic diversification and development in the CIS economies. Overall, reform initiatives should focus on those areas that have a general impact on the cost of economic activities, including basic infrastructures, where public investment plays a central role. In this context, as the private sector becomes the means of achieving public goals, public policy should foster private sector development and entrepreneurship by reducing the cost of doing business and establishing a conducive environment for the attraction of both domestic and foreign investment.[45] Further efforts are also needed to improve public and corporate governance and eliminate the existing numerous market imperfections.

The broader policy agenda should also target innovation and human capital development, which are key factors of long-term growth and competitiveness. In fact, many of the CIS countries (in particular Russia and other larger economies) are better placed to pursue an innovation-driven diversification agenda than some of the resource-rich developing countries due to their already existing human capital endowment. But policy should also seek to eliminate existing structural rigidities that may hamper the transformation of human capital endowments into innovative entrepreneurial activity.

The development of the financial system is of particular importance in fostering productive investment and hence diversification. Facilitating credit access would ease a key constraint on the development of new economic activities and the promotion of innovation. A well-functioning banking system in resource-rich economies is also required to efficiently channel the surpluses generated in fast-growing, commodity-based activities to investment opportunities in other sectors.

Wider regional economic cooperation and further integration into the global economy can also serve to foster economic diversification by increasing the effective size of the market and encouraging FDI outside the resource sectors. This is particularly relevant for the smaller CIS economies, where the role of external demand for economic development is more obvious and for many landlocked countries where transit issues are more painfully felt. But as a word of caution, trade liberalization alone may not necessarily stimulate new economic activities (as evidenced by recent experience); for these to materialize, the integration efforts should complement domestic policies fostering diversification. In addition, it is crucial that trade and transit arrangements that increase market access are perceived as stable and not subject to possible reversals if those beneficial effects are to be obtained.

In addition, diversification policies require specific skills from the government agencies that will be involved in implementation. A public administration with adequate capacity is in fact a precondition for engaging in any large-scale government-sponsored programmes. Capacity building efforts thus emerge as an important policy step that should be assigned high priority, especially in the lower-income CIS countries. Obviously, this is also an area where targeted assistance by the international community (which will not necessarily require large-scale funding) can generate high returns in terms of its welfare effect in the recipient countries.

Economic diversification in the CIS region should be regarded as a long-term policy goal. Given the economic structures that prevail at present, dependence on commodity exports is likely to remain a dominant feature of many CIS economies for some time to come. Successful economic diversification requires an integrated and consistent policy framework that relies on comprehensive reforms in many areas and calls for a lasting and dedicated policy effort.

(iv) Financial vulnerability in the ECE emerging market economies

The level of net capital inflows and the corresponding current account deficits of the majority of the ECE emerging market economies (EME) have been relatively large for the last decade. This has allowed investment and consumption to be maintained at levels above those that would have been possible in their absence. Growth can be increased with external finance since the level of domestic investment is no longer constrained by domestic savings. These capital inflows have allowed the EME to partially rebuild their productive capital stocks that were inadequate for a market economy.[46] In addition, this inflow allowed consumption levels to be partially maintained despite the

---

[44] D. Rodrik, op. cit.

[45] Reducing the cost of doing business concerns not only explicit burdens, such as taxes and social contributions, but also other types of regulatory and administrative costs.

[46] Early in the transition process, moreover, some enterprise capital assets were stripped due to the lack of adequate corporate and public governance. It is possible that capital market liberalization contributed to this since it allows capital to be hidden abroad where it cannot be seized. K. Hoff and J. Stiglitz, "After the Big Bang? Obstacles to the emergence of the rule of law in post-communist societies", *American Economic Review*, Vol. 94 No. 3, June 2004, pp. 753-763.

collapse in economic activity during the transition phase. Although these advantages are very important, the EME should remain cognisant of a number of additional constraints and qualifications that apply to a development strategy based upon a strong reliance on external finance. These primarily include more stringent constraints on macroeconomic policy, the opportunity cost of holding increased amounts of international reserves, and the loss of national income during a currency crisis if one should occur. Due to these constraints, the benefits of capital market openness may well be smaller for emerging markets than for more advanced economies.[47]

Given the significant levels of capital inflows into the EME, there is the possibility that for some of these economies capital account liberalization may have proceeded too rapidly given their domestic institutional reforms. Since boom-bust cycles seem to characterize emerging market economies throughout the world, especially given the current international financial architecture, additional prudence towards adjusting both current account and fiscal deficits to sustainable levels during this period of relatively favourable performance would be in order.

It is difficult to assess the degree to which the EME current account deficits are likely to be problematic for economic stability.[48] Almost all analyses of previous exchange rate crises have concluded that large or increasing current account deficits were a significant contributing factor. However, the risk posed by a current account deficit cannot be evaluated solely by its size; it will also depend on how it is being financed, how it is being used, the exchange rate regime, current debt levels, the size of international reserves, the health of the financial system and the country's overall macroeconomic condition. Although there has been some progress in understanding the factors that may eventually trigger a currency crisis, there remain significant gaps in knowledge, and each crisis appears to be somewhat different from previous ones.[49] The fundamental problem is that current account deficits that appear sustainable under current conditions may no longer be viewed as such after some unforeseen, and perhaps totally external, shock. The question of sustainability is often raised for countries with current account deficits

significantly above their GDP growth rates. This is especially the case for those countries with double-digit current account deficits and high levels of external debt relative to official reserves or GDP (data on these variables is provided in chapter 6.1). Most of the EME have maintained current accounts deficits below 10 per cent of GDP, the level of Mexico's deficit in the years prior to its financial crisis in 1994. However, many have deficits that are larger than several of the east Asian countries prior to their financial crises in 1997-1998.[50] Given that the region has limited experience with open capital accounts and a susceptibility to currency crises,[51] including Bulgaria in 1996,[52] the Czech Republic[53] and Romania in 1997,[54] Russia in 1998,[55] Turkey in 2000-2001, and several speculative attacks against Hungary in 2003,[56] concern about possible future currency instability would seem to be warranted. Attention towards current account deficits and possible financing difficulties needs to be heightened during periods, such as the current one, when global liquidity is being tightened.

If a currency crisis were to occur in eastern Europe, the ability of the IMF to deal with it would depend to a large degree on how much contagion was involved since IMF funds are limited. The degree to which the EU would provide additional support is another significant factor. The ECB's focus on price stability, however, may limit its ability to intervene to support currencies in the ERM-2.[57] The United States special assistance to Mexico

[47] M. Obstfeld, *Globalization, Macroeconomic Performance and the Exchange Rates of Emerging Economies*, Bank of Japan Institute for Monetary and Economic Studies, Discussion Paper Series, 2004-E-14 (Tokyo), 2004.

[48] The sustainability of the current account deficits of the EU-10 is examined by P. Zanghieri, *Current Account Dynamics in New EU Members: Sustainability and Policy Issues*, CEPII Working Paper 2004-07 (Paris), July 2004. Concerns about specific countries have been raised in the press, e.g. E. Yeldan and M. Weisbrot, "Is Turkey the next Argentina?", *International Herald Tribune*, 4 December 2004.

[49] Even when the fundamentals are reasonably sound it is possible to have a self-fulfilling crisis that need not have occurred. Speculators will attack a currency when there is reasonable confidence that the attack will succeed regardless of the fundamentals.

[50] According to Joseph Stiglitz, the major contributing factors to the east Asian currency crisis were: 1) an exchange rate peg, 2) sterilization of capital inflows, 3) liberalization of capital accounts, and 4) inadequate financial regulation; speech delivered to the Council on Foreign Relations, *The Role of International Financial Institutions in the Current Global Economy* (Chicago), 27 February 1998.

[51] Exactly what constitutes a crisis is somewhat ambiguous; some define it as any time the nominal exchange rate depreciates by at least 20 per cent within 10 trading days, other criteria include changes in additional variables such as currency reserves and interest rates. These different measures are discussed in A. Brüggemann and T. Linne, *Are the Central and Eastern European Transition Countries Still Vulnerable to a Financial Crisis? Results from the Signals Approach*, Bank of Finland, Institute for Economies in Transition, Discussion Papers, No. 5 (Helsinki), 2002.

[52] For an analysis of this crisis and an earlier, milder one in 1994, see UNECE, *Economic Survey of Europe, 1996-1997*, chap. 3.1(iii).

[53] UNECE, *Economic Survey of Europe, 2001 No. 2*, p. 128, box 5.2.1.

[54] Although there was a significant and rapid depreciation of the Romanian leu during 1997, it did not result in a more generalized financial or economic crisis.

[55] Russia had a trade and current account surplus in the years prior to its crisis; see UNECE, *Economic Survey of Europe, 1998 No. 2*, chap. 1.2(ii).

[56] The attacks on Hungary's currency are described in UNECE, *Economic Survey of Europe, 2004 No. 1*, p. 51, box 3.1.1.

[57] Some argue that the ECB could intervene believing it would not increase the euro area money supply by enough to significantly affect inflation. K. Gern, F. Hammermann, R. Schweickert and L. Vinhas de Souza, *European Monetary Integration after EU Enlargement*, Kiel Discussion Paper, No. 413 (Kiel), September 2004.

in 1994-1995 was considerable and played an important role in containing that crisis. The lack of any special bilateral assistance from any of the major economies in the Asian crisis (although Japan offered to supply it) contributed to its magnitude.

Current account deficits should mainly finance investment

A major consideration in evaluating the sustainability of current account deficits is the degree to which the associated capital inflows are being invested or used for consumption. Although the emphasis on international financial integration is often on the potential for increasing fixed investment, empirical analysis finds that reduced savings instead of increased investment is often the main effect of capital market openness.[58] The lower interest rates that can result from capital account liberalization encourage private households to borrow for consumption purposes. Although additional consumption in the EME is not necessarily inappropriate, especially given the initial fall in living standards throughout much of the EME, it must be recognized that net foreign debt will have to be paid back with trade surpluses at some time in the future.[59] When current account deficits are used to increase fixed investment in the tradeables sector, they thereby contribute to growth and an increased capacity to earn the foreign exchange required to service and repay foreign debt; consumption driven deficits do not have this property. One lesson from the Mexican and east Asian crises is that investment in non-traded sectors such as real estate are of little value when foreign exchange is needed for debt repayment.

Although it is clear theoretically that current accounts deficits should ideally finance additional investment instead of additional consumption, it is difficult to determine empirically if this is actually happening. One possible approach that analysts use to address this question is to examine current account balances and investment over time to see how the former affects the latter. However, for the EME it would be inappropriate to use the pre-market years, and the early transition years when national income was falling were obviously not typical. Thus, the EME do not have an historical record that can be appropriately used to make this comparison.

Given that empirical analysis finds that financial liberalization is likely to lower domestic savings, and given the difficulty of altering private sector savings

behaviour, the most effective way to counter this fall in domestic savings is to increase public saving. However, this may not be desirable if fiscal deficits are being used to finance infrastructure investment. Investment can be directed into the tradeable sectors by giving those sectors favourable tax treatment. In terms of macro-stability, investment from equity is preferable to debt,[60] and FDI to portfolio investment.[61] Public policy should therefore be directed at providing incentives for FDI in the traded goods sectors. However, any incentives need to be carefully designed to minimize rent-seeking behaviours. In addition, any FDI promotion policy should also include complementary measures to increase positive technological spillovers. Research on EME economies has generally found that knowledge spillovers from FDI are weak[62] since firms have an incentive to limit spillovers to domestic competitors. The public policy emphasis should be on encouraging linkages to upstream and downstream firms in less direct competition.[63] In addition, the effects of foreign firms on market structure need to be monitored to ensure that these firms, which generally have superior technology, are not able to monopolize markets.

Currency arrangements complicate external finance

The task of managing capital market openness can be further complicated by currency arrangements that may constrain the set of potential policy options. This is especially the case for those economies that are attempting to fix or peg their exchange rates.[64] Countries with open capital accounts and pegged exchange rates will find it especially difficult to maintain domestic

---

[58] O. Blanchard and F. Giavazzi, "Current account deficits in the euro area: the end of the Feldstein-Horioka puzzle?", *Brookings Papers on Economic Activity*, 2 (Washington, D.C.), 2002, pp. 147-209.

[59] Technically, if creditors can be found debt never needs to be repaid, it can just be continuously rolled over. However, given limits to debt levels, higher current account deficits today imply lower current account deficits in the future and thus lower future domestic absorption than would have occurred otherwise.

[60] And long-term debt is preferable to short-term debt. A definitive verdict has yet to be reached on the advisability of capital account restrictions, as in Chile, that attempted to tilt the structure of investment by maturity from short term to long term.

[61] Most crises are accompanied by a significant stock market decline as equity investors try to get out; large and destabilizing reversals of portfolio investment were a central aspect of the crises in Argentina, Brazil, Mexico, the Republic of Korea and Russia.

[62] S. Djankov and B. Hoekman, "Foreign investment and productivity growth in Czech enterprises", *World Bank Economic Review*, Vol. 14, No. 1, January 2000, pp. 49-64; J. Konings, "The effects of foreign direct investment on domestic firms", *Economics of Transition*, Vol. 9, No. 3, November 2001, pp. 619-633.

[63] For a detailed analysis see UNCTAD, *World Investment Report 2001: Promoting Linkages* (United Nations publication, Sales No. E.01.II.D.12). Recent evidence for backward linkages in Lithuania is described in B. Javorcik, "Does foreign direct investment increase productivity of domestic firms? In search of spillovers through backward linkages", *American Economic Review*, Vol. 94, No. 3, June 2004, pp. 605-627.

[64] Estonia, Lithuania and Slovenia have joined the Exchange Rate Mechanism (ERM-2) as a preliminary step to adopting the euro; Latvia is expected to follow. All of the EU-10 are scheduled to adopt the euro by 2010, and must maintain a fixed exchange rate (around a band of ±15 per cent) in the two years prior to joining. Other countries such as Ukraine have maintained a de facto peg with the dollar, and Bosnia and Herzegovina and Bulgaria have implemented currency boards.

balance.[65] It will be a major policy challenge for them to reap the benefits of foreign borrowing without falling victim to a currency crisis. The fundamental problem facing the EU-10, as well as the other EME that attempt to maintain a fixed exchange rate, is the so-called trilemma of international finance – with open capital markets and a fixed exchange rate a country loses control over domestic monetary policy. In practical terms this means that the monetary authorities do not have sufficient instruments to achieve exchange rate stability and price stability at the same time. The EU-10, however, have macroeconomic targets for inflation and interest rates, and in addition limits on fiscal deficits, which they must meet as part of the Maastricht criteria to qualify for entry into the EMU. Therefore there is the possibility that these targets will not be consistent with one another and thus cannot be achieved simultaneously.[66] It is also possible that with these targets to satisfy, these countries will be forced to ignore, as their richer counterparts have, what should perhaps be the most important target – employment. The "classical" view, that if the other macroeconomic targets are achieved then macroeconomic policy is not needed to take care of employment, which is implicit in the Maastricht criteria, has proven to be a costly delusion.

Given that countries will be quite vulnerable once they are in the ERM-2, they are well advised to choose carefully the moment at which they embark on this stage of currency integration.[67] One of the main economic benefits from entry into the euro is the elimination of the possibility of a currency crisis and the absence of stabilization costs.

Increased international reserves could provide important insurance

A significant step that the EME may take to limit the possibility of a currency crisis is to increase the level of their official reserve assets. Concern about unexpected external shocks is a significant factor behind the tripling of international reserve assets by developing countries between 1993 and 2002. This has been especially the case for the east Asian countries, which are especially sensitive to potential risks given their experience in the 1997-1998 crises. These countries have also attempted to create a regional market for domestic currency debt as added insurance. However, the accumulation of international reserves, although providing some protection from a currency crisis, entails significant opportunity

costs. The reserves, normally held as short-term euro or dollar bills, pay interest rates that are relatively low, while real resources, in terms of foregone imports, must be sacrificed. In addition, the accumulation of reserves presents a fiscal burden in that in order to sterilize them (in order to avoid monetary growth and inflation), higher interest rate domestic bonds must be issued, while the government receives a much lower rate on its holdings of foreign bonds. The opportunity costs of holding international reserves can be reduced by purchasing slightly more risky assets with higher yields such as long-term government bonds or equity indexed funds; the overall risk is likely to be smaller by having more but riskier reserves than by having a smaller amount of less risky assets.[68] Another alternative that allows accumulation of reserves without an immediate decline in consumption, is for the central bank to borrow abroad long-term and invest the funds in liquid international securities. Although this has a cost due to the interest rate differential, the overall social costs are lower since the probability of an attack is lower and the interest spread on private debt and equity capital may fall as well.[69] As a further fall in the dollar would erode the value of existing official reserves, a re-evaluation of the currency allocations of current reserve portfolios would be prudent.

(v) Upcoming challenges posed by globalization in manufacturing and services

In order to reap the benefits of international trade integration, just as with financial integration, it is necessary to have in place the necessary complementary domestic institutions and policies. The failure to do so can be just as costly although not as dramatic as a currency crisis resulting from an institutional failure under financial integration. In the case of trade integration, the result can be increased unemployment, lower investment and increased inequality. The traditional benefits of increased specialization from trade openness can be easily negated if the displaced workers become unemployed, and the benefits of higher national income can be lost if it is more unequally distributed.

Each of the EME subregions will need to find a niche for themselves in the global production system. The EU-10 should be able to find a place in the manufacturing chain given their open access to the EU market, their relatively high levels of human capital but considerably lower wages. Market fragmentation and limited institutional reform are continuing to limit manufacturing in some of the south-east European countries. Currently, the CIS economies appear to be

---

[65] Even Brazil with a flexible exchange rate was subject to capital flight and a currency crisis in 2002.

[66] For a more detailed analysis see UNECE, *Economic Survey of Europe, 2002 No. 1*, chap. 5.

[67] The possibility of a currency crisis in the new EU members is examined in H. Gibson and E. Tsakalotos, "Capital flows and speculative attacks in prospective EU member states", *Economics of Transition,* Vol. 12 No. 3, 2004, pp. 559-586.

[68] M. Feldstein, *Aspects of Global Economic Integration: Outlook for the Future*, NBER Working Paper, No. 7899 (Cambridge, MA), September 2000.

[69] M. Feldstein, "A self-help guide for emerging markets", *Foreign Affairs*, Vol. 78, No. 2, March/April 1999, pp. 93-109.

largely outside the global manufacturing network; this is due to both the devastation of their manufacturing sectors during the transition phase and their natural competitive advantage in natural resource products. However, these primary commodities will not provide these countries with the basis to become dynamic growth economies.

Over the last half-century, countries in the middle of the global income distribution, which were also integrating into the world trading system, had relatively good growth rates and were able to converge towards the per capita income levels of the richer countries.[70] If this historical pattern were to hold in the coming decades, most of the EME, which clearly fit into this middle zone, would be expected to do relatively well. However, over the last half-century, those industrializing middle-income countries were not under a significant competitive threat from industrializing countries with even lower per capita incomes. In the coming decades, however, the EME will have to compete with countries such as Brazil, China and India; these countries have not only much lower wages but are in many areas as advanced or even more advanced technologically than the EME.[71] There are of course some high-tech niche markets in the EME, but they are not sufficient to employ large numbers of people.[72] Thus, the challenge will be to determine the sectors in which they will have a comparative advantage and also the potential for technological growth along with high and increasing wages. To avoid the undesirable situation of having to compete on the basis of low wages, the EME would appear to have little choice but to create knowledge-based societies by increasing investment in human capital formation and implementing policies to promote more entrepreneurship and innovation.

The outsourcing of services takes off

The issue of outsourcing,[73] especially of services, received intense public scrutiny during the last year. Although still a relatively minor activity, the concern was more a reflection of its longer-run potential to eliminate large numbers of service sector jobs in the advanced economies. For the east European countries and the CIS, service sector outsourcing represents more of an opportunity for employment and wage growth. Outsourcing is basically an expansion of trade and allows a further increase in the international division of labour and the productivity gains associated with it. For manufactured goods this has been an ongoing process for decades. More specifically multinational corporations have tended to move the assembly stage of production, which is generally a low-skilled labour-intensive activity, to low-wage low-skilled countries. The major factors which limit the ability of firms to engage in this activity are the costs of transporting the components and final products, the ability to manage and coordinate the outsourced stage in a distant location, the costs of maintaining larger inventories, the availability of complementary social infrastructure such as roads and ports, the availability of a sufficiently skilled workforce, and concerns about the protection of intellectual property rights.

With the significant decline in international telecommunications costs and the expansion of service activities that can be conducted over the phone or the Internet, certain service sector activities began during the 1990s to follow the pattern of manufacturing and began to be located in lower wage countries. Many of the same factors that limit manufacturing outsourcing also limit service sector outsourcing, but the disadvantages of transportation costs and distance are much less significant for many services. In fact, some service industries have used distance as a plus by taking advantage of the time differences that come with distance. Call centre or other activities can be maintained around the clock, and items can be processed during the night as a way to improve the speed and efficiency of operations. Since the workers performing many of these service sector jobs must have far more interaction with residents in the home country, or documents in the home country language, linguistic similarity appears to be a far more important consideration for service sector outsourcing than is the case for manufacturing. For this reason, the United Kingdom and the United States have been particularly interested in India – a country where 150 million people have English as their primary language and where wages are often one tenth of United States wages for comparable occupations.

Firms in western European countries have also outsourced to India, but for a variety of reasons including linguistic dissimilarity, they have not been as active in outsourcing service sector operations. Estimates for the next decade suggest that west European firms are likely to outsource only about 1.2 million service sector jobs or only one third as many jobs as United States firms are likely to outsource.[74] Nevertheless, a recent McKinsey

---

[70] C. Jones, "On the evolution of the world income distribution", *Journal of Economic Perspectives*, Vol. 11, No. 3, 1997, pp. 19-36; D. Ben-David, "Equalizing exchange: trade liberalization and income convergence", *Quarterly Journal of Economics*, Vol. 108, No. 3, 1993, pp. 653-679.

[71] This development is already becoming apparent. G. Garrett, "Globalization's missing middle", *Foreign Affairs,* November/December 2004, pp. 84-96.

[72] The recent acquisition by Microsoft Corporation of a Romanian software firm as the center for its anti-virus software is such an example.

[73] Outsourcing is defined as the process where firms split up the production process into smaller steps with each step located in a different geographical area depending on where each step can be produced at the lowest cost; these different steps may be produced by the same or by different firms. The term generally implies that an activity, which had previously been produced domestically, has been moved to a different country.

---

[74] A. Parker, "Two-speed Europe: why 1 million jobs will move offshore", Forrester Research (Cambridge, MA), 18 August 2004.

study reports that 40 per cent of western Europe's 500 largest companies have begun moving some of their service operations offshore. European firms, for now at least, seem to be staying closer to home and outsourcing more of their service activities to eastern Europe. For example, 60 per cent of German outsourcing goes to eastern Europe and only about 40 per cent to Asia. However, because of higher wages and infrastructure costs in eastern Europe, the cost savings are lower than going to Asia. Outsourcing provides western European firms a significant benefit, which is only marginally important for United States firms, in that they can adjust the size of their labour force without being subject to domestic labour regulations.

Given the high proportion of services in the GDPs of the advanced market economies, the rise of service sector outsourcing provides additional opportunities for the EME, particularly in the light of the prevailing high rates of unemployment in many of them. The usual factors which attract FDI apply to services as well; these include a skilled workforce, social infrastructure and appropriate regulatory institutions. A number of the EME have attracted some service sector FDI investment. Call-centre jobs have gone to the Czech Republic, Hungary, Poland and Slovakia; billing and back office jobs have gone to the Czech Republic, Hungary and Poland, while software and ICT jobs have gone to the Czech Republic, Hungary, Poland and Russia. Bulgaria, Estonia, Romania and Serbia and Montenegro are also beginning to be considered as possible destinations. Russia has the potential to become a significant destination for higher-skilled ICT services due to its large number of math and science graduates. Other major destinations outside the EME, especially for United States outsourced services, include China, Malaysia, the Philippines and Singapore.

As with trade generally, given the long-run full employment assumptions, the effect of outsourcing of either goods or services is to increase national income. Distributional problems arise, however, where certain groups of workers by skill category might lose from this development or where conditions of less than full employment exist; since the latter plagues much of Europe, there are legitimate employment concerns about outsourcing. So far, however, the level of outsourcing has not been large enough to significantly affect the level of unemployment. However, the most significant implication of service sector outsourcing is its potential to significantly increase the number of sectors and workers whose prices and wages will be determined in global markets which, in turn, will tend to put downward pressure on the wages of the unskilled in the advanced economies.[75]

A number of international economists have downplayed the potential for trade in goods to adversely affect wages in the advanced economies by arguing that the amount of trade is too small to dominate domestic employment conditions. With so many jobs in the "protected" non-traded sectors, foreign wages and prices can only have a minimal impact on the overall domestic employment situation. Therefore the possibility, suggested by some simple trade models, of factor price equalization – where wages for similar skill levels are the same throughout the world – is unlikely. Thus the wages of the unskilled in the advanced economies become unhooked from global wages as these countries fully specialize in non-traded goods and skill-intensive traded goods. The wage pressure from the traded sector is therefore limited by its small size. However, if a significant portion of the so-called "non-traded" service sector is actually tradeable, then this insulation of wages from global influences falls away, and the tendency towards factor price equalization returns. However, there are many services that cannot be outsourced, so there remains a question as to how extensive outsourcing and its effects are likely to be. An additional concern is that in some countries workers displaced by the outsourcing of services are not covered by trade adjustment assistance or by other types of job protections that may have evolved in the past to protect workers in the manufacturing sectors when they were subject to external shocks. In the countries receiving the outsourced services, which may include many of the EME, the distributional effects may be positive as new and better jobs are created for medium-skilled workers.

Many of the benefits from trade derive not from relative differences in factor costs, but from trade in differentiated products. Services are similar; trade among countries at similar levels of development can increase both the variety of services available and national income without creating significant distribution problems or adjustment costs.[76] The basic arguments for and against free trade in goods generally apply to trade in services. Although the political process has been slow, those in the advanced economies that have benefited from more open trade in goods have been able to convince enough of the losers (unskilled labour) that the general welfare is served by their gains. To some degree this has been due to the fact that many of those that lose from trade, such as unskilled labour in the non-traded sectors, do not perceive the way they are harmed through trade's impact on the unskilled labour market, but only appreciate the lower prices of goods. However, when large segments of the labour force see more directly how service sector outsourcing may harm them, this social consensus for open trade may dissolve.

[75] R. Shelburne, "Trade and inequality: the role of vertical specialization and outsourcing", *Global Economy Journal*, Vol. 4, No. 2, 2004 [www.bepress.com/gej/].

[76] R. Shelburne and J. Gonzalez, "The role of intra-industry trade in the service sector", in M. Plummer (ed.), *Empirical Methods in International Trade: Essays in Honor of Mordechai Kreinin* (London, Edward Elgar Press, 2005), pp. 110-128.

One approach to resolve this dilemma may be for the winners to provide more compensation to the losers. The system of public finance provides for various mechanisms and channels through which an additional redistribution could be performed. For example, more public funds could be allocated to training and skill upgrading of the affected workforce that could facilitate their reintegration into the more skilled segments of the labour market. More generally, national public policies targeting human capital development will strengthen the future competitive position of a country and allow it to benefit from expanding trade in services. Although in time, firms in the EME may also begin outsourcing services to even lower wage countries, over the next several years at least, workers in the EME, especially skilled workers, are likely to benefit from the opportunities provided by outsourcing. As with FDI generally, it would be highly beneficial if these investments in the EME service industries did not produce isolated clusters but could produce technological spillovers, stimulate competition and promote human capital formation.

CHAPTER 2

THE GLOBAL CONTEXT

2.1 The broad picture

A strong global recovery, but losing momentum

The global economic recovery continued in 2004. World output increased by some 5 per cent, up from 3.9 per cent in 2003.[77] This was the fastest average annual rate of increase in 30 years. The strong growth in output led to a marked acceleration in world trade of goods and services, which increased in volume by nearly 9 per cent in 2004, double its growth rate in 2003. The annual average, however, masks the fact that the global recovery had started to lose momentum after the first quarter of 2004. A major factor behind this deceleration in the course of the year appears to have been the sharp rise in oil prices; but the gradual withdrawal of the economic policy stimulus in the major economies has also played a role. Moreover, the depreciation of the dollar, which resumed in the second of half of the year, recalled the fact that large financial imbalances remain a major downside risk for the global economy. Against the backdrop of uncertain labour market prospects and the adverse effect of higher energy prices on households' purchasing power, consumer confidence fell in the United States and remained subdued in western Europe throughout the second half of 2004. Business confidence in the United States fell after the first quarter of 2004 and in western Europe, a modest strengthening of industrial confidence petered out into stagnation in the second half of the year.

Among the major economies, the United States and China provided the main stimuli to global growth in 2004. The rate of economic expansion in the other six major economies slowed down significantly between the second and third quarters of 2004. Real GDP in the G7 combined (which does not include China) slowed to 0.6 per cent in the third quarter compared with 1 per cent in the first quarter. Virtually all of this slowdown was due to weak growth in Japan and the four major west European economies. A direct consequence of the latter was a marked deceleration in the rate of economic growth in the euro area. But there were also indications of a weakening, albeit moderate so far, of the still buoyant growth of the Chinese economy.

Looking at 2004 as a whole, all the major regions shared in the global recovery, although growth rates varied, reflecting the differences in the strength of external and domestic demand as well as the stance of economic policy. The continued dynamism of the Asian economies stood out, reflecting especially the continued strong growth in China and India and the accelerating growth in south-east Asia. There has also been remarkably rapid growth in the CIS largely because of the boom in commodity prices. Economic activity also picked up strongly in Latin America, and in most of central and eastern Europe, economic activity continued at high momentum. The euro area, as in 2003, remained the laggard of the global recovery.

Changing preoccupations of policy makers

In early 2003, policy makers were still concerned at the prospect of continued sluggish growth in the aftermath of the bursting of the ICT and stock market bubbles in 2000. But the progressive lowering of interest rates by the major central banks to historically low levels (chart 2.1.1) contributed, together with a massive fiscal stimulus in the United States, to a gradual recovery of the world economy, which strengthened in the second half of 2003 and continued into 2004. Attention has now switched to the risks of higher inflation and overheating, as well as the emergence of asset price bubbles which have followed the surge in global liquidity. The main challenge now is to withdraw this massive monetary stimulus without undermining the sustainability of the global recovery.

In the United States, where the recovery was well entrenched, the Federal Reserve started to raise its key policy interest rate (the target for the federal funds rate) gradually from 1 per cent in June 2004 in four steps to 2 per cent in November 2004. In the United Kingdom, the Bank of England's Monetary Policy Committee already started to tighten monetary policy in November 2003, a process that continued during the first eight months of 2004. The central banks of Canada and Switzerland also raised their key policy rates. In contrast, in the euro area, the ECB has so far maintained a wait-and-see attitude in view of the still fragile recovery of output, leaving its main refinancing rate unchanged at 2 per cent (chart 2.1.1). There has also been a tightening of monetary controls and an increase in interest rates (among other policy measures) in China, which for a long time has

---

[77] Based on national GDPs using weights at purchasing power parity rates. Using weights based on market exchange rate, global real GDP rose by 4.1 per cent in 2004, up from 2.4 per cent in 2003. Consensus Economics, *Consensus Forecasts* (London), 6 December 2004.

CHART 2.1.1

Key official interest rates of major central banks, January 1999-November 2004

(Per cent per annum)

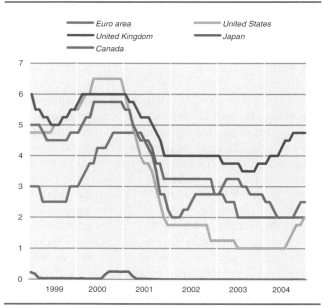

Source: Central bank publications.

Note: Euro area: main refinancing rate; Canada: target for overnight rate; Japan: uncollaterized overnight rate; United States: intended federal funds rate.

been "disconnected" from the international business cycle, to prevent overheating and ensure a "soft landing". Fiscal policy (as judged by changes in cyclically adjusted primary balances) was slightly expansionary in the United States, but somewhat restrictive on average in the euro area in 2004. In Japan, there was a more pronounced fiscal tightening. Governments are increasingly preoccupied by the need to consolidate the public finances in the face of the mounting fiscal challenges presented by ageing populations.

A major and more immediate concern of policy makers remains the large current account imbalances across the main regions of the world economy. The United States current account deficit rose to record levels in 2004 and further increases are forecast for the next two years. The main counterparts to this deficit are large current account surpluses in Japan and Asia (especially China), and to a lesser extent in the euro area (mainly Germany). These imbalances reflect not only the differential strength of domestic demand in the United States and the rest of the world, but also the misalignment of exchange rates among the major currencies. The latter remains a potential source of disruption to the pattern of international capital flows, given the unsustainability of the large United States current account deficit and the consequent cumulative increase in net foreign debt. These concerns appeared to be the main factor behind the strong depreciation of the dollar against other major currencies in November and December 2004. The gradual reduction of the United States current account deficit without

endangering the sustainability of the global recovery is therefore the other major policy challenge.

Buoyant growth in developing markets

Real GDP in the developing countries grew by an estimated 6.1 per cent in 2004, the largest increase in three decades.[78] While this largely reflects the dynamism of Asian economies, economic growth accelerated in all developing regions. Economic activity was reinforced by a faster rate of expansion of international trade, and stimulated by competitive exchange rates, strengthening domestic demand, favourable international financing conditions, and in some regions high commodity prices.

Net private capital flows to developing markets rose somewhat in 2004 to an estimated $226 billion, their highest level since the east Asian crisis.[79] Investors were attracted by the economic performance of these economies, ample liquidity and the relatively low rates of return to financial assets in industrialized countries. The increase in capital flows was due entirely to foreign direct investment (FDI), other types of net financial flow either falling or remaining more or less stable. The bulk of the FDI went to Asia (which received a net $62 billion), where China accounted for over 80 per cent of the regional total (amounting to some $50 billion). Emerging market borrowers intensified their bond emissions, so that the estimated value of their gross issuance reached the record set in 1997.[80] This reflects borrowers' efforts to lock in low interest rates and extend maturities, in anticipation of higher borrowing costs from 2005. Spreads over United States treasury bills finished the year close to the level of early 2004, when they had reached record low levels.

In developing Asia economic growth accelerated to 7 per cent in 2004, matching the pace of 2000, which was the highest since the crises of 1997-1998.[81] Growth was favoured by the rise in global spending on ICT products[82] and the dynamism of regional and global trade. The strengthening of fixed investment and the continued strong growth of domestic consumption has meant that growth became more broadly based. Rising domestic demand led to a rapid increase in imports, so that the region's current account surplus fell somewhat from its four-year high in 2003. Nevertheless, the accumulation of foreign reserves continued on a large scale in the region.

---

[78] World Bank, *Global Economic Prospects 2005* (Washington, D.C.), November 2004 [www.worldbank.org].

[79] Institute of International Finance, *Capital Flows to Emerging Market Economies* (New York), 2 October 2004 [www.iif.com].

[80] BIS, "International banking and financial market development", *BIS Quarterly Review* (Basel), December 2004 [www.bis.org].

[81] Asian Development Bank, *Asian Development Outlook Update* (Manila), October 2004 [www.adb.org].

[82] Worldwide spending on ICT grew by an estimated 4.6 per cent in 2004, after a rhythm of 1.4 per cent in the previous year. EITO, *EITO Update 2004*, October 2004 [www.eito.com].

In China, economic growth has been accelerating since 2001, accompanied by a rapid expansion of credit and fixed investment to the point where higher rates of inflation and capacity bottlenecks began to emerge in some sectors. In order to fend off the dangers of overheating, the authorities have introduced since mid-2003 a number of largely administrative macro-control measures to cool down the economy. In late October 2004, the central bank raised interest rates, albeit only slightly, for the first time in nine years, a first step towards greater emphasis on market-driven mechanisms for slowing the growth of loans and fixed investment. At the same time, the ceiling on bank lending rates was abolished, a move which should help to increase the efficiency of financial intermediation. While there are signs that the growth of investment and imports were slowing down during 2004, real GDP still rose by nearly 9 per cent. In India economic growth was 6.5 per cent in 2004, high but clearly below the 8.2 per cent in 2003. The slowdown was brought about by significantly less favourable conditions in the agricultural sector, which strongly influences personal income and consumption.

In Latin America, GDP growth accelerated to an average 5.5 per cent in 2004, the fastest rate in over 25 years.[83] This was the first time in seven years that all economies in the region grew (except for Haiti). They benefited from the strong import demand in the United States and Asia (particularly China), increased receipts from tourism, favourable external financing conditions and from higher commodity prices.[84] The current account surplus increased somewhat from 2003, when the region had a current account surplus for the first time in more than a quarter of a century. The external stimulus was underpinned by competitive exchange rates and prudent macroeconomic policies. The combination of rising exports, improving confidence and a more positive economic outlook helped to stimulate domestic demand.

In the Middle East, economic growth was supported by the surge in oil prices. But the stimulus from the latter was partly offset by the uncertainties created by political tensions, terrorist attacks and war. In Africa, real GDP rose by some 4.5 per cent in 2004 compared with 3.7 per cent in 2003. A fairly stable macroeconomic environment contributed to the improvement as did higher commodity prices, which led to significantly improved terms of trade. There was also an increase in FDI. There were, however, large differences in economic performance across the continent, reflecting, in addition to macroeconomic fundamentals, differences in factor and natural resource endowments, in socio-political stability and in climatic conditions.

---

[83] ECLAC, *Preliminary Overview of the Economies of Latin America and the Caribbean 2004* (Santiago), December 2004 [www.eclac.org].

[84] The main commodities exported by Latin America are petroleum and petroleum products, coffee, bananas, soya beans and oil, meat, copper and iron ore.

A boom in international commodity markets

International commodity prices rose strongly in 2004 in response to unexpectedly strong demand combined with low stock levels and a relatively weak supply response. The pressure on prices appears to have been accentuated by the activities of speculative investment funds seeking alternatives to low returns on financial assets, although their actual influence on developments is difficult to gauge. Non-energy commodity prices in 2004 were some 22 per cent higher than in 2003, the biggest increase in 10 years. They were driven by metal prices, which increased on average by almost 40 per cent during the year (table 2.1.1), led by copper, lead, tin, nickel and ferrous raw materials. Demand for metals was spurred by the growth of world industrial output, particularly in China and other Asian countries. But the sharp rise in non-energy prices levelled off and was partly reversed in the second half of the year (chart 2.1.2).

Oil prices rise to record levels

Oil prices were rising rapidly during the first 10 months of 2004. They peaked at a nominal record of $52.3 per barrel (Brent spot) in the second half of October 2004, but fell back to $37 per barrel by mid-December (chart 2.1.3). World oil demand in 2004 rose by an estimated 3.4 per cent[85] – the largest increase in over two decades – driven by the strengthening of world economic activity and, particularly, by rising consumption in China and the United States. The large increase in demand occurred in a context of very low margins of spare capacity. Actual or potential supply disruptions in several major producing areas (Gulf of Mexico, Iraq, Nigeria, Norway, Russia, Venezuela) thus had a strong additional impact on prices. Oil prices started to retreat from their peaks in November, reflecting the emergence of excess of supply over demand and rising inventories. In November 2004, the average monthly oil price (Brent crude) was 50 per cent higher than 12 months earlier; in euros, the increase was 35 per cent. The average price for the first 11 months of 2004 was $38 per barrel, some $9.2 (or 32 per cent) higher than during the same period of 2003. Given the appreciation of the euro against the dollar, the rise in the euro price of oil was about 20 per cent over the same period.

In real terms (deflating nominal oil prices by an index of unit values of manufactures exported by developed countries), prices in 2004 were some 22 per cent above those of 2003 but they were still some 30 per cent below the level reached after the second oil price shock in 1980-1981 (chart 2.1.3).

---

[85] International Energy Agency, *Oil Market Report* (Paris), 10 November 2004 [www.iea.org].

TABLE 2.1.1

International commodity prices, 2002-2004
(Annual percentage change)

Items	Weights	Prices in dollars			Prices in euros		
		2002	2003	2004[a]	2002	2003	2004[a]
Energy	67.4	-0.4	14.4	35.6	-5.9	-3.9	23.0
Non-energy raw materials	32.6	2.7	14.2	21.6	-2.6	-4.5	10.6
Industrial raw materials	22.6	-1.6	17.3	25.6	-6.5	-2.1	14.2
Non-ferrous materials	9.1	-4.2	11.9	38.1	-8.8	-6.8	25.5
Iron ore, scrap	3.4	2.7	17.9	38.4	-2.6	-1.4	25.6
Agricultural raw materials	10.1	-0.6	21.6	10.5	-5.8	1.7	0.5
Food	9.9	12.0	8.1	13.2	6.1	-9.4	2.9
Total above	100	0.6	14.4	30.9	-4.8	-4.2	18.9

Source: Hamburg Institute of International Economics (HWWA).

Note: Weights correspond to the average shares of the various product categories in total OECD commodity imports in 1999-2001.

[a] January-November.

CHART 2.1.2

Non-energy commodity prices, January 2000-November 2004
(Selected commodity groups, indices, 2000=100)

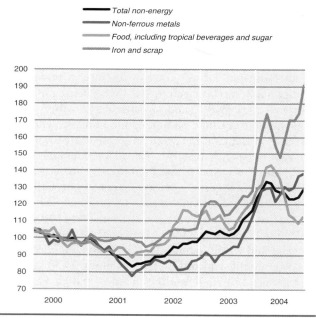

Source: Hamburg Institute of International Economics (HWWA).

Note: Indices calculated on the basis of current dollar prices and weighted by the average shares of the various product categories in total OECD commodity imports in 1999-2001.

Equity markets remain lacklustre

In the international equity markets there was a great deal of volatility during 2004. After a buoyant start in the first quarter – sustained by positive prospects for world economic growth, improved corporate earnings and a renewed willingness of investors to take risk – global equity markets moved erratically around a basically flat trend. Investor confidence appears to have been depressed by lingering geopolitical uncertainties, concerns about the oil price, a possible hard landing in

CHART 2.1.3

Nominal and real crude petroleum prices, 1980-2004
(Dollars/barrel, index)

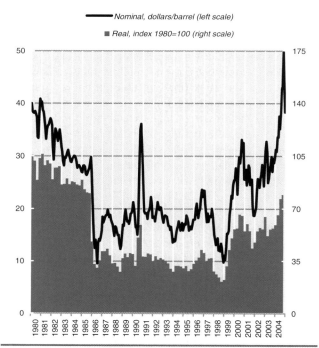

Source: United States Department of Energy, *Weekly Status Petroleum Report* (Washington, D.C.), various issues [www.eia.doe.gov]; IMF, *International Financial Statistics* (CD-Rom); United Nations, Common Database.

Note: Brent crude spot price, monthly averages for nominal prices and quarterly averages for real prices. The real price of crude oil was calculated by deflating the nominal price index by the unit value index of manufacturing exports of developed market economies.

China and the lowering of global growth forecasts for 2005. In late 2004, when oil prices fell sharply from their record levels in October, equity prices rallied again in the wake of renewed confidence in the continuation of the global recovery. All told, between January 2004 and end-November, prices in the major equity markets increased on average by only 5 per cent.

The dollar depreciation continues

The main development on the foreign exchange markets in 2004 was the further weakening of the dollar in the second half of the year, which accelerated in November and more than reversed an appreciation in the first five months of the year (chart 2.1.4). This slide of the dollar has been mainly due to the increasingly perceived need for a fundamental realignment of the exchange rate in order to correct the large United States current account deficit and the associated rise in external financial liabilities. Concerns about the large and persistent government budget deficit have likely also played a role.

The exchange rate between the dollar and the euro rose to a record $1.33 in early December 2004. The yen/dollar rate fell to Y102.6, a five-year low, with no apparent attempt by the Japanese authorities to intervene in

CHART 2.1.4

Bilateral exchange rates between the dollar, the euro and the yen, January 1999-November 2004

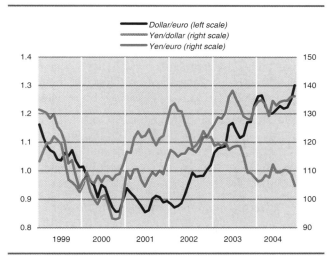

Dollar/euro (left scale)
Yen/dollar (right scale)
Yen/euro (right scale)

Source: Eurostat, NewCronos Database; Board of Governors of the Federal Reserve System [www.federalreserve.gov].

Note: Average monthly values.

CHART 2.1.5

Nominal effective exchange rate indices of the dollar, the euro and the yen, January 1995-November 2004
(Indices, 1997=100)

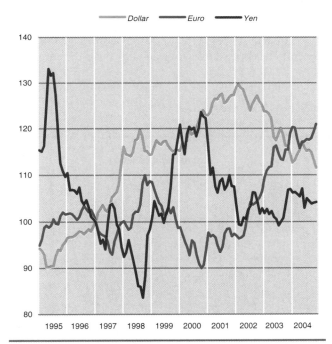

Dollar   Euro   Yen

Source: Dollar: Board of Governors of the Federal Reserve System [www.federalreserve.gov]; euro: ECB [www.ecb.int]; yen: Datastream.

Note: Broad index for the dollar and the euro.

the market. Since reaching a monthly low in February 2002, the euro had appreciated by nearly 50 per cent against the dollar in November 2004. The yen has risen against the dollar by some 27.5 per cent over the same period. The dollar also weakened markedly against other

major currencies, such as the UK pound and the Swiss franc, as well as several Asian currencies, in late 2004. The Chinese monetary authorities, however, maintained the parity of their currency peg to the dollar for the ninth consecutive year, although there have been increasing pressures from speculative capital inflows and from the United States for a revaluation.

From its previous high in February 2002, the nominal trade-weighted exchange rate of the dollar had fallen 15 per cent by November 2004 (chart 2.1.5). Over the same period, the nominal effective exchange rate of the euro appreciated by some 25 per cent. In contrast, the effective exchange rate of the yen rose by only about 5 per cent over the period between February 2002 and November 2004.

2.2 The United States and Japan

(i) The United States

Recovery continues, driven by domestic demand and exports

In the United States, economic activity grew at a brisk pace in 2004, driven by domestic demand. Exports picked up in a favourable external environment and helped by the weaker dollar. But the ongoing surge in imports meant that the change in real net exports continued to be a drag on domestic output. Real GDP rose by 4.4 per cent, significantly above the trend rate of output growth of some 3¼ per cent; as a result, the gap between potential and actual output became quite small in 2004.[86] Private consumption, supported by a slowly recovering labour market, low interest rates and the wealth effects from the booming housing market, was the mainstay of economic activity (table 2.2.1). Households also lowered their savings rate from its already low level of 1.4 per cent of disposable income in 2003. Buoyed by continued low mortgage rates, the housing market remained strong, with a solid expansion of residential investment and a record number of home sales. Some cooling in house sales, however, appears to have dampened the rise in house prices in late 2004. The growth in consumer spending also appears to have levelled off in the final months of 2004 against a background of declining consumer confidence, high energy prices and expectations of more moderate economic growth in 2005 with associated concerns for the labour market (chart 2.2.1).

Business spending on equipment and software was buoyant, stimulated by improved profitability, rising capacity utilization rates and tax incentives. The decline in spending on industrial buildings in the previous three years appears to have bottomed out in 2004. But business confidence declined after the first quarter of

---

[86]   *OECD Economic Outlook No. 76*, Preliminary edition (Paris), November 2004.

TABLE 2.2.1

Changes in real GDP and main expenditure items in the United States, 2003QIII-2004QIII

(Percentage change over previous period)

	2003		2004		
	QIII	QIV	QI	QII	QIII
Private consumption	1.2	0.9	1.0	0.4	1.2
Final consumption expenditure of general government	-0.3	0.5	0.5	0.2	0.8
Gross fixed capital formation	3.7	2.1	1.1	3.1	1.5
Stockbuilding [a]	0.1	0.1	0.3	0.2	-0.2
Total domestic expenditure	1.6	1.2	1.2	1.1	1.0
Exports of goods and services ...	2.7	4.1	1.8	1.8	1.6
Imports of goods and services ...	0.7	4.0	2.6	3.0	1.5
Net exports [a]	0.2	-0.2	-0.2	-0.3	-0.1
GDP	1.8	1.0	1.1	0.8	1.0

Source: United States Department of Commerce, Bureau of Economic Analysis.

Note: Data are seasonally adjusted. 2004QIII figures are preliminary estimates.

[a] Percentage point contribution to real GDP growth.

2004, against the background of a less optimistic economic outlook (chart 2.2.1). This is also reflected in the downward tendency of the ISM business activity indicators, although they remained well above the threshold of 50, a pointer to the ongoing expansion of business activity (chart 2.2.2).

Labour markets improve gradually

The recovery, with an unusually long lag, was also reflected in an upturn of employment, although this was relatively subdued by historical standards. Non-farm payrolls in November 2004 were 1.9 million higher than

at the beginning of the year, an increase of 1.4 per cent. The number of employees, however, was still slightly below its previous peak in March 2001. The unemployment rate fell by only 0.2 percentage points to 5.4 per cent over the same period, reflecting an increase in the labour supply. Slowing productivity growth in the third quarter of 2004 combined with rising wage costs put some upward pressure on unit labour costs, which have nevertheless remained moderate. Intense competition has limited the ability of producers to pass on the higher cost of energy.

Consumer price inflation edged up somewhat, largely because of higher energy prices. The headline inflation rate averaged 2.5 per cent, year-on-year, during the first 10 months of 2004, but the rate of core inflation, which excludes food and energy products, was only 2 per cent.

External imbalances deteriorate further

The trade deficit surged to record levels in 2004, increasing by some $100 billion to around $605 billion. The current account deficit amounted to some $670 billion or 5.7 per cent of GDP, up from 4.8 per cent in 2003. The gap between the current account and trade deficits widened in 2004 (a trend which is expected to continue in 2005 and 2006) due to a deterioration in the net balance of factor income, a result of the net outflow of dividend and interest payments to foreigners holding dollar denominated financial assets.

A gradual reversal of the expansionary monetary policy stance

Against a background of economic growth, the Federal Reserve started to gradually raise the target for

CHART 2.2.1

Business and consumer confidence in the United States, January 2001-November 2004

(Business confidence, balances; consumer confidence, index 1985=100)

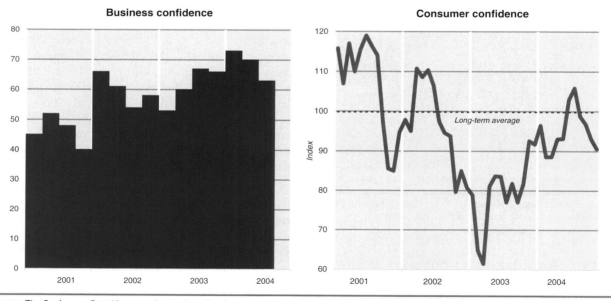

Source: The Conference Board [www.conference-board.org].

Note: For business confidence, a value above 50 indicates more positive than negative responses (quarterly values, 2001QI-2004QIII). Long-term average value of consumer confidence for 1990-2003.

CHART 2.2.2

Surveys of business activity in the United States, January 2001-November 2004
(Per cent)

Manufacturing sector: Purchasing Managers' Index (PMI)
Non-manufacturing sector: business activity index

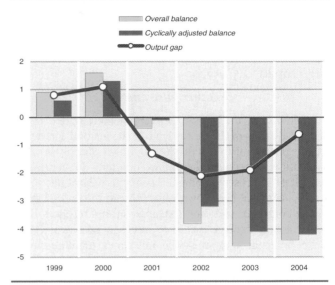

Source: Institute for Supply Management (Arizona) [www.ism.ws].

Note: An index value above (below) 50 indicates that the sector is generally expanding (contracting). Long-term average of PMI for 1990-2003.

CHART 2.2.3

General government financial balance in the United States, 1999-2004
(Per cent of GDP)

Overall balance
Cyclically adjusted balance
Output gap

Source: OECD Economic Outlook No. 76 (Paris), November 2004.

Note: Overall balance as a per cent of actual GDP; cyclically adjusted balance as a per cent of potential GDP. Figures for 2004 are estimates.

the federal funds rate, which had been at a 46-year low of 1 per cent since June 2003. The target rate was raised in four steps each of a quarter of a percentage point to 2 per cent between June and November 2004. Monetary policy, however, is still very supportive of economic growth. Real short-term interest rates (based on the CPI) continued to be negative. Moreover, the moderate tightening of monetary policy was offset by the further depreciation of the dollar in the second half of 2004. At the long end of the maturity spectrum, yields on 10-year treasury bonds rose by 90 basis points to 4.7 per cent between March and June 2004, reflecting, *inter alia,* concerns about the inflationary impact of higher oil prices and the large fiscal deficits. Long-term yields fell back to 4.2 per cent in November in the face of expectations of weaker growth in 2005. Contemporaneous real long-term yields were close to 2 per cent in 2004.

Following two years of strong fiscal stimuli (chart 2.2.3), fiscal policy was only slightly expansionary in 2004. The general government deficit is estimated at 4.4 per cent of GDP, compared with 4.6 per cent in 2003. The bulk of this deficit is structural.[87]

Short-term prospects remain favourable

The short-term outlook for the United States is for continued expansion but at a rate more in line with the

underlying trend of output growth. Real GDP is forecast to increase by 3.5 per cent in 2005. The level of employment is expected to pick up somewhat and the unemployment rate to fall again. The stimulus from monetary policy will be further reduced in 2005. Long-term interest rates are thus expected to edge upward during 2005. At the same time, fiscal policy is expected to have a small contractionary impact on economic activity, *inter alia,* a reflection of the phasing out of special investment incentives for the business sector and smaller income tax refunds. Against this background, the recovery will continue to be supported by a strong, albeit moderating, growth of private consumption. The personal savings rate is expected to remain below 1 per cent of disposable income in 2005. Non-residential business investment should remain buoyant, stimulated by shrinking margins of idle capacity and favourable prospects for profitability. The boom in residential investment is expected to level off, partly because of the rise in interest rates. Exports should benefit from the favourable global environment and the depreciation of the dollar. Changes in real net exports, moreover, will exert less of a drag on overall economic activity. The current account deficit is expected to rise to a level corresponding to more than 6 per cent of GDP.

Apart from high oil prices, the major downside risks to this benign scenario include uncertainty about the spending behaviour of private households in the face of high levels of debt, a fading house price boom and less favourable financing conditions due to rising interest rates. If labour market performance were to be less

_____
[87]   Ibid.

favourable than expected, that would also weigh on consumer confidence and risk an increase in the household savings rate with a corresponding reduction of demand. The current account deficit in combination with the large government budget deficit may trigger adverse reactions in the international financial markets with concomitant upward pressures on interest rates in the bond markets.

(ii) Japan

Another false dawn?

In Japan, the strong recovery, which started in the second quarter of 2003, faltered in the second quarter of 2004. Economic growth slowed down sharply to near stagnation in the second and third quarters. Nevertheless, real GDP still rose by some 3.4 per cent in 2004 due to the strong statistical carry-over effect[88] from the end of 2003. While consumer spending remained strong, business fixed investment and the growth of exports slowed down. At the same time, the cuts in public investment continued at a rapid rate. The loss of cyclical momentum was also visible in a weakening of industrial production and the continuing fall of prices in 2004. The decline of the consumer price index decelerated in 2004, in contrast to the continued rapid decline of the GDP deflator, the broadest measure of price changes in an economy. Land prices also continued to fall. The financial sector, however, has made progress

in the consolidation of non-performing loans, and the long-term decline in bank lending appears to be bottoming out. The stance of monetary policy remained unchanged in 2004, with the central bank's overnight lending rate being held at virtually zero per cent. Yields on 10-year government bonds were only 1.5 per cent in late 2004. Interventions in the foreign exchange market designed to stem the appreciation of the yen against the dollar appear to have ceased after the first quarter of 2004 leading to some tightening of overall monetary conditions. Fiscal policy was contractionary in 2004. The actual government budget deficit is estimated at some 6.5 per cent of GDP in 2004, down from 7.7 per cent in 2003.

The assessment of the underlying cyclical momentum, however, has been made more difficult than usual by revisions to the national accounts statistics.[89] Based on currently available data, forecasts are for economic growth to slow down in 2005 to an average annual rate of 1.5 per cent. This reflects both a moderate increase in domestic demand and a weaker growth of exports. Given the dependence of the Japanese economy on exports, a strong appreciation of the yen will risk an even further weakening of economic growth. Given the explosive trajectory of government debt, which was equivalent to 170 per cent of GDP in 2004, the main medium-term challenge for policy makers in Japan is to correct and consolidate the public finances.

---

[88] Maintaining real GDP throughout 2004 at the level of the final quarter of 2003 would anyway have ensured an average annual growth rate of 2 per cent.

[89] Preliminary estimates of GDP based on a new (chain-linked) deflation method, put the annual average rate of economic growth in 2003 at 1.3 per cent compared with an estimate of 2.5 per cent based on the old methodology. Based on the latter method, real GDP rose by 4.4 per cent, year-on-year, during the first three quarters of 2004. Preliminary revised data using the new methodology put the growth for the same period at only 3.2 per cent.

CHAPTER 3

WESTERN EUROPE AND THE NEW EU-10

3.1 Western Europe

(i) Euro area

Recovery fails to gain momentum

After a very promising start in the first quarter of 2004, the economic recovery progressively lost momentum. Between the second and third quarters, real GDP rose by only 0.3 per cent, equivalent to a seasonally adjusted annual rate of 1.2 per cent and significantly below the trend rate of output growth. Real exports, which had been leading the recovery, slowed markedly in the face of a weakening external economic environment and, possibly, the euro appreciation (table 3.1.1). In contrast, the volume of imports accelerated into the third quarter, so that the impact of real net exports on GDP growth became strongly negative. The strong upturn in exports since the third quarter of 2003 has failed to stimulate final domestic demand, which remained rather sluggish. The weakening of foreign demand occurred in a context where domestic demand had failed to become a source of sustained growth (chart 3.1.1). Higher inventory investments made a significant contribution to growth in the third quarter of 2004, but it is unclear to what extent this was voluntary or due to an unexpected shortfall of demand.

Persistent weakness of demand

For the year as a whole, real GDP in the euro area is estimated to have increased by 2 per cent, up from an average annual growth rate of 0.5 per cent in 2003. Private household consumption was lacklustre, held back by low consumer confidence, a sluggish employment recovery in most countries, and a dent in real disposable incomes due to rising energy prices. Consumer confidence, having improved somewhat during 2003, stabilized at a subdued level below its long-term average. This partly reflected uncertainties concerning the economic outlook and the medium- and longer-term income effects of ongoing or planned reforms of social security systems in several countries. Following declines in the three preceding years, fixed investment picked up somewhat in 2004, but failed to gather significant momentum. Business fixed investment was held back by uncertainties regarding the medium-term outlook for demand as well as the surge in oil prices. This appears to have offset the potentially better conditions for investment spending due to continued progress in

TABLE 3.1.1

Quarterly changes in real GDP and major expenditure items in the euro area, 2003-2004QIII

(Percentage change over previous period, seasonally adjusted)

	2003				2004		
	QI	QII	QIII	QIV	QI	QII	QIII
Private consumption	0.2	–	0.3	–	0.6	0.2	0.2
Final consumption expenditure of general government	-0.1	0.4	0.6	0.5	0.1	0.4	0.8
Gross fixed capital formation	-0.8	-0.2	0.3	1.0	-0.3	0.3	0.6
Total domestic expenditure	0.6	-0.1	–	1.0	0.2	0.3	1.1
Exports of goods and services	-1.7	-0.8	2.6	0.3	1.5	3.1	1.2
Imports of goods and services	-0.4	-0.7	1.3	2.0	0.5	2.8	3.2
GDP	–	-0.2	0.5	0.4	0.7	0.5	0.3

Source: Eurostat, NewCronos Database.

redressing corporate balance sheets, supportive financial conditions, and improved profitability on the back of a cyclical recovery in productivity combined with wage moderation. Capacity utilization in manufacturing, moreover, increased following the rise in output (chart 3.1.2). Influenced by international developments, industrial confidence improved only moderately during 2004. Government spending contributed marginally to economic growth in 2004.

A moderate upturn in labour markets

Labour markets in the euro area remained generally weak throughout 2004. Employment was only 0.5 per cent higher than in 2003. The elasticity of employment with regard to changes in output has fallen in recent years, after being on a rising trend in the second half of the 1990s (chart 3.1.3). The latter increase in the employment elasticity (or the "employment content of growth") may have been a reflection of the labour market reforms that encouraged short-term contracts and part-time work in the second half of the 1990s. Conversely, the recent decline probably reflects the waning impact of these measures as well as the effects of labour hoarding in the cyclical downturn. The steady fall in the unemployment rate since 1997, when it stood at 10.8 per cent, bottomed out at 8 per cent in 2000, the peak of the previous growth cycle. Since then, unemployment edged up to 8.9 per cent in 2004 (chart 3.1.4), mainly reflecting

CHART 3.1.1

The contribution of major expenditure items to quarter-to-quarter changes in real GDP in the euro area, 2003-2004QIII
(Percentage points)

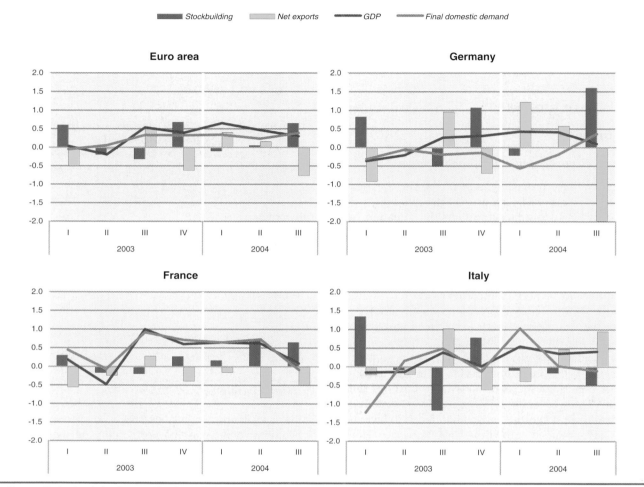

Source: National statistics; Eurostat, NewCronos Database.
Note: Data are seasonally adjusted.

the cyclical downturn but also the fading effects of the labour market reforms that supported the demand for labour in the second half of the 1990s.

Inflation remains moderate

Consumer price inflation has remained moderate, averaging 2.1 per cent, year-on-year, for the first 10 months of 2004. For the year as a whole an increase of 2.2 per cent is expected. Upward pressure on the headline inflation rate from the sharp rise in oil prices was partly offset by lower prices for unprocessed food that were mainly due to a statistical base effect that arose as a result of the long, dry summer in 2003, which had led to large price increases. But higher prices for services (especially administered prices such as those for health care) and increases in tobacco taxes in some countries kept the core inflation close to 2 per cent in 2004 (chart 3.1.5). Higher oil and commodity prices were also reflected in industrial producer prices during 2004, but they only rose by less than 2 per cent, year-on-year, in the first nine months of 2004. Overall, there are no

indications of a build-up in medium-term inflationary pressures in the euro area, as wage growth remains moderate in a context of modest real GDP growth and weak labour markets. Due to stronger productivity increases, the growth of unit labour costs moderated significantly in 2004.

Differences in the inflation rate among the member countries of the euro area, and of western Europe at large, remained considerable in 2004 (chart 3.1.6). It is notable that, with the exception of Finland, the countries with the lowest average rates of inflation in 2004 (January to October) are all non-euro area members, namely, Denmark, Norway, Sweden, Switzerland and the United Kingdom.

Differential sources of growth in the member states of the euro area

Among the three major economies of the euro area, real GDP in Germany grew by 1.7 per cent in 2004, following three years of stagnation. Given their relative

CHART 3.1.2

**Manufacturing output and capacity utilization in the euro area,
January 2000-September 2004**
(Index, percentage)

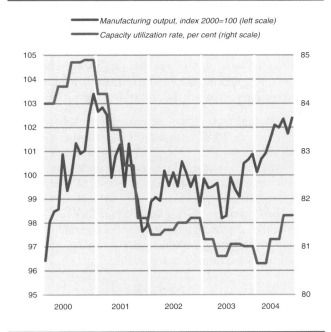

Source: Eurostat, NewCronos Database; European Commission, *Business and Consumer Survey Results* (Brussels), various issues.

Note: Capacity utilization rates are available only for January, April, July and October of each year. Data shown are approximations of quarterly data calculated as the arithmetic average of January and April data (first quarter), April and July (second quarter), etc. All data are seasonally adjusted.

CHART 3.1.3

Elasticity of employment with regard to changes in real GDP in the euro area and the EU-15, 1995-2004
(Percentage points)

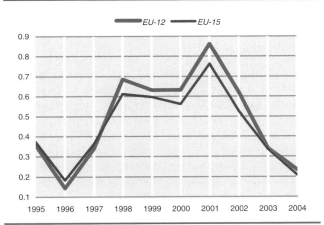

Source: UNECE secretariat calculations.

Note: The elasticity indicates the percentage point change in employment that is associated with a change in real GDP by 1 percentage point. Calculated as the ratio of annual growth rates of employment to annual growth rates of real GDP. Data for 2004 are estimates.

CHART 3.1.4

Unemployment rate in the euro area and EU-15, January 1995-October 2004
(Per cent of labour force)

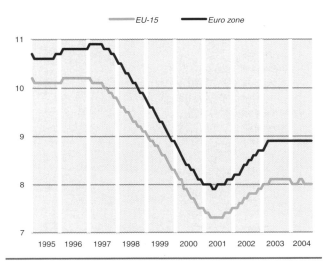

Source: UNECE Statistical Database and Eurostat, NewCronos Database.
Note: Standardized unemployment rate as defined by Eurostat/ILO.

CHART 3.1.5

Consumer prices in the euro area, January 2001-October 2004
(Percentage change over the same month of the previous year)

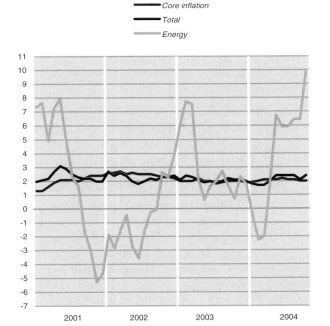

Source: Eurostat, NewCronos Database.
Note: Harmonized Index of Consumer Prices (HICP). Core inflation is defined as the change in total HICP excluding unprocessed food and energy.

specialization in investment goods, German exporters took advantage of the upswing in the global investment cycle. As a result of the export boom, the current account surplus of Germany almost doubled to an estimated €85 billion in 2004, corresponding to 3.9 per cent of GDP. Final domestic demand fell marginally, reflecting depressed private consumption and lacklustre fixed investment. Construction investment continued to fall (as has been the case in 9 of the last 10 years), as the hangover from the

CHART 3.1.6

Inflation differentials in western Europe, January 2004-October 2004

(Per cent)

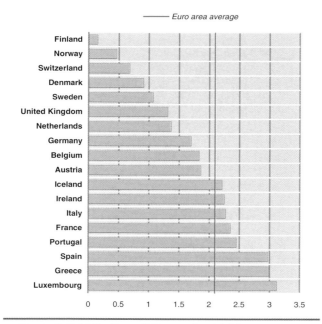

——— Euro area average

Source: Eurostat, NewCronos Database; national statistics.

Note: Average changes in consumer price indices compared with the same period of 2003. Harmonized consumer price indices for all countries, except Switzerland for which the national consumer price index is used.

post-reunification boom has still not been completely unwound. Further measures of economic reform were adopted – as part of the government's "Agenda 2010" reform programme – designed to create incentives for unemployed persons to seek jobs.

In France, the recovery was more reliant on domestic demand in 2004, in contrast to Germany and Italy. Consumer spending, which was the main factor behind economic activity, was supported by a further reduction in the savings rate, given that employment was stagnant and real disposable incomes rose only marginally. Following two years of decline, fixed investment picked up with the largest increase in four years. To a large extent, this reflected an increase in spending on machinery and equipment, stimulated by increasing profit margins. At the same time, housing construction accelerated strongly. Export growth was relatively weak and changes in net exports subtracted a full percentage point from real GDP growth in 2004. Nevertheless, the average annual growth rate was relatively strong at 2.4 per cent, up from a meagre 0.5 per cent in 2003. This average figure, however, masks a weakening of the cyclical momentum in the second half of 2004.

Activity also picked up in Italy in 2004, following two years of near stagnation. Real GDP rose by 1.2 per cent, the slowest rate among the large west European economies. The Italian economy reacted only belatedly

to the more positive international environment, due to its continued loss in competitiveness, which is reflected in the falling shares of Italian products in international markets. This, in turn, is the result of unfavourable specialization patterns and cost developments. (Unit labour costs have been rising continuously above the average of the euro area.) The total number of jobs has continued to grow in recent years in spite of weak economic growth, thanks to the prolonged effects of measures, adopted at various times since the mid-1990s, to promote labour market flexibility (e.g. part-time work).

Growth also strengthened in the other economies of the euro area in 2004, except for Greece, where activity slowed down as the strong impulse of the Olympic Games started to wane. Activity was mainly driven by domestic demand in Belgium, Finland, Luxembourg, Portugal and Spain, while in Austria and Ireland the sources of growth were more balanced. In the Netherlands, the external impulse accounted for the rebound from the previous year's recession, while domestic demand remained depressed.

A mildly supportive fiscal policy

Fiscal policy was slightly expansionary in the euro area in 2004, as indicated by a small decline (corresponding to 0.2 percentage points of potential output) of the surplus on the cyclically adjusted primary balance.[90] The support from fiscal policy to economic activity had been quite modest during the preceding cyclical downturn, a reflection, at least in part, of the rigid constraints imposed by the rules of the Stability and Growth Pact. The actual general government budget deficit averaged 2.9 per cent of GDP in 2004. Budget deficits were significantly above the threshold of 3 per cent in France, Germany and especially Greece. In the latter, revised fiscal statistics show that budget deficits were already significantly above the 3 per cent threshold in 2000-2003.

Against a background of the crisis around the Stability and Growth Pact,[91] which broke in November 2003, the European Commission made proposals in late summer 2004 to increase the flexibility of the fiscal rules. This is to be achieved, *inter alia*, by taking more account of country specific circumstances and putting greater emphasis on levels of public debt in the surveillance process. But a consensus of governments on these proposals may not be easy to achieve.

Monetary policy remains on hold

Against a background of fragile domestic sources of growth and moderate inflationary expectations, the European Central Bank (ECB) has left its key

---

[90]   *OECD Economic Outlook No. 76* (Paris), November 2004.

[91]   UNECE, *Economic Survey of Europe, 2004 No. 1*, pp. 10-15.

CHART 3.1.7

Nominal short-term and long-term interest rates in the euro area, the United Kingdom and the United States, January 2000-November 2004
(Per cent per annum)

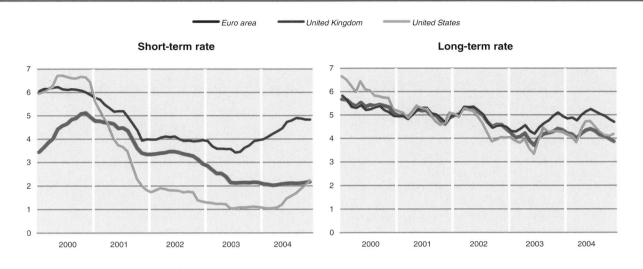

Euro area   United Kingdom   United States

Short-term rate   **Long-term rate**

Source: European Central Bank [www.ecb.int]; OECD, *Main Economic Indicators* (Paris).

Note: Average monthly values. Short-term rates are three-month money market rates; long-term rates are yields on 10-year government bonds.

refinancing rate unchanged at 2 per cent since June 2003. In the money market, three-month interest rates (EURIBOR) remained slightly above 2 per cent in the course of 2004. The gradual tightening of monetary policy in the United States led to the positive interest rate differential in favour of euro area short-term interest rates virtually disappearing in November 2004 (chart 3.1.7). Real short-term interest rates in the euro area, based on the Harmonized Index of Consumer Prices (HICP), were close to zero for most of 2004.

Different perspectives on the stance of monetary policy

While the low short-term interest rates suggest an expansionary stance of monetary policy in the euro area, a more coherent framework against which monetary policy can be judged is the Taylor rule. This is an estimated interest rate feedback rule describing how central banks are changing interest rates away from their neutral level in response to deviations of inflation from its desired rate and to emerging output gaps, i.e. to deviations of actual from potential output. The rule is best understood as an approximation to the behaviour of central banks, which are also likely to take other variables besides inflation and output gaps into account in their decision-making process. But it is plausible to assume that central banks will aim to dampen fluctuations of inflation and output gaps.[92] So-called Taylor interest rates have to be taken with a grain of salt, given that key variables such as the neutral interest rate and the output gap cannot be directly observed but have to be estimated. In any case, the estimated Taylor rates (chart 3.1.8)

support the view that the monetary policy stance of the ECB continued to be expansionary in 2004, insofar as the actual short-term interest rate has been persistently below the predicted Taylor rate.[93]

While the central bank can control interest rates at the shorter end of the maturity spectrum, the monetary transmission mechanism is also influenced by changes in the real exchange rate, which is outside the direct control of the central bank. The real effective exchange rate of the euro weakened in early 2004, a tendency which bottomed out in April. Since then it has been rising, and at an accelerated pace in late 2004. In November, the real effective exchange rate was 4.1 per cent higher than in April 2004, although only just 0.3 per cent above its level in January 2004.

The combined impact of changes in real short-term interest rates and the real effective exchange rate on economic activity can be gauged with a monetary conditions index (chart 3.1.9). This index has been rising since the beginning of 2002, reflecting a tightening of monetary conditions. This was solely due to the real effective appreciation of the euro, in the presence of low and relatively stable real short-term interest rates. This rise in the real effective exchange rate, in turn, is largely due to the depreciation of the dollar. The strengthening of the dollar in early 2004 temporarily reversed this trend, but since May, the depreciation of the dollar resumed and

---

[92] M. Woodford, "The Taylor rule and optimal monetary policy", *American Economic Review*, Vol. 91, No. 2, May 2001.

[93] In the specification of the estimated equation, the reaction function of the central bank allows for interest rate smoothing, given that central banks typically try to avoid "surprises". D. Gerdesmeier and B. Roffia, *Empirical Estimates of Reaction Functions for the Euro Area*, ECB Working Paper, No. 206 (Frankfurt am Main), January 2003.

CHART 3.1.8

Actual short-term interest rate and the Taylor rate in the euro area, 2000-2004QIII

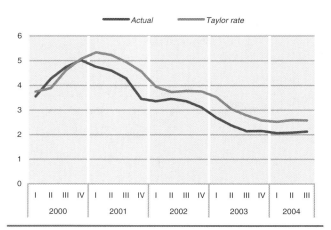

Source: UNECE secretariat calculations.

Note: The short-term interest rate is the nominal three-month EURIBOR. The Taylor rate is computed by fitting the following monetary policy rule with interest rate smoothing: $i_t = (1-\rho)\alpha + (1-\rho)\beta\pi_t + (1-\rho)\gamma(y-\bar{y}) + \rho i_{t-1}$ where i is the short-term nominal interest rate, π is the HICP inflation rate, $(y-\bar{y})$ is the output-gap, α is a constant term, β is the coefficient of monetary policy response to inflation, γ is the coefficient of monetary policy response to the output gap, ρ is the smoothing coefficient and t is the time index. The output gap has been determined by fitting a linear trend to the seasonally adjusted quarterly GDP data. The values of the coefficients are set as follows: α=1.8, β=1.93, ρ=0.87, γ=0.28. These values are drawn from the empirical estimates reported in D. Gerdesmeier and B. Roffia, *Empirical Estimates of Reaction Functions for the Euro Area*, ECB Working Paper, No. 206 (Frankfurt am Main), January 2003. Alternative sets of numerical values for the coefficients are available from R. Clarida, J. Gal and M. Gertler, "Monetary policy rules in practice – new research in macroeconomics", *European Economic Review*, Vol. 42, Issue 6, June 1998, pp. 1033-1067. These alternative values yield a pattern of the Taylor rate which is not significantly different from the one depicted in the chart.

accelerated strongly in November, producing a renewed tightening of monetary conditions in the euro area. The net result, therefore, is that monetary conditions were not supporting economic growth in 2004.

Long-term interest rates remain low

In the bond markets, yields on 10-year government bonds reached a peak of 4.4 per cent in June 2004, but fell thereafter in tandem with bond yields in the United States. In November 2004, 10-year yields averaged 3.9 per cent in the euro area; in the United States, they fell to 4.2 per cent, down from 4.7 per cent in June. A major factor behind the fall in long-term yields were expectations of a more moderate outlook for economic growth in 2005. Contemporaneous real long-term interest rates were only 2 per cent in October 2004, and even lower in the United States at 1 per cent.

The economic recovery in the euro area is expected to continue in 2005

For the euro area as a whole, real GDP is expected to increase by some 2 per cent in 2005, much the same as in 2004. Continuing strong demand from the rest of the

CHART 3.1.9

Monetary conditions index for the euro area and the United States, January 2000-October 2004

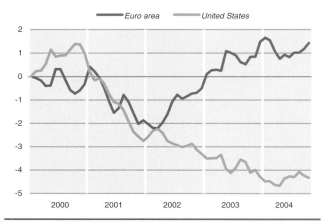

Source: UNECE secretariat calculations.

Note: The monetary conditions index is computed as $MCI = \theta_R(R_t - R_0) + \theta_e(e_t - e_0)$ where R is the three-month real short-term interest rate, e is the real effective exchange rate (in logs), θ_R and θ_e are weights and t is a time index. A fall in the index denotes loosening of monetary conditions. The base period ($t = 0$) is January 2000. Weights are set to $\theta_R = 0.2$ and $\theta_e = 0.8$ for the euro area and $\theta_R = 0.1$ and $\theta_e = 0.9$ for the United States. These are the weights commonly used in the literature and reflect empirically estimated output elasticities. The real short-term interest rate is computed as the nominal rate deflated by the core inflation rate. Core inflation is given by the all-items inflation index minus unprocessed food and energy.

world should support exports, which will remain the mainstay of growth. But, as in 2004, changes in real net exports will continue to make only a modest contribution to growth. An important assumption underlying the current forecasts is that domestic demand will strengthen, albeit moderately in 2005. This is due to stronger business fixed investment in response to favourable financing conditions and the pent-up need to replace machinery and equipment, such as ICT products, with relatively short service lives. Private consumption will also strengthen somewhat, supported by a slight improvement in the labour markets. In Germany, the major west European economy, the annual growth rate will only be about 1.5 per cent in 2005, down from 1.7 per cent in 2004. This slowdown, however, partly reflects the smaller number of working days in 2005. Although there has been further progress with economic reforms in Germany, their impact on economic performance is difficult to gauge and, in any case, will take time to materialize.

The situation in the labour markets in the euro area is expected to improve slightly in 2005, reflecting a combination of a further modest increase in employment and a small decline in unemployment. The inflation outlook remains benign with upside risks mainly related to developments in the price of oil.

Against this background, and in the face of continued strong reliance on exports as a main support of the cyclical upturn, monetary policy should leave interest rates unchanged until the recovery is stronger and supported by a sustained improvement in domestic demand. In fact, a sharp, real effective appreciation of the euro may even necessitate a lowering of interest rates, for which there is sufficient scope. The stance of fiscal policy is expected to be either broadly neutral or possibly even slightly restrictive in 2005.

Given its strong reliance on foreign demand, the recovery in the euro area continues to be very vulnerable to a deterioration in the external environment. Besides adverse trends in the oil markets, downside risks are also related to the risk of a more pronounced than expected weakening of growth in the global economy. A further sharp appreciation of the euro would also weigh on business confidence and risk choking the growth of exports.

(ii) Other western Europe

The United Kingdom business cycle is at a more advanced stage

In the United Kingdom, the growth of real GDP accelerated to 3.2 per cent in 2004, up from 2 per cent in 2003. As in the euro area, the rate of expansion slowed markedly after the second quarter of 2004. But the United Kingdom business cycle is at a much more advanced stage, with strong growth during the past few years having led to tight labour markets and little remaining spare capacity in the economy. Private consumption was again the mainstay of economic growth in 2004, supported by wealth effects originating in the housing market boom. But non-residential private sector fixed investment also rose strongly, following a decline in 2003, as did private housing investment. Inflation remained significantly below the government's target of 2 per cent in 2004, partly because of the strong exchange rate, which led to falling import prices. Fiscal policy was slightly restrictive in 2004, following two consecutive years of strong fiscal stimulus. The fortuitous timing of government spending programmes has been an important factor behind the resistance of the United Kingdom's economy to the global economic downturn after 2000. But the general government budget deficit is likely to have risen above the 3 per cent Maastricht threshold in 2004. The gradual tightening of monetary policy led to a series of increases in the central bank's base rate from 3.5 per cent in November 2003 to 4.75 per cent in August. A major concern of monetary policy is to ensure a gradual correction of the sharp rise in house prices, which have attained levels above their trend values that are generally regarded as unsustainable. But the rise in interest rates since November 2003 does appear to have had a somewhat cooling effect on the housing market, as suggested by the deceleration of house price increases in the second half of the year.

The cyclical momentum is expected to weaken somewhat in 2005 and fall closer in line with the potential growth rate, which is estimated at some 2.5 per cent. The slowdown reflects to a large extent the impact of fading wealth effects in the housing market on private household's spending propensity, which is expected to decline. Apart from adverse changes in the external environment, the downside risks include the possibility of a sudden sharp reversal of the rise in house prices, with consequent negative wealth effects on private household consumption and the overall rate of economic growth.

Favourable growth performance in the other smaller economies

In Denmark and Sweden, economic growth recovered strongly in 2004, with output rising at a rate above its long-term trend. Following a strong performance in 2003, real GDP in Sweden rose by 3.4 per cent in 2004, driven by exports (especially of ICT goods and vehicles) and fixed investment (with large increases in both equipment and housing construction). In Denmark, tax cuts supported consumer spending which, together with strong exports, underpinned economic growth. Economic performance in the west European economies outside the EU (Iceland, Norway and Switzerland) was also quite favourable in 2004. Driven by booming domestic demand, economic growth in Iceland accelerated to 4.3 per cent; economic policy was subsequently tightened to prevent overheating. In Norway strong domestic demand led to a sharp acceleration in GDP growth to an average annual rate of 3.4 per cent. In Switzerland, the economy emerged from the recession of 2003, supported by expansionary monetary and fiscal policies. Real GDP rose by 1.8 per cent. The stance of monetary policy was slightly tightened in response to an increased risk of higher inflation. In all five countries, the recovery is set to continue at a relatively strong rate of expansion in 2005, although perhaps at a somewhat more moderate rate in Switzerland.

3.2 The new EU member states

The growth of GDP in the 10 new member states (EU-10) picked up in 2004, exceeding by a significant margin the average rate in the old member states (EU-15). However, the labour markets in the EU-10 continued to be weak, with low employment and high unemployment rates. The increase in GDP was broadly based in most of the EU-10 economies, and with relatively high levels of confidence and industrial orders, their prospects for output and productivity growth in 2005 are good. Risks to this outlook include a further slowdown of activity in the euro zone, higher than expected energy prices, and a weakening of budgetary discipline. Aside from the need for sustainable fiscal consolidation, the most pressing policy challenge facing the new member states is to create conditions for a strong growth of employment.

(i) The policy agenda

EU membership raises a number of policy challenges. On the structural front, it implies a commitment to the so-called Lisbon strategy that aims to transform the EU into the world's most competitive knowledge-based economy by 2010. This presupposes catching up with the productivity and employment levels of the United States economy. On the macroeconomic front, the new members are expected to meet the Stability and Growth Pact criteria pertaining to inflation, long-term interest rates, government deficits, public debt and exchange rate stability, and eventually to enter the Economic and Monetary Union (EMU).[94]

The medium-term strategy of the EU-10 is broadly consistent with the official economic policy guidelines for the EU member states.[95] The strategy requires of each member country prudent macroeconomic policies and structural reforms to improve its trend rate of output growth. Similar guidelines were laid down for the formulation of the individual pre-accession strategies of the new members. The implementation of these strategies should enable the 10 economies to achieve sustainable nominal convergence and join the EMU after a transitional period in the European Monetary System, ERM-2.[96]

In recent years, the new member states have been relatively successful in raising per capita income levels while moving towards the EMU nominal convergence targets.[97] Despite the progress achieved to date, a number of major policy challenges continue to face policy makers in the EU-10.

The real convergence challenge: how to overcome the large gaps in per capita income levels?

The average per capita GDP level (at purchasing power parity) in the EU-10 is currently less than one half of the comparable level in the euro zone, reflecting low labour productivity and low employment rates in the former (chart 3.2.1). Productivity levels and employment rates differ significantly across the EU-10 economies, some of them being closer to the characteristic pattern of

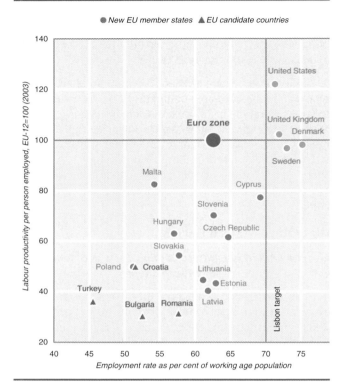

CHART 3.2.1

Employment rates and productivity gaps in the new EU member states and candidate countries, 2003

● *New EU member states* ▲ *EU candidate countries*

Source: Eurostat.

Note: Labour productivity refers to GDP in purchasing power standards per person employed. Employment rates are ratios of total employment in the 15-64 years age group to the total population of working age (15-64 years).

the EU candidate countries than that of the euro zone or the three mature EU economies remaining outside the EMU. While a strong productivity catch-up has occurred in recent years, the gap in employment rates has not diminished.

The real convergence challenge is amplified by shortcomings in the human capital stock. The intensity of R&D spending in the EU-10 is less than one half of the EU-15 average. There is no obvious development strategy that would be able to transform the EU-10 into dynamic knowledge-based economies in the medium term, given the deficiencies of their education systems.[98] Policies to deal with these issues can be classified into two major categories: the "liberal" model (based on the British or Irish experience over the last quarter century) or the "dynamic welfare state" model (based on the Austrian or Scandinavian experience).[99] However, the experience of

---

[94] Unlike Denmark and the United Kingdom, which were able to negotiate special clauses that allow them to opt out of the euro, the new member states are legally obliged to join the euro zone. The current EMU status of each new entrant is comparable to that of Sweden, i.e. that of a member state with temporary derogation.

[95] These guidelines were approved by the Council of EU member states in June 2003 and updated in April 2004. Commission of the European Communities, *Commission Recommendation on the 2004 Update of the Broad Guidelines of the Economic Policies of the Member States and the Community (for the 2003-2005 period)*, COM (2004) 238 (Brussels), 7 April 2004.

[96] ERM-2 is an exchange rate framework that precludes crawling-peg regimes, pegs to currencies other than the euro as well as floating regimes without a mutually agreed central rate. Only after a country has been a member of ERM-2 for at least two years without major problems, can it apply for full EMU membership.

[97] For the first official assessments of the convergence process in the EU-10 economies, see European Central Bank, *Convergence Report 2004* (Frankfurt am Main), 20 October 2004 and European Commission, *Convergence Report 2004* (Brussels), 20 October 2004.

[98] A number of EU-10 countries participated in the OECD PISA project assessing student performance: in most cases they achieved below-average results and significantly lagged behind the leading countries such as Finland or the Republic of Korea, although performing somewhat better than the United States.

[99] According to a special report on Ireland, published in the *The Economist* on 16 October 2004, policy makers in the eight new EU member states from central and eastern Europe would like to emulate

TABLE 3.2.1

Economic and Monetary Union nominal convergence criteria

Criterion	Inflation	Fiscal criteria		Interest rate
Measure	HICP ª annual average (percentage change) Sep. 2003-Aug. 2004	Government deficit (per cent of GDP) 2003	Public debt (per cent of GDP) 2003	Long-term interest rates (annual average, per cent) Sep. 2003-Aug. 2004
Reference value	2.4	3	60	6.4
Cyprus	2.1	*6.4*	*70.9*	5.2
Czech Republic ᵇ	1.8	*5.3*	37.8	4.7
Estonia	2.0	-3.1	5.3	..
Hungary	*6.5*	*6.2*	59.1	*8.1*
Latvia	*4.9*	1.5	14.4	5.0
Lithuania	-0.2	1.9	21.4	4.7
Malta ᵇ	*2.6*	*6.5*	*71.1*	4.7
Poland ᶜ	*2.5*	*5.4*	45.4	*6.9*
Slovakia	*8.4*	*3.7*	42.6	5.1
Slovenia	*4.1*	2.0	29.4	5.2

Source: European Commission and UNECE secretariat estimates.

Note: Numbers in bold italics signify non-compliance.

ª Harmonized Index of Consumer Prices.

ᵇ Government deficits for the Czech Republic and Malta exclude one-off charges to improve cross-country comparability.

ᶜ Government deficit for Poland includes the estimated impact of a reclassification of the defined contribution pension scheme to improve cross-country comparability.

economies that joined the EU in earlier rounds of expansion, and which have been successful in catching up, suggests that neither approach can work without credible fiscal consolidation. A discussion of alternative approaches to real convergence is presented in chapter 7.

Nominal convergence: a multi-speed project

Fiscal consolidation remains a serious problem in most of the new member states, including the relatively large central European economies as well as Cyprus and Malta (table 3.2.1). The majority of the 10 economies have also failed so far to satisfy the EMU inflation criterion, which partly reflects the ongoing process of productivity catch-up.[100] None of the 10 new member states examined in the recent convergence reports of the ECB and the EC fulfil the exchange rate stability and legal requirements necessary for entry into the euro zone. The legal criteria include the independence of the central bank in pursuit of price stability and other legal norms of the EMU.

But it is fiscal consolidation that remains the principal macroeconomic policy challenge in most new member states, including the relatively large central European economies as well as Cyprus and Malta (table 3.2.1). These countries exceeded the 3 per cent threshold for the deficit to GDP ratio in 2003 and 2004; Cyprus,

Hungary and Malta in addition exceeded or were close to exceeding the 60 per cent ceiling for the government debt to GDP ratio. But government debt has also been growing rapidly in the Czech Republic and Poland. Fiscal consolidation is particularly urgent in order to set public finances on a sustainable path in the face of rapidly ageing populations, which will put added pressures on public pension and health-care systems in the medium to long term.

To ensure sustainability, the EU fiscal framework also calls for the member states to achieve a medium-term, cyclically adjusted budget position of close to balance or in surplus. However, strict abidance by the EU fiscal framework may impose unnecessary rigidities for some of the new member states. In particular, these economies need to undertake a lasting effort to improve their public infrastructure, which is an essential precondition for a successful catching up to higher productivity and income levels. In turn, this implies the need for maintaining relatively high levels of public infrastructure spending in the medium and longer term. Discussions on the possible reform of the EU's fiscal rules are still underway and the new EU members, now full-fledged participants in this debate, can voice their concerns. Even more than the most developed current members of the EU, the new members would benefit from a possible relaxation of some of the constraints on government borrowing for financing public investment. Relaxing these constraints would help prevent counterproductive fiscal tightening in these economies.[101]

_____

the impressive economic transformation of Ireland in recent decades and to draw relevant policy lessons. They are also interested in the policies pursued by Finland and other dynamic welfare states. See, for example, the presentation of the Governor of the Czech National Bank, Z. Tuma, "Czech fiscal policy in the light of European fiscal policy lessons", *Forum Populini* (Prague), 23 October 2003 [www.cnb.cz/en/pdf/Tuma_Forum_populini.pdf].

[100] For a comprehensive discussion of the Stability and Growth Pact (Maastricht) criteria, see UNECE, *Economic Survey of Europe, 2004 No. 1*, pp. 10-15.

_____

[101] The available data show that in recent years the level of public investment in most new member countries was indeed higher than the average level in the EU-15 (table 3.2.2). This average reflects significantly lower spending by the most developed current members of

TABLE 3.2.2

Selected fiscal indicators for the new EU member states, 1998-2007
(Per cent of GDP)

	Cyclically adjusted general government deficit, 2003	Targeted cyclically adjusted general government deficit, 2007	Public investment, average 1998-2003
Cyprus	5.4	1.6	3.1
Czech Republic	5.2[a]	3.6	3.6
Estonia	-2.6	-0.1	4.2
Hungary	6.2	2.7[b]	3.7
Latvia	1.4	2.0	1.4
Lithuania	1.8	1.8	2.6
Malta	5.4[c]	0.2	4.3
Poland	5.0[d]	3.7[d]	3.4
Slovakia	3.7	3.1	2.9
Slovenia	1.5	0.7	2.2
Memorandum item:			
EU-15	1.6	..	2.3

Source: Table 3.2.1; Convergence Programs; European Commission, *General Government Data* (Brussels), Autumn 2004; UNECE secretariat calculations.

[a] Adjusted for the one-off charge for state guarantees granted for the restructuring of the banking system.

[b] 2008.

[c] Adjusted for the one-off charge for restructuring the debt of the shipyards.

[d] Adjusted for the estimated impact of a reclassification of the defined contribution pension scheme.

For example, the so-called golden rule that allows for public borrowing to finance public investment has been successfully followed by the United Kingdom in conjunction with a self-imposed upper limit on net public debt, without unduly restricting the operation of automatic stabilizers.

In their most recent Convergence Programs, only Estonia and Malta aim to balance their cyclically adjusted deficits by 2007, and Slovenia plans to bring its deficit below 1 per cent in relation to GDP (table 3.2.2).[102] However, most of the other countries target cyclically adjusted deficits that are slightly lower than or close to their ratios of public investment to GDP. Such fiscal targets are in fact consistent with the golden rule mentioned above. This approach would provide for the infrastructure spending necessary for successful convergence, while avoiding a slowdown in economic growth through excessive fiscal restriction. Nevertheless, further fiscal consolidation efforts will be required to reach the golden rule compatible deficits (which seem to have averaged 3.5 per cent of GDP in the larger new member states in recent years) in a sustainable manner.

Overall each new member state has developed its medium-term macroeconomic policy framework on the basis of its own evaluation of the desirability of an early entry into the euro zone.[103] Apparently, the estimated benefits of early entry are judged to exceed the associated costs in the three EU-10 economies (Estonia, Lithuania and Slovenia) that joined ERM-2 in the second month of their EU membership.[104] Estonia and Lithuania have preserved their euro-based currency board, which is effectively a pledge to keep their exchange rates fixed vis-à-vis the euro. The Slovene authorities abandoned managed floating and the tolar is now allowed to fluctuate around its central parity within a relatively large band (±15 per cent). Given their comparatively good fiscal positions and commitment to strong monetary discipline, the adoption of the euro by Estonia, Lithuania and Slovenia may well take place in 2007.

Cyprus, Latvia, Malta and Slovakia also appear to be committed to a relatively early adoption of the euro. In the case of Latvia, ERM-2 entry is expected in 2005, once the authorities implement their plan to replace the SDR-linked currency peg with one based solely on the euro. Both Cyprus and Malta also intend to join ERM-2 in 2005. In Slovakia, the government has made considerable progress in fiscal consolidation and expects to reduce its deficit below the 3 per cent reference value by 2007, while the central bank is aiming to meet the EMU inflation criterion in 2006. The Slovak authorities plan to join ERM-2 in the first half of 2006 and adopt the euro in January 2009.[105] The key question is whether the current medium-term fiscal programme will be adhered to.

The remaining three new EU member states from central Europe (Czech Republic, Hungary and Poland), which account for the bulk of economic activity and population in the EU-10, are unlikely to adopt the euro before 2010. This reflects their weak fiscal positions and the fact that their public expenditure and tax reforms are still at an early stage. Moreover, such reforms could still be subverted by the electoral spending cycle.[106] Until the public finances have been consolidated, entry into the euro zone is unlikely to be pursued by policy makers in these three countries. The ability to devalue a national currency still remains a useful policy option to cope with asymmetric shocks prior to ERM-2 entry.

_____

[103] For an example of such evaluation, see National Bank of Poland, *A Report on the Costs and Benefits of Poland's Adoption of the Euro* (Warsaw), March 2004.

[104] The only other state with temporary derogation that meets all the nominal convergence criteria is Sweden. However, Swedish voters have repeatedly rejected adoption of the euro in national referenda. Similarly, the citizens of Denmark, the only current ERM-2 member from western Europe, have repeatedly rejected entry into the euro zone.

[105] National Bank of Slovakia, *Specification of the Strategy for Adopting the Euro in the SR* (Bratislava), 2004.

[106] National elections will take place in Poland by September 2005 and in the Czech Republic and Hungary during the first half of 2006.

_____

the EU, while at the same time, Greece, Portugal and Spain on average spent slightly more on public investment than the four larger new member countries, i.e. the Czech Republic, Hungary, Poland and Slovakia.

[102] Malta's Convergence Program foresees a massive fiscal consolidation equivalent to some 5 per cent of GDP over four years. This target certainly looks ambitious.

TABLE 3.2.3

Quarterly real GDP and industrial output in the new EU member states, 2003QIII-2004QIII
(Percentage change over the same period of the preceding year)

	GDP					Industrial output				
	2003QIII	*2003QIV*	*2004QI*	*2004QII*	*2004QIII*	*2003QIII*	*2003QIV*	*2004QI*	*2004QII*	*2004QIII*
Cyprus [a]	1.7	2.8	3.6	4.0	3.5	2.1	2.1	2.5	0.6	-0.7
Czech Republic	4.0	4.0	3.5	3.9	3.6	6.0	6.1	9.0	12.6	8.7
Estonia	5.2	6.2	6.8	5.9	6.2	10.0	9.4	7.4	7.1	7.4
Hungary	3.0	3.8	4.3	4.2	3.7	6.5	10.1	10.4	10.4	6.0
Latvia	7.3	7.5	8.8	7.7	9.1	7.8	4.2	9.2	6.5	3.9
Lithuania	9.3	11.5	7.1	7.3	5.8	20.0	19.3	9.8	17.4	7.3
Malta	-1.6	3.0	2.1	-1.6	1.4	..	..	..	..	..
Poland	4.0	4.7	6.9	6.1	4.8	9.1	11.8	18.9	16.6	9.7
Slovakia	4.5	5.2	5.4	5.5	5.3	2.3	4.2	6.6	5.7	3.8
Slovenia	2.3	2.5	3.8	4.6	4.9	0.2	4.9	4.1	7.4	5.7
Memorandum items:										
Euro area [a]	0.3	0.8	1.9	2.4	1.6	-0.3	1.4	1.0	3.0	2.6
EU-15 [a]	0.5	1.1	2.1	2.4	2.3	-0.1	1.2	1.0	2.8	2.0
EU-25 [a]	0.7	1.2	2.2	2.6	2.3	0.3	1.6	1.6	3.3	2.4

Source: National statistics; Eurostat; OECD; UNECE secretariat estimates.

[a] Industrial output adjusted for the number of working days.

CHART 3.2.2

Economic sentiment indicator in the new EU member states, January 2000-November 2004
(Balance of positive and negative replies, seasonally adjusted)

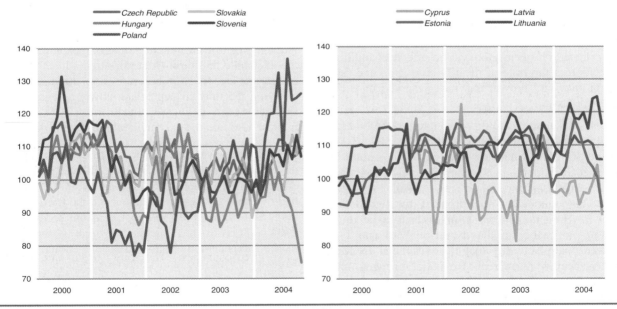

Source: European Commission, Directorate General for Economic and Financial Affairs.

Note: The economic sentiment indicator is scaled to have a mean of 100 and a standard deviation of 10 over 1990-2003. The weights of the component indicators are as follows: industry – 40 per cent; services – 30 per cent; consumers – 20 per cent; construction – 5 per cent; retail trade – 5 per cent.

(ii) Recent economic developments

Economic growth was strong throughout the EU-10 in 2004 (table 3.2.3). In central Europe, it accelerated and became more broadly based, underpinned by strong private consumption and fixed investment as well as robust external demand. The three Baltic economies continued to grow very rapidly. Economic confidence in the new EU economies is broadly consistent with continued economic dynamism (chart 3.2.2), the economic sentiment indicator in November remaining above its long-term average in the majority of the EU-10.[107]

---

[107] The economic sentiment indicator and its components are not available for Malta.

TABLE 3.2.4

Components of real final demand in the new EU member states, 2002-2004
(Percentage change over the same period of the preceding year)

	Private consumption expenditure			Government consumption expenditure			Gross fixed capital formation			Exports of goods and services			Imports of goods and services		
	2002	2003	2004 QI-QII	2002	2003	2004 QI-QII	2002	2003	2004 QI-QII	2002	2003	2004 QI-QII	2002	2003	2004 QI-QII
Cyprus	1.5	2.6	6.8	7.5	4.7	11.3	8.1	-2.2	15.5	-5.2	-1.4	4.0	-0.5	-0.4	15.4
Czech Republic	2.8	4.9	3.0	4.5	4.2	-1.1	3.4	4.8	10.0	2.1	7.3	18.4	4.9	7.9	18.8
Estonia	10.3	5.7	6.1	5.9	5.8	4.5	17.2	5.4	6.1	0.9	5.7	18.7	3.7	11.0	16.7
Hungary	10.2	8.0	4.2	5.0	5.4	-0.3	8.0	3.4	13.5	3.7	7.6	18.4	6.2	10.4	18.6
Latvia	7.4	8.6	9.3	2.2	1.9	2.3	13.0	10.9	19.3	5.2	5.0	7.6	4.6	13.0	18.4
Lithuania	6.1	12.4	11.1	1.8	4.0	6.1	11.1	14.0	15.9	19.5	6.9	3.7	17.6	10.2	14.6
Malta	-0.4	1.6	0.4	3.8	1.6	-0.4	-29.6	41.4	-4.1	6.6	-3.8	2.7	-2.4	7.1	0.1
Poland	3.4	3.1	3.8	0.4	0.4	2.0	-5.8	-0.9	3.6	4.8	14.7	13.6	2.6	9.3	9.8
Slovakia	5.5	-0.6	3.0	4.9	2.7	1.2	-0.6	-1.5	2.4	5.6	22.5	16.1	5.5	13.6	14.6
Slovenia	0.3	2.7	3.5	1.7	2.6	0.8	3.1	6.3	7.3	6.7	3.2	11.5	4.9	6.8	12.9

Source: National statistics; Eurostat; OECD; UNECE secretariat estimates.

GDP growth remains vibrant in central Europe...

The available national accounts and industrial production data indicate that economic activity continued to expand briskly throughout central Europe, although slowing somewhat in the third quarter of 2004. Growth was driven by large increases in consumption and investment and by strong external demand. Exports grew rapidly and the central European economies continued to increase their shares of west European markets. The underlying factors include the expanding capacities of export-oriented FDI firms, the one-off effects of full trade liberalization at the time of the EU accession, and rapid labour productivity growth that has preserved their cost competitiveness.

Real consumer spending accelerated in the first half of 2004 in Poland, Slovakia and Slovenia (table 3.2.4). The rapid growth of final consumption slowed somewhat in the Czech Republic and Hungary, reflecting more moderate increases in real wages. Real investment increased throughout central Europe in the first half of 2004. In Hungary, business investment expenditure picked up noticeably in the export-oriented and FDI-dominated manufacturing sector. Investment spending gathered pace in the Czech Republic, growing most rapidly in the government and household sectors but also picking up in the key non-financial business sector where it was driven by improved corporate profitability. Real investment also accelerated in Slovenia. In Poland and Slovakia, fixed capital formation increased after two years of decline. Improved profitability in the non-financial corporate sector underpinned business investment in both countries.

Imports grew rapidly throughout the region, in response to the expansion of both domestic demand and exports. Net trade continued to support GDP growth in Poland and Slovakia in the first half of 2004, while its contribution was negative in the other three central European countries; this pattern most probably continued in the second half of the year.

Macroeconomic policies were broadly supportive of growth. The cyclical upturn in economic activity contributed to relatively favourable budget out-turns in the Czech Republic, Poland, Slovakia and Slovenia. Consequently, the Czech and Polish central banks raised policy rates less aggressively in the face of rising inflationary pressures than would otherwise have been the case with less favourable fiscal outcomes. In Slovakia, the central bank continued to ease monetary conditions with repeated cuts to policy rates, while reducing the upward pressure of strong capital inflows on the exchange rate through sterilization. In Slovenia, the central bank reduced policy rates until June 2004, while allowing the tolar to depreciate slowly against the euro. Following the country's entry into ERM-2, market interest rates and the exchange rate remained stable.

Hungary was an exception to these generally benign developments due to the carryover effects from financial destabilization in late 2003 and early 2004.[108] Inflation had overshot the targeted range since the third quarter of 2003 and only started to subside in the second half of 2004. This, as well as the apparent stabilization of market expectations, allowed the National Bank of Hungary (NBH) to start cautiously reducing its policy rates; however, they have remained at comparatively high levels, reflecting the country's serious twin-deficit problem and the underlying lack of progress with fiscal stabilization. The government's attempt to reduce interest rates more rapidly (and thus the cost of financing the relatively large public debt) through increased political pressure on the central bank is unlikely to succeed and could even backfire through its impact on market expectations.[109]

---

[108] For details of the financial destabilization, see UNECE, *Economic Survey of Europe, 2004 No. 1*, pp. 51-52, box 3.1.1.

[109] The government attempted to influence monetary policy by pushing through parliament a radical amendment to the Central Bank

...while the Baltic states continue to enjoy the fastest growth rates in the EU...

Rapid GDP growth continued throughout the Baltic region in the first three quarters of 2004. The pace slowed somewhat in Lithuania while picking up in Estonia and Latvia, the latter being the fastest growing EU economy in 2004. The strong growth of output and productivity in the Baltic economies is likely to continue, given the soundness of their underlying competitive positions.[110] Domestic demand remained the principal source of growth throughout the region. Buoyant consumption and rising exports by FDI-firms led to a rapid growth of imports.[111] The contribution of net exports to GDP growth was negative, especially in Latvia and Lithuania. The relatively large current account deficits of the Baltic states appear to be manageable in the short term, given the underlying factors and continuing inflows of FDI (see table 6.1.2).

Both fiscal and monetary policies were supportive of growth and in Estonia and Lithuania there was no change after their entry into ERM-2 in June 2004. The Latvian authorities intend to repeg the lats to the euro in January 2005 and to maintain their unilateral commitment to a narrow (±1 per cent) exchange rate band. Given the strong acceleration of growth and signs of overheating in 2004, the planned entry into ERM-2 in the near future and early adoption of the euro may well require a tightening of fiscal policy to prevent excessive inflation.[112]

...and Cyprus and Malta experience diverging output trends

Following the recent liberalization of all capital account transactions with non-residents, and the uncertainty arising from the failed attempt to unify the country prior to EU accession, the Central Bank of

---

Act. The NBH published a strong objection to the amendment on its website [www.mnb.hu] on 20 October 2004. According to the NBH, the government's attempt to encroach on its independence may "ultimately discredit Hungary as a new member state of the European Union". Although parliament approved the controversial amendment in November, it remains unclear whether it will be implemented.

[110] R. Burgess, S. Fabrizio and Y. Xiao, *Competitiveness in the Baltics in the Run-up to EU Accession*, IMF Country Report No. 03/114 (Washington, D.C.), April 2003.

[111] The importance of foreign-invested firms can be illustrated by the example of Elcoteq Tallin, an Estonian subsidiary of the Finnish-owned Elcoteq Network Corporation. This affiliate has assembled electronic communications products since 1994; its output accounted for 14 per cent of Estonia's exports in 2003. In 2004, it rapidly increased its production and workforce, becoming one of the largest Estonian employers. This expansion was driven by strong global demand for its products and competitive hourly labour costs (€3 in Estonia vs. €20 in Finland). "Finnish-owned Elcoteq to become one of largest employers in Estonia", *Enterprise Estonia News*, 4 November 2004 [www.investinestonia.com/index].

[112] For a brief discussion of ERM-2 and exchange rate issues, see "Aide-Mémoire: IMF Staff Visit to the Republic of Latvia", 13-15 October 2004 [www.imf.org/external/np/ms/2004/101504.htm].

TABLE 3.2.5

Consumer prices in the new EU member states, 2002-2004
(Percentage change)

	Consumer prices, total					
	Over preceding year		2004 (year-on-year)			Sept. over previous Dec.
	2002	2003	QI	QII	QIII	2004
New EU member states ...	2.7	2.0	3.1	4.1	4.9	3.6
Cyprus	2.8	4.1	1.4	1.6	3.0	2.4
Czech Republic	1.8	0.2	2.4	2.6	3.3	2.3
Estonia	3.5	1.1	0.7	3.4	4.1	3.9
Hungary	5.4	4.9	6.9	7.4	7.0	5.0
Latvia	1.9	3.0	4.4	5.9	7.5	6.0
Lithuania	0.4	-1.2	-1.3	0.4	2.3	2.5
Malta	2.2	0.7	2.7	2.7	3.0	1.2
Poland	1.9	0.7	1.7	3.3	4.6	3.3
Slovakia	3.3	8.5	8.4	8.1	7.5	6.2
Slovenia	7.6	5.7	3.8	3.8	3.7	2.6
Memorandum item:						
EU-8	2.7	2.0	3.1	4.2	4.9	3.6

Source: UNECE secretariat estimates, based on national statistics.

Cyprus tightened monetary policy with a steep rise of its interest rates. Fiscal policy was tightened less resolutely through a gradual withdrawal of fiscal stimulus in 2004 that will be followed by spending restraint in 2005. In the first half of 2004 output growth picked up, driven by robust consumption, increased investment and exports of goods and services. The key tourism sector appears to have recovered from the slump in 2003. It remains unclear whether the pace of economic growth will be sustained when the planned fiscal tightening materializes in 2005.

In Malta, GDP growth appears to have remained sluggish in 2004. The impact of strong investment spending and improving net exports on aggregate output was moderated by subdued final consumption. On the supply side, the deceleration in output growth reflected the poor performance of the manufacturing sector.

Disinflation came to a halt

The headline rate of consumer price inflation picked up or remained in high single digits in most of the 10 new member states of the European Union in the first three quarters of 2004 (table 3.2.5). The reversal of the downward trend of the last three years was prompted by a combination of factors. Some of them were expected one-off factors arising from their entry into the EU, such as deregulation of a broad range of prices, and increases in indirect taxes and excise duties. There were other temporary or exogenous factors, such as the rise in food and domestic fuel prices and a surge in imported inflation following the increase of world commodity prices, particularly of oil and natural gas. In some of these economies, the external price pressures were partly offset by the appreciation of their currencies vis-à-vis the dollar and the currencies of other major trading partners; this was particularly the case in Lithuania and Slovakia.

Exchange rates depreciated in nominal effective terms only in Latvia and Poland. Other factors, such as buoyant consumer demand and tighter labour markets, also contributed to the revival of inflationary pressures in some of these economies.

It should also be noted that core inflation, which excludes volatile food and energy price changes and is an indicator of underlying inflationary pressures, was lower than the headline inflation in all these economies in 2004; however, the pace of deceleration was much less than in 2003.

Wage pressures intensified but were offset by surging productivity

The rate of change in industrial producer prices, which is a measure of the overall inflationary pressure originating from the supply side, also accelerated in the first three quarters of 2004 and rose even faster than consumer prices except in Hungary and Slovakia (but in the latter, producer prices rose more than in the same period of 2003).

The moderation of wage inflation came to a halt in 2004 and average gross wages in industry rose faster than the increase in the sector's producer prices. These increased wage pressures, however, were more than offset by surging labour productivity, a reflection of dynamic but jobless output growth. Productivity grew at double-digit rates in the first half of 2004 in all countries except Estonia, Slovakia and Slovenia, while industrial unit labour costs continued to decline in both nominal and real terms. Given strong external and domestic demand, the pricing power of firms rose significantly. This allowed them to increase their operating surpluses in tandem with accelerated wage inflation, particularly in those economies where appreciation of the exchange rate mitigated the pressure of higher import prices on industrial material input costs.

Industrial labour productivity rose significantly in the central European and Baltic economies between the end of 1999 and mid-2004 (chart 3.2.3). In the Czech Republic, Lithuania and Poland, the increase in productivity was greater than the rise in wages. In the other remaining economies, wage inflation in 2000-2004 exceeded the rise in productivity.[113] These wage increases, in excess of labour productivity growth, are recognized by the authorities as a major problem that needs to be addressed in order to achieve and sustain price stability.

Labour markets were generally weak

The relatively strong growth of output in the EU-10 area had only a very slight impact on their labour markets. The average level of employment in the first half of 2004 was only 0.2 per cent higher than in the same period of 2003, while unemployment remained substantially

unchanged throughout the first three quarters of the year (table 3.2.6). Employment declined or stagnated in the Czech Republic, Estonia, Hungary, Lithuania and Slovakia. In contrast, there was a modest increase in Poland for the first time in several years, although it continued to fall in the manufacturing sector. Employment growth was comparatively strong in Cyprus and Latvia. The large rise in Slovenia was largely the result of a one-shot increase of employment in the public sector.

Concerns at low employment rates...

The failure of the EU-10 to generate new employment on a significant scale is a cause of major concern, especially since employment rates in these countries remain, with the exception of Cyprus, significantly below the 70 per cent target set in the Lisbon agenda for 2010.[114] Starting from an employment rate of 60 per cent (the current average for the EU-10) in 2005, hitting the Lisbon target by 2010 would require an average employment growth rate of about 1.5 per cent a year, assuming a roughly constant population of working age. With the exception of the Baltic states, none of the EU-10 have been able to sustain this rate of employment growth over the past few years.

Weak employment growth in the EU-10 area results from the combination of two broad sets of factors. On the one hand, rapid labour productivity growth, as achieved in most EU-10 economies in recent years, tends to keep employment growth down in the short run. This is the case over and above the labour-shedding that is associated with restructuring in the enterprise sector. The available empirical evidence, however, suggests that such a trade-off is likely to vanish over the longer term. Continued high rates of economic growth should therefore lead eventually to higher levels of employment. On the other hand, a number of rigidities have created distortions on both the demand side and the supply side of the labour market. The issue appears to be particularly relevant to the central European economies, where the tax-benefit systems have adversely affected the incentives to work and the extent of labour mobility across regions.[115] To overcome these rigidities, reforms to strengthen the incentives to work, job-search facilitation services and programmes to minimize the mismatch of skills are required.[116] Moreover, while the overall degree of

---

[113] The differential was largest in Slovenia where the gains in productivity were about one third of the rise in wages.

[114] Indeed, it should be pointed out that if the part of Cyprus under Turkish administration was included in the employment statistics, the overall employment rate for Cyprus would likely fall significantly short of its current 69 per cent.

[115] For an elaboration of this point, see UNECE, *Economic Survey of Europe, 2004 No. 2*, chap. 1, pp. 26-27.

[116] In Slovakia, despite recent tax and benefit reforms that have introduced strong work incentives, job creation has stalled. This disappointing result reflects to some extent the lack of specific employment programmes targeted at the large Roma minority. OECD, *Economic Surveys: Slovak Republic* (Paris), March 2004. It may also reflect the uncertainty of firms about the permanence of the recent tax cuts. If these cuts are not reversed following the 2006 election, business investment and job creation in Slovakia could pick up strongly.

CHART 3.2.3

Gross nominal wages and labour productivity in industry in the eight new EU member states, 1999QIV-2004QII
(Indices, 1999QIV=100; seasonally adjusted)

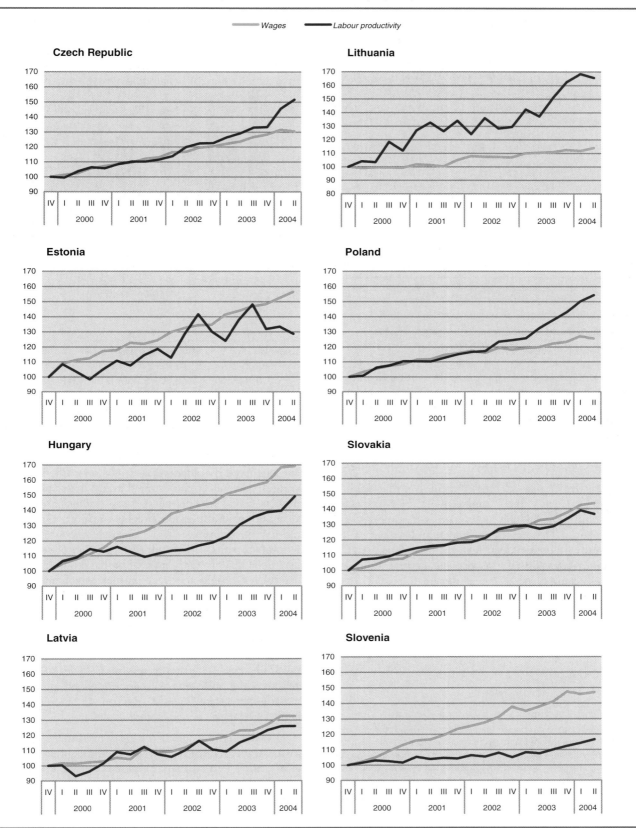

Source: UNECE secretariat estimates, based on national statistics.

TABLE 3.2.6

Rates of unemployment and employment growth in the new EU member states, 2002-2004

(Per cent, percentage change)

	Unemployment (per cent of labour force)			Employment (per cent change over the previous period)		
	2002	2003	2004 [a]	2002	2003	2004 [b]
New EU members states	14.8	14.3	14.2	-0.8	–	0.2
Cyprus	3.9	4.4	4.8	1.3	1.0	2.7
Czech Republic	7.3	7.8	8.4	-0.4	-0.7	-0.8
Estonia	9.5	10.1	9.5	1.4	1.5	0.2
Hungary	5.6	5.8	5.8	0.1	1.3	–
Latvia	12.6	10.5	9.8	2.8	1.8	1.2
Lithuania	13.5	12.7	11.1	4.0	2.3	-0.6
Malta	7.5	8.2	7.4	-0.7	-0.7	-0.1
Poland	19.8	19.2	18.9	-2.2	-0.7	0.5
Slovakia	18.7	17.5	18.2	0.2	1.8	-0.4
Slovenia	6.1	6.5	6.1	0.6	-0.8	4.8
Memorandum items:						
Euro area	8.4	8.9	8.9	0.6	0.2	0.5
EU-15	7.7	8.1	8.1	0.5	0.2	0.5

Source: UNECE Statistical Database; Eurostat; NewCronos Database; European Commission, *European Economy Forecasts* (Brussels), Autumn 2004.

Note: Standardized unemployment rate as defined by Eurostat/ILO.

[a] Average of the first three quarters of 2004, seasonally adjusted.

[b] First half of 2004 change over first half of 2003.

employment protection legislation in central European countries is not particularly high by OECD standards, further flexibility can be achieved through the deregulation of temporary work, especially in Hungary and Poland.[117]

...and to employment of older workers in particular

The overall rate of employment is influenced by developments in the employment of specific demographic groups, such as women, young people and older workers. The significant underemployment of this latter group is a striking feature of several EU-10 economies (chart 3.2.4). Again, the central European economies stand out, as employment rates of older workers, on average, are 16 percentage points below the EU-15 average.

Various factors have reduced the employment rate of older workers.[118] Generous pension benefits have

CHART 3.2.4

Employment rates of older workers in the new EU member states, 2000 and 2003

(Per cent of population aged 55-64)

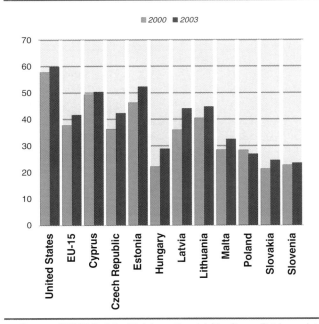

Source: UNECE Statistical Database; Eurostat, NewCronos Database; data for the United States are from the OECD, *Employment Outlook* (Paris), 2004.

Note: The employment rate is the proportion of employed persons aged 55 to 64 in the total population in the same age group.

contributed to early retirement in Hungary and Poland; much less so in the Czech Republic and Slovakia, where income replacement ratios are significantly smaller, even by OECD standards. Moreover, on the assumption that jobs freed by older workers would be filled by young workers, several countries in the past have placed high implicit taxes on continued work, either through non-actuarially neutral pension systems or through other social transfer programmes (i.e. unemployment-related and disability benefits). There are also a number of demand-side distortions that are fairly general in this group of countries. One relates to rigid age-wage profiles, which are often due to employment protection legislation. Another has to do with difficulties of older workers in updating their skills in the face of rapid technological progress. This problem is exacerbated by firms' unwillingness to train older workers because of the shorter time horizon of such investment. Taken together these two factors make older workers less attractive to employers. Age discrimination appears to be particularly strong against women in secretarial and clerical jobs in the private sector.

While the incentives for early retirement have been progressively reduced in several countries, thus leading to an overall (albeit still small) increase in the employment rate of older workers between 2000 and 2003, further action is needed to foster labour utilization in this demographic group. A first important step will be the

---

[117] Empirical analysis of the determinants of unemployment in the central European economies has identified other factors that contribute to weak labour market performance, particularly in Poland and Slovakia. These include the combination of restructuring with tight monetary policy, poor rule of law (which in turn limited FDI inflows) and demographic changes. Some of these factors are cyclical while others appear to be of a more structural nature. If not properly addressed, such problems could then reduce the expected positive impact on employment dynamics of labour market reforms. S. Ederveen and L. Thissen, *Can Labour Market Institutions Explain Unemployment Rates in New EU Member States?*, CPB Document No. 59 (The Hague), April 2004.

[118] See, for instance, R. Duval, *The Retirement Effects of Old-age Pension Systems and Other Social Transfer Programmes in OECD*

Countries, OECD Economics Department Working Papers, No. 370 (Paris), November 2003.

reform of the pension system to strengthen its actuarial fairness and at the same time to move away from pay-as-you-go, non-funded mechanisms. Such reforms have already been launched in Hungary, Latvia, Poland and some other new member states.[119] In Poland, however, the still high replacement ratios have probably offset some of the positive effects that the pension reform might have had on the employment rate. A second step is to increase the flexibility of wage growth by age. This can be achieved both within a decentralized wage-setting structure, where wages are more likely to be determined by actual productivity, and a centralized system, where economy-wide considerations are internalized by industry or sector encompassing unions. It is more difficult to achieve this greater flexibility with the intermediate degrees of concentration of wage bargaining that prevail in the EU-10 economies. Additional efforts will also need to be made to reduce age discrimination, especially against minorities, such as the Roma in central Europe and, generally, against women. Finally, retraining programmes to update the skills of older workers need to be strengthened. Some empirical evidence for the OECD countries shows that to be effective training programmes should be designed with a strong on-the-job component and be associated with the provision of efficient job placement services.[120] However, it must be acknowledged that low labour mobility across regions might significantly hinder the effectiveness of such programmes as people receiving training in one region might not be willing or able to move to another region where there are suitable job openings. For this reason, in countries with sharp regional disparities (e.g. Hungary, Poland and Slovakia), it is important to combine training programmes with policies that facilitate labour mobility (for example, housing and rental policies).

(iii) The short-term outlook

Rapid output and productivity growth should continue in 2005...

The prospects for continued strong output growth in the EU-10 in 2005 are relatively good (table 1.1.1) but subject to a number of risks. The pace of expansion may well be only slightly below that of 2004, assuming slow but steady GDP growth in western Europe. Economic sentiment has remained remarkably robust in Poland, the economy that dominates trends in the EU-10. This, together with strong industrial orders in recent months, indicate that activity is likely to remain vigorous in the short term. On the supply side, the capacity-increasing effects of foreign direct investment should continue to play a key role in the growth process. The slowly improving business environment and EU membership have coincided with a noticeable growth of greenfield

FDI projects that are likely to improve the quality of the ongoing economic restructuring and to underpin a continued strong performance of exports.[121]

...but prospects for employment growth remain bleak

Strong output growth in the EU-10 area, however, is still unlikely to induce significant employment gains, given the slow progress of labour market reforms and the aggressive industrial restructuring taking place in the dominant economies. The persistent duality of the labour market is apparent in the coexistence of skilled labour bottlenecks with the absence of vacancies for the low-skilled jobseekers that dominate the ranks of the long-term unemployed. The tax-benefit systems still create poverty traps that reduce significantly the work incentives of low-skilled labour. Heavy taxes on labour and excessive regulation limit job creation in the private sector. Moreover, fiscal consolidation in most EU-10 economies precludes employment gains in the government sector.

...and there are considerable risks to the outlook

An important downside risk to the above outlook is the possibility of a sharp slowdown of economic growth in the euro zone and a subsequent weakening of external demand. Another major short-term risk is the possibility of further increases in world commodity prices, particularly of oil and natural gas.[122] This would not only exert direct upward pressure on production costs and prices but could also affect the rates of growth of industrial output and productivity, which were instrumental in offsetting the impact of accelerated wage inflation in 2004. Such developments could result in rising core inflation and a consequent monetary tightening that would eventually reduce the pace of output growth.

Aside from those mentioned above, the most serious risk to the outlook is posed by the fragile nature of fiscal consolidation in central Europe ahead of the upcoming general elections. Traditionally, national elections in the region have been preceded by large increases in public sector wages and social transfers. If this electoral spending pattern is repeated in 2005, it could undermine policy credibility and erode confidence, possibly triggering monetary tightening, lower FDI inflows and reduced competitiveness.

---

[119] On pension reforms designed to increase actuarial fairness see A. Lindbeck and M. Persson, "The gains from pension reform", *Journal of Economic Literature*, Vol. 41, No. 1, March 2003.

[120] J. Martin, "What works among active labour market policies: evidence from OECD countries' experiences", OECD, *Economic Studies No. 30* (Paris), 2001/1.

[121] According to a recent report, the number of FDI projects in the first half of 2004 rose much faster in Hungary, Poland and the Czech Republic than in the mature EU economies. Relative to other European economies, Hungary was in the third position with 84 new FDI projects, Poland in fifth place with 69 new projects and the Czech Republic in eighth place with 63 new projects. Slovakia did not rank among the top 10 countries but nevertheless received more new FDI projects than the Netherlands. *Ernst & Young European Investment Monitor*, First Half 2004.

[122] The energy intensity of the EU-10 economies still significantly exceeds that of their west European counterparts. The adverse impact of higher energy prices on economic growth is therefore likely to be stronger in the new EU economies than in the old ones. For a country-specific estimate of this impact, see National Bank of Hungary, *Inflation Report*, August 2004, pp. 75-79.

CHAPTER 4

SOUTH-EAST EUROPE

4.1 The policy agenda

With the entry of 10 new members of the EU in 2004, the agenda for the next round of enlargement focuses on candidates from south-east Europe. In 2004, Bulgaria and Romania closed all the negotiation chapters and are scheduled to join the EU in 2007. The start of accession negotiations with Croatia and Turkey is expected to give a strong impetus to their ongoing economic reforms. The emergence of a new, regional group of potential EU members will undoubtedly have a wide-ranging and positive economic impact on the whole south-east European region.

The experience of the east European economies that have just joined the EU provides strong evidence that the realistic prospect of EU membership has been the single most important stimulus to the economic transformation of these countries. The preparation for accession to the EU defines a broad reform agenda with clearly specified goals and the means to achieve them, and establishes strong and clear incentives for policy makers. Moreover, the institutionalization of the policy commitments within a tight schedule of accession negotiations helps both to accelerate and provide direction to the reform process.

The recent experience of the south-east European EU candidate countries supports the view that a virtuous cycle of strong growth and accelerating reforms can emerge during the final years of preparation for EU membership. A similar process was also observed in the central European and Baltic countries prior to their accession to the EU. This experience indicates that, through its powerful effect on expectations, the realistic prospect of EU accession (especially when accompanied by a clear timetable for membership) can act as a major, albeit indirect, stimulus to economic growth. In particular, the recent increase of FDI in Bulgaria, Romania and, to a lesser extent, Croatia, largely reflects the change in investors' expectations with regard to the prospect of these economies becoming part of the EU in the not too distant future. In turn, the large flows of inward FDI have undoubtedly contributed to the restructuring of these economies, giving a boost to economic activity.

The current economic revival in Turkey has a somewhat different character in that it is largely associated with a successful stabilization programme and a faster pace of reform; but, at the same time, it also bears some resemblance to what has been happening in other parts of south-east Europe (box 4.1.1). It can be expected that the eventual start of accession negotiations with the EU will also provide strong support to the economic and legislative reforms being pursued in this country.

The policy process and agenda in the other parts of south-east Europe, however, lack the clear direction that can be seen in the EU candidate countries. In Serbia and Montenegro, the largest of these economies, the reform effort has lost some momentum and focus, largely because of a difficult political situation (involving four rounds of election in 12 months). Very high and persistent levels of unemployment in most of these countries remain an acute problem that policy makers in the region have yet to solve.

In recent years, all the south-east European economies have made considerable progress in macroeconomic and financial stabilization, and 2004 has generally been no exception in this respect: Turkey and Romania, with the highest inflation rates in the region, are also the countries that have made the most progress in reducing them. The emergence of a more stable and predictable macroeconomic environment has undoubtedly contributed to the strengthening of economic activity in south-east Europe. In turn, this has had a beneficial effect on domestic financial markets where both nominal and real interest rates have generally been falling in recent years (table 4.1.1).

The economic outlook of south-east Europe as a whole depends on several key policy-related issues and factors. The first is whether individual countries will be successful in their attempts at integration with the EU. As mentioned already, unambiguous progress in this process can trigger a virtuous cycle of strong economic growth and focused market reforms. However, in order to get to this point, clear, long-term policy goals need to be established as national priorities and accepted as such by a significant majority of their populations. The absence of such a consensus about the general direction of reform in some of these countries is one of the major stumbling blocks to their economic transformation.

Box 4.1.1

Economic turnaround in Turkey: can the momentum be sustained?

In early 2001, the Turkish economy was on the brink of financial default. A long period of political instability, persistently double-digit rates of inflation, growing public sector debt and deteriorating bank portfolios triggered a massive loss of investor confidence. The crisis led to a full-blown run on the banking system (forcing a massive government bailout of failing banks) and the collapse of the crawling peg exchange rate regime.[1]

The policy response to the 2000-2001 crisis

In spring 2001, the government launched a series of policy reforms (based on the national programme for convergence with the EU's *acquis communautaire*) supported by a standby agreement with the IMF. Further measures (the so called Urgent Action Plan) were adopted in 2002. This ambitious programme envisaged wide-ranging structural reforms targeting macroeconomic stabilization and a higher trend rate of growth. It also included important changes in macroeconomic policy such as a considerable tightening of fiscal policy, the introduction of a floating exchange rate regime and the granting of operational independence to the central bank.

In the following three years the main macroeconomic targets of the programme were exceeded by a significant margin. Year-on-year consumer price inflation fell from more than 70 per cent at the end of 2001 to single digits in May 2004, the lowest rate in more than 30 years (chart 4.1.1). In November 2004, the 11-month cumulative rate of inflation was 8.8 per cent compared with the central bank's year-end target of 12 per cent. Rising confidence in the central bank's commitment to pursue and maintain price stability is reflected in the fact that the gap between consensus inflation forecasts and the official inflation target (a proxy for the credibility of the central bank) turned negative for the first time. Further evidence of rising investor confidence is provided by the spreads on Turkey's eurobonds, which fell by 290 basis points, and by the equity market index (ISE-100), which rose by nearly 25 per cent in dollar terms between mid-May and end-September 2004.

After a sharp recession in 2001, the economy recovered rapidly: the cumulative real GDP growth in 2002 and 2003 was more than 14 per cent, and the current forecast is for a rise of some 9 per cent in 2004 (well above the initial forecast of 5 per cent). A strong rebound in productivity was the key factor behind this remarkable, non-inflationary rate of growth. It may also be surmised that there has been an increase in potential output growth since 2001, at least in part because of the favourable effects of successful stabilization policies on business investment and productivity. The sharp fall in the rate of inflation has allowed the monetary authorities to lower interest rates significantly which, in turn, have stimulated investment in the private sector. Thus, real gross fixed investment rose by more than 50 per cent year-on-year in the first half of 2004, mainly due to a nearly 95 per cent increase in business spending on machinery and equipment.

There has been remarkable progress in fiscal consolidation since 2001. The primary surplus of the consolidated public sector financial balance was more than 6 per cent of GDP in 2003, up from 3 per cent in 2000, and is forecast to reach 6.5 per cent in 2004, in line with the government's programme. The ratio of total public net debt to GDP is forecast to fall to about 70 per cent at the end of 2004, down from more than 90 per cent in 2001. As part of the debt is held in foreign currency, the appreciation of the lira also contributed to the reduction in the debt to GDP ratio. Productivity driven falls in unit labour costs have prevented losses in cost competitiveness despite the appreciating lira and these have helped to strengthen merchandise exports.[2] Foreign reserves reached some $36 billion in September 2004, up from $17 billion at the end of 2002, and well above the amount envisaged in the stabilization programme.

In December 2004, the European Council acknowledged that Turkey had met the Copenhagen political criteria for EU membership with a view to opening accession negotiations on 3 October 2005. This positive outcome should provide Turkey with an important external anchor for domestic policy, contributing to a further strengthening of investor confidence and a general improvement in expectations.

The challenges ahead

The major challenge for the government is to sustain the pace of reform in the face of mounting political and social pressures. In the past, policy reversals have resulted in major economic setbacks on several occasions. Sustaining the hard-won macroeconomic stability and keeping the economy on a high growth track thus requires a lasting and dedicated policy effort.

Despite its reduction, the ratio of total public debt to GDP still remains high, implying net interest payments above 10 per cent of GDP in 2004. The large and rising current account deficit (around 5 per cent of GDP in 2004) remains a concern for policy makers as it is largely financed by volatile short-term capital. Inward FDI is relatively low despite a recent upturn.[3] In view of the external vulnerability, a number of measures have been introduced to curb the growth of consumer demand and imports (see section 4.1 and chapter 6.2).

Further progress in reducing inflation is needed (to low single-digit rates) if interest rates are to continue to fall. This would not only lower domestic debt service payments but would also stimulate further productive investment and help to sustain a high rate of economic growth. Indeed, a shift to a higher trend rate of growth will be needed in order to reduce the unemployment rate which has reached 13 per cent in urban areas. In view of the rapid growth of population and very low participation rates this will remain a major policy concern in the medium and long term.[4] Growing unemployment has been accompanied by a rise in poverty and the expansion of informal economic activities.[5]

Box 4.1.1 (concluded)

Economic turnaround in Turkey: can the momentum be sustained?

Further structural reforms are needed to sustain the fiscal consolidation. The efficiency of public spending needs to be improved, together with further reforms of the system of taxation. At present, three quarters of total budgetary expenditures are non-discretionary, which reduces the room for manoeuvre in public spending. In order to enable more spending on public investment and a more effective social safety net, the pension and health-care systems will have to be reformed (some preliminary work is already underway). The current system of taxation, heavily dependent on excise duties, also calls for major changes. Tax reforms will need to be mainly focused on broadening the tax base which, if successful, should boost public revenue.

Efforts also need to be made to reduce the exposure of the economy to volatile short-term capital flows, and to attract more FDI. This, in turn, will require further improvements in the business environment, and the continuation of structural reforms. Privatization needs to be given high priority in order to strengthen the basis of the market economy.

The consolidation of macroeconomic gains also requires microeconomic adjustments. The present stabilization programme has so far been based on sound macroeconomic policies and structural reforms mainly in the public sector. The next round of reforms should focus on labour markets, competition policy and corporate governance in order to make both the product and labour markets more efficient and to lay the basis for further gains in productivity and competitiveness which should stimulate employment growth in the longer term.

Thus, sustaining the current momentum requires consistent implementation of the new policy framework and a deepening of the reform effort. So far the indications are that the government is committed to these goals, as evidenced in the announced new three-year standby agreement with the IMF (due to start in February 2005 when the present one expires). The government has also pledged to maintain its fiscal consolidation effort: according to the budget proposal for 2005 the primary fiscal surplus should remain at 6.5 per cent of GDP in spite of the projected slowdown in GDP growth. However, it is still too early to judge whether or not the recent economic recovery and the associated policies have paved the way to a new era for the Turkish economy.

---

[1] As a result public net debt rose from less than 60 per cent of GDP in 2000 to more than 90 per cent in 2001. The ex-post cost of cleaning up the banking system is estimated at around $50 billion, corresponding to some 30 per cent of GDP in 2002 and more than half of total banking assets at the end of that year.

[2] Merchandise exports increased by nearly one third, year-on-year, in the first three quarters of 2004.

[3] In January-September 2004, net FDI inflows reached $1.6 billion (or some $23 per capita), significantly below the levels recorded in other ECE emerging market economies.

[4] According to the household labour force survey, the labour force participation rate was 49.2 per cent (44.1 per cent in urban areas) in the second quarter of 2004, down from 57 per cent in 1990. The employment rate for the whole economy fell to 44.6 per cent (38.4 per cent in urban areas).

[5] Even though food poverty is negligible in Turkey, 27 per cent of the population was living below the food and non-food poverty line in 2002. According to official estimates, informal activities accounted for more than 50 per cent of total employment in 2004.

Structural and institutional reforms remain an important challenge for the whole south-east European region. The reforms of health care and pension systems are either at an early stage or have not yet started at all. Public institutions for a market economy in most of these countries are still underdeveloped and this has a negative effect on the business environment: the protection of property rights, including law and contract enforcement, is generally weak; the public administration is widely perceived as inefficient and lacking in transparency; and corruption is still widespread. Significant reform in these areas is a fundamental requirement for successful economic integration with the EU.

All the south-east European economies still have per capita incomes, which are much lower than those in the more developed market economies. A key prerequisite for closing the gap, namely sustaining relatively high rates of economic growth for a sufficiently

long period of time, is the development of human capital. This is an important determinant of national competitiveness and a key factor of their long-term growth. Hence human capital development should be among the principal priorities of public policy in the countries of south-east Europe.

It also needs to be borne in mind that social cohesion is a crucial dimension of human capital development. The lingering social tensions amid widespread poverty in some of the south-east European countries will require a leading role for public policy if they are to be eliminated or defused. In this regard, an integrated set of structural reforms focused on increasing employment (employment rates being excessively low at present) is one of the areas where success could bring wide-ranging benefits. Policies aimed at reducing inequality – without diluting incentives to work – can also have a positive effect on future growth prospects. In

TABLE 4.1.1

Short-term interest rates and credit to the non-government sector in selected south-east European economies, 2002-2004
(Per cent per annum, per cent of GDP)

| | Interest rates on short-term credits (per cent) | | | | | | Interest rates on short-term deposits (per cent) | | | | | | Total credit [a] (per cent of GDP) | | |
| | Nominal | | | Real | | | Nominal | | | Real | | | | | |
	2002	2003	2004 [b]	2002	2003	2004 [b]	2002	2003	2004 [b]	2002	2003	2004 [b]	2002	2003	2004 [b]
Albania	15.3	14.3	12.1	21.5	14.3	10.0	8.5	8.4	6.9	3.1	5.7	3.6	6.3	6.6	7.8
Bosnia and Herzegovina	12.7	10.9	10.4	12.0	11.0	8.1	4.5	4.0	3.6	3.5	3.4	3.2	32.7	39.2	43.0
Bulgaria	9.8	9.2	9.1	8.5	4.0	3.9	3.0	3.1	3.2	-2.6	0.8	-2.6	16.5	22.8	28.6
Croatia	13.0	11.6	11.8	13.4	9.5	9.3	1.9	1.5	1.8	0.0	-0.6	-0.6	47.1	54.6	56.1
Romania	35.4	25.7	26.3	8.6	3.9	5.6	19.1	11.0	11.9	-2.8	-3.8	-1.5	10.7	12.5	13.8
Serbia and Montenegro	24.3	16.5	15.9	14.3	11.4	8.5	21.2	14.3	14.3	4.0	4.5	5.0	12.0	15.9	14.8
The former Yugoslav Republic of Macedonia	18.3	16.0	12.6	19.4	16.3	13.1	9.6	8.0	6.6	7.6	6.7	5.4	16.2	16.4	17.9
Turkey	..	..	..	..	..	..	50.5	37.7	24.5	3.8	9.9	11.6	13.5	13.8	15.3

Source: National statistics and direct communications from national statistical offices to the UNECE secretariat; IMF, *International Financial Statistics* (Washington, D.C.), various issues.

Note: Definition of interest rates:

Credits – Bulgaria: average rate on short-term credits; Croatia: weighted average rate on new credits to enterprises and households only; Romania: average short-term lending rate; The former Yugoslav Republic of Macedonia: median rates for short-term loans to all sectors. The real lending rates are the nominal rates discounted by the average rate of increase in the PPI for the corresponding period.

Deposits – Bulgaria: average rates on one-month time deposits; Croatia: weighted average rate on new deposits; Romania: average short-term deposit rate; The former Yugoslav Republic of Macedonia: lowest reported interest rate on household deposits with maturities of three to six months. The real deposit rates are the nominal rates discounted by the average rate of increase in the CPI for the corresponding period.

[a] Total outstanding claims of commercial banks on the non-government sector. GDP data for 2004 are preliminary estimates.

[b] January-September.

CHART 4.1.1

Quarterly GDP growth and changes in the consumer price index in Turkey, 2000-2004QIII
(Year-on-year, percentage change)

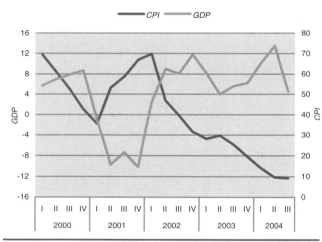

Source: National statistics.

particular, greater social solidarity will help to create a general consensus about the nature and direction of the reform process which, in turn, will increase the probability of it being maintained.

4.2 Recent macroeconomic developments

Turkey's economy is booming

Aggregate GDP growth in south-east Europe generally strengthened in 2004, thanks to a robust performance in most of the EU candidate countries.

During the first half of 2004, Turkey, the largest economy in the region, was expanding at double-digit rates (table 4.2.1). The upturn was broadly based but industry (mining, manufacturing and utilities) contributed most of the increase. In the third quarter, the pace of industrial output slowed down somewhat (chart 4.2.1) but industrial capacity utilization continued to rise and in September it stood at 84.8 per cent, the highest rate in the last seven years. Domestic demand (both private consumption and, especially, fixed investment) was unusually buoyant, reflecting the positive shift in expectations. With domestic demand outpacing GDP growth, net exports contributed negatively to GDP growth, despite a continued robust increase in the exports of goods and services (table 4.2.2 and chart 4.2.2). However, the rapid import growth contributed to a further widening of the already large current account deficit, which remains a major policy concern. As discussed in more detail in box 4.1.1, the current boom reflects the positive outcomes (including macroeconomic stabilization) of the reform programme initiated in 2001.

Economic activity also strengthened in other south-east European countries...

A broad-based economic recovery in Bulgaria and Romania gained further ground in 2004, underpinned by several factors. On the supply side, there was a notable acceleration in the pace of economic restructuring and modernization of these economies, largely driven by the recent surge in inward FDI.[123] The upgrading and expansion

_____

[123] Thus, car production in the Romanian automobile industry, recently restructured with FDI, grew by almost one third, year-on-year, in January-September 2004.

TABLE 4.2.1

Changes in real GDP in south-east Europe, 2003-2004QIII

(Percentage change over the same period of the preceding year)

	2003	2004 [a]	2003				2004		
			QI	QII	QIII	QIV	QI	QII	QIII
South-east Europe	5.1	7.9	6.3	4.0	5.1	5.3	8.2	10.3	5.9
Albania	6.0	6.0	..	..	..	..	..	..	..
Bosnia and Herzegovina	3.2	4.0	..	..	..	..	..	..	..
Bulgaria	4.3	5.5	3.5	4.2	4.4	4.9	5.3	6.0	5.8
Croatia	4.3	4.0	4.9	5.0	3.9	3.3	4.2	3.8	3.6
Romania	4.9	7.5	4.4	4.3	5.4	4.6	6.1	7.0	10.2
Serbia and Montenegro	1.5	7.0	..	..	..	..	..	..	..
The former Yugoslav									
Republic of Macedonia	3.4	2.5	2.4	3.6	5.8	1.9	-3.2	-0.1	1.5
Turkey	5.8	9.0	8.1	3.9	5.5	6.1	10.1	13.4	4.5
Memorandum item:									
South-east Europe excluding Turkey	4.2	6.4	3.9	4.1	4.6	4.1	5.6	6.2	7.8

Source: National statistical offices.

Note: The aggregates are computed by the UNECE secretariat using weights based on purchasing power parities. In the cases when countries do not report quarterly national accounts data, their annual GDP growth rates were used to compute the quarterly regional aggregates.

[a] Preliminary estimate.

CHART 4.2.1

Real industrial output in selected south-east European economies, 2001-2004QIII

(Indices of 12-month output, corresponding period of the preceding year=100)

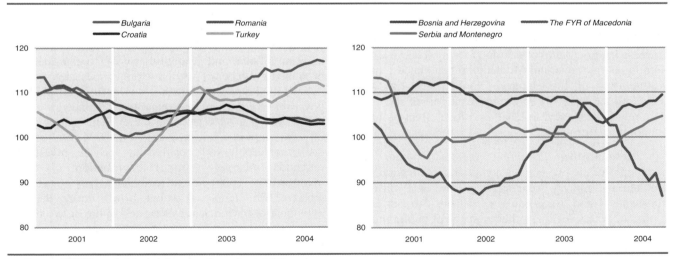

Source: UNECE secretariat calculations, based on national statistics.

of their manufacturing production capacities and the accompanying productivity gains set the stage for a large rise in merchandise exports in 2004 despite the general sluggishness of their main market, western Europe. Output in the relatively large agricultural sectors of the two countries was boosted by good harvests, especially in Romania. In Bulgaria, industrial output surged in 2004 (chart 4.2.1) while the rapidly expanding tourism industry registered record revenues for a third consecutive year. Other business services also contributed to the strong growth of aggregate output in both Bulgaria and Romania.

On the demand side, the strengthening of investor and consumer confidence has translated into a sustained upturn in their final domestic demand which, in both countries, continued to support domestic activity levels in 2004. Since 2001, the pattern of final demand contributions to GDP growth in the two countries has been broadly similar (chart 4.2.2). A relatively new phenomenon, which became even more visible in 2004, has been the surge in demand for consumer durables. This is similar to that observed in central Europe several years ago. Investment demand remained strong in both Bulgaria and Romania, with gross fixed capital formation growing at double-digit rates in the first half of the year (table 4.2.2). During the same period their domestic absorption continued to grow faster than GDP, resulting in negative contributions of net exports to GDP growth.

TABLE 4.2.2

Components of real final demand in selected south-east European economies, 2002-2004QII
(Percentage change over the same period of the preceding year)

	Private consumption expenditure [a]			Government consumption expenditure [b]			Gross fixed capital formation			Exports of goods and services			Imports of goods and services		
	2002	2003	2004 QI-QII	2002	2003	2004 QI-QII	2002	2003	2004 QI-QII	2002	2003	2004 QI-QII	2002	2003	2004 QI-QII
South-east Europe	3.2	7.0	11.3	1.0	0.5	-0.7	3.0	10.5	32.8	11.1	13.1	12.9	12.8	21.1	23.9
Bulgaria	3.5	6.4	5.2	4.1	7.2	2.5	8.5	13.8	12.6	7.0	8.0	9.6	4.9	14.8	14.2
Croatia	7.3	4.1	3.8	-1.8	-0.3	-0.5	12.0	16.8	8.2	1.3	10.1	5.0	8.8	10.9	5.6
Romania	4.8	7.1	9.5	-8.9	6.1	4.9	8.2	9.2	10.8	17.6	11.1	17.5	12.0	16.3	19.7
The former Yugoslav Republic of Macedonia	12.5	..	..	-11.1	..	..	17.6	..	..	-5.5	..	..	10.3	..	..
Turkey	2.0	7.2	13.5	5.4	-2.4	-3.5	-1.1	10.0	52.1	11.1	16.0	13.1	15.8	27.1	32.0
Memorandum item:															
South-east Europe excluding Turkey	5.2	6.7	7.7	-5.0	4.9	3.2	9.2	11.3	10.5	10.9	9.6	12.7	9.6	14.7	15.5

Source: National statistical offices.

Note: The aggregates are computed by the UNECE secretariat using weights based on purchasing power parities.

[a] Expenditures incurred by households and non-profit institutions serving households.

[b] Expenditures incurred by the general government on both individual consumption of goods and services and collective consumption of services.

In 2004, a marked recovery was also underway in Serbia and Montenegro, after a rather sluggish performance in 2003. The turnaround was underpinned by an upturn in industry, after two years of a difficult adjustment of local firms to the comprehensive market reforms initiated in 2001 (chart 4.2.1), and a large increase in agricultural output due to a good harvest. The authorities in Serbia and Montenegro negotiated a major restructuring of the country's foreign debt in 2004, including the write-off of a significant part of it.[124] The debt relief is expected to have a positive effect on future economic performance.

Despite their common national border, the economies of the two entities comprising the federal state are almost entirely separated. They use different currencies (and, accordingly, adhere to different monetary policy regimes), their systems of public finance (and therefore, their fiscal policies) are entirely disconnected, and the two entities do not even maintain a customs union.[125] Given the absence of strong economic links, the two parts of the federal state may display quite divergent patterns of economic performance. In fact, the upturn in 2004 is almost entirely due to the strengthening of output growth in Serbia.

Albania's economy maintained a relatively fast pace in 2004, thanks to the large agricultural sector which also contributed to an upturn in the food processing industry.

...but growth remained moderate in some parts of the region

In 2004 output growth in Croatia decelerated for a second consecutive year, largely because of the tightening of macroeconomic policy. Croatia's chronic twin deficit problem (a combination of fiscal and current account deficits) and a rapidly growing foreign debt has prompted a number of restrictive policy measures seeking to curb final domestic demand. In the first half of 2004, government consumption expenditure continued to fall in real terms, year-on-year (table 4.2.2). The scaling down of public infrastructure investment in 2004 resulted in a declining, albeit still positive (as private investment remained relatively strong) contribution of fixed investment to GDP growth in the first half of the year (chart 4.2.2). Industrial output growth during the first three quarters of the year was modest, more or less in line with the increase in exports. On the supply side it was mostly market services (tourism as well as transport and communications) that made the largest contribution to GDP growth in the first half of the year.

In Bosnia and Herzegovina, the economy continued to grow at a moderate pace, with industrial output growth accelerating in the course of the year. Several years of aid-driven, post-war reconstruction has allowed the rebuilding of most of the country's infrastructure and the reinstatement of most public services. However, the progress in institutional and structural reforms as well as in private sector development has been rather slow and the economy still appears to be incapable of a self-sustained recovery.[126] The two entities that form the country (the

---

[124] As a result of three consecutive deals with Russia, the London Club and the Paris Club of creditors, a total of $2.5 billion of foreign debt (or some 17.5 per cent of the debt prior to the restructuring) was written off in 2004.

[125] The absence of a common system of tariffs is one of the important stumbling blocks to progress in trade negotiations with the EU.

[126] At a Consultative Group meeting held in Sarajevo on 22-23 September, donors pledged a total of $1.2 billion of financial aid to Bosnia and Herzegovina over the period 2004-2007, especially for support of the country's poverty reduction programme. "Bosnia-

CHART 4.2.2

Contribution of final demand components to GDP growth in selected south-east European economies, 2001-2004
(Percentage points)

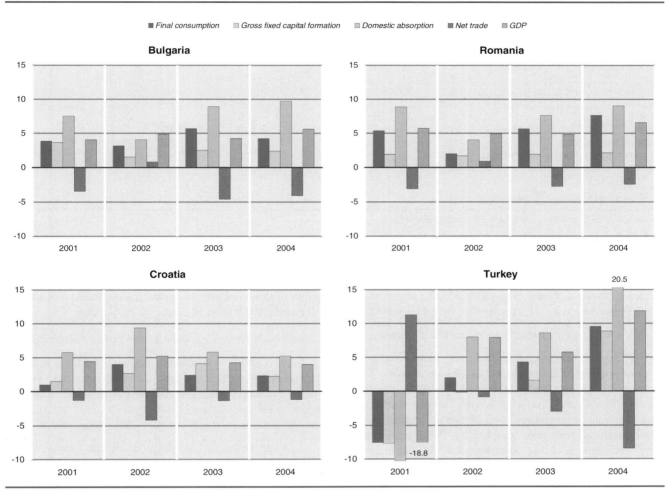

■ *Final consumption*   ▨ *Gross fixed capital formation*   ▨ *Domestic absorption*   ■ *Net trade*   ▨ *GDP*

Source: National statistics.

Note: The contributions shown for 2004 refer to the first half of the year and are calculated over the same period of 2003.

Federation of Bosnia and Herzegovina and Republika Srpska) still remain to a large extent economically segregated.

Improving financial intermediation

The progress of financial reforms in some south-east European countries (in particular, Bulgaria and Croatia and, to a lesser extent, Romania) has given an additional boost to economic activity. A great number of commercial banks in these countries have already been privatized, in many cases to strategic foreign investors. The ensuing overhaul of the banking sector together with the strengthening of financial regulation and supervision have greatly improved financial intermediation in these economies. Thanks to the government's restructuring effort and the lowering of inflation – which resulted in a sharp reduction of interest rates – banking and credit activity in Turkey has been recovering rapidly, especially

Herzegovina: poverty reduction strategy programme is last chance for progress", *Oxford Analytica*, 8 November 2004.

during 2004. The rapid expansion of credit in recent years, particularly in Bulgaria, Croatia and Turkey (table 4.1.1), has boosted both business activity and investment, and final consumer demand.

Several more specific developments also merit attention in this regard. The ongoing restructuring of the banking sector in some of the more economically advanced countries of the region has been accompanied by growing competition among the banks. One result has been the appearance of an increasing variety of new financial products on the domestic markets. Moreover, the banks have been increasingly turning their attention to the retail market, a development that not only benefits households and small businesses but also supports economic performance in general. Thus the proliferation of credit cards is not only a convenience for the customers but is having an overall positive effect on consumer demand. Furthermore, the surge in the demand for consumer durables (including automobiles) is to a large extent related to the availability of, and easy access to, various credit facilities. Similarly, the rapid growth of

TABLE 4.2.3

Consumer prices in south-east Europe, 2002-2004

(Percentage change)

| | Consumer prices, total | | | | | | | | Food | Non-food | Services |
| | Over preceding year | | | 2004, year on year | | | September over previous December | | | | |
	2002	2003	2004[a]	QI	QII	QIII	2003		2004		
South-east Europe	35.0	21.0	12.1	12.9	9.4	9.6	11.8	4.9	..	..	..
Albania	5.3	2.5	3.1	3.9	2.8	2.5	-0.4	-1.6	-8.2	..	..
Bosnia and Herzegovina	0.9	0.2	–	0.9	-0.5	-1.1	-1.3	-3.7	-5.6	-4.5	0.6
Bulgaria	5.8	2.3	6.1	6.4	6.7	6.6	1.2	1.8	-3.4	4.5	6.8
Croatia	1.8	2.2	2.3	2.7	2.0	1.8	2.1	1.1	-1.8	0.7	4.2
Romania	22.5	15.4	13.1	13.6	12.3	11.8	9.7	6.6	4.4	8.4	8.4
Serbia and Montenegro	19.3	9.6	9.3	8.2	9.7	11.5	4.9	9.0	10.6	9.1	8.5
The former Yugoslav Republic of Macedonia	2.3	1.1	0.4	1.9	-0.5	-1.6	1.4	-3.0	-6.4	0.5	2.7
Turkey	44.9	25.4	12.9	14.0	9.3	9.6	13.9	4.7	..	..	..
Memorandum item:											
South-east Europe excluding Turkey	16.2	10.7	10.0	10.2	9.6	9.6	6.6	5.5	..	..	..

Source: UNECE secretariat estimates, based on national statistics.

[a] For the 12 months ending September 2004 over the preceding 12 months.

house construction in some south-east European countries partly mirrors the concomitant expansion of mortgage finance. Small businesses are also beginning to enjoy better access to credit and other financial services.

Consumer price inflation was on the decline...

Rates of consumer price inflation continued to fall in most south-east European economies in the first three quarters of 2004 (table 4.2.3) thanks to relatively tight fiscal policies and, in some cases, nominal effective exchange rate appreciation. Food prices (a major item in the household consumer baskets of these economies) were declining and this contributed to the lowering of inflation rates.

Disinflation in Romania continued gradually in 2004, a positive outcome of fiscal consolidation (see below). Although the year-on-year rate in September remained in double digits, the nine-month cumulative rate of change in September was 6.6 per cent and the year-end target of 9 per cent may well be within reach. In Turkey, the rate of inflation continued to fall rapidly for a third consecutive year, a reflection of the government's successful reform programme (box 4.1.1). The year-on-year rate of consumer price inflation fell to single digits in May 2004 and the nine-month cumulative rate was down to 4.7 per cent in September, suggesting that the year-end outcome may be well below the target of 12 per cent. In Croatia, the tightening of macroeconomic policy stance (accompanied by exchange rate appreciation) led to another fall in the already low inflation rate in 2004. In Albania, Bosnia and Herzegovina and The former Yugoslav Republic of Macedonia, consumer prices actually fell during the first nine months of 2004 mainly due to declining food prices but also in some cases (particularly Albania), to a tightening of fiscal policy.

In the first nine months of 2004, year-on-year rates of consumer price inflation accelerated only in Bulgaria and Serbia and Montenegro, largely because of increases

in administered energy prices and excise duties. However, core inflation in Bulgaria remained low, and despite the effect of these one-off increases, the cumulative rise in the 10 months to October remained just 2 per cent.

...but producer prices were under rising cost pressures

In 2004, industrial producer price inflation accelerated in most south-east European countries (Turkey being the exception) and the increases were generally larger than those in the consumer prices (chart 4.2.3). This development was largely due to higher energy prices.

Wage inflation (as measured by the change in the average gross wage in industry) varied in the first half of 2004. According to the available data, wage growth continued to moderate in Bosnia and Herzegovina, The former Yugoslav Republic of Macedonia and in Turkey, while in Croatia the rate was more or less unchanged.[127] In contrast, industrial wages in Bulgaria and Romania rose faster than during the same period of 2003.

The dynamics of industrial unit labour costs in the four EU candidate countries have been rather varied in recent years. Between the end of 2001 and mid-2004 they declined by nearly 20 per cent in Bulgaria while increasing by almost two thirds in Romania. In Turkey, in spite of a relatively favourable performance since mid-2003, unit labour costs in mid-2004 were nearly one fifth above their level at the end of 2001. In Croatia, wage growth has followed the slow increase in labour productivity and so unit labour costs have remained more or less stable.

The factors behind these changes highlight the related policy challenges. While labour productivity in both Bulgaria and Turkey has increased by some 30 per cent over the last two and a half years, wages in Turkey

_____

[127] Data for Albania and Serbia and Montenegro were not available.

CHART 4.2.3

Consumer and industrial producer prices in south-east Europe, January 2000-September 2004
(Year-on-year, monthly percentage change)

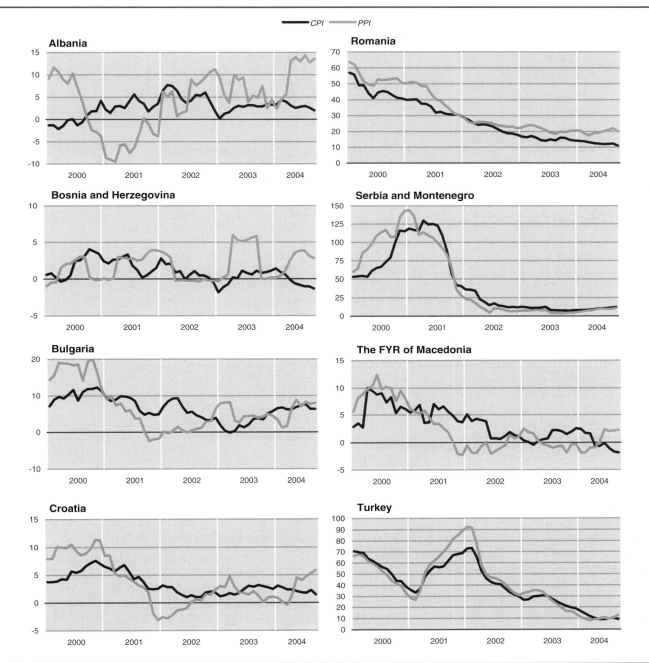

Source: National statistics.

grew nearly five times faster than in Bulgaria (chart 4.2.4). Wage inflation was even more rapid in Romania while its productivity growth was much weaker. Increases in labour costs which are not matched by rising productivity lead to losses in competitiveness and, if unchecked, may weaken the growth potential of these economies and undermine their catch-up prospects. While wages in the catching-up economies are likely to continue to grow rapidly, an excessive rate of growth will involve an obvious trade-off, as income gains in the short run may come at the expense

of long-term income. Maintaining an appropriate balance between the growth rates of wages and labour productivity should thus be given high priority in the policy agenda of catching-up economies.

Labour market performance remained uneven across the EU candidate countries...

Of the four EU candidate countries, Bulgaria continues to be the one with the most rapid growth of employment (table 4.2.4). This reflects a number of

CHART 4.2.4

Gross nominal wages and labour productivity in industry in selected south-east European economies, 2001QIV-2004QII

(Indices, 2001QIV=100, seasonally adjusted)

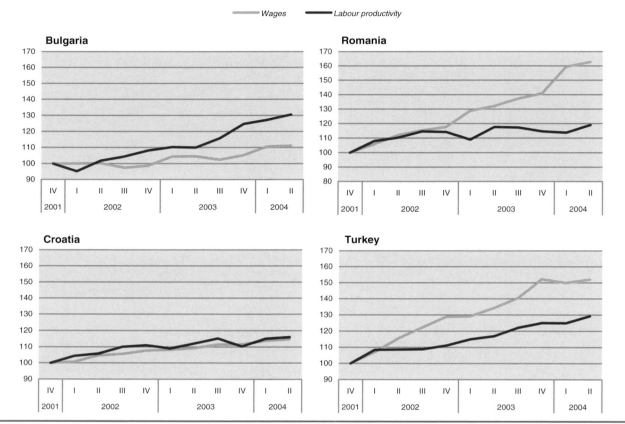

Source: UNECE secretariat estimates, based on national statistics.

underlying factors, including strong economic growth, robust inflows of FDI and a cautious incomes policy, which has moderated wage growth in the public sector and in state-owned enterprises. To some extent, the reported increases in both the labour force survey (LFS) and in the payroll employment data reflect the temporary measures launched in 2003.[128] Total employment rates have continued to increase from comparatively low levels for all age groups, including older workers (55-64 years of age). Employment growth in industry has slowed down while remaining positive. Both registered and LFS-based unemployment rates continued to decline in 2004 (table 4.2.5).

It is uncertain whether the strong employment growth in Bulgaria will continue, given the ongoing privatization and restructuring of state-owned enterprises and a recent amendment to the labour code that introduces a number of obligations on employers that could have a dampening effect on job creation in the private business

sector.[129] The very low employment rates of ethnic minorities are unlikely to be improved through market forces alone and need to be addressed by specific programmes, as elsewhere in south-east Europe.[130]

Unemployment declined in Croatia in the first half of 2004, continuing a downward trend that started in 2001. Total employment, however, stopped growing in the second quarter while industrial employment was falling from the beginning of the year. The disappointing rate of job creation may be partly due to an employment protection system that favours "insiders" (current job holders). Public sector employment in Croatia accounts for one quarter of total employment. This comparatively

_____

[128] These include a public works programme for long-term unemployed as well as wage subsidies to encourage firms to hire unemployed persons.

_____

[129] For more details see "Bulgaria: labour code amended", *European Industrial Relations Observatory On-Line*, 11 August 2004 [www.eiro.eurofound.eu.int].

[130] The comparatively low activity and employment rates of ethnic minorities show up in poverty statistics. In 2003, the poverty rate of ethnic Bulgarians was 9.4 per cent. Poverty rates of the Turkish and Roma minorities were considerably higher, at 23.5 per cent and 64.3 per cent, respectively. (The poverty line was set at 60 per cent of median total expenditure per capita.) "Bulgaria: survey finds one in seven people below poverty line", *European Industrial Relations Observatory On-Line*, 25 August 2004 [www.eiro.eurofound.eu.int].

TABLE 4.2.4

Total and industrial employment in south-east Europe, 2003-2004QII

(Percentage change over the same period of preceding year)

	Total employment [a]						Employment in industry [a]					
	2003				2004		2003				2004	
	QI	QII	QIII	QIV	QI	QII	QI	QII	QIII	QIV	QI	QII
South-east Europe	0.3	1.0	0.9	0.5	0.6	-0.2	-0.1	-1.0	1.2	1.8	-1.7	2.6
Albania	0.9	1.1	1.0	0.7	-0.8	-0.6	..	..	..	..	..	..
Bosnia and Herzegovina [b]	-4.2	-0.8	-0.8	-0.8	–	–	-5.5	-4.7	-4.7	-4.8	-3.3	-4.1
Bulgaria	2.0	2.7	4.6	4.5	2.9	3.3	2.9	3.5	1.7	1.6	0.4	0.2
Croatia	1.7	2.7	0.1	2.7	1.2	-0.2	–	1.1	-1.2	2.0	-0.3	-1.2
Romania	-0.1	0.4	–	-0.8	0.1	-1.0	0.2	-2.2	2.0	2.5	-2.2	4.6
Serbia and Montenegro [c]	-5.0	-4.5	-3.1	-3.3	-3.5	-1.3	..	..	..	..	..	..
The former Yugoslav Republic of Macedonia	-5.0	-2.1	-1.8	-3.2	-4.1	-5.8	-3.9	-3.5	-2.7	-4.5	-5.2	-6.9
Turkey	..	..	..	-1.0[d]	-1.7	2.3	..	..	..	..		

Source: National statistics and direct communications from national statistical offices to UNECE secretariat.

[a] Regional quarterly aggregates of total employment exclude Turkey, and Serbia and Montenegro; those of industrial employment also exclude Albania.

[b] Figures cover only the Bosnian-Croat Federation.

[c] Data relate to Serbia only.

[d] Annual average.

TABLE 4.2.5

Registered and labour force survey unemployment in south-east Europe, 2003-2004

(Per cent of labour force)

	Registered unemployment [a]						Labour force survey unemployment					
	2003			2004			2003				2004	
	Jun.	Sep.	Dec.	Mar.	Jun.	Sep.	QI	QII	QIII	QIV	QI	QII
South-east Europe	16.1	15.5	15.8	16.3	15.4	..	..	..	..	..	..	..
Albania	15.2	15.0	15.3	14.9	14.8	..	..	..	..	..	..	..
Bosnia and Herzegovina	43.1	43.8	44.1	44.5	44.6	..	..	..	..	..	..	..
Bulgaria	13.7	12.8	13.5	13.7	12.2	11.7	15.6	13.7	12.7	12.7	13.3	12.0
Croatia	18.9	18.3	19.1	19.1	17.4	17.6	..	14.1[b]	..	14.4[b]	..	13.8[b]
Romania	7.3	6.7	7.2	7.7	6.5	6.0	8.1	6.9	6.2	6.7	8.8	7.7
Serbia and Montenegro [c]	28	28	28	32	32	..	..	..	..	15.2[d]	..	..
The former Yugoslav Republic of Macedonia	44.4	44.6	45.3	45.9	46.0	45.2	..	36.7[e]	..	..	37.1	36.8
Turkey	..	..	..	..	..	..	12.3	10.0	9.4	10.3	12.4	9.3

Source: National statistics and direct communications from national statistical offices to UNECE secretariat; for Bosnia and Herzegovina: The Economist Intelligence Unit (these figures cover only the Bosnian-Croat Federation; data for Republika Srpska are not available).

[a] Registered unemployment rates in Serbia and Montenegro and The former Yugoslav Republic of Macedonia are UNECE secretariat estimates. Both national statistical offices report only the number of registered unemployed. The rates have been calculated as a percentage of the registered unemployed in the labour force as reported in the labour force surveys.

[b] Average for the first and the second half of the year.

[c] Data exclude Kosovo and Metohia. Since 2004, data relate to Serbia only.

[d] October.

[e] April.

large share and the fiscal consolidation programme of the government imply that the public sector cannot be expected to act as the employer of last resort and that jobs will have to be created in the private sector. Despite the recent amendments to the labour code that weaken somewhat the stringent employment protection rules, much remains to be done to encourage job creation.[131]

Total employment in Romania declined in the first half of 2004 while payroll employment in industry increased. According to LFS, the unemployment rate increased over the same period of 2003 as a result of layoffs in state-owned mines and other redundancies related to restructuring.[132] The overall employment rate

---

[131] High payroll taxes may be partly responsible for a large share of informal jobs in total employment.

[132] It should be noted that different indicators give conflicting views of changes in unemployment in Romania. Thus, according to registration data, the rate of unemployment in the first half of 2004 was down from the same period of 2003. However, the LFS data are generally considered to present a more accurate picture of the underlying trend.

declined further, while the employment rate of older workers was the lowest of all the EU candidate countries. Given the continuing restructuring of state-controlled enterprises, employment rates for all age groups may decline further over the next couple of years. The authorities have introduced a number of tax changes that seek to stimulate job creation and to enhance work incentives.

The strong growth of output in Turkey in recent years did not result in net job creation until the second quarter of 2004. The employment rate continued to fall from an already low level in 1999 until the first half of 2004, and the decline in the unemployment rate largely reflects a falling participation rate.[133] Given the rapid growth of the working-age population, a reversal of this unsustainable trend is of key importance if Turkey is to move towards EU membership. In addition to the ongoing structural reforms in the product and financial markets, policies that address the very low degree of utilization of the available labour reserves are of the utmost importance for sustaining the successes of the macroeconomic stabilization and reform effort (box 4.1.1).[134]

On the whole, employment rates in the EU candidate countries are still comparatively low and fall far short of the Lisbon target of 70 per cent (chart 3.2.1). The employment rate of older workers remains very low in all four countries and this may have serious long-term fiscal implications. A possible policy response is to realign incentives away from early retirement. Labour market policies that strike a proper balance between flexibility and security are also required for low-skilled workers in order to reduce the high levels of structural unemployment prevailing in the candidate countries.

...while high unemployment persisted in western Balkans

Among the remaining four south-east European economies, the employment gains of 2003 were reversed in Albania where total employment declined in the first half of 2004. Both total and industrial employment continued to fall in The former Yugoslav Republic of

Macedonia. Total employment stagnated in the Federation of Bosnia and Herzegovina, while in Serbia payroll employment declined in the first eight months of 2004, stabilizing at a relatively low level in the summer.[135] Registered unemployment fell somewhat in Albania in the first half of 2004, but remained close to 15 per cent. It stabilized at 45 per cent in Bosnia and Herzegovina and The former Yugoslav Republic of Macedonia, and at 32 per cent in Serbia. The few available labour force surveys for the four countries indicate that involuntary unemployment tends to be significantly lower than the measure based on registration due to the large numbers employed in the informal economy.

Macroeconomic policy: coping with fiscal and current account deficits

The excessive macroeconomic disequilibria that featured prominently throughout the south-east European region only several years ago, now seem to be in the past. Nevertheless, several economies still face important macroeconomic policy challenges such as large fiscal and current account deficits. Although such deficits do not appear to pose immediate threats to macroeconomic stability, the inherent risks associated with them – as plainly revealed by the financial crisis in Turkey in 2001 – remain a source of concern for policy makers.

In Romania, the main policy focus in recent years has been the chronically high inflation rate, a result of the combination of a relatively loose fiscal policy and delayed structural reforms. As noted above, there was notable progress in lowering inflation in 2004, largely a positive outcome of the policy reforms. A key factor has been the successful, albeit gradual, fiscal consolidation in recent years, involving a major reform of tax administration (which has raised the efficiency of tax collection), a restructuring of expenditures as well as the reduction of various forms of implicit subsidies (mostly in the form of budgetary arrears by state-owned firms).[136] The strong economic upturn has also helped to reduce the general government deficit in 2004.[137] The fiscal consolidation and disinflation efforts in Romania have been underpinned by a relatively tight monetary policy.[138]

In Serbia and Montenegro, the general government fiscal deficit widened considerably in 2002 and 2003 (reaching more than 4 per cent of GDP in both years), a

---

[133] Had the participation rate remained constant over the last five years, the unemployment rate in the second quarter of 2004 would have been 15.4 per cent rather than 9.3 per cent. If account is taken of discouraged workers, the rate rises to 19.5 per cent. S. Çevik, "Turkey: affluent future of a jobless society", *Morgan Stanley Global Economic Forum*, 28 October 2004 [www.morganstanley.com].

[134] According to OECD assessments, the problems to be addressed include heavy taxation of formal employment, excessive protection of regular workers against dismissal (the strictest among the OECD countries), low educational attainment coexisting with rapid urbanization and gender discrimination, political instability and large regional disparities with respect to the business environment. Despite the heavy taxes on labour, government revenues from this source are limited due to the extent of informal employment that accounts for one half of total employment. In turn, the very low participation and employment rates of women are partly explained by ongoing urbanization. Women from the families migrating from the countryside to large cities are often unable to find gainful employment. OECD, *Economic Surveys: Turkey* (Paris), 2004.

---

[135] No recent information about Montenegro and Republika Srpska was available at the time of writing this *Survey*.

[136] The monetization of the large quasi-fiscal deficit associated with such subsidies was an important source of the high rate of inflation in Romania.

[137] The cash deficit is expected to shrink to around 1.5 per cent of GDP in 2004, down from 2.3 per cent in 2003. On a cash basis, Romania's fiscal deficit has been falling since 2000.

[138] In recent years the Romanian monetary authorities have been using the exchange rate as the main nominal anchor, in combination with relatively high central bank interest rates and capital controls on short-term capital flows. In the second quarter of 2005, the central bank intends to switch to inflation targeting.

result of the costs of the market reforms initiated by the government. The cash deficit in 2004 is expected to be halved; as in Romania, this reflects the combined result of tighter policies and a strong economic recovery.

Several south-east European economies have chronically large current account deficits (table 6.1.2). In most cases these cannot be regarded as excessive as they are a consequence of their rapid economic growth, which has been accompanied by an expansion of their export-oriented production capacity; moreover, these deficits have been largely financed by inflows of FDI. However, in Croatia the macroeconomic risks are compounded by the "twin deficit" problem. The conventional policy approach of dealing with a current account deficit that is regarded as excessive is by (fiscal or monetary) policy tightening focused on various components of domestic demand. In the case of a twin deficit, fiscal tightening is generally considered to be the more efficient policy and this was the option chosen by the Croatian government in 2004.

Although the current account deficit of Turkey is not excessively high in relative terms, it is considered to be a source of macroeconomic vulnerability as it is mostly financed by short-term capital.[139] Reducing the current account deficit thus remains a priority for Turkey's macroeconomic policy: both fiscal and monetary policy are set to remain relatively tight in the short run, in an attempt to curb domestic demand for imports. In Bulgaria, the sharp widening of the current account deficit in 2003 and the first half of 2004 was partly driven by the credit boom in this period. However, under the currency board arrangement the authorities have no instruments to directly control the money supply. At the same time, with public finances in surplus, a further fiscal tightening did not appear to be an efficient policy option. The Bulgarian authorities have therefore attempted to check the current account deficit in 2004 by resorting to various non-conventional policy measures to curtail the pace of credit expansion.[140] So far, these appear to have been successful as the current account deficit has stopped growing.

4.3 The short-term outlook

Despite some deceleration, economic growth is likely to remain strong...

Most south-east European economies are set to preserve strong rates of growth in 2005. Supply-side

restructuring and the associated productivity gains are likely to continue to drive economic growth particularly in the EU candidate countries. If market reforms remain on course, the inflow of FDI – which is an important component of this process – should continue and even intensify. The expected further shift towards a more restrictive macroeconomic policy stance in some economies is likely to have only a marginal effect on their domestic demand. At the aggregate level, this negative impact may be partly offset by the positive effects of improved financial intermediation (in particular, easier access to a growing number of financial products and services). Overall, domestic demand in south-east Europe as a whole should remain buoyant and provide a solid support to economic activity. In contrast, with growth in western Europe possibly losing some momentum in 2005, the demand for south-east European exports is likely to weaken to some extent.

Compared with 2004, the average rate of economic growth in south-east Europe is likely to slow down in 2005. Given the expected changes in the domestic and international environment, it is unlikely that the exceptionally high rates of GDP growth in some of them in 2004, especially Turkey but also Romania, can be sustained in 2005. As these are the two largest economies in south-east Europe, this will result in a somewhat slower rate of GDP growth in the region as a whole. Nevertheless, the rate of GDP growth in Turkey and Romania, as well as in Bulgaria, is still expected to be above 5 per cent in 2005. In the other south-east European economies, GDP growth should be more moderate, in a range of between 3.5 per cent and 4.5 per cent.

...but important risks still remain

The main risks to the outlook for south-east Europe are possible negative external shocks. Thus a more pronounced and protracted sluggishness of western European import demand would have a perceptible negative impact on exports from the region, despite the expected improvements in their competitiveness. In addition, if the recent surge in world energy prices were to translate into a lasting upward shift (and even more so if they continue to rise), the rise in import prices could threaten to check or reverse the process of disinflation in the region. In turn, this could prompt an even more restrictive policy stance, which would intensify the dampening effect on economic activity. Finally, the large current account deficits in some of the south-east European economies carry certain macroeconomic risks that should not be neglected by policy makers. In any case, the underlying determinants of the deficits should be subject to careful and continuous monitoring. If a deficit reflects the expansion of productive investment in export-oriented industries, then it can be regarded as a normal feature of a healthy-growing emerging market economy; however, the risks are significantly larger if the deficit is caused by an unsustainable growth in consumer spending – in this case, a timely policy response is appropriate.

---

[139] As a share of GDP Turkey's current account deficit is much below the levels prevailing in other south-east European countries; however, in most of these economies a much larger share of the deficit is financed with FDI than is the case in Turkey (table 6.1.2).

[140] In particular, the government withdrew most of its funds held in commercial banks and redeposited them with the central bank. Another set of measures undertaken by the central bank effectively increased the mandatory reserves of the commercial banks. In addition, the provisioning requirements on various types of credit were tightened. All these measures have a negative effect on the money supply and hence on credit.

CHAPTER 5

THE COMMONWEALTH OF INDEPENDENT STATES

5.1 The policy agenda

In 2003 and 2004, the CIS emerged as one of the fastest growing regions in the world economy, all 12 members posting solid, albeit varying, rates of GDP growth. This outcome followed more than a decade of uneven economic performance and setbacks that accompanied the difficult economic and political transformation in the region. The current economic boom is all the more welcome as it has contributed to a recovery of living standards in these countries. It also reflects the progress made in some of the CIS economies with the market reforms introduced some years previously.

The rapid rates of economic growth in the region, especially in the commodity exporting countries, owe much to a favourable external environment characterized by rising prices and robust demand for most basic commodities. High commodity prices have also boosted fiscal revenues in the commodity exporting CIS economies, and the generally high rates of GDP growth have contributed to more balanced fiscal positions throughout the region (table 5.1.1). Resources channelled into the recently established stabilization funds in Azerbaijan, Kazakhstan and Russia have grown rapidly, creating a cushion in the event of negative external shocks. Nevertheless, in 2004 there has been a general pattern of procyclical fiscal loosening in many of the CIS economies, in some cases (such as Kazakhstan and Ukraine) reflecting an increase in pre-electoral spending. Monetary policy was generally accommodative in 2004. Rates of inflation continued to fall in most of the CIS economies in 2004 but inflationary pressures re-emerged in the course of the year due to higher energy prices and expansionary fiscal policies. In many countries the year-end inflation targets announced at the beginning of 2004 are unlikely to be met. Rapid economic growth, however, has had relatively limited impact on employment, with Azerbaijan, Georgia, Kyrgyzstan, Russia and especially Kazakhstan being the only countries where new jobs were created in 2004.

In some countries, particularly Russia, the persistently large current account surplus associated with growing oil exports (chart 5.1.1) has created dilemmas for macroeconomic policies. An outflow of private capital (box 5.1.1) has only partly offset the macroeconomic effect of this surplus, which has put a strong upward pressure on the exchange rate. The Russian monetary authorities have tried to prevent an excessive appreciation of the rouble, and so reduce the pernicious effects of the so-called "Dutch Disease",,[141] while at the same time preserving control over the rate of inflation.[142] Despite the central bank's massive interventions, the real appreciation of the rouble continued in 2004, especially when measured on the basis of international differences on producer prices (chart 5.1.2).

The Russian experience clearly shows that monetary policy alone is incapable of dealing with the negative implications of the "Dutch Disease" for competitiveness. Given their considerable dependence on commodity exports, other CIS economies also face similar problems. The focus of their policy approach therefore needs to be considerably broadened in order to encompass a wider set of factors that have an effect on competitiveness. Public policy should aim to establish well-functioning product, labour and financial markets, in order to create an environment that encourages firms to increase efficiency through active restructuring (which is key for preserving and raising competitiveness in the face of real exchange rate appreciation). More generally, policy makers in these economies will have to continue to progress with key systemic institutional and structural reforms.

Compared with eastern Europe, market reforms in the CIS have been complicated by the legacy of a greatly distorted economic structure, the lack of unequivocal political and popular support for reform, and the absence of an external anchor for the reform process, such as a realistic expectation of EU membership. Nor are the CIS countries close to the large west European markets. Despite these disadvantages, reforms in the CIS have nevertheless advanced, although at a slower pace and with significant differences across countries.[143]

---

[141] The term "Dutch Disease" denotes the real appreciation of the exchange rate and its negative repercussions on the tradeable sector as a result of resource windfalls. In Russia, during the last several years there have been a series of shifts in the current account position due to increasing shipments and rising prices of oil. As can be seen in chart 5.1.2, these have led to a considerable cumulative real appreciation of the rouble.

[142] As discussed in section 5.2(i), this inconsistent policy led to conflicting objectives in monetary management.

[143] For an overview of the reform process in the CIS, see UNECE, "Progress in systemic reforms in the CIS", *Economic Survey of Europe, 2003 No. 1*, chap. 5, pp. 123-147.

TABLE 5.1.1

Fiscal deficits and public debt in the CIS economies, 2000-2005
(Per cent of GDP)

	Consolidated general government deficit (-) / surplus (+)						Public debt [a]				
	2000	*2001*	*2002*	*2003*	*2004* [b]	*2005 target*	*2000*	*2001*	*2002*	*2003*	*2004* [c]
Armenia	-6.4	-3.7	-0.3	-1.1	-1.3	..	..	45.3	46.6	40.9	..
Azerbaijan	-1.3	1.2	-0.4	-2.0	-1.2	..	..	..	..	..	..
Belarus	-0.2	-1.9	-1.8	-1.0	-1.5	-1.5	15.0	..	13.1	10.6	9.4
Georgia	-4.7	-2.0	-2.2	-1.3	-1.2	-0.5	60.3	57.7	55.0	54.3	..
Kazakhstan	-0.8	2.7	1.4	3.0	2.3	1.6	25.5	20.4	17.7	15.5	14.4
Kyrgyzstan	-9.9	-5.5	-6.3	-5.5	-4.7	-4.5	112.4	100.4	103.0	101.6	..
Republic of Moldova	-2.8	-0.5	-2.0	0.2	-0.7	-0.5	73.2	60.7	56.9	47.1	39.1
Russian Federation	3.1	2.7	0.6	1.1	3.2	1.5	63.3	50.8	43.2	32.1	28.1
Tajikistan	-0.6	-3.2	-2.4	-1.8	-3.5	..	..	..	..	..	..
Turkmenistan	..	-1.1	-0.7	-0.9	–	–	..	..	..	..	..
Ukraine	-1.3	-1.6	0.5	-0.7	-4.3	-1.3	..	31.0	29.2	25.0	23.1
Uzbekistan	..	-1.3	-3.0	-2.2	-1.1	-1.0	..	..	..	..	..

Source: UNECE secretariat estimates and calculations, based on direct communications from national ministries of finance, central banks and national statistical offices; IMF, *International Financial Statistics* (Washington, D.C.), various issues and country studies; TACIS publications.

Note: The consolidated general government deficit, or financing requirement, is reported in accordance with the IMF GFS method. National reporting practices may, in some cases, differ from this methodology. The 2005 targets are official budget deficits, forecast in the initial budget proposals, necessarily involving GDP and inflation projections as well as fiscal data. The definitions of the target deficits as well as some of the preliminary estimates of the deficits in 2004 may differ from the above definition. Definition of public debt: central government debt for Belarus, Kyrgyzstan and the Russian Federation; central government and government guaranteed for Armenia; consolidated general government debt for Georgia, Kazakhstan, Republic of Moldova and Ukraine.

a End of period values.

b Forecast.

c June.

CHART 5.1.1

Russia's current account balance and official foreign exchange reserves, 1995-2004QIII
(Billion dollars)

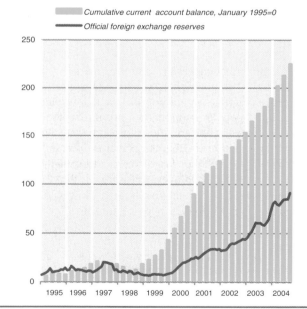

Source: UNECE secretariat calculations, based on national statistics.

Most of the progress has been concentrated in basic market reforms, such as price and trade liberalization and small-scale privatization. Structural and institutional reforms – for example, of major institutions (the judiciary, public administration, health care, the pension system), labour markets, the banking system, competition policy, the establishment of effective bankruptcy procedures, etc. – have been much patchier. Compared with the basic reforms, the latter are more complicated as they require the creation and development of the structures and institutions that govern a market economy. In other words, they involve a transformation of the role of the state from direct participant in economic activity to regulator and institution-builder in a market context. The new institutional structures are required to define and implement policy, without directly interfering in the functioning of markets, and to enable these functions to be performed in an efficient, transparent and predictable manner.

In general, the pace of institutional and structural reforms in the CIS has slowed down in recent years, including 2004. In effect, policy makers have failed to take full advantage of the favourable economic circumstances during this period to accelerate the pace of systemic change. Electoral cycles may have affected the pace of reform in a number of countries that until recently had led the reform process in the region, such as Kazakhstan, Russia and Ukraine. Weak "state capacity" (the capacity of the public administration to initiate and implement reforms) appears to be an important constraint on structural and institutional reforms in the low-income CIS countries.

The loss of momentum in the reform process in the CIS is regrettable, given the daunting challenges that these economies face. Despite their strong economic performance

BOX 5.1.1

Capital outflows from the Russian Federation

Large capital outflows historically have had a weakening effect on Russia's balance of payments. In the immediate pre-devaluation period, substantial external financing was required to offset these outflows, as the current account balance did not provide the necessary funds.[1] Since then, the economic and political situation has changed radically, resulting in a much stronger balance of payments position. However, capital flight remains a significant problem.

There is no agreement on the definition of capital flight in the economic literature; different studies use diverse definitions. Moreover, conceptual differences may not yield operational indicators because of measurement problems. Thus, the definition of capital flight as outflows that exceed the amounts that could be explained by legitimate portfolio diversification is appealing but not easy to apply in practice. Broader definitions have the merit of avoiding difficult-to-make distinctions while capturing the overall impact on financing and foreign exchange supply.

The Central Bank of Russia (CBR) regularly presents figures on net private capital outflows, which include transactions by banks, non-financial companies and households (i.e. the non-financial private sector). Net errors and omissions in the balance of payments are included in their entirety and attributed to this latter sector. However, it is conceivable that this partly reflects unrecorded imports, which would have the effect of overstating both the reported current account surplus and capital outflows. Overall, net private capital outflows represent a broad measure of capital flight. Only public sector transactions are excluded, which comprise public debt transactions, foreign currency reserves and, since 2004, resources channelled into the Stabilization Fund.

It is possible to distinguish three periods in the overall dynamics of net private capital flows in Russia. The most critical phase was during the period 1997-1998, when large outflows were accompanied by a current account that was roughly in balance. In the subsequent two years (1999-2000), net outflows increased slightly, but they were accompanied by large current account surpluses, with the coverage ratio improving dramatically. In 2001-2003 there was a steady decline in net outflows, while the current account surplus remained large. As a result, these outflows represented only 6 per cent of the surplus in 2003. This evolution is consistent with the reduction of macroeconomic and political instability during this period. Empirical studies show that variables which measure instability, including expectations of a devaluation and the state of public finances, appear to have been the main determinants of capital flight.[2] In addition, there was less uncertainty over public policy, once the policy framework became easier to predict.

While the Russian Federation's current account remains healthy, estimates for the first three quarters of 2004 indicate that net capital outflows picked up again, with an increase of more than $7 billion from the same period in 2003. However, changing perceptions regarding the policy environment may now be exerting a negative influence.

As a net measure, net private capital outflows – the indicator of capital flight referred to so far – reflect transactions related to various types of assets held by both Russians and non-Russians. While from a macroeconomic point of view it is the aggregate result that matters, the implications of the dynamics of the various components are different, and should therefore be considered separately. Three main trends have emerged in recent years, each exerting a significant influence on overall net outflows: the growth of Russian foreign direct investment abroad, renewed confidence in the rouble, and increased access by Russian corporations to foreign financing.

Balance of payment figures show that net FDI inflows were negative since 2002, turning positive in the first nine months of 2004. The expansion of Russian corporations abroad has mainly involved the purchase of assets by natural resource companies as part of their efforts towards the global integration of their production networks or to secure market access. More recently, companies in other sectors, such as automotive, telecoms and information and communication technologies (ICT), have also sought to establish a direct presence abroad.[3] Outward FDI is not necessarily a reflection of the lack of domestic opportunities; rather, it is a sign of the strength of emerging Russian companies. On the other hand, the real appreciation of the rouble since 1999 (following its devaluation in 1998) has suppressed domestic demand for foreign exchange, as reflected in the balance of payments figures that indicate a fall in foreign cash assets since 2003.

Rating upgrades and favourable financing conditions for emerging markets have allowed Russian non-bank corporations to raise a significant amount of funds abroad since late 2001, with borrowing by the banking sector taking off somewhat later.[4] Access to international capital markets has allowed them to bypass the still inefficient domestic financial system, although at the cost of increasing foreign exchange risk. Massive borrowing caused recorded net private capital outflows to reach their lowest level in 2003. This was the result of a large increase in the liabilities (which appear in the balance of payments as a positive entry) of the banking and non-banking sectors by $33.3 billion. In contrast, the pace of accumulation of assets abroad by non-bank corporations slowed somewhat in the first nine months of 2004 ($1.7 billion less than in the same period of the preceding year, including errors and omissions, according to CBR estimates), and the increase in net outflows can be explained mainly by the decrease in liabilities and the accumulation of further assets by the banking sector. Driven by the rise in interest rates and the financial turmoil in mid-2004, movements in interest-sensitive flows appear to have been the main factor contributing to the increase in net capital outflows, in what seems to have been a reversal of the borrowing which took place in 2003. Despite some emerging concerns regarding the direction of economic policy and the protection of property rights in the Russian Federation, evidence of any significant impact on net private capital outflows is so far limited.

BOX 5.1.1 (concluded)

Capital outflows from the Russian Federation

On the basis of CBR data, it is possible to construct a narrower measure of capital flight (chart 5.1.3), which includes estimates of non-repatriated export revenues, fictitious import contracts, and errors and omissions in the balance of payments. In absolute terms, the ratio of this measure to the current account surplus declined sharply after the devaluation of the rouble; it then drifted upwards after 2001 only to fall again in 2004. A broader coverage along with measurement difficulties may partially explain these movements.

As argued earlier, the distinction between unrecorded capital outflows and broader measures has little significance from the point of view of the overall financing available to the economy. The new currency control law, which was enacted in June 2004, envisages a gradual elimination of most capital controls by 2007, which would make this difference even less meaningful.

Given the net private capital outflows, averaging almost $17 billion annually during the period 1996-2003, Russian residents may have accumulated a large stock of capital abroad, even allowing for some consumption and possible capital losses. This represents a significant pool of foreign assets from which reversals of previous outflows could take place. However, since some of these capital outflows reflect portfolio diversification, part of the cumulated stock is likely to remain abroad, even if adverse incentives for domestic investment are removed. The origin of some of the capital flowing into the Russian Federation suggests that some reversal has already been taking place. Insofar as Russian investors may display a superior knowledge of the domestic situation, such a reversal could imply a greater endorsement of national policies. However, it is arguable whether policy should specifically aim to reverse the flow of capital. A more appropriate stance would be to establish a favourable investment climate for foreign and domestic investors alike.[5] This would require mainly an effective protection of property rights, predictability of relations with the administration and further development of the financial system. However, institutional upgrading is a lengthy process that requires consistent actions over a long period of time.[6]

Moreover, a sharper than observed reduction in net capital outflows in recent years would have created even more problems for monetary management through increased upward pressure on the rouble. Successful economic restructuring requires sustained investment, which, apart from the evolution of oil prices, should erode the current account surplus. Declining net capital outflows are required as a counterpart to this desirable development.

---

[1]   The balance of payments identity implies that a surplus in the current account must be accompanied by a net accumulation of foreign assets. This is reflected in an aggregate deficit of the capital and financial accounts, including the accumulation of foreign reserves, which appear with a negative sign in the balance of payments. Capital outflows that exceed the financing possibilities of the current account surplus (or which add to the financing requirements of the current account deficit) must be offset by capital inflows, including a loss of reserves, which enter the balance of payments with a positive sign.

[2]   A useful review of empirical studies on the determinants of capital flight is given in N. Hermes, R. Lensik and V. Murinde, *Flight Capital and its Reversal for Development Financing*, United Nations University/World Institute for Development Economics Research, Discussion Paper No. 2002/99 (Helsinki), 2002. This confirms that the broad definitions are the most commonly used.

[3]   UNCTAD, *World Investment Report 2004: The Shift Towards Services* (United Nations publication, Sales No. E.04.II.D.36), pp. 72-73. Low inward FDI figures partly reflect the fact that some transactions have been conducted offshore.

[4]   However, this does not appear excessive when compared with the overall increase in borrowing and equity issuance by emerging markets. International Monetary Fund, *Russian Federation: Selected Issues*, IMF Country Report No. 04/316 (Washington, D.C.), 2004.

[5]   In the recent past, some countries, such as Italy and South Africa, have declared an amnesty with the aim of recovering past tax losses due to the outflows. This, however, requires strong government credibility and avoidance of moral hazard problems. W. Buiter and I. Szegvari, *Capital Flight and Capital Outflows from Russia: Symptom, Cause and Cure,* European Bank for Reconstruction and Development Working Paper, No. 73 (London), 2002.

[6]   There is a difference between the announcement effect of changes and the actual consequences of their implementation, which are only likely to appear after a certain time lag. P. Hanson, "Putin and Russia's economic transformation", *Eurasian Geography and Economics*, Vol. 45, No. 6, 2004.

---

in recent years, the CIS economies still lag behind eastern Europe in terms of the recovery of output to its pre-transition level.[144] Overall, compared with eastern Europe, there has also been less progress in transforming the economic structures of the CIS countries. Much of the new investment in the CIS has been in the extractive industries, while relatively little has gone to other sectors of economic activity. And probably most important, the current pattern of economic growth in the CIS, heavily reliant on rising commodity exports, is not sustainable in the medium and long run. A failure to respond adequately to such problems will only make them more acute. They require instead a widening, deepening and acceleration of the reform process.

Economic diversification, which in the smaller commodity exporting CIS economies is closely linked to their efforts to reduce the incidence of poverty, constitutes an important policy challenge for most countries in this region. While large windfall revenues may tempt policy makers to engage in activist fiscal intervention (in the form of industrial policies involving increasing amounts of public funds), such a strategy runs a significant risk of introducing distortions. The case for intervention may be stronger in the provision of basic infrastructure services or improving education, as opposed to favouring specific sectors or activities. Plans

---

[144]   While aggregate GDP in eastern Europe as a whole had surpassed its 1989 level by 2001, in the CIS in 2003 it was still some 75 per cent of its 1989 level.

CHART 5.1.2

The rouble's real exchange rate against the dollar, January 1995-September 2004

(Indices, January 1995=100, per cent)

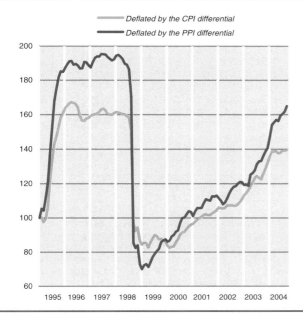

Source: UNECE secretariat calculations, based on national statistics.

CHART 5.1.3

Capital flight in Russia, narrow definition,[a] 1999-2004QIII

(Percentages)

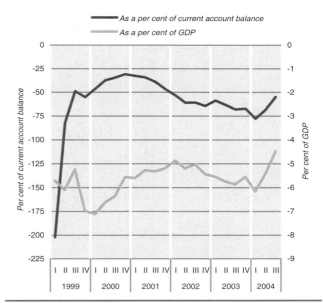

Source: Central Bank of Russia; UNECE Common Database.

   [a] The narrow definition includes non-repatriated export revenues, fictitious import contracts and errors and omissions. The values in the chart refer to rolling, cumulative four quarter indicators. The values for 2004QIII are Central Bank of Russia estimates.

in these areas will require a realistic assessment of the absorptive capacity of the economy and the ability of the institutional structures to implement them. Reforming the so-called "natural monopolies" (in particular, the electricity sector) remains a challenge in many countries including Russia. An important objective is to ensure the reduction of waste by means of an appropriate price structure and to provide the industry with the necessary funds for its long-term investment needs.

Labour market reforms are another key ingredient of the broad reform agenda of the CIS economies, and should be assigned high priority. Moreover, compared with eastern Europe, the CIS economies have made less progress in reforming their labour markets. Unfinished restructuring, as gauged by the share of loss-making enterprises in many countries and incomplete privatization, indicate the potential for further labour shedding. Policies fostering labour mobility, including the removal of bottlenecks in the housing market and of obstacles to the creation of new companies, are required to absorb the excess labour released from particular activities and companies. Unemployment benefit systems in the CIS (which appear to be rather inefficient in stimulating labour adjustment and active job search)[145] also require a radical overhaul. But most importantly, in order to lay the foundations for sustained and high rates of growth, these economies need to foster job creation in

modern, high value added manufacturing and market services.

Financial reforms are another key component of the reform agenda as financial development can foster the growth of investment and promote the desired economic diversification. There are substantial differences in the depth of CIS financial sectors (table 5.1.2) but even in the countries with more sophisticated financial sectors, comparative indicators highlight the need for further progress. The prevalent large spreads on domestic interest rates indicate high levels of risk and widespread inefficiencies in the banking sectors. Improvements in the business environment and increased competition should be encouraged in order to address these deficiencies. Difficult access to credit is often quoted as a constraint on the development of small and medium enterprises (SME), which are expected to play a significant role in the development of activities outside the commodities sector. Poor corporate governance and outdated accounting practices, as well as weak banking supervision add to the underlying vulnerabilities of the region's financial systems, as evidenced by the recent turmoil in Russia's banking sector.

Financial development needs to start with the creation of a modern and efficient banking system but the importance of other non-banking financial intermediaries, such as insurance companies, pension funds and the organization of capital markets, should not be neglected. To some extent, the roots of the underdevelopment of the financial system are related to the ineffectual protection

---

   [145] For details see UNECE, "Changes in unemployment benefit systems in eastern Europe and the CIS", *Economic Survey of Europe, 2003 No. 1*, chap. 7.1, pp. 191-198.

TABLE 5.1.2

Short-term interest rates and credit to the non-government sector in selected CIS economies, 2002-2004

(Per cent per annum, per cent of GDP)

| | Interest rates on short-term credits (per cent) | | | | | | Interest rates on short-term deposits (per cent) | | | | | | Total credit [a] (per cent of GDP) | | |
| | Nominal | | | Real | | | Nominal | | | Real | | | | | |
	2002	2003	2004 [b]	2002	2003	2004 [b]	2002	2003	2004 [b]	2002	2003	2004 [b]	2002	2003	2004 [c]
Armenia	21.1	20.8	18.6	18.1	10.9	-2.0	9.6	6.9	5.0	8.5	2.1	-2.6	6.7	5.4	5.6
Azerbaijan	17.4	15.4	15.2	20.2	-0.6	10.1	8.7	11.5	9.3	5.7	9.2	3.5	6.4	7.2	8.6
Belarus	37.3	24.0	17.7	-2.2	-9.9	-6.4	27.2	17.4	13.0	-10.9	-8.6	-5.5	12.2	14.3	15.7
Georgia	31.8	32.3	34.5	24.4	29.3	29.8	9.8	9.3	7.8	3.9	4.2	2.4	9.1	9.9	9.2
Kazakhstan	15.6	15.5	14.6	15.2	5.7	0.9	11.3	10.6	9.5	5.0	3.7	2.2	16.4	19.3	22.1
Kyrgyzstan	36.2	24.3	21.5	29.1	15.7	10.2	7.9	5.5	5.3	5.7	2.3	0.8	3.8	4.1	4.7
Republic of Moldova	23.5	19.3	20.9	18.0	10.7	14.6	14.2	12.6	15.0	8.5	0.7	1.9	15.8	18.7	19.2
Russian Federation	15.7	13.0	11.7	-1.2	-0.1	-9.2	5.0	4.5	3.8	-9.5	-8.0	-6.3	16.0	18.6	21.9
Tajikistan	14.2	16.6	20.9	4.5	1.4	4.1	9.2	9.7	9.9	-2.7	-5.7	2.3	18.6	15.9	14.9
Ukraine	25.4	17.9	17.4	21.7	9.6	-1.3	7.9	7.0	8.1	7.1	1.7	–	14.3	21.1	25.3

Source: National statistics and direct communications from national statistical offices to the UNECE secretariat; IMF, *International Financial Statistics* (Washington, D.C.), various issues.

Note: Definition of interest rates:

Credits – Armenia: weighted average rate charged by commercial banks on new loans in domestic currency with maturities of 15 days to less than a year; Azerbaijan: weighted average rate charged by commercial banks on 12-month loans in national currency; Belarus: weighted average rate on short-term loans; Georgia: weighted average rate charged by commercial banks on three-month loans in national currency; Kazakhstan: weighted average interest rates for new credits; Kyrgyzstan: weighted average rate on loans in soms for one- to three-month maturities; Russian Federation: weighted average rate on loans of up to one-year maturity; Tajikistan: weighted average rate charged by commercial banks on loans of all types and maturities in national currency to non-bank sectors; Ukraine: weighted average rate on short-term loans. The real lending rates are the nominal rates discounted by the average rate of increase in the PPI for the corresponding period.

Deposits – Armenia: weighted average rate charged by commercial banks on new deposits in domestic currency with maturities of 15 days to less than a year; Azerbaijan: weighted average rate offered by commercial banks on 12-month deposits in national currency; Belarus: weighted average rate on short-term deposits; Georgia: weighted average rate offered by commercial banks on three-month deposits in national currency; Kazakhstan: weighted average interest rate (for new deposits); Kyrgyzstan: weighted average rate offered on time deposits of three-month maturities; Russian Federation: prevailing rate for time deposits with maturity of less than one year; Tajikistan: weighted average rate offered by commercial banks on time and savings deposits of various maturities in national currency; Ukraine: weighted average rate on short-term deposits. The real deposit rates are the nominal rates discounted by the average rate of increase in the CPI for the corresponding period.

[a] Total outstanding claims of commercial banks on the non-government sector. GDP data for 2004 are preliminary estimates.

[b] January-September; for Georgia, Kyrgyzstan and Tajikistan: January-August.

[c] January-September; for Armenia, Kazakhstan, Kyrgyzstan and Tajikistan: January-June.

of property rights, the absence of an efficient and impartial judicial system, weaknesses in the legal framework and the lack of transparency in corporate accounts. Ultimately, an underdeveloped financial system – which is a drag on economic growth – is a mirror of the overall economic and institutional conditions in a country. Financial reforms should thus be regarded as an integral part of a broader and more comprehensive programme of institutional and structural reform.

5.2 Recent macroeconomic developments

(i) Russia and other European CIS countries

(a) Macroeconomic performance

Growth remained vigorous in Russia for a second consecutive year...

Russia's economy continued to grow strongly in 2004, reaping windfall gains from the high world market prices of oil (table 5.2.1). However, economic activity started to lose some momentum in the third quarter, suggesting that the annual increase in GDP might be less than in 2003.[146] This deceleration reflects a combination

of factors, including the real appreciation of the rouble, rising production costs and the negative impact of the turmoil in the banking system on access to credit.[147] In particular, a number of leading manufacturing branches seem to have suffered losses in competitiveness as a result of the rising real exchange rate. Construction activity also slowed down, most likely as a result of the banking crisis. In contrast, the growth of services has remained robust, particularly in communications.

While the average profitability of the corporate sector in Russia has been improving in recent years, there is still a large, albeit declining, group of loss-making companies.[148] This indicates the persistence of a segmented economic structure, partly the result of significant barriers to exit, characterized by costly allocative inefficiencies. Aggregate industrial performance figures (including

---

[146] Quarterly industrial output grew by 4.9 per cent, year-on-year, in the third quarter, down from 7.6 per cent in the first quarter and 7.1 per cent in the second.

[147] In the summer of 2004, Russia's central bank withdrew the banking licences of several banks, which caused a temporary havoc and withdrawals of deposits from the banking system. However, with most banks in a relatively sound financial position, the turmoil did not escalate into a full-blown banking crisis.

[148] While net aggregate corporate profits (excluding agricultural and financial companies) rose by 52.2 per cent, year-on-year, in the first nine months of 2004, 37.5 per cent of companies reported losses. Ministry of Economy of the Russian Federation, *Monitoring za yanvar'-oktyabr' 2004* (Moscow), 2004.

TABLE 5.2.1

Changes in real GDP in the CIS, 2003-2004
(Percentage change over the same period of the preceding year)

			2003				2004		
	2003	2004 [a]	QI	QII	QIII	QIV	QI	QII	QIII
CIS	7.7	7.9	7.5	8.1	6.7	8.5	8.2	8.5	8.1
Armenia	13.9	10.0	11.8	16.7	15.9	11.3	7.5	10.2	11.2
Azerbaijan	11.2	9.5	7.9	12.2	11.3	13.2	10.6	10.6	8.6
Belarus	6.8	10.0	5.6	4.7	7.3	8.9	9.3	11.0	11.7
Georgia	11.1	6.0	6.5	12.3	10.2	14.8	9.2	9.2	1.7
Kazakhstan	9.3	9.3	10.5	9.6	7.7	9.2	9.0	9.2	9.1
Kyrgyzstan	6.7	6.5	4.6	0.8	7.8	10.8	5.7	12.2	4.8
Republic of Moldova	6.3	8.0	5.4	7.3	5.9	6.5	6.1	6.8	7.7
Russian Federation	7.3	6.8	7.5	7.9	6.5	7.6	7.5	7.4	6.4
Tajikistan	10.2	11.0	12.1	5.2	6.6	16.8	9.1	13.2	15.5
Turkmenistan [b]	6.8	6.0	..	..	..	..	..	..	..
Ukraine	9.4	12.4	8.4	10.0	6.8	12.1	12.3	13.2	14.3
Uzbekistan	4.4	7.6	2.2	5.4	4.4	5.9	4.8	7.5	14.2
Memorandum items:									
CIS without Russian Federation	8.5	10.1	7.5	8.5	7.3	10.2	9.6	10.8	11.6
Caucasian CIS countries	11.7	8.6	8.3	13.2	12.0	13.2	9.5	10.1	7.1
Central Asian CIS countries	7.5	8.4	7.4	7.3	6.6	8.4	7.3	8.7	10.2
Three European CIS countries	8.6	11.6	7.5	8.4	6.9	11.0	11.3	12.4	13.4
Low-income CIS countries	7.7	8.1	5.4	7.9	7.7	9.7	7.0	9.2	10.4

Source: National statistics; CIS Statistical Committee; direct communications from national statistical offices to UNECE secretariat.

Note: The CIS countries defined by the IFIs as low-income countries are: Armenia, Azerbaijan, Georgia, Kyrgyzstan, Republic of Moldova, Tajikistan and Uzbekistan. The aggregates are computed by the UNECE secretariat using weights based on purchasing power parities.

a Preliminary estimate.

b The annual changes of real GDP in Turkmenistan are UNECE secretariat estimates. On the methodology used, see box 5.2.1. These annual GDP growth rates were also used in computing the corresponding quarterly regional aggregates.

industrial productivity) thus mask large differences among firms and industries, underlining the need for further restructuring.

On the demand side, private consumption was the main source of growth, with the national accounts showing a significant acceleration in the first half of the year (tables 5.2.2 and 5.2.3). Retail trade figures suggest that this continued into the third quarter (table 5.2.4). Strong wage growth, new job creation and an improved terms of trade on households' income have supported buoyant consumption. Although gross fixed investment also rose strongly in the first half of the year, the latest figures indicate a certain loss of momentum, possibly related to the financial turmoil in the summer, which is likely to result in an overall deceleration for the year as a whole. There were also signs of diversification in fixed investment,[149] an acceleration of which would be welcome as it could bring about the productivity increases required to accommodate a stronger rouble.

Import growth continued to accelerate in 2004, bolstered by the strong domestic demand increasing the share of imports in domestic markets. The rapid rise in imports of 2004 was also driven by an increased demand

for investment equipment.[150] In contrast, export volumes trailed behind and were losing some steam in the course of the year. The poor performance of industries that rely on the domestic market, against the background of rapid import growth, is yet another sign of the loss of competitiveness by domestic producers, implying a diminishing impact of final demand on domestic economic activity.[151] Income effects and supply constraints may have also played a role, as the increasing wealth of middle and upper class Russian consumers is shifting their preferences towards high-quality goods that are not always supplied by local producers.

...and accelerated in Belarus and Ukraine

A favourable external environment, coupled with solid domestic demand, fuelled a marked acceleration in Ukraine's GDP growth in 2004. In particular, the strong demand for Ukraine's key exports (chemicals, metals and some engineering products) boosted exporters' earnings, especially in the first half of the year, with positive spillovers

---

[149] There was a sharp drop in the share of investment going to the fuel-related industries (which, however, still remain the dominant sectors), with gains in communications, transport, agriculture and ferrous metallurgy.

[150] In the first nine months of 2004, the share of machinery, equipment and motor vehicles in total imports from non-CIS countries increased by 5.2 percentage points to 45.3 per cent. Ministry of Economy of the Russian Federation, op. cit.

[151] Output in light industry fell by 6.7 per cent, year-on-year, in the first 10 months of 2004, while in the food industry it grew by 3.8 per cent. In contrast, machine-building, with a 12 per cent increase in the same period, seems to be benefiting from the strength of investment.

TABLE 5.2.2

Components of real final demand in selected CIS countries, 2002-2004QII

(Percentage change over the same period of the preceding year)

	Private consumption expenditure [a]			Government consumption expenditure [b]			Gross fixed capital formation			Exports of goods and services			Imports of goods and services		
	2002	*2003*	*2004 QI-QII*	*2002*	*2003*	*2004 QI-QII*	*2002*	*2003*	*2004 QI-QII*	*2002*	*2003*	*2004 QI-QII*	*2002*	*2003*	*2004 QI-QII*
CIS	9.0	9.5	12.1	1.0	4.2	1.8	5.7	14.2	15.0	10.1	12.3	11.1	10.7	16.6	17.0
Armenia	8.9	8.4	9.6	2.2	14.0	13.6	33.1	33.7	9.2	35.8	29.0	1.3	18.9	27.0	-2.4
Azerbaijan	8.0	9.7	..	14.5	22.1	..	84.0	61.5	..	-6.3	19.6	..	16.4	57.6	..
Belarus	10.9	7.0	10.4	0.4	0.6	0.7	6.7	17.7	22.5	10.1	9.4	11.7	9.1	10.4	15.6
Kazakhstan	12.2	22.2	..	-4.3	7.5	..	10.2	8.9	..	22.6	5.5	..	4.3	-4.1	..
Kyrgyzstan	4.7	11.2	9.3	-0.2	-1.2	2.1	-7.4	-1.4	29.0	8.1	2.5	23.2	13.1	1.8	28.8
Republic of Moldova	6.3	16.7	8.4	30.3	-0.5	-15.4	5.7	13.3	15.9	19.0	18.9	10.4	15.7	25.0	7.5
Russian Federation	8.7	7.8	12.1	2.6	2.2	2.5	3.5	12.2	13.2	9.6	13.7	10.5	14.6	19.5	21.9
Ukraine	9.0	12.1	15.1	-6.7	14.8	-2.7	3.4	15.8	12.1	7.4	10.3	15.8	3.3	16.4	10.5

Source: National statistics; CIS Statistical Committee; direct communications from national statistical offices to UNECE secretariat.

Note: The aggregates are computed by the UNECE secretariat using weights based on purchasing power parities.

[a] Expenditures incurred by households and non-profit institutions serving households.

[b] Expenditures incurred by the general government on both individual consumption of goods and services and collective consumption of services.

TABLE 5.2.3

Contributions of the major components of final demand to changes in real GDP in selected CIS economies, 2002-2004QII

(Percentage points)

	Final consumption expenditure			Gross fixed capital formation			Changes in stocks			Total domestic expenditure [a]			Net exports		
	2002	*2003*	*2004 [b] QI-QII*	*2002*	*2003*	*2004 [b] QI-QII*	*2002*	*2003*	*2004 [b] QI-QII*	*2002*	*2003*	*2004 [b] QI-QII*	*2002*	*2003*	*2004 [b] QI-QII*
Armenia	8.6	8.9	10.5	5.9	7.1	2.0	-1.4	–	–	13.0	16.0	12.6	0.4	-4.1	2.3
Azerbaijan	6.9	8.8	..	19.2	21.0	..	-1.9	0.3	..	24.3	30.1	..	-8.7	-20.4	..
Belarus	6.4	4.3	7.4	1.5	3.9	5.4	-0.9	0.3	0.6	7.0	8.5	13.4	0.4	-1.0	-4.6
Kazakhstan	6.5	13.9	..	2.4	2.1	..	0.6	-0.2	..	9.5	15.8	..	8.4	4.5	..
Kyrgyzstan	3.0	7.4	7.3	-1.2	-0.2	2.9	0.1	-0.1	0.2	1.9	7.0	10.4	-1.9	0.2	-4.2
Republic of Moldova	9.8	13.8	3.9	1.0	2.2	2.5	-0.7	-0.3	0.7	10.0	15.7	7.1	-2.2	-9.4	-0.6
Russian Federation	4.8	4.5	6.5	0.7	2.2	2.0	-1.1	0.5	0.4	4.3	7.2	8.9	–	–	-1.7
Ukraine	3.8	9.6	8.2	0.7	3.0	2.3	-1.0	-0.4	-1.5	3.5	12.2	9.0	2.3	-2.6	3.9

Source: National and CIS Statistical Committee data; direct communications from national statistical offices to UNECE secretariat.

Note: The sum of the component changes does not add up to the GDP change for some CIS economies because of a reported statistical discrepancy, which appears on the expenditure side because the statistical offices base total GDP on the production side rather than the components of expenditure.

[a] Total consumption expenditure plus gross capital formation.

[b] Over the same period of 2003.

to other activities. However, the dynamics of industrial output suggest a certain moderation in the third quarter (chart 5.2.1), possibly indicating a weakening of demand. Agricultural output, which was badly affected by poor weather in 2003, recovered strongly in 2004 (thanks, in particular, to a record grain harvest), and made an important contribution to GDP growth. Construction activity was also on the rise, reflecting increasing incomes and a high level of fixed investment. Both domestic and external demand contributed to the high rate of GDP growth in the first half of 2004, Ukraine being one of the few CIS economies where net exports made a positive contribution to the increase in GDP (table 5.2.3). Real private consumption expenditure increased at a double-digit rate (table 5.2.2), fuelled by large wage increases. Quarterly figures for retail trade

suggest that consumer demand remained strong in the third quarter as well (table 5.2.4). Gross fixed capital formation also continued to grow very rapidly.

While the recent economic performance in Ukraine has been impressive, the strong export-led growth is very narrowly based and vulnerable to a worsening of the external environment. The existence of a large current account surplus, despite the obvious investment needs of the country, suggests the presence of significant barriers to investment that need to be removed by further progress in structural reforms.

In 2004, economic growth also accelerated in Belarus. While the upturn was broadly based, the main supply-side impetus came from manufacturing, with industrial production accelerating in the course of the

TABLE 5.2.4

Volume of retail trade and real investment outlays in selected CIS economies, 2001-2004
(Percentage change over the same period of the preceding year)

	Volume of retail trade				Real investment outlays			
	2001	2002	2003	2004[a]	2001	2002	2003	2004[a]
Armenia	15.5	15.6	14.5	9.4	6.0	45.0	41.0	16.0
Azerbaijan	9.9	9.6	10.9	12.5	21.0	84.2	73.5	45.3
Belarus	28.2	11.5	9.9	11.3	-3.0	6.0	21.0	20.0
Georgia	7.3	3.7	8.8	6.3	11.0	18.0	68.0	22.0
Kazakhstan	15.7	8.2	10.0	10.0	44.7	10.6	10.6	10.0
Kyrgyzstan	6.2	8.2	13.5	18.7	-14.5	-9.6	-6.6	9.0
Republic of Moldova	14.8	34.2	18.2	9.7	11.0	11.0	16.0	12.0
Russian Federation	10.7	9.2	8.0	11.5	8.7	2.6	12.5	11.6
Tajikistan	1.6	17.5	24.5	21.9	..	..	..	..
Ukraine	11.6	16.2	21.0	18.7	20.8	8.9	31.3	34.5
Uzbekistan	9.6	1.7	5.1	3.1	3.7	3.8	4.5	3.0

Source: National statistics; CIS Statistical Committee; direct communications from national statistical offices to UNECE secretariat.

Note: Retail trade covers mainly goods in Kazakhstan and the Russian Federation; it comprises goods and catering in other CIS countries. The coverage in 2004, based on current monthly statistics, may differ from the coverage of annual statistics. Investment outlays mainly refer to expenditure on construction and installation works, machinery and equipment. Gross fixed capital formation is usually estimated by adding the following components to "capital investment": net changes in productive livestock, computer software, original art, the cost of mineral exploration and the value of major renovations and enlargements of buildings and machinery and equipment (which increase productive capacity or extend the service life of existing fixed assets).

[a] January-September.

year (chart 5.2.1). On the demand side, growth was predominantly driven by the continuing recovery of domestic absorption (particularly of fixed investment – table 5.2.2). With imports outpacing exports, net exports contributed negatively to GDP growth (table 5.2.3), despite the strong growth in exports, especially to Russia. In the Republic of Moldova, economic growth remained relatively strong in 2004. Good harvests contributed to a notable upturn in the important sector of agriculture and the related food-processing industry. Private consumption continued to rise strongly, partly driven by remittances from abroad.

Inflationary pressures are re-emerging in the large economies

During the course of the year, inflationary pressures were rising in both Russia and especially Ukraine, largely a consequence of the loosening of macroeconomic policy. In Russia, the cumulative inflation rate in January-September 2004 was 8.1 per cent, only a fraction lower than in the same period of 2003. The official target of 8 to 10 per cent for the cumulative year-end inflation rate (it was 12 per cent in 2003) appears unlikely to be achieved. The persistence of a relatively high rate of consumer price inflation reflects the effect of a highly expansionary monetary policy (see below) against a background of buoyant consumer demand. In Ukraine, the resurgence of inflationary pressure was even more pronounced, consumer prices rising faster than in the same period of 2003 (table 5.2.5). This largely reflects the effect of the pre-election loosening of fiscal policy (discussed below), which is likely to carry over into 2005. The hryvnia depreciated rather strongly in nominal effective terms and this added further upward pressure on prices.

In both Russia and Ukraine, industrial producer prices rose even faster than consumer prices in the period January-September 2004 (chart 5.2.2), suggesting the likelihood of a further inflationary boost if the price rises incurred by producers are passed onto consumers.

In contrast, inflation rates continued to fall in Belarus and the Republic of Moldova in 2004, and the downtrend was more pronounced for producer than for consumer prices (chart 5.2.2). Despite the improvement, however, the average annual rate of consumer price inflation in Belarus remained the highest in the CIS, reflecting a highly accommodating monetary stance.[152] The fact that the rise in consumer prices in 2004 lagged behind that of producer prices probably reflects the influence of administrative price controls, which are still extensive at the retail level. In the Republic of Moldova, food prices rose more slowly than in 2003 (due to better harvests) and a significant appreciation of the nominal effective exchange rate helped to keep imported inflation to relatively modest levels.

Labour market performance lags behind the economic upturn

In Russia, total employment, as measured by the labour force survey (LFS) has been rising since the final quarter of 2003, and the unemployment rate had fallen to 7.4 per cent by the third quarter of 2004 (tables 5.2.6 and 5.2.7).

_____

[152] The main instrument of monetary expansion in Belarus is directed soft lending by state-owned banks to state-owned firms. This is equivalent to hidden subsidies and is a form of quasi-fiscal activity in support of the government's industrial policy. Despite some recent reduction, the flow of such credits still remained significant in 2004.

CHART 5.2.1

Real industrial output in selected CIS economies, January 2001-September 2004

(Indices of 12-month output, same period of the preceding year=100)

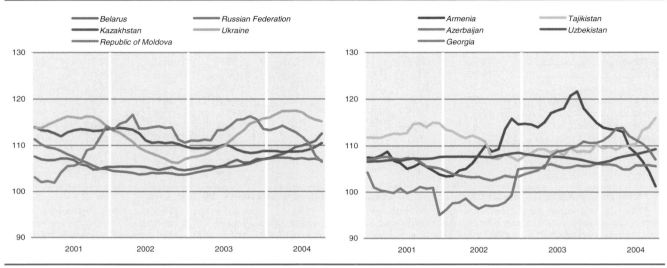

Source: UNECE secretariat calculations, based on national statistics.

TABLE 5.2.5

Consumer prices in the CIS, 2002-2004

(Percentage change)

	Consumer prices, total								Food	Non-food	Services
	Over preceding year			2004, year on year			September over previous December				
	2002	2003	2004ᵃ	QI	QII	QIII	2003		2004		
CIS	15.0	13.3	11.4	11.2	10.6	1.2	8.4	7.4	..	..	..
Armenia	1.0	4.7	7.7	7.8	7.3	8.3	1.1	-1.3	-2.1	-0.3	0.9
Azerbaijan	2.8	2.1	5.0	5.5	6.3	5.2	0.2	1.7	2.6	-0.1	-0.2
Belarus	42.8	28.5	21.3	22.4	19.7	17.0	18.5	9.1	9.5	5.7	11.0
Georgia	5.7	4.9	5.7	5.9	4.8	5.4	1.9	0.9	0.6	2.0	0.7
Kazakhstan	6.0	6.6	7.1	6.7	6.9	7.6	3.0	4.0	4.0	4.3	2.9
Kyrgyzstan	2.1	3.1	4.7	5.3	2.9	5.6	-0.1	0.3	-0.9	0.8	1.2
Republic of Moldova	5.3	11.7	13.8	14.6	13.0	11.1	11.4	6.5	4.0	8.0	9.1
Russian Federation	16.0	13.6	11.1	10.8	10.3	11.1	8.6	8.1	7.1	5.5	14.3
Tajikistan	12.2	16.3	9.5	8.5	5.7	8.7	8.5	4.6	4.8	5.5	0.3
Turkmenistan	..	..	..	..	..	..	..	..	..	..	..
Ukraine	0.8	5.2	8.0	7.4	7.4	9.6	3.3	5.6	6.5	3.8	4.5
Uzbekistan	..	..	..	..	..	..	..	..	..	..	..
Memorandum items:											
CIS excluding Russian Federation	13.1	12.6	12.1	12.2	11.3	11.4	8.1	5.9	..	..	..
Caucasian CIS countries	3.4	3.8	5.9	6.2	6.0	6.0	1.1	0.6	..	..	..
Central Asian CIS countries	..	..	..	..	..	..	..	..	..	..	..
Three European CIS countries	16.4	16.0	14.7	14.9	13.7	13.4	10.8	7.5	..	..	..

Source: UNECE secretariat estimates, based on national statistics.

ᵃ For the 12 months ending September 2004 over the preceding 12 months.

Payroll employment in industry increased significantly in the second quarter of 2004 after a two-year period of relatively aggressive restructuring.[153] The state sector's share in total employment has fallen slowly over the last few years, as in other CIS economies (chart 5.2.3). The cuts in payroll tax envisaged for 2005 should boost employment by reducing non-wage labour costs, although at the same time it may have an adverse effect on the public pension system.[154] The authorities contemplate a 20

---

[153] For an analysis of the underlying issues of industrial competitiveness, see OECD, *Economic Surveys: Russian Federation* (Paris), 2004, chap. 2.

[154] The government aims to offset the revenue losses associated with the reduction of the Unified Social Tax rate with the aid of new measures which, however, will have repercussions for the ongoing pension reform. While it is practically impossible to project precisely the overall effect of the payrolls tax cut, the estimates of the Russian authorities tend to be more optimistic than those of outside observers. OECD, op. cit., pp. 118-119.

CHART 5.2.2

Consumer and industrial producer prices in selected CIS economies, January 2000-September 2004
(Year-on-year, monthly percentage change)

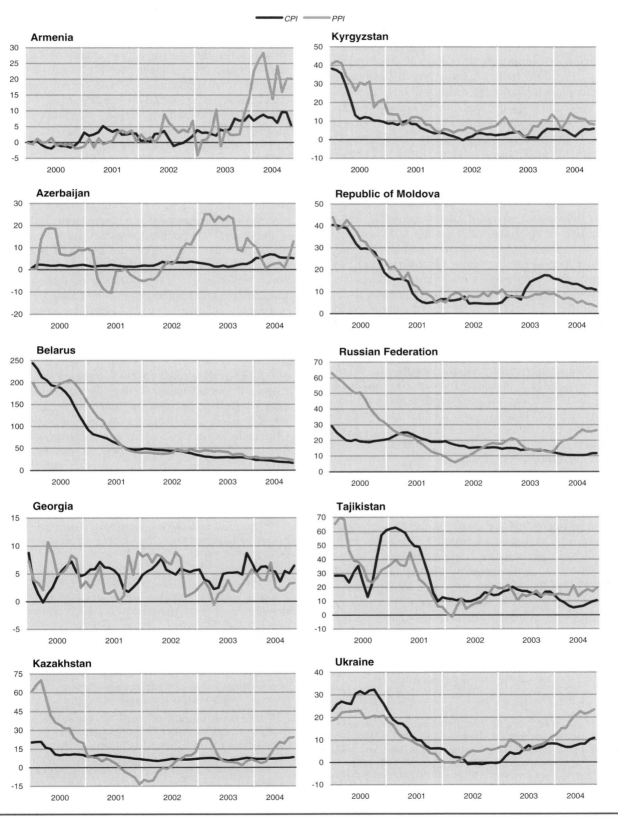

per cent increase in the minimum wage in 2005; this could reduce the demand for low-skilled workers and induce a strong wage inflation through a subsequent realignment of relative wages, unless some offsetting measures are implemented.

In Ukraine, total employment appears to have declined in the first half of 2004 despite a significant acceleration of output growth. Payroll employment in industry also fell (table 5.2.6). At the same time, involuntary unemployment, estimated on the basis of labour force surveys, declined in the second quarter of 2004, implying a drop in the participation rate. However, changes in the frequency of the labour force surveys and incomplete reconciliation of labour force statistics with the population census mean that the actual employment, unemployment and participation trends may differ from those shown in the available data.[155]

In Belarus, total payroll employment fell slowly in the first half of 2004 and more rapidly in industry. The fall in the number of registered unemployed over the same time period implies either increasing inactivity or some growth of employment in the small business sector that has not been captured by the official statistics.[156] However, the relatively large number of workers on long-term leave and the rather cumbersome registration rules for obtaining unemployment benefit imply that involuntary unemployment may be much higher than registered unemployment.[157] In the Republic of Moldova, there were large falls in employment in 2003 and the first half of 2004, and the unemployment rate, based on the quarterly labour force survey, was increasing through 2004. However, the postponement of the planned population census means that the reported unemployment rates are increasingly unreliable.

The combination of a rapid output growth and relatively stable levels of employment suggests large gains in industrial labour productivity, and the available statistics confirm this for most of the CIS economies. However, with wages often growing even more rapidly, there were no major improvements in cost competitiveness, as measured by unit labour costs (chart 5.2.4). Given the prevailing pressures for real exchange rate appreciation, this makes life very difficult for local producers who need to achieve still larger gains in efficiency if they are to preserve or improve their competitiveness. This points yet again to the need to accelerate and deepen major structural reforms in the domestic product, labour and financial markets.

---

[155] The annual LFS data for 2003 have been revised according to the 2001 population census. However, no revised data for the preceding period or for the individual quarters of 2004 have yet been published. Furthermore, beginning in 2004, the samples are taken on a monthly rather than a quarterly basis, and the two may not be fully comparable.

[156] The official monthly data for total and industrial employment exclude employment in small firms and self-employment.

[157] Economist Intelligence Unit, *Country Report. Belarus* (London), September 2004.

(b) Selected macroeconomic policy issues

In Russia, monetary management is under strain...

The persistent rise in its current account surplus has put monetary management in Russia under considerable strain. The Central Bank of Russia (CBR) has in fact been targeting simultaneously two monetary goals – inflation (in the pursuit of its main objective, price stability) and the exchange rate (in an effort to prevent excessive real appreciation) – with only one instrument: intervention in the foreign exchange market.[158] However, this policy arrangement cannot guarantee success in meeting the two targets, given that the dynamics of the current account (which is a key driver of domestic monetary developments) is beyond the control of the monetary authorities. Day-to-day monetary management is likely to encounter consistency problems due to the possible emergence of conflicting objectives, forcing the monetary authorities to abandon one target at the expense of the other.[159] In addition, the current policy framework may have a destabilizing effect through its impact on the expectations of market participants. The CBR's revealed policy preference in 2004 appears to have been to prevent an excessive real appreciation of the rouble. However, if perceptions of a shift towards renewed importance of the inflation target emerge among market participants, even larger capital inflows could result as speculators seek to benefit from an expected appreciation of the rouble.[160]

One of the principal flaws in the present system of monetary management is that its success hinges on external factors, such as the price of crude oil, which largely determines Russia's current account position. Ultimately, monetary policy cannot successfully target the real exchange rate; at best, it can only have a temporary influence on the speed at which the real exchange rate changes.[161] Despite its shortcomings, the

---

[158] The scope for using the central bank's policy rate in monetary management has been limited by the large amount of excess liquidity in the banking system. UNECE, *Economic Survey of Europe, 2004 No. 2*, chap. 1, p. 43.

[159] Consistency problems were obvious in 2004 due to the continued rise in Russia's current account surplus. The ensuing upward pressure on the exchange rate effectively precluded the CBR from meeting its targets of year-end inflation of between 8 per cent and 10 per cent, and a real effective exchange rate appreciation of between 5 and 7 per cent. Although the control of inflation has been declared the main goal of monetary policy, in 2004 the CBR de facto abandoned the inflation target as its main goal (which is likely to be missed for the year as a whole) at the expense of the real exchange rate target (which is likely to be achieved).

[160] The recent volatility of capital flows to Russia partly reflects the effect of this inconsistency on financial markets. Thus, capital outflows in early 2004 (box 5.1.1) followed a perceived shift in the CBR's policy towards a reduced emphasis on inflation; in turn, this was partly a reversal of previous inflows that had been generated by earlier expectations of rouble appreciation. There are indications that perception of increased tolerance of rouble appreciation may have been encouraging capital inflows in the closing months of 2004.

[161] The scope for sterilization operations, which offset the liquidity creation impact of foreign exchange purchases, has increased since the CBR started to issue its own bonds. This, however, may prove to be insufficient.

TABLE 5.2.6

Total and industrial employment in selected CIS economies, 2003-2004QII

(Percentage change over the same period of preceding year)

	Total employment [a]						Employment in industry [a]					
	2003				2004		2003				2004	
	QI	QII	QIII	QIV	QI	QII	QI	QII	QIII	QIV	QI	QII
CIS	-0.7	-0.1	-0.9	1.1	0.2	1.4	-1.8	-5.1	-1.8	-0.6	-1.5	2.2
Armenia	0.2	1.1	1.1	-0.5	0.7	-1.6	..	..	..	..	..	..
Azerbaijan	0.5	0.5	0.6	0.4	0.3	0.3	–	1.6	0.8	-2.0	0.1	0.2
Belarus	-1.1	-1.4	-0.9	-0.3	-1.2	-0.6	-5.4	-3.3	-2.5	-2.0	-1.0	-1.4
Georgia	1.2	3.6	7.3	9.6	4.0	0.2	..	..	..	..	..	..
Kazakhstan	2.2	4.0	4.0	5.2	7.0	1.8	6.7	8.2	7.7	5.8	4.3	2.5
Kyrgyzstan	1.3	1.3	1.3	1.3	1.0	1.0	-2.5	-2.8	-2.7	-2.7	0.8	1.2
Republic of Moldova	-11.4	-7.8	-8.8	-11.7	-6.7	-3.7	–	1.8	-3.6	-14.0	-9.2	-3.5
Russian Federation	-1.4	-0.7	-1.2	1.1	1.3	2.7	-1.7	-6.7	-2.2	-0.5	-1.8	3.5
Tajikistan	2.6	1.6	1.2	0.6	-1.0	-1.4	-6.6	-7.4	-5.7	-5.7	2.7	–
Turkmenistan	..	..	..	2.2[b]	..	..	..	..	..	2.4[b]	..	..
Ukraine	0.7	0.8	-1.6	1.4	-4.3	-1.2	-2.7	-2.1	-1.5	-0.8	-1.6	-1.4

Source: National statistics; TACIS; direct communications from national statistical offices to UNECE secretariat.

[a] Regional quarterly aggregate of total employment excludes Turkmenistan and Uzbekistan for which data are not available; that of industrial employment excludes Armenia and Georgia.

[b] Annual average.

TABLE 5.2.7

Registered and labour force survey unemployment in the CIS economies, 2003-2004

(Per cent of labour force)

	Registered unemployment					Labour force survey unemployment						
	2003		2004			2003				2004		
	Sep.	Dec.	Mar.	Jun.	Sep.	QI	QII	QIII	QIV	QI	QII	QIII
CIS	2.4	2.4	2.7	2.6	2.4	..	..	..	..	..	..	..
Armenia	9.8	9.8	9.8	9.3	9.1	..	..	..	..	..	..	..
Azerbaijan	1.4	1.4	1.4	1.4	1.4	..	..	..	..	..	..	..
Belarus	3.2	3.1	3.0	2.4	2.2	..	..	..	..	..	..	..
Georgia	..	2.5	..	..	..	13.5	11.4	10.5	10.7	13.0	11.9	..
Kazakhstan	2.0	1.8	1.9	1.9	1.6	9.3	8.3	7.9	9.1	8.9	7.8	7.9
Kyrgyzstan	3.0	3.0	3.0	2.9	3.0	13.7	8.3	7.1	10.7	..	..	..
Republic of Moldova	1.5	1.2	2.0	1.5	1.6	9.8	6.9	6.6	8.7	11.3	7.2	7.4
Russian Federation	2.1	2.3	2.3	2.2	2.2	8.9	8.0	7.9	8.2	8.9	7.5	7.4
Tajikistan	2.5	2.4	2.3	2.2	2.2	..	..	..	..	..	..	..
Ukraine	3.5	3.6	3.9	3.5	3.3	9.4	8.8	9.2	9.0	9.6	7.8	..

Source: National statistics; TACIS; direct communications from national statistical offices to UNECE secretariat.

current regime is unlikely to be abandoned as long as preventing an excessive appreciation of the exchange rate remains a significant policy concern. An eventual switch towards inflation targeting, as announced in Kazakhstan, would also raise difficult issues (section 5.2(iii)) and would require the development of a wider range of instruments of monetary management in line with an increased role of interest rates.

...while fiscal policy is squeezed between efficiency concerns and pressures for relaxation

Given the current strains in monetary management, fiscal policy in Russia can play a significant role in addressing competitiveness concerns. The launch in 2004 of a Stabilization Fund to accumulate the excess fiscal revenues arising from high oil prices has emerged as a powerful tool to reduce the pressure for rouble

appreciation.[162] Unlike the foreign exchange interventions of the CBR, there are no domestic monetary implications (such as liquidity creation) associated with its operation, as the resources placed in the Stabilization Fund are to be invested abroad.

High commodity prices and strong economic growth resulted in a sizeable fiscal surplus in 2004, which was partly channelled into the Stabilization Fund.[163] In

---

[162] A credible fiscal rule governing the functioning of the stabilization fund would be an important component of the overall framework for macroeconomic policy, facilitating an eventual shift towards a regime of formal inflation targeting. However, this component is still missing.

[163] The growth of official foreign exchange reserves picked up strongly in the fourth quarter, partly as a result of the introduction of higher oil export tariffs (leading to increased repatriation of earnings

CHART 5.2.3

Share of total employment in the state sector in selected CIS economies, 2001 and 2003

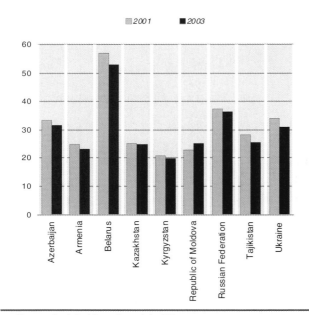

Source: Statistical Committee of the CIS.

fact the fund is likely to have reached its statutory ceiling already by the end of its first year of existence.[164] With the rapid accumulation of fiscal reserves in the Fund, a political debate has intensified about the rules that govern its functioning and the use of its resources, and political pressures to use the Fund's resources to finance various items of current expenditure have been increasing. However, policy makers will need to resist the temptation of using this resource in response to populist demands, if the role of the Stabilization Fund as an instrument of macroeconomic management is not to be compromised. Moreover, the current rule that excess resources in the Fund can be spent once the ceiling has been reached, without reference to the current oil price, creates the risk of procyclical spending.[165]

In fact, there are already signs that the significant cyclical improvement in Russia's cash fiscal balance is prompting a procyclical relaxation of fiscal policy. Thus

by oil exporters). The resulting increase in fiscal revenues were diverted to the Stabilization Fund without affecting the money supply.

[164] In accordance with its statutory operating rules, excess fiscal revenues arising from a price for Urals oil blend above $20 per barrel are channelled to the Stabilization Fund. (A recent proposal has been to raise the oil price threshold.) Once the fund amounts to 500 billion roubles any excess can be used for other purposes, such as the repayment of public foreign debt. The rules for allocating such surpluses, however, are not clearly spelled out. The 500 billion rouble ceiling is expected to be reached (and even exceeded) by the end of 2004.

[165] Thus, if the accumulated funds were used to finance domestic public expenditure, the Stabilization Fund would fail to perform its role of sterilizing part of the foreign exchange inflows associated with the current account surplus, while the increase in expenditure would increase the pressure of domestic demand.

the draft budget for 2005 contains a number of policy measures with a possible procyclical effect. In particular, it is envisaged that the revenue loss associated with the planned reductions in payroll tax rates will only be partly offset by higher oil taxes.[166] The budget also envisages the expansion of a number of government financed programmes. The planned rise in public spending appears to be procyclical given the current strength of the Russian economy and the windfall revenue from the high oil price. At the same time, the envisaged policy changes are likely to increase the vulnerability of the budget to sudden falls in the price of oil.

Macroeconomic policy in Ukraine stumbled prior to the elections...

The political cycle in Ukraine led to a significant relaxation of fiscal policy as the presidential elections drew closer. Although this is a widespread phenomenon, some of the populist pre-election moves (such as the large increases in pensions in September and the planned rise in public sector wages) will have lasting negative fiscal implications as they are equivalent to a general increase in government spending. As a result, the underlying structural fiscal balance is likely to have deteriorated significantly in 2004. As shown by the experience of some east European countries (for example, Hungary) this type of fiscal loosening (involving notable wage increases) can have a lasting and damaging effect on macroeconomic stability. Furthermore, the negative fiscal implications of such moves are very difficult to reverse or offset, especially during a downturn in the growth cycle.

Ukraine's recent macroeconomic performance actually provides some early evidence of the potentially destabilizing effect of the fiscal loosening. Already in October, the sharp rise in aggregate incomes boosted the demand for foreign currency (still preferred as the vehicle for saving). At the same time, concerns about the course of policy after the election triggered increasing outflows of capital. The mounting pressure on the exchange rate soon gave rise to liquidity problems in the banking sector. The National Bank of Ukraine (NBU) was forced to intervene on both the interbank and the foreign exchange markets to prevent a banking crisis and a collapse of the exchange rate.[167] However, inflationary pressures were also mounting as a result of the excessive liquidity injected into the economy. Concerns about rising inflation forced another intervention by the monetary authorities who raised the central bank's interest rates in

[166] The negative net fiscal impact of the reduction in payroll taxes is estimated at around 1 per cent of GDP, even in an environment of high oil prices. International Monetary Fund, *Russian Federation: Selected Issues,* Country Report No. 04/316 (Washington, D. C.), September 2004. Lower payroll taxes can have a positive impact on job creation in the longer run.

[167] As a result of these interventions, during the month of October alone Ukraine's official foreign exchange reserves dropped by 13 per cent, to $9.15 billion.

CHART 5.2.4

Industrial productivity and the dynamics of labour cost pressures in selected CIS economies, 2000-2004QII
(Cumulative percentage change, 1999=100)

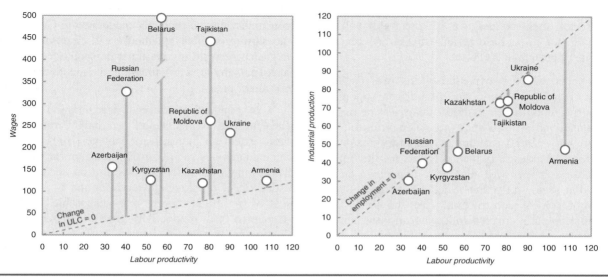

Source: UNECE secretariat estimates and national sources.

Note: Industry=mining+manufacturing+utilities; wages: average nominal gross wages in industry; labour productivity: gross industrial production per worker; unit labour costs (ULC): average gross wages in industry deflated by labour productivity. The data for Armenia are for the period 2000-2003. Belarus: cumulative wage growth in 2000-2004 was 1,080 per cent. The distance (perpendicular line) between the country-value and the dotted line measures the cumulative increase in unit labour costs on the left-hand chart and the cumulative fall in employment on the right-hand chart.

November. At that point the NBU was confronted with conflicting objectives, as the tightening of policy could have an adverse effect on the banks' liquidity position, something that it had sought to prevent with its previous interventions. This episode highlights the risks associated with an excessive relaxation of fiscal policy in an environment of immature and volatile financial markets. Maintaining macroeconomic and financial stability in this environment requires a high degree of coordination between monetary and fiscal policy.

...and the macroeconomic situation deteriorated in their aftermath

While policy makers in Ukraine managed to prevent an outbreak of financial turmoil in the run-up to the elections – by sacrificing some of the relatively large foreign exchange reserves – there has since been a considerable deterioration in the general economic situation. The major uncertainties regarding the resolution of the ensuing political crisis constituted a major shock to investor confidence, causing turmoil in the financial markets. It is likely that political uncertainty and disruption in the financial system will have negative implications for economic activity in the short run.

(ii) The Caucasian Rim

Robust growth continued in 2004...

Economic growth in Azerbaijan continued to be fuelled by large inflows of FDI in the oil and gas sectors. The growth of fixed investment remained considerable

(real investment outlays rising by 45 per cent, year-on-year, in the period January-September – table 5.2.4) but nevertheless was lower than in 2002-2003. The expansion in the construction and service sectors reflected positive spillovers from the oil and gas sectors. Real money incomes grew at double-digit rates, supporting an acceleration in the volume of retail trade (table 5.2.4). However, there is a growing divide between the oil and gas industry and the rest of the economy. The relatively small and underdeveloped agricultural sector remains the main source of employment and therefore its evolution has a major impact on welfare. As elsewhere in the region, agriculture has the potential to make a significant contribution to the diversification of exports and the improvement of living standards, but in order to do so the sector needs a major restructuring and investment to produce the needed gains in efficiency.

In Georgia, the economy has benefited greatly from its role as a transit corridor for oil and natural gas. In 2004, the construction sector was boosted by the ongoing work on the Baku-Tbilisi-Ceyhan oil pipeline and the Shah-Deniz gas pipeline, which have provided employment and generated demand for business services.[168] Industrial output, particularly manufacturing,

---

[168] These projects accounted for 69.3 per cent of construction output in the first half of the year. Housing construction also grew strongly. Georgian-European Policy and Legal Advice Centre, *Georgian Economic Trends*, No. 3 (Tbilisi), 2004.

grew strongly in the first half of the year, but more recent figures indicate a slowdown in the second half. Expansion in the services sector contributed most to the increase in GDP in the first three quarters of 2004. In contrast, output in agriculture, which remains the second largest sector after services, was sluggish although this was partly due to a base-period effect reflecting the strong rate of growth in 2003.

Armenia, which is bypassed by the two pipelines, has not benefited from the FDI-driven boom in neighbouring countries. In 2004 there was a marked slowdown of industrial output (after two years of very strong growth - chart 5.2.1) due to temporary disruptions in the diamond industry (which accounts for the bulk of its exports). There was also less dynamism in the construction sector reflecting a decline in foreign grant financing for local construction. At the same time, agricultural output recovered following improvements in infrastructure and a good harvest. Strong consumer demand (supported by wage increases and large remittances from abroad, which appear to have reached record levels in 2004) supported an expansion in trade and other business services, which partly offset the deceleration in construction and industry. Overall, the growth of GDP remained strong in 2004 and for the year as a whole is likely to exceed earlier expectations.

...and there was some increase in employment

The available labour market information indicates some increase in aggregate employment in the Caucasian region, although not in all the individual countries. In Armenia, total employment started to fall in the second quarter of 2004 while at the same time registered unemployment continued its slow decline (tables 5.2.6 and 5.2.7). It remains unclear whether these trends reflect a declining participation rate or rising activity in the informal sector. Total and industrial employment increased slightly in Azerbaijan, reflecting job creation as a result of the large energy infrastructure projects. Employment in Georgia has risen steadily since the second quarter of 2003, stimulated in part by the same infrastructure projects. Nevertheless, weak employment growth in the official sector has to be seen against a background of extensive self-employment that accounts for about two thirds of total employment in Georgia. Involuntary part-time employment remains widespread.[169]

Inflation remains low

In the three Caucasian rim economies consumer price inflation remained low in the first three quarters of 2004. Over January-September, consumer prices actually fell in Armenia and rose less than 2 per cent in both Azerbaijan and Georgia. As in 2003, these were among the lowest nine-month cumulative rates of consumer

price inflation in the CIS. Food prices weakened over the summer and had a dampening effect on the overall level of consumer prices. In Armenia and Georgia, imported inflation also moderated, thanks to the appreciation of their currencies in nominal effective terms. Furthermore, consumer demand probably moderated in Georgia due to the slow growth of real household disposable incomes. In Azerbaijan, strong consumer demand does not seem to have put any upward pressure on the overall level of consumer prices.

In contrast, producer price inflation accelerated, especially in Armenia and Azerbaijan, reflecting to a large extent an intensification of cost pressures. In all three economies such cost pressures appear to be strong. These may eventually put pressure on consumer prices, especially if employment recovers and if the growth in real wages (and hence real disposable incomes) is decoupled from productivity growth. In Azerbaijan, the continuing surge in capital inflows could trigger inflationary pressure (as in Russia), unless they can be sterilized by government intervention through the State Oil Fund.

Seeking more flexibility in fiscal policy

The recent boom in the oil and gas sectors of Azerbaijan has given a strong boost to public revenue, not only in absolute terms but also as a share of GDP. The resulting improvement in the fiscal position has provided the government with more flexibility to pursue its agenda and allowed it to increase spending on social and developmental needs. Thus the 2004 budget envisaged a substantial increase in expenditure on health and education. Nurturing the development of the non-oil sectors, which is a key strategic policy, may eventually result in tax cuts that can be accommodated by projected increases in revenue. In contrast to Azerbaijan, Armenia and, particularly, Georgia, face the immediate challenge of raising public revenue and widening the tax base, while at the same time improving the structure of taxation.

Following the political change in November 2003, the government of Georgia embarked on a major effort to improve the efficiency of tax collection and of the customs administration.[170] The new strategy combines measures to strengthen enforcement with a tax reform, to be enacted in 2005, that will reduce both the rates and the number of taxes. These changes will be grounded in a general overhaul of the administration that will address governance issues in the public sector and seek to increase the efficiency of policy interventions. Economic performance in 2004 was satisfactory as progress in clearing arrears increased the credibility of the new

---

[169] Georgian-European Policy and Legal Advice Centre, op. cit., pp. 42-48.

[170] Public revenue as a proportion of GDP in Georgia is well below the average for countries with similar levels of GDP per capita. H. Lorie, *Priorities for Further Fiscal Reforms in the Commonwealth of Independent States*, IMF Working Paper, No. WP/03/209 (Washington, D.C.), October 2003.

measures. A significant increase (by 20 per cent) in tax revenue is expected already in 2005, the first year of the tax reform.[171] At the same time Georgia is faced with the need for fiscal consolidation due to the precarious state of its external finances.

In Armenia, a sharp fall in foreign grants weakened the overall budgetary position in 2004 but this was partly offset by improvements in tax collection, which have served to cushion the impact on spending.[172] Despite further projected increases in tax revenues (resulting from measures intended to strengthen the tax and customs administrations), the large increases in social expenditures may lead to a deterioration of the structural fiscal balance. As in Georgia, however, continued progress with reform may serve to mobilize external financial support.

Capacity constraints in public administration are a recurrent problem throughout the region, and these help to explain the low levels of efficiency in collecting public revenue. However, this is just one aspect of a vicious cycle, as improving this capacity requires public spending. Azerbaijan may be closer to escaping from this vicious cycle, as the oil-related rise in public revenue will provide the government with the opportunity to invest more resources in public administration.

At the same time, the scope for increased public spending on infrastructure and human capital needs is constrained by the absorptive capacity of these economies. Increasing that capacity requires major improvements in the legal and administrative environment in which public projects are undertaken. In any case, the proper management of public expenditure and continued efforts to reduce non-transparent, quasi-fiscal activities, particularly in the energy sector, remain important policy challenges.

Exchange rates face upward pressures

Upward pressures on exchange rates continued to mount in 2004. Appreciation vis-à-vis the dollar reflected the latter's weakness, but gains also occurred in relation to the euro and the Russian rouble. In Azerbaijan, the increased demand for the national currency is connected to the considerable oil-related capital inflows. The traditional response has been to

maintain a relatively loose monetary policy, with foreign exchange intervention being the main instrument to contain upward pressures. However, this strategy will come under increasing strain as exports take off, following the completion of the infrastructure projects, while the scope for rapid increases in money demand narrows.[173] In Georgia, improved tax collection increased the demand for the domestic currency; this also had a dampening effect on inflation.[174] The strengthening of the balance of payments position led to the appreciation of the Armenian dram. This development was not resisted by the Central Bank of Armenia, as it remains more concerned with the control of inflation, which accelerated in 2003, and has refrained from targeting the exchange rate.

(iii) The central Asian CIS economies

Commodity exports continued to drive growth

Booming world commodity markets and strong import demand in its main export markets continued to underpin economic growth in the region in 2004. The continuing expansion of the oil and gas sectors, coupled with robust domestic demand, continued to drive economic growth in Kazakhstan. The strategic character of investments in this sector (supported by a steady inflow of FDI) suggests that these sectors will continue to expand even in the face of less favourable prices. The non-oil sectors also benefited from spillovers from the oil sector through income effects and increased demand for local inputs. The share of services in total GDP continued to increase, with transport and communications services benefiting from strong demand in the oil and gas industries. The growth of industrial output accelerated (chart 5.2.1), mainly due to the extractive industries, but manufacturing also performed well, with chemicals, plastics and engineering providing evidence of diversification.

Kyrgyzstan's industrial base is still rather narrow, dominated by gold extraction. The resumption of full-scale production in the Kumtor mine played a large role in the recovery of total industrial output early in the year but this one-off base effect eventually faded away. Similarly, soaring industrial output in Tajikistan largely reflected the export-driven expansion of aluminium production. A relatively strong recovery also continued in Turkmenistan, underpinned by growing output of natural gas and a good grain harvest; nevertheless, the actual rate of GDP is likely to have been well below the officially reported figures (box 5.2.1).

---

[171] *BBC Monitoring Former Soviet Union*, 1 October 2004. On the basis of a stronger than projected revenue performance and increased grants, the government expects the ratio of total expenditures (including net lending) to GDP to grow by 4.6 percentage points to 25 per cent of GDP in 2005-2008. Government of Georgia, *The Government's Strategic Vision and Urgent Financing Priorities*, Donor's Conference (Brussels), 16-17 June 2004.

[172] In 2002-2003, grants accounted for around one fifth of total public revenue. However, the tax base did not grow in line with GDP, as grant-financed construction and diamond polishing are tax exempt. Tax revenue has been boosted by the introduction of a minimum corporate tax of 1 per cent of total sales.

---

[173] A more efficient policy may be the introduction of suitable sterilization instruments and increasing the rate of accumulation in the State Oil Fund.

[174] The National Bank of Georgia accommodated the increased demand for lari through a reduction of commercial banks' minimum reserve requirements in June 2004.

Box 5.2.1

Alternative estimates of real GDP growth in Turkmenistan

The official statistics produced since 2000 by the National Institute of Statistics and Forecasting (NISF) of Turkmenistan raise a number of questions. The officially reported rates of real GDP growth (an annual average rate of 19 per cent for the period 2000-2003, table 5.2.8) suggest that in this period Turkmenistan has been the fastest growing economy in the world. These rates diverge considerably, however, from the reported changes in the physical volume of output of the country's key commodities.[1] The implicit GDP deflators in the official statistics (an annual average of 8.4 per cent for 2000-2003) also appear to be inconsistent with the reported growth in the average nominal wage in the economy (an annual average increase of 52 per cent for the same period – table 5.2.8). Moreover, in 2002 the NISF stopped publishing GDP statistics reflecting valued added, and started reporting figures for aggregate gross output instead. The reporting of demographic statistics has been modified: the NISF replaced the previously published time series on the "resident" population with the number of persons "actually living" in the country. The latter implies a 4-5 per cent increase in the population per annum since 2000. The reported actual population for 2004 exceeded the resident population by about 20 per cent or 1 million people (table 5.2.8).

The UNECE secretariat has produced alternative estimates of real GDP growth for Turkmenistan. These were derived from output data in volume for some of the main products that shape the performance of Turkmenistan's resource-based economy. As most of these products are basic commodities, their weighted output growth, calculated from data in physical units, should be a good proxy for real output growth in the main economic sectors. The real change in total output (a proxy for GDP) is then calculated as a weighted average of output growth in these sectors.

More specifically, the changes in real agricultural output have been estimated on the basis of the reported production of grain, cotton, meat (slaughter weight), milk and vegetables. The production volumes of electricity, natural gas, oil, cotton yarn, flour, fertilizers, copper cable, wire, meat products and milk products were used to compute a proxy for industrial output; the volumes of cement, iron-reinforced structures and bricks – for construction; and the freight and passenger turnover – for transport and communication. Public sector employment served as a proxy for estimating the changes to the real output of the public sector. The rates of real output growth by main economic sectors (agriculture, industry, construction, transport and communication, trade and others) were then weighted by their shares in GDP to compute the rates of change of real aggregate output (GDP). The corresponding sectoral data for the years through 2001 are the officially reported statistics; for subsequent years the 2001 fixed weights were used. Within industry and agriculture, the weights of individual products were estimated on the basis of the previous year's structure of gross output.

The resulting estimates of the changes in real GDP for Turkmenistan are reported in table 5.2.8. A comparison with the corresponding official statistics for the years before the reporting methodology was changed suggest that the alternative measure of total output is reasonably reliable: although the latter differ somewhat from the official figures for 1997, 1998 and 1999, both series yield similar growth rates of real GDP in this period. Notably, the alternative estimates capture the dependence of Turkmenistan's economy on the output of a few key commodities (such as natural gas and cotton and, to a lesser extent, oil, grain and textiles). Thus, the 50 per cent fall in the output of natural gas in 1997, when Turkmenistan suspended gas exports to Ukraine because of the latter's non-payment, was the main factor behind the drop in real GDP in that year. Conversely, the rapid GDP growth in 1999 was the result of a combination of large increases in the production of natural gas, oil and oil products, cotton and textiles. Both the official figures for real GDP in these years and the alternative estimates reflect these fluctuations.

In contrast, from 2000 the alternative measure suggests much lower rates of real GDP growth than the official figures. During this period, there have been major fluctuations in the output of some key products (equivalent to shocks to the economy), which do not appear to have been captured in the official statistics. Thus, whereas the output of natural gas, after doubling in 2000 remained stable through 2004 (to meet demand from Russia and Ukraine), grain and cotton harvests were uneven and indeed poor in some years. The alternative estimates in table 5.2.8 reflect the impact of volatile commodity output on the rate of growth of real GDP. In addition, the implicit GDP deflators used in the alternative estimates for 2000-2003 are more plausible than the implicit deflators derived from the official statistics and are more closely in line with the reported changes in the average nominal wage. Finally, the alternative estimates of the changes in real GDP in Turkmenistan look more realistic when compared with the rates of real GDP growth in neighbouring countries with similar economic structures, such as Azerbaijan, Kazakhstan and Uzbekistan.

The alternative UNECE estimates of real GDP growth in Turkmenistan have been used in the relevant statistical tables of this *Survey*.

_____

[1] The official statistics seems to follow the overambitious long-term economic targets set in the recently adopted political document: "Strategia ekonomicheskogo, politicheskogo i kul'turnogo razvitiya Turkmenistana na period do 2020" [www.turkmenistan.gov.tm/countri/gos&prog.html]. Using 2000 as the base year, this strategy envisages a 28-fold increase of aggregate gross output, a 26-fold increase for industrial output and an 18-fold increase of agricultural output by 2020.

TABLE 5.2.8

Selected economic indicators for Turkmenistan (officially reported and estimated), 1997-2004

	1997	1998	1999	2000	2001	2002	2003	2004 [a]
Officially reported statistics								
Nominal GDP (billion manats)	11 109.0	13 995.0	20 056.0	25 648.0	35 119.0	45 240.0	55 709.0	..
Real GDP, rate of change (per cent per annum)	-11.4	7.1	16.5	18.6	20.4	20.5	17.1	..
Implicit GDP deflator (per cent per annum)	61.7	17.6	23.0	7.8	13.7	6.9	5.2	..
Average nominal wages, rate of change (per cent per annum)	156.9	46.3	21.8	80.5	47.1	42.4	40.0	..
Actual population (thousand persons)	4 710.4	4 846.8	4 993.5	5 200.0	5 369.4	5 640.0	5 893.8	..
Total employment (thousand persons)	1 815.9	1 838.7	1 851.9	1 908.3	1 947.3	1 996.1	2 039.7	..
Public sector employment (per cent of total employment)	53.5	46.4	42.8	35.5	31.0	27.9	26.5	..
Production of main commodities								
Electricity (million kwh)	9 498.0	9 416.0	8 860.0	9 943.0	10 615.0	10 700.0	10 900.0	11 000.0
Gas (billion cubic metres)	17.3	13.3	22.9	47.2	51.3	53.5	59.1	62.0
Oil and refinery products (million tonnes)	8.6	10.9	11.8	12.2	13.0	14.7	17.2	18.1
Cotton (thousand tonnes)	635.0	705.0	1 304.0	1 031.0	1 137.0	489.0	714.0	750.0
Grain (thousand tonnes)	760.0	1 290.0	1 544.0	1 091.0	1 238.0	1 287.0	1 310.0	2 130.0
GDP by main sectors of economic activity [b]								
Agriculture (per cent of total)	20.0	25.2	24.8	22.9	24.7	24.0	24.0	24.0
Industry (per cent of total)	32.9	27.5	31.4	35.0	36.6	37.0	37.0	37.0
Construction (per cent of total)	11.3	13.1	12.2	6.8	5.7	9.0	9.0	9.0
Transport and communication (per cent of total)	10.3	7.8	6.7	6.6	5.4	6.0	6.0	6.0
Trade (per cent of total)	3.6	3.6	4.1	3.5	4.2	4.0	4.0	4.0
Other (per cent of total)	21.8	22.8	20.8	25.1	23.5	20.0	20.0	20.0
Estimates by the UNECE secretariat								
Rates of change of real output								
Aggregate output (proxy for GDP, per cent per annum)	-11.6	5.1	13.8	6.1	4.1	1.8	6.8	6.0
Agriculture (per cent per annum)	16.4	22.3	24.6	-6.8	4.1	-8.5	8.2	10.6
Industry (per cent per annum)	-21.2	7.6	23.4	26.6	9.0	5.1	8.1	4.6
Construction (per cent per annum)	-4.6	1.3	2.1	-15.3	-3.4	12.9	12.0	10.0
Services (per cent per annum)	-7.2	-5.5	2.6	4.1	0.6	4.0	2.4	3.1
Implicit GDP deflator (per cent per annum)	61.7	17.6	23.0	20.6	31.6	26.5	15.3	10.0
Resident population (thousand persons)	4 605.5	4 681.3	4 738.2	4 790.4	4 845.3	4 900.8	4 957.0	5 013.8

Source: National Institute of Statistics and Forecasting of Turkmenistan; UNECE secretariat estimates.

a Preliminary estimates.

b Officially reported through 2001, UNECE secretariat estimates thereafter. See box 5.2.1 in this *Survey*.

Domestic demand remained buoyant in most of the central Asian economies with the possible exception of Uzbekistan (table 5.2.4). Consumption, boosted by large increases in real wages, continued to be a key support of economic growth. In Kyrgyzstan and, particularly, Kazakhstan, increased employment provided additional support for consumption. In Kazakhstan, wage rises were relatively large in low pay sectors, such as public health care and education, enhancing the impact on consumption. In addition, worker remittances from abroad have been rising in Kyrgyzstan and Tajikistan, underpinning consumption and the growth of domestic demand.

In Kazakhstan, total investment remained strong and there were signs of diversification: large increases in metallurgy and services (especially real estate) more than offset weaker investment in the extractive industries.[175] Investment accelerated sharply in Kyrgyzstan, partly reflecting the low base period following three years of

contraction. In contrast, investment appears to have been sluggish in Uzbekistan.[176]

Strong domestic demand throughout the region has led to large increases in imports, which have exceeded the growth of exports.

Risks of overheating in Kazakhstan

In Kazakhstan, an expansionary fiscal policy, matched during most of the year by an accommodative monetary stance, prevented any further decline in the rate of inflation in 2004. The continuing strong growth of real household incomes and the steep rise in labour costs and material input prices added to the inflationary pressures. In September, the nine-month cumulative rate

---

[175] Despite a 7 per cent year-on-year fall during the first three quarters of 2004, investment in the extractive industries still accounted for 40 per cent of the total.

[176] While official data indicates a strong pick-up in GDP growth in Uzbekistan in 2004 (8.9 per cent in the first three quarters against 4 per cent in the same period of 2003), these figures have been questioned by some observers. Stagnation in the hydrocarbons sector and electricity consumption suggest a lower figure. Economist Intelligence Unit, *Country Report. Uzbekistan* (London), September 2004. The situation is similar in Turkmenistan, where the reported growth of oil and gas output (the country's key industry) is not consistent with the official figures for the growth of total industrial output (box 5.2.1).

of change of consumer prices reached 4 per cent and the year-end CPI target band of 5-7 per cent looked increasingly difficult to reach. This prompted the National Bank of Kazakhstan to signal in October its intention to tighten its policy stance by reducing its intervention in the foreign exchange market.[177] At present Kazakhstan's booming economy shows signs of overheating; the prevention of a further increase of inflationary pressures will ultimately depend on a tightening of fiscal policy.

In Kyrgyzstan, there was virtual price stability in terms of consumer and producer prices in 2004. Unit labour costs declined thanks to soaring productivity gains and moderate wage growth in industry, while the exchange rate remained relatively stable. In Tajikistan, inflation continued to fall throughout the first three quarters as a result of tighter monetary policy. The strong recovery of labour productivity largely offset the continued rise in wages (those in industry rose some 40 per cent, year-on-year, during the first three quarters).

Labour market performance remained uneven

In Kazakhstan, the labour markets continued to improve, employment growth being by far the most dynamic in the CIS. However, the government sector continues to account for one quarter of total employment and two fifths of dependent employment.[178] This suggests structural weakness in the private business sector that prevents it from increasing its share of total employment. The prospects for employment growth are good, provided that the government implements its ambitious plans for economic diversification without unduly restricting the development of product markets. Total employment increased in Kyrgyzstan in the first half of 2004. In contrast, it fell in Tajikistan, although industrial employment started to recover slowly. No labour market data for 2004 are available for Turkmenistan and Uzbekistan. The latest available labour market statistics for Turkmenistan show that in the early 2000s the growth of total and industrial employment was slowing down.

Fiscal revenues are highly dependent on commodity prices

High oil and gas prices, robust economic growth, and, in some cases, improvements in tax collection, boosted fiscal revenues in a number of central Asian economies in 2004. Revenues rose sharply in Kazakhstan, despite a number of tax cuts at the beginning of the year. However, the windfall from higher than

projected oil prices was absorbed by increased expenditures. The relaxation of fiscal policy reflected increased spending on health and education (with sharp wage increases in both sectors), larger social outlays and an extensive housing programme. Nevertheless, the consolidated general budget remained in surplus and the reserves in the National Fund continued to grow.

The fiscal loosening reflects a policy choice to share the oil and gas windfall more widely, a preference that could strengthen social cohesion. While the expansion of the oil and gas sectors has helped to strengthen the public finances, financing extensive redistribution policies from temporary sources carries important risks. In particular, considerable fiscal prudence is needed with regard to programmes involving recurrent, non-discretionary spending as their unbalanced expansion may lead to a chronic deterioration in the structural fiscal balance.

The government of Kazakhstan has announced its intention to introduce tax incentives to promote high-technology and export-oriented industries as part of a broader strategy to encourage economic diversification.[179] In addition, specialized financial institutions have been set up to sustain this effort. The identification of favoured industries and their support with public funds carries a potential risk of wasteful use of public resources and the emergence of activities that are unable to survive under normal competitive conditions. An effective institutional framework for economic diversification can involve strategic partnerships between the government and the private sector, that associate closely the private sector to public goals, ensuring transparency in the provision of public support and promoting competition as the ultimate guarantor of sustained gains in productivity.[180] In any case, a careful review of the efficiency of budgetary spending in Kazakhstan should accompany the plans for its expansion.

Economic diversification is an even more pressing challenge in Kyrgyzstan, where, in the absence of new discoveries, the projected phasing out of gold production

---

[177] As in Russia, the large commodity-related export revenues have prompted massive purchases of foreign exchange by Kazakhstan's central bank and, at present, this is one of its key policy instruments.

[178] Kazakh Statistical Agency, *Ekonomicheskaya aktivnost' naseleniya Kazakhstana* (Almaty), 2004.

---

[179] Further tax reforms are scheduled for 2005, including changes in the amortization schedule of fixed assets with a fiscal cost equivalent to 0.4 per cent of officially projected GDP. Diversification is also expected to reduce the reliance of the budget on oil and gas revenues. Official projections indicate that in 2007, oil and gas revenues will account for 17.6 per cent of total revenues (national definition), down from 22.2 per cent in 2005. Government of the Republic of Kazakhstan, *Srednesrochnaya fiskal'naya politika Pravitel'stva Respubliki Kazakhstan na 2005-2007 gody*, Postanovlenie No. 918, 31 August 2004 [www.government.kz]. However, changes in the taxation of oil and mining revenues imply an increase in the government share of new contracts.

[180] Competition appears as a more important factor than infrastructure provision or administrative interference in explaining differences in productivity at the firm level in a recent sectoral survey of the investment climate in a number of eastern European and central Asian countries. F. Bastos and J. Nasir, *Productivity and the Investment Climate: What Matters Most?*, World Bank Policy Research Working Paper, No. 3335 (Washington, D.C.), June 2004.

will greatly reduce export capacity over the medium term. The envisaged tax reforms are intended to create better conditions for the development of small and medium enterprises and provide support for the development of alternative activities.[181] However, the precarious state of the public finances greatly reduces government's ability to implement these policies. Early figures suggest that there was some modest progress in fiscal consolidation in 2004 but this effort needs to be sustained.[182] Plans to increase development spending depend crucially on the ability to raise public revenue, including through a number of recent tax innovations where implementation has been lagging. Mobilizing additional external financial support, including through a possible debt rescheduling agreement with the Paris Club of creditors in 2005, could be vital for the success of Kyrgyzstan's development effort, given its large foreign debt burden.

The sharp fall of cotton prices from their high level at the beginning of 2004 has had a negative impact on public sector revenue in the other countries of the region. Despite the fall, average cotton prices for the year were roughly unchanged from 2003 and public sector revenue benefited from the exports of other commodities. In Tajikistan, an important challenge is to broaden the tax base in the emerging private sector in order to reduce the impact of volatile commodity prices on fiscal revenues. A more general policy issue for Tajikistan (as well as for other central Asian economies) is to sustain the effort to reform and streamline government administration and to create the right incentives for efficient governance through extensive civil service reform. These changes are necessary conditions for improving the efficiency of tax collection and public spending. Lack of timely data and extensive quasi-fiscal operations make it difficult to assess the position of public finances in Turkmenistan and Uzbekistan.

Monetary policy remained accommodative

Strong inflows of foreign capital have continued to pose problems for the conduct of monetary policy in Kazakhstan, which have been compounded by the procyclical loosening of fiscal policy. Although the main policy goal is the control of inflation, the monetary authorities (as in Russia) have intervened heavily in the foreign exchange market in order to avoid an excessive appreciation of the exchange rate.[183] In addition, the growth of foreign borrowing by Kazakh banks and corporations has further increased the pressure on the exchange rate.[184] The intended gradual liberalization of the capital account may help to ease the upward pressure on the exchange rate, as investing abroad will become easier for residents.[185] At the same time, it will increase the vulnerability of the economy to sudden capital outflows.

The intended policy shift towards inflation targeting raises further problems for policy makers in Kazakhstan. Such a regime of monetary management will require a greater degree of exchange rate flexibility, particularly in view of the intention to pursue a more activist fiscal policy. Inflation targeting will also require a wider range of policy tools for intervention on the domestic money markets in order to increase the role of interest rates in monetary management.[186] The extent of monetization has increased but it still remains low (table 5.1.2), which makes money demand difficult to predict, while the responsiveness of the economy to changes in interest rates may be limited.

In Kyrgyzstan, monetary policy has been conducted in an environment characterized by low inflation and a reduction in the cash fiscal deficit. Thanks to rising money demand, a rapid expansion of the money supply was absorbed without putting undue pressure on prices. In Tajikistan, monetary policy was tightened in order to

---

[181] Interfax Central Asian News, 13 September 2004. Turkmenistan has also announced a programme of tax cuts, including the reduction of the VAT rate, BBC Monitoring Central Asia, 23 October 2004.

[182] The sale in 2004 of a part of the government's stake in the Kumtor gold mine on the Toronto stock exchange raised a total of $252.6 million, which helped to ease the public sector's financing constraints. However, in addition to the reported cash fiscal deficit, the public sector continues to incur a large quasi-fiscal deficit through extensive quasi-subsidies (implied levels of electricity tariffs that are well below cost recovery prices). In 2003, this was equivalent to 10.4 per cent of GDP and in 2004 it is expected to amount to 9.2 per cent of GDP. The government intends to reduce such quasi-subsidies to 4.8 per cent by 2007. Ministry of Finance of the Kyrgyz Republic, *Srednesrochnyi Prognoz Byudzheta Kyrgyzskoi Respubliki na 2005-2007 gody* (Bishkek), 2004.

[183] The purchases of foreign exchange have been partially sterilized through the sale of central bank notes but, in general, monetary policy has remained expansionary. The operations of the National Oil Fund (which has accumulated part of the windfall due to oil exports) are also equivalent to partial sterilization. However, the expansionary fiscal policy reduced to some extent the impact of this sterilization.

[184] Public external debt expressed in dollars has remained roughly unchanged but non-guaranteed private debt rose by 34.4 per cent in the year to the end of the second quarter of 2004. Commercial banks have raised long-term funding through syndicated loans, which has facilitated the lengthening of maturities in domestic lending. The access of banks and corporations to international capital markets is a reflection of good credit ratings, but it also indicates the limitations of the domestic banking system, which is nevertheless one of the most developed in the CIS.

[185] Other policy options being discussed are the introduction of higher minimum reserve requirements on commercial banks and compulsory deposits on foreign borrowing. *Dow Jones International News*, 22 October 2004.

[186] A conventional policy step would be to strengthen the central bank's portfolio of government securities in order to increase the scope of open market operations. In the case of Kazakhstan, however, this is complicated by the solid fiscal position and the reluctance of current holders to dispose of these assets. National Bank of the Republic of Kazakhstan, *Obzor inflyatsii 2 kvartala 2004 goda* (Almaty), 2004.

reduce inflation and correct previous policy slippages. Despite a sharp deceleration in the growth of monetary aggregates, the somoni resumed its slide in relation to the dollar in the second quarter, following some recovery early in the year.

The absence of monetary statistics prevents any comprehensive assessment of the situation in the other countries in the region. In Uzbekistan, the refinancing rate was lowered in July from 20 per cent to 18 per cent on the basis of a reported low rate of inflation. However, administrative credit constraints rather than cost are the main determinants of the access to finance. Support for the official exchange rate, which was unified in October 2003, is likely to have required continued restrictions and a de facto tight monetary stance.[187] In Turkmenistan, there is evidence of increasing spreads between official and black market rates, which are indicative of growing macroeconomic imbalances.

5.3 The short-term outlook

Growth may lose some momentum in 2005

Economic activity in the CIS as a whole is expected to lose some momentum in 2005 but will nevertheless remain quite strong. The major external factors that affect the short-term growth prospects of the CIS economies – the evolution of world commodity prices and demand in their main regional markets – point to some slowdown in the rate of growth. However, while commodity prices are expected to soften somewhat, they are still likely to be relatively high by historical standards. Domestic demand in the CIS should generally remain buoyant but its effect on domestic economic activity will depend on the extent to which local producers improve their responsiveness to demand. Macroeconomic policy will continue to be generally supportive, with an increasing risk of procyclical fiscal loosening in a number of countries.

GDP growth in Russia is set to weaken again in 2005, as a result of the combined effect of softer commodity prices and a strong rouble. Both the output and exports of oil are likely to slow down after several years of very strong growth. The influence of the planned fiscal expansion in supporting economic activity will probably be limited in view of the weak responsiveness of supply to rising domestic demand (partly a consequence of declining competitiveness). Nevertheless, GDP growth in Russia will still remain relatively high at around 6 per cent in 2005.

Output growth is also expected to decelerate in neighbouring Belarus and Ukraine, partly reflecting weaker Russian demand for their exports. In Ukraine, the

political crisis following the 2004 election increases the risk of financial and macroeconomic destabilization and this is likely to have a negative effect on economic activity. GDP growth in Kazakhstan is expected to decelerate by around 1 percentage point to some 8 per cent in 2005, in line with the output targets for oil and natural gas production, and also influenced by somewhat weaker import demand in its main markets (Russia and China). While monetary policy may tighten in response to emerging inflationary pressures, the procyclical bias in fiscal policy is set to be carried forward into 2005.[188]

The Caucasian region is on the brink of a major transformation, with economic growth being driven by a major expansion of the regional pipeline system transporting Azeri oil.[189] This is expected to produce a sharp acceleration of GDP growth (to two-digit rates in 2005), with the main source of growth shifting from massive FDI (which will remain large), to growing exports, resulting in a reduction of external imbalances.[190] Macroeconomic policy, however, will have to cope with even greater pressures from strong capital inflows. Developments in Azerbaijan are expected to feed into the Georgian economy, through the impact of pipeline construction, growing transit fees and enhanced opportunities for trade. Georgia's new government has launched a new reform programme that has managed to attract considerable donor support.[191] Armenia is unlikely to benefit from the oil boom, as it is bypassed by the pipeline routes. GDP growth is expected to decelerate somewhat in 2005, as the momentum of grant-financed construction projects fades away.

GDP growth in Kyrgyzstan is likely to moderate in 2005, the result of a less favourable external environment and the fading of the base period effect associated with the recovery of output in the Kumtor gold mine. Macroeconomic policy will have to be more cautious in view of the need for fiscal consolidation, which is a condition for obtaining vital debt relief from the Paris Club of creditors. After several years of strong

---

[187] Public access to cash remains restricted, resulting in significant discounts on cash transactions. Asian Development Bank, *Asian Development 2004 Update* (Manila), 2004.

[188] The new parliament, elected in September-October 2004, adopted an amendment to the draft budget, agreed by the outgoing parliament, which increases the planned expenditure for 2005 by 101.4 billion tenge (or 0.2 per cent of GDP).

[189] The expected completion of the Baku-Tbilisi-Ceyhan oil pipeline in 2005 will allow Azerbaijan to greatly increase its exports. Pipeline construction will continue to boost economic activity in the region. The South Caucasus Gas Pipeline is expected to be finished in time to deliver the first contracted exports to Turkey in 2006.

[190] Azerbaijan's GDP is projected to double in dollar terms in the next four years, increasing its lead as the largest economy in the region. IMF, *Azerbaijan Republic: Third Review Under the Three-Year Arrangement Under the Poverty Reduction and Growth Facility-Staff Report*, Country Report No. 04/9 (Washington, D.C.), January 2004.

[191] In June 2004, a donor conference pledged $1 billion. However, further reforms will be needed to improve the absorptive capacity of the economy and to boost consumer and investor confidence.

growth, partly reflecting the impetus of post-conflict recovery, a more moderate but still robust pace of expansion is expected in Tajikistan in 2005. The conclusion of a debt-for-equity swap agreement with Russia may encourage further foreign direct investment. As in Kyrgyzstan, remittances will remain a significant support to domestic demand. In the remaining CIS countries, GDP is expected to continue to grow at rates similar to those in 2004, provided there are no negative external shocks.

Risks to the outlook: high vulnerability to external shocks and competitiveness losses

Whereas GDP throughout the CIS, and especially in the resource-rich CIS economies, has been growing at remarkably high rates during the last couple of years, economic growth in the region is not soundly based. The current boom in world commodity markets has greatly benefited the resource-abundant economies but it has also increased their exposure to external shocks caused by possible reversals in prices and/or world demand. The main vulnerability of these economies is their high degree of dependence on the exports of natural resources and low value added manufactured products. Besides, the current rate of export growth is clearly not sustainable for most of the CIS commodity exporters and even if external conditions remain favourable, the sources of this resource-based growth are likely to be exhausted in the not-too distant future.

While generating unusually large windfall revenue gains, high commodity prices have in some cases led to potentially damaging macroeconomic side effects, in particular the so-called "Dutch Disease". There are already signs, especially in Russia, that the loss of competitiveness due to real exchange rate appreciation, is an increasing burden on local producers and is choking off aggregate domestic economic activity. The capacity of macroeconomic policy to address these negative implications is fairly limited, moreover, given the relatively narrow set of instruments at the disposal of policy makers. Unless local producers are able to respond at the micro level through further restructuring, negative repercussions on output growth are likely in the affected countries, especially in their manufacturing industries.

Long-term prospects depend on diversification and economic reform

The current sources of rapid economic growth in the CIS region (rising volumes of exports of natural resources and favourable world commodity prices) could soon evaporate.[192] The recent rates of rapid GDP growth

were possible because of increased utilization of existing productive capacity and largely reflect a recovery from the deep transformational recession in these economies. None of these factors is likely to continue for very long. Sustaining high rates of economic growth will therefore call for major changes in its composition and direction.

At the same time, current policies which are seeking to contain real exchange rate appreciation in order to preserve the competitiveness of local producers (as is the case in Russia) have obvious limitations. This is not a sustainable direction for policy and may prove a distraction from the necessary efforts to accelerate the pace of structural reforms in the resource-rich CIS economies. Ultimately, through diversification and modernization, these economies (Russia, in particular) will need to achieve significant productivity gains. Increased productivity will not only allow some of the negative implications of the real exchange rate appreciation to be offset, but it will also set the stage for sustainable high rates of economic growth and consequent increases in living standards.

The economic diversification and modernization of these economies is a long-term process that is likely to take years to materialize even under favourable circumstances and in a supportive policy environment. In order to restructure and develop, the CIS economies will have to be capable of attracting and absorbing vast amounts of private fixed investment, including FDI. That is, their economic environment should not only offer direct investors attractive and attainable future returns but should also facilitate the implementation of investment projects.

Public policy can play an important role in the successful restructuring of these economies. An important condition for this to materialize is the development of human capital, which is a key factor in long-term growth. Public policy can also play a leading role in the development of infrastructure. A crucial requirement, however, is to improve the quality and capacity of public administration and other institutions in order to enhance the impact of public intervention and limit distortions. Broadly speaking, public policy should target the removal of existing obstacles to the development of the private sector. In turn, this implies further deepening and broadening of key reforms in product and financial markets. In any case, a strategy of economic diversification relying on the mobilization of fixed investment calls for credible long-term policy commitments on the part of governments that will improve and then stabilize investors' long-term expectations.

---

[192] Thus according to medium- and long-term forecasts of the International Energy Agency, Russia's share in the global supply of oil is likely to fall after 2010. IEA, *World Energy Outlook 2004* (Paris), 2004, chap. 9.

CHAPTER 6

FOREIGN TRADE AND PAYMENTS IN THE EU-10, SOUTH-EAST EUROPE AND THE CIS

During 2004, the ECE emerging market economies (EME) continued to make significant progress in integrating themselves into the global trading and financial system. The further enlargement of the EU eastward was historic for both economic and political reasons. Although the EU-10 had already achieved high levels of trade and financial integration with the EU-15 prior to accession, the enlargement is likely to further intensify these trade and investment relations in the coming years. The difference in the commodity structure of the trade of the EME explains to a large degree the current account trends which developed during this period. The increase in the price of crude oil was particularly important for several of the CIS countries; the energy exporters and Ukraine had trade surpluses and were able to use their increased export earnings to further strengthen their economies and accumulate international reserves. Robust growth in all three regions – the EU-10, south-east Europe and the CIS – stimulated trade among themselves, as well as imports from the rest of the world. Exports from these economies benefited from strong global growth although exports to western Europe, their major market for manufactured goods, were dampened by the continued relatively slow growth there.

The continual integration of the ECE emerging market economies into the global financial market has eliminated the requirement that their national savings must limit their national investment. Low interest rates in the United States and western Europe increased the attractiveness of these regions to investors searching for higher yields. FDI inflows into the EU-10 declined slightly from last years' levels, while investment into south-east Europe and the CIS continued to increase.

6.1 The balance of payments and external financial flows

(i) The balance of payments in the EU-10, south-east Europe and the CIS

During the last 12 months to June 2004, net capital inflows into the EME totalled $53.4 billion, with $29.1 billion flowing in the first half of 2004; this amounted on average to about 3.3 per cent of the region's yearly GDP.[193]

Over the same period, the international reserve assets of the EME increased by $45.2 billion, which is approximately 2.8 per cent of the region's GDP. On a net basis therefore, most of the capital inflow was channelled into international reserves. In the sense that a reserve accumulation can be considered as a capital outflow, the region was only a small net recipient of savings from the rest of the world. Excluding Turkey, the other emerging market economies accumulated more reserves than they imported capital and were thus net exporters of capital. The overall goods and services account balance for the EME in aggregate was just slightly in surplus over the last year, so the region produced slightly more than it consumed. There were significant differences among the subregions: the EU-10, south-east Europe and the energy-importing countries of the CIS[194] had large current account deficits while the energy-exporting CIS members[195] were in surplus. The fact that the majority of the economies of the region were large capital importers, while the region as a whole imported very little capital (when international reserves are included), reflects the economic weight of the CIS energy exporters that account for 38 per cent of the region's total GDP aggregated on the basis of current exchange rates.

The level of net foreign borrowing (excluding reserves) has remained relatively stable as a percentage of GDP for the last several years, both for the entire region and for the major subgroups – the EU-10, south-east Europe (excluding Turkey)[196] and the CIS; however there are considerable differences among these economies in their capital accounts and in the annual changes.

---

[193] The analysis of this section (table 6.1.1) primarily uses variables expressed as percentages of GDP. This allows for a more meaningful comparison across countries and also eliminates much of the distortion created by the relatively large fluctuations in the dollar and euro exchange rates.

[194] Armenia, Belarus, Georgia, Kyrgyzstan, the Republic of Moldova and Tajikistan.

[195] The CIS energy exporters include Azerbaijan, Kazakhstan, Russia, Turkmenistan, Ukraine and Uzbekistan. Ukraine is grouped with the energy exporters despite the fact that it is not a major oil exporter (although it exports significant amounts of coal) and actually imports significant amounts of energy. Ukraine's major export product is steel and the increase in the world price for steel has been as large as that for oil. Uzbekistan exports some energy (oil, gas, electricity) but cotton is its major export; by end of 2003, cotton prices were up significantly from mid-year or the beginning of the year but have since subsided. In this sense Ukraine and Uzbekistan are in a similar economic situation to that of the energy exporters and are therefore grouped with them.

[196] Turkey's current account has deteriorated over the last two years.

TABLE 6.1.1

The balance of payments and external financing for ECE emerging market economies, 2003QIII-2004QII
(Per cent of GDP)

	Balance of flows by accounts						External financial indicators		
	Merchandise trade	Trade in services	Income and transfers	FDI inflows	Other capital[a]	Reserve changes[b]	Cumulative FDI inflows[cd]	Gross debt[d]	Total reserves[d]
New EU members	-4.3	1.4	-1.7	2.7	2.9	0.9	33.1	52.4	19.8
Cyprus[e]	-25.7	21.3	-0.9	8.6	0.1	3.3	52.4	38.1	22.6
Czech Republic	-2.3	0.5	-4.5	3.1	3.6	0.3	43.8	35.8	26.9
Estonia	-18.7	9.8	-6.1	8.9	7.8	1.7	45.7	81.6	13.5
Hungary	-3.3	-0.9	-5.1	3.0	5.9	-0.4	43.4	68.9	14.2
Latvia	-20.0	4.7	3.8	3.5	9.6	1.6	28.8	87.1	12.4
Lithuania	-10.1	3.1	-1.6	1.7	8.5	1.7	21.2	45.6	16.0
Malta	-13.5	8.8	-1.6	7.6	-2.4	-1.1	56.9	33.7	49.4
Poland	-2.6	0.5	0.4	2.0	1.1	1.3	26.1	51.2	16.0
Slovakia	-2.1	0.8	-0.6	2.1	3.2	3.4	31.0	50.7	32.3
Slovenia	-2.6	2.2	–	0.9	-1.8	-1.1	13.4	58.1	26.2
South-east Europe	-11.4	4.3	1.1	2.6	6.1	2.6	12.7	53.3	15.5
Albania[f]	-20.0	-1.1	14.5	4.3	4.7	2.4	18.7	20.0	15.4
Bosnia and Herzegovina[f]	-56.7	4.2	22.7	6.0	31.2	7.3	18.9	50.6	26.5
Bulgaria	-13.9	3.2	2.2	8.7	6.9	7.0	35.0	66.6	32.2
Croatia	-26.8	17.4	2.1	4.9	4.5	2.1	32.2	80.5	24.7
Romania	-8.5	–	2.3	3.8	7.0	4.7	19.6	33.4	16.7
Serbia and Montenegro[g]	-28.3	1.5	15.6	7.3	8.3	4.3	15.6	57.1	15.3
The former Yugoslav Republic of Macedonia	-19.6	-0.6	10.6	3.2	6.9	0.4	22.2	36.4	16.7
Turkey	-7.2	4.3	-1.7	1.0	5.1	1.6	6.3	54.6	12.5
CIS[h]	11.1	-2.4	-2.3	2.5	-4.5	4.5	13.0	40.1	16.4
Armenia	-14.3	-2.7	10.9	6.4	0.6	0.9	31.5	59.4	16.3
Azerbaijan[f]	-2.0	-25.2	-4.4	50.4	-16.3	2.4	132.9	18.4	10.6
Belarus	-7.6	3.1	0.9	1.1	2.3	-0.2	9.5	19.1	3.5
Georgia	..	..	..	..	..	..	..	43.6	6.1
Kazakhstan[i]	13.7	-7.9	-6.8	8.5	-1.1	6.4	50.4	68.2	17.0
Kyrgyzstan	-4.7	-0.3	3.2	..	..	..	..	110.8	17.8
Republic of Moldova	-31.1	-3.3	26.0	3.2	6.3	1.2	38.0	85.2	13.3
Russian Federation[i]	13.6	-2.5	-3.2	1.3	-4.8	4.5	8.2	38.2	16.8
Tajikistan	..	..	..	..	..	..	..	60.0	7.8
Turkmenistan	..	..	..	..	..	..	..	..	..
Ukraine	3.1	2.9	3.2	2.9	-6.3	5.8	13.7	47.1	17.0
Uzbekistan	..	..	..	..	..	..	..	..	..
Total emerging market economies[h]	0.1	0.6	-1.2	2.6	0.7	2.8	19.6	47.6	17.3
Memorandum items:									
EU-8	-3.7	0.8	-1.7	2.5	3.0	0.9	32.3	53.0	19.4
South-east Europe without Turkey	-18.8	4.3	5.8	5.3	7.7	4.3	23.7	51.1	20.7
CIS without Russian Federation[h]	3.0	-2.0	0.4	6.4	-3.5	4.4	28.9	46.4	15.1
CIS energy exporters[h]	12.3	-2.6	-2.7	2.5	-4.9	4.7	12.8	40.2	16.9
CIS energy importers[h]	-11.3	1.5	4.7	3.1	2.7	0.7	18.2	38.3	6.8

Source: UNECE secretariat calculations, based on national statistics; IMF statistics.

[a] Includes errors and omissions.

[b] A negative sign indicates a decrease in reserves.

[c] From 1988.

[d] As of 30 June 2004 unless otherwise noted.

[e] Debt only to December 2003.

[f] Debt not reported using standard IMF definitions.

[g] Serbia only.

[h] Totals include UNECE secretariat estimates for missing values.

[i] Debt only to March 2004.

Current account surpluses for the energy exporters

Over the last 12 months to June 2004 and especially in the first half of 2004, the EME current account balances, and their merchandise trade component, were affected by the rise in commodity prices. This was most noticeable for the major oil exporters (Kazakhstan and Russia), which accumulated large trade surpluses exceeding 10 per cent of GDP. Due to large increases in the price of steel, Ukraine was in a similar position with a trade surplus of 3.1 per cent of GDP. Turkmenistan and Uzbekistan also had large trade surpluses based on price increases for their exports of fuels and in addition, cotton for Uzbekistan. Exceptionally, the oil exporter Azerbaijan had a trade deficit and the largest current account deficit (as a per cent of GDP) of any EME. This largely reflected Azerbaijan's large imports of capital equipment for pipeline infrastructure and oil and gas exploration. All of the CIS energy exporters (except Ukraine) were in deficit on their service accounts; these imported services are often directly related to the development of the their energy industries.

Since the energy exporters have gained an essentially temporary boost in income (historically, previous oil price increases have been followed by declines) it should be expected that they would attempt to save a portion of this to iron out fluctuations in their consumption and investment patterns, and thus the expectation of improvements in their current accounts. An additional factor in explaining the increased external surpluses of the energy exporters is their specialized export structure. Generally, countries with highly concentrated commodity exports tend to have more volatile terms of trade, and many of them attempt to minimize this effect by increasing precautionary savings and thereby running more positive current accounts than more diversified economies.[197]

The CIS energy exporters have used their oil revenues to accumulate significant amounts of official reserve assets.[198] In absolute terms, Russia dominates with a net increase of $22.5 billion over the last year (or 4.5 per cent of its GDP), and its total reserve assets in October 2004 were in excess of $100 billion.[199] Although large as an absolute amount, as a per cent of its GDP (16.8 per cent) its official reserves are not particularly large compared with the other ECE emerging market

economies. In terms of their proportion to GDP, several other CIS energy exporters including Kazakhstan (with reserve accumulation equalling 6.4 per cent of its GDP), Ukraine (5.8 per cent), and possibly Turkmenistan had even higher rates of reserve growth than Russia. Although such accumulation provides some insurance against future currency instability and allows some smoothing of consumption over time, a major motivation over the last year has been to check currency appreciation in order to limit possible "Dutch Disease" effects.

Current account deficits for east Europe and CIS energy importers

All of the EU-10, south-east Europe and the energy-importing CIS countries are primarily energy importers and all had both current account and merchandise trade deficits during 2003QIII-2004QII (table 6.1.1). The current account deficit of the south-east European region was the largest at 6 per cent of GDP (8.7 per cent excluding Turkey), while the EU-10 had a slightly smaller deficit of 4.7 per cent and the CIS energy importers one of 5.1 per cent. There was more variation in their trade deficits, which varied from 4.3 per cent of GDP for the EU-10 to 11.4 per cent for south-east Europe (18.8 per cent without Turkey); the CIS energy importers fell in between with a trade deficit of 11.3 per cent of GDP. Each of these three subregions has a current account deficit that has been increasing over the last two and a half years (table 6.1.2).

These increasing current account deficits seem consistent with the more general pattern of how a spurt in income growth affects current accounts in emerging markets. The response of the current account to an increase in income above the past trend differs between small open advanced economies and emerging markets.[200] When an advanced economy experiences growth, agents tend to view it as a positive transitory income shock, and they therefore increase savings as a way to smooth consumption and this generally offsets any increase in investment. The current account therefore follows a procyclical pattern (i.e. surpluses during periods of rapid growth). In emerging markets, however, there is a tendency to interpret a period of high growth not as a transitory shock (likely to be reversed) but as an increase in the likely long-run growth rate.[201] Since an expected increase in the growth rate implies that future income will increase by more than current income, consumption increases relative to income, and the current account deteriorates. The recent rapid increases in the GDP of the ECE emerging market economies are translating into growing expectations that their per capita income levels will tend to converge toward those of western Europe. The previous experiences of

---

[197] Empirical evidence for this is provided by A. Ghosh and J. Ostry, "Export instability and the external balance in developing countries", *IMF Staff Papers*, Vol. 41 (Washington, D.C.), June 1994, pp. 214-235.

[198] Official external debt has also been retired. Russian foreign debt has declined from 90 per cent of GDP at the time of the 1998 crisis to about 28 per cent by mid 2004; significant amounts of oil profits have also been diverted into a stabilization fund.

[199] This gives Russia the eighth largest amount of official reserves of any country in the world economy, larger even than those of the United States.

---

[200] M. Aguiar and G. Gopinath, *Emerging Market Business Cycles: The Cycle Is the Trend*, NBER Working Paper, No. 10734 (Cambridge, MA), September 2004.

[201] It is this basic tendency of adjusting expectations about the long-run prospects of an economy based upon short-run developments that contributes to the underlying volatility in emerging markets.

TABLE 6.1.2

Trends in trade and external balances of the ECE emerging market economies, 2002-2004

(Per cent)

	Trade and services balance (per cent of GDP)			Current account (per cent of GDP)			FDI inflows (per cent of GDP)			Total reserves to gross debt (per cent)		
	2002	2003	2004 Jan.-June	2002	2003	2004 Jan.-June	2002	2003	2004 Jan.-June	2002	2003	2004 June
New EU members	-3.1	-3.0	-3.0	-4.3	-4.4	-5.0	5.5	2.5	3.1	44	39	38
Cyprus [a]	-1.0	-1.5	-12.8	-4.4	-3.4	-12.5	10.4	7.8	6.6	70	60	59
Czech Republic	-2.0	-2.2	-0.2	-5.6	-6.2	-4.2	11.5	2.9	4.4	87	77	75
Estonia	-7.1	-8.0	-9.9	-10.2	-13.2	-16.4	4.0	9.8	9.2	21	19	17
Hungary	-2.5	-4.7	-4.1	-7.3	-9.0	-10.1	4.7	2.8	2.5	26	22	21
Latvia	-10.2	-12.9	-15.8	-6.8	-8.3	-13.6	2.8	2.7	5.3	18	15	14
Lithuania	-5.6	-5.6	-7.0	-5.2	-6.6	-9.9	5.2	1.0	4.6	38	39	35
Malta	1.2	-5.3	-7.2	0.3	-5.6	-8.9	-10.2	6.2	3.9	162	166	147
Poland	-3.3	-2.5	-2.2	-2.6	-2.2	-2.1	2.2	2.0	2.1	34	31	31
Slovakia	-6.9	-1.2	-1.4	-8.0	-0.9	-3.2	16.6	1.7	3.7	67	65	64
Slovenia	1.5	-0.1	-0.4	1.4	-0.4	-0.5	7.4	1.2	0.9	58	52	45
South-east Europe	-4.8	-5.9	-10.3	-3.4	-5.2	-9.4	1.7	2.3	2.7	26	29	29
Albania [b]	-25.8	-23.4	-18.1	-9.3	-6.7	-5.4	3.0	2.9	5.5	71	72	77
Bosnia and Herzegovina [b]	-57.7	-53.5	-48.2	-31.0	-29.6	-27.1	4.9	5.5	6.4	52	70	53
Bulgaria	-7.2	-9.5	-13.0	-5.3	-8.4	-11.1	5.8	7.1	11.3	39	48	48
Croatia	-10.9	-7.9	-18.1	-8.4	-7.2	-17.2	4.9	6.9	3.4	38	35	31
Romania	-5.7	-7.7	-9.5	-3.4	-5.7	-7.2	2.5	3.2	5.2	46	44	50
Serbia and Montenegro [c]	-23.2	-23.3	-28.5	-11.0	-9.8	-13.7	3.0	6.9	2.8	18	24	27
The former Yugoslav Republic of Macedonia	-22.0	-18.3	-22.6	-9.5	-6.0	-14.4	2.1	2.0	3.3	45	49	46
Turkey	0.3	-1.5	-6.0	-0.8	-3.4	-7.8	0.6	0.7	1.2	21	23	23
CIS [d]	7.9	8.7	10.1	6.6	6.5	8.0	1.9	2.8	3.2	28	36	41
Armenia [e]	-17.2	-17.9	-22.9	-6.2	-6.8	-10.3	4.7	4.3	8.7	41	29	28
Azerbaijan [b]	-7.3	-24.0	-25.8	-12.3	-28.3	-31.0	22.3	46.0	50.2	52	57	58
Belarus	-3.3	-3.9	-3.1	-2.1	-3.0	-2.3	1.7	1.0	0.7	20	17	18
Georgia [b]	-12.5	-14.6	..	-6.8	-10.0	..	4.9	8.5	..	11	10	14
Kazakhstan [f]	0.7	6.1	8.1	-3.4	-0.1	0.5	10.5	6.8	9.9	14	19	25
Kyrgyzstan [e]	-3.7	-4.0	-8.7	-1.6	-1.2	-5.1	0.3	2.4	..	16	16	16
Republic of Moldova [e]	-24.7	-33.8	-32.7	-3.1	-7.3	-3.7	7.0	3.0	3.7	16	15	16
Russian Federation [f]	10.5	11.4	11.9	8.4	8.3	9.1	1.0	1.8	2.0	29	39	44
Tajikistan	-13.1	-9.8	..	-1.2	-0.3	..	3.0	2.0	..	9	11	13
Turkmenistan	..	..	..	..	..	..	..	..	..	..	..	..
Ukraine [e]	4.4	2.6	11.5	7.5	5.8	15.0	1.6	2.9	3.3	33	28	36
Uzbekistan	..	..	..	..	..	..	..	..	..	..	..	..
Total emerging market economies [d]	0.8	0.8	0.6	0.2	-0.3	-0.7	3.2	2.6	3.0	33	35	36
Memorandum items:												
EU-8	-3.2	-3.0	-2.6	-4.3	-4.4	-4.8	5.5	2.4	3.0	42	38	37
South-east Europe without Turkey	-13.2	-13.4	-17.6	-7.5	-8.2	-12.0	3.6	5.1	5.3	38	40	40
CIS without Russian Federation [d]	0.2	0.3	3.9	1.1	0.8	4.1	4.7	5.6	7.1	26	27	32
CIS energy exporters [d]	8.8	9.7	11.1	7.1	7.1	8.7	1.9	2.8	3.2	29	37	42
CIS energy importers [d]	-7.8	-9.0	-10.0	-3.1	-4.3	-5.2	2.7	2.6	3.1	18	17	18

Source: UNECE secretariat calculations, based on national statistics and direct communications from national statistical offices; IMF statistics.

[a] Debt only to December 2003.

[b] Debt not reported using standard IMF definitions.

[c] Serbia only from 2003.

[d] Totals include UNECE secretariat estimates for missing values.

[e] Debt not reported using standard IMF definitions prior to 2003.

[f] Debt only to March 2004.

Portugal, Spain and to a lesser extent Greece further contribute to this expectation. Generally it is thought that countries that have expectations of future growth rates of income above the world level (or that of the regions in which they are highly integrated) are likely to run current account deficits, while slower growing countries are likely

to run surpluses.[202] An additional possible explanation for the increasing deficits is that the higher fuel prices and

_____

[202] O. Blanchard and F. Giavazzi, "Current account deficits in the euro area: the end of the Feldstein-Horioka puzzle?", *Brookings Papers on Economic Activity*, 2 (Washington, D.C.), 2002, pp. 147-209.

higher domestic GDP growth increased imports, while the monetary authorities attempted to partially or fully maintain exchange rates.

In the EU-8, the three Baltic countries had the largest merchandise trade deficits – all above 10 per cent of GDP. These three economies also had the largest surpluses in their services accounts, but these were much smaller than their trade deficits. These service surpluses are primarily due to the shipment of freight coming from and going to Russia through Baltic ports. Estonia also receives extensive revenue from tourism. The Czech Republic, Estonia, and Hungary had sizeable deficits of over 4 per cent of GDP in their income and transfers account. Cyprus and Malta also had large current account deficits due to large trade deficits. Both of these countries also have a large surplus in their service account due to tourism and the provision of business services. Generally the current account deficits of the new EU members are significantly larger than those of the three southern EU members during an equivalent period after their accession. In the coming years the current accounts of the EU-10 should benefit from increased transfers from the EU structural and cohesion funds and increased worker remittances.[203] Net capital inflows into the EU-8 amounted to 5.5 per cent of their GDP between July 2003 and June 2004, and their official reserves grew by 0.9 per cent of GDP or 16 per cent of the net capital inflow.

The south-east European countries had sizeable trade deficits ranging from a deficit of 7.2 per cent of GDP in Turkey to the extremely large deficit of 56.7 per cent in Bosnia and Herzegovina; Albania, Croatia, Serbia and Montenegro, and The former Yugoslav Republic of Macedonia also had sizable trade deficits of over 19 per cent. These large deficits were offset to some degree by either a significant surplus (i.e. over 10 per cent of GDP) in the services account as in Croatia (tourist services), or a large surplus in the transfer account as in Albania (primarily workers' remittances), Bosnia and Herzegovina (mostly workers' remittances), Serbia and Montenegro, and The former Yugoslav Republic of Macedonia. Net capital inflows into south-east Europe amounted to 8.6 per cent of their GDP with 2.6 per cent of GDP allocated to reserves.

Each of the CIS energy importers had a sizable merchandise trade deficit with a smaller current account deficit due to a surplus in the income and transfers account. The Republic of Moldova's trade deficit of 31.1 per cent of GDP was particularly large and similar to that in the previous year. Armenia, Georgia and Tajikistan had trade deficits of over 10 per cent of GDP with smaller but still significant current account deficits; Georgia's current account has deteriorated over the last few years. Net capital inflows into the energy-importing CIS countries were equivalent to 5.8 per cent of GDP while the change in reserves amounted to 0.7 per cent of GDP.

The levels of gross external debt and total official reserves for the three regions are remarkably similar, the EU-8 and the south-east European countries (excluding Turkey) being almost identical. Turkey's official reserves are comparatively low. Reserves of the CIS energy importers are less than half the levels of the other regions (including the CIS energy exporters) although their external debt is only slightly lower.[204] All of the CIS energy importers stand out as having relatively low levels of reserves, especially in relation to the levels of their external debt. Much of this debt is public debt and much of it is owed to official creditors (box 6.1.1).

(ii) Foreign direct investment

Of the various types of capital flows, foreign direct investment (FDI) is generally considered to be the most desirable. Capital inflows such as bank loans and bond funds, tend to crowd out domestic investment; however FDI tends to increase national investment in an equal amount.[205] FDI is generally considered less volatile during financial crises and unlike debt, which is fixed in nominal terms, it is re-priced as conditions evolve and does not involve a currency or a maturity mismatch.[206] FDI can also provide the EME with much needed technological and managerial expertise. A country may gain the benefits from FDI without also being dependent on net capital inflows or increasing its net external debt. Two recent growth experiences highlight this distinction. Both Ireland during 1991-1999 and China during 1990-2002 (except for 1993) received large FDI inflows that are generally credited with playing an important role in their growth performance, yet during these periods both countries had current account surpluses every year. Given the clear advantages of FDI over debt, a more active policy to shape the structure and volume of such capital inflows may be warranted.

During 2003 worldwide FDI flows stabilized after declining in the previous two years due to the slowdown in economic activity during this period that reduced the supply of internal company funds available for investment.[207] FDI inflows into the EME totalled $42 billion from July 2003 through June 2004; this is only

---

[203] Complete mobility of labour for the EU-10 will not be fully implemented until 2010. Currently, however, there are no significant restrictions in Ireland, Sweden and the United Kingdom.

[204] Debt levels in many of the CIS countries (see the notes to table 6.1.1) are not reported using standard IMF concepts and caution should be used in making cross-sectional comparisons.

[205] B. Bosworth and S. Collins, "Capital flows to developing economies: implications for savings and investment", *Brookings Papers on Economic Activity,* 1 (Washington, D.C.), 1999, pp. 143-169.

[206] The theoretical and empirical evidence that FDI is a safer form of finance for countries that are unable to issue long-term debt in their own currency is reviewed by E. Fernandez-Arias and R. Hausmann, "Capital inflows and crisis: does the mix matter?", *Foreign Direct Investment Versus other Flows to Latin America* (Paris, OECD, 2001), pp. 93-110.

[207] According to UNCTAD, reported worldwide inflows of FDI declined in 2003 while outflows increased; in theory these should equal, but different reporting practices and timing issues result in different sums. UNCTAD, *World Investment Report 2004: The Shift Towards Services* (United Nations publication, Sales No. E.04.II.D.33).

Box 6.1.1

Debt sustainability in the low-income CIS countries

External debt sustainability remains an important policy issue in five low-income CIS countries (Armenia, Georgia, Kyrgyzstan, the Republic of Moldova and Tajikistan). While much has been accomplished in these five economies in terms of macroeconomic stability, fiscal consolidation, institutional development and resumption of growth, one area that remains a potential concern is external debt, which has reached very high levels in a number of them. From a situation of virtually no debt in 1992, these five countries have seen a rapid increase in the ratio of external debt to output during the late 1990s.[1] This increase in debt occurred even as their currencies appreciated and the average interest rate on the debt declined during this period. However, since 2001, driven by robust export performances, these countries have experienced sustained growth in real GDP. External debt service indicators have also improved in all five countries with a general decline in various debt ratios. As of June 2004, the ratio of gross external debt to GDP ranged from a low of 44 per cent in Georgia to a high of 111 per cent in Kyrgyzstan.[2] By the end of 2003, the debt service to exports ratio ranged from a low of 7.5 per cent in Armenia to a high of 20.9 per cent in Kyrgyzstan.[3]

Against this background, individual country performances have varied. While Armenia, Georgia and Tajikistan have grown out of their debt problems, Kyrgyzstan and the Republic of Moldova continue to have debt indicators that are sources of concern for both the national policy makers and the creditors.

Country performances

Buoyed by a favourable debt restructuring and strong economic growth resulting from, among other factors, structural reform, external debt is expected to remain fiscally sustainable in the medium term in Armenia, Georgia and Tajikistan. Armenia concluded a favourable debt restructuring in 2003. For Georgia, the conclusion of an agreement with the IMF paved the way for a Paris Club rescheduling on Houston terms in July 2004.[4] The recently concluded debt-for-equity swap agreement between Russia and Tajikistan will result in a significant reduction of debt service ratios in the future as this agreement implies the cancellation of the Russian debt, which accounts for about a third of Tajikistan's total debt stock.

In Kyrgyzstan, on the other hand, more than half of its external debt is owed to multilateral organizations, while bilateral debts account for about one third. The scheduled debt service weighs heavily on the budget, absorbing about one third of total revenue and constraining the development of social protection and poverty reduction programmes. This debt overhang could be potentially discouraging to many foreign investors. The government has recently approved a debt reduction strategy which calls for a streamlining of the public investment programme, accepting new loans only with a high grant element, and a programme of debt repayments using potential proceeds from privatization, debt equity swaps and other sources.

Although the stock of public and publicly guaranteed debt in the Republic of Moldova as a ratio of GDP has seen a recent decrease, debt service obligations absorb over 40 per cent of central government expenditures, reducing resources available for social expenditures in particular and for the country's development in general.[5] More than half of the outstanding public and publicly guaranteed debt is owed to IFIs, while debt to bilateral official donors represents about another quarter.[6] Although recent *non-concessional* debt restructurings with commercial and bilateral creditors have provided temporary cash flow relief, they have increased future debt service obligations. There is a potential risk that the substantial financing gap will be difficult to meet, while remaining current on debt service obligations. This raises questions regarding Moldova's capability to meet these obligations in full, without seeking debt rescheduling and/or debt relief. However, there are some encouraging signs pointing to a possible increase in the country's trend output growth in the medium term. Relatively modest FDI inflows have contributed to an improving export performance in recent years while shipments to western Europe have increased. Further, the authorities intend to intensify cooperation with the EU within the framework of the Stability Pact for south-east Europe and through a closer association in 2007 when neighboring Romania joins the EU. This could provide the Republic of Moldova with a much needed anchor for its systemic reforms that would enhance significantly the business environment and make economic development more sustainable.

Debt reduction strategy

A major motivation for debt relief arises from the presumption that a deleterious interaction exists between a heavy debt burden (or a debt overhang) and economic growth. The widely discussed "debt overhang theory" suggests that a heavy debt burden creates a disincentive for private investment due to concerns for future taxes and/or debt-induced crises. This reduces investment spending leading to a slowdown in economic growth. The cycle continues with further reduction in investment following the economic slowdown, an increase in the debt-income ratio, and a reinforcement of the disincentive effect, which ultimately leads to stagnation.

The healthiest way out of the debt trap is strong economic growth. Since 2001, these five countries have experienced strong growth, which has eased the debt situation in most of them. The major challenge for these governments will be to sustain the pace of growth and maintain macroeconomic stability by making the necessary structural reforms.

In addition, the governments have recognized the importance of a debt reduction strategy, including strong fiscal adjustment, and a number of them have already embarked on the process. External debt sustainability in these countries requires a delicate balance between the potentially conflicting needs to spend more on health, education, infrastructure and other poverty reduction initiatives, while at the same time maintaining a tight fiscal stance. In order to meet this challenge, a debt reduction strategy

Box 6.1.1 (concluded)

Debt sustainability in the low-income CIS countries

should include, among others: a substantial fiscal adjustment and strengthening of public finance institutions, including tax policy changes with a view to broadening the tax base and strengthening and simplifying the tax and customs administration to improve compliance and governance;[7] acceleration of structural reforms that support growth and poverty reduction;[8] ongoing work with IFIs and bilateral donors to attract technical assistance,[9] as well as *concessional loans* and grants consistent with commitments made with respect to attainment of the Millenium Development Goals; and not contracting any new *non-concessional* debt.[10]

The attraction of non-debt sources of financing, in particular foreign direct investment, should be deemed a policy priority. This requires sustained efforts to improve the business climate, which would also have a positive impact on growth rates, thus reducing the relative debt burden. Privatization can obviously play an important role in this area. However, the divestiture of state assets must take place within the framework of well-designed programmes to avoid the revenue damaging effects associated with distress sales.

Notwithstanding the recent improved economic performance, the downside risk arises from a high concentration of exports in commodities like gold in Kyrgyzstan, aluminium in Tajikistan and diamond polishing in Armenia, and potential external liabilities from the stock of energy sector arrears in Georgia (up to 6 per cent of GDP and 18 per cent of exports in 2003) and the Republic of Moldova (6 per cent of GDP and 12 per cent of exports in 2003).[11] One possible way to meet this downside risk would be through export diversification in Armenia, Kyrgyzstan and Tajikistan.[12]

While strong economic growth based on structural reform coupled with successful implementation of a debt strategy programme have eased the debt situation in Armenia, Georgia and Tajikistan by making it fiscally sustainable, Kyrgyzstan and the Republic of Moldova will continue to have debt indicators that are close to the thresholds established under the enhanced Heavily Indebted Poor Countries (HIPC) Initiative of the IMF and World Bank. These two countries will require additional assistance in the form of debt relief and highly *concessional* financing in order to achieve debt sustainability and sustained economic growth.[13]

A *non-concessional* flow rescheduling under the Paris Club Houston terms would only defer the problem for the time being, as it would only temporarily relieve the liquidity constraint by providing cash relief. It may even make the situation more difficult on a cash basis as debt service would suddenly jump back to high levels at the end of the consolidation period. Large amounts of *concessional* financing and grants under the Paris Club Naples terms, on the other hand, would result in smaller financing gaps so that debt sustainability indicators would keep declining and return to a sustainable level. Nevertheless, in order to avoid vulnerability to internal and external shocks, the potential debt relief must also be accompanied by cautious external borrowing and maintenance of official reserves coverage at levels significantly higher than those in other CIS countries.

---

[1]   Lending to most of the CIS-5 countries was more restricted before 1995 due to political instability and internal military conflicts. For a detailed discussion of the factors leading to debt accumulation in these countries, see UNECE, *Economic Survey of Europe, 2001 No. 1*, pp. 159-163.

[2]   UNECE Statistical Database.

[3]   International Monetary Fund and World Bank, *Recent Policies and Performance of the Low-income CIS Countries. An Update of the CIS-7 Initiative* (Washington, D.C.), 23 April 2004, p. 15.

[4]   The Paris Club refers to the meetings between government creditors, mainly OECD countries and debtor countries under the auspices of the French government. For a brief history of debt relief provided under different terms of the Paris Club see, among others, W. Easterly, "How did highly-indebted poor countries become highly indebted? Reviewing two decades of debt relief", *World Development*, Vol. 30, No. 10, October 2002, pp. 1677-1696.

[5]   Latest figures from the National Bank of Moldova show that, at the current exchange rate, the ratio of public and publicly guaranteed debt to GDP has decreased from 49 per cent in 2003 to 36 per cent in June 2004 [www.bnm.org/english/docs/comments/108_3659.pdf].

[6]   National Bank of Moldova.

[7]   Fiscal consolidation through expenditure cuts may be counterproductive as this may suppress growth. So the main focus should be on raising revenue without risking negative implications on economic activity. As emphasized in previous issues and in this *Survey* (see chap. 5), a major concern in this regard is the low efficiency of tax collection.

[8]   The acceleration of domestic structural reforms remains an essential ingredient of a strategy oriented towards reducing the debt burden and serving to unlock the necessary support from the IFIs and other creditors.

[9]   A relatively small amount of external aid in terms of technical assistance focused on raising the efficiency of tax collection could have very high returns.

[10]   The World Bank granted IDA-only status to these countries in 2000. These countries also have access to *concessional* resources from the IMF, including those under the Poverty Reduction and Growth Facility. For official creditors as a group, the grant element of new loan commitments to these countries jumped from around half in the late 1990s to about three fourths in 2003.

[11]   For these figures, see International Monetary Fund and World Bank, op. cit.

[12]   On the benefits of diversification, see chap. 1.2(iii).

[13]   For example, without further rescheduling, the ratio of debt service to fiscal revenue in Kyrgyzstan would increase from 17 per cent in 2004 to 28 per cent in 2005.

slightly above the rate over the last two years. FDI inflows into the EU-8 declined considerably in 2003 to $11.3 billion from $22.6 billion in 2002; in the last four quarters inflows continued at the lower rate and amounted to $12.7 billion. Although it rose 21 per cent (year-on-year) during the first six months of 2004 ($7.9 billion), FDI remains at a significantly lower level than during the 1999-2002 period. This decline, however, was not the result of any general disenchantment with the economic prospects of the EU-8, but a reflection of the general unwinding of the privatization process, primarily in the Czech Republic, Hungary and Slovakia. Over the last year, FDI inflows as a per cent of GDP were particularly large for Estonia (8.9 per cent) and particularly low for the EU-8's richest member, Slovenia (0.9 per cent), which has not encouraged FDI. Cyprus and Malta received significant FDI inflows amounting to 8.6 and 7.6 per cent of their respective GDPs.

FDI likely to increase

For a number of reasons FDI inflows into the EU-10 are expected to increase in the coming years. A stronger world economy is likely to generate additional corporate profits and thus the world supply of investible funds for FDI is likely to increase. The attractiveness of the EU-10 as a location for FDI should also increase with EU membership, since the business climate has improved now that they have adopted the full body of EU law. In the immediate years after accession, FDI inflows increased significantly in Portugal and Spain but not in Greece. The provision of €21.5 billion of EU Structural Funds for infrastructure enhancement over the 2004-2006 period is likely to crowd-in additional private investment. In order to fulfil the government deficit and debt level requirements of the Maastrict Treaty for euro adoption, a number of countries are likely to privatize additional public companies as a way to obtain funds. The ability to obtain funds in this manner raises the possibility of "excessive privatization" where companies are privatized not on grounds of economic efficiency but to meet fiscal revenue requirements. In addition, several of the EU-10 have lowered corporate tax rates from already low rates, as a means of attracting FDI. There are, however, aspects of EU membership that could act to reduce FDI inflows, such as higher labour and environmental standards that could increase the costs of operating in the new member states.

The belief that FDI can be an important factor contributing to growth is well established, although the empirical evidence is more nuanced than is generally believed and the evidence for technological spillovers to domestic firms is weak. Undoubtedly, FDI is like other aspects of international integration such as trade openness, in that a country needs to have in place the appropriate domestic institutions in order to fully benefit from it. For example, regression analysis finds that the benefits to growth of FDI depend on the trade openness of the economy; the real advantage of FDI appears to lie

in its ability to promote trade integration with the rest of the world.[208] For the EU-8 countries, there was a negative relationship between the level of FDI (as a percentage of GDP) and the real growth rate during 1994-2001. There was also no statistical relationship between FDI and the level of gross fixed investment. It has been argued that the normal pattern of FDI in increasing investment did not hold for these countries due to the unique circumstances that prevailed during the transition phase. More specifically, FDI during this period was dominated by acquisitions related to privatization rather than greenfield investment, and the proceeds were largely consumed, often by financing government expenditure.[209]

FDI inflows (as a per cent of GDP) into the south-east European economies have been increasing over the last several years, and during the first six months of 2004 the FDI inflow percentage of GDP was greater than the rate in either 2002 or 2003 in all of the south-east European economies except Croatia and Serbia and Montenegro. Over the last four quarters, FDI inflows as a per cent of GDP were similar for the EU-8, south-east Europe and the CIS at about 2.5 per cent of GDP. However, with the exception of Turkey, south-east European inflows were almost twice as large as those to the other regions, and each of these countries had inflows greater than the EU-10 average of 2.7 per cent. This is surprising given the historic opportunities present in the EU-10 and the political uncertainty and more limited progress with institutional reform in the south-east European countries (excluding Turkey). One explanation is that although the inflows were relatively large, the cumulative stock of FDI inflows (23.7 per cent of GDP excluding Turkey) in the south-east European countries is lower than in the EU-10 (33.1 per cent), and that there were more privatizations to attract inflows. FDI inflows were particularly large in Bulgaria (8.7 per cent of GDP) and Serbia and Montenegro (7.3 per cent). Bosnia and Herzegovina is noteworthy for its very large net capital inflows amounting to 37 per cent of its GDP; however, only 6 percentage points of this consisted of FDI inflows, the rest being composed largely of capital transfers and long-term borrowing. FDI inflows into Turkey over the last 12 months were quite low, at only 0.9 per cent of GDP; this is only slightly above the low annual rates in 2002 and 2003.

FDI inflows into the CIS have been on a moderate upward trend since 2000. Over the last 12 months, inward FDI into the CIS was essentially the same as the EU-8 average of 2.5 per cent of GDP. However, the CIS average is dominated by Russia whose FDI inflow was quite low at 1.3 per cent of GDP; for the CIS excluding

---

[208] OECD, *Open Markets Matter: The Benefits of Trade and Investment Liberalization* (Paris), 1998.

[209] J. Mencinger, "Does foreign direct investment always enhance economic growth?", *Kyklos*, Vol. 56, Issue 4, 2003, pp. 491-508. In some cases the proceeds were also used to pay off foreign debt.

Russia, their inflows amounted to 6.5 per cent of GDP, well over twice the level for the EU-8. Cumulative FDI inflows as a per cent of GDP for the CIS excluding Russia are only slightly below the EU-8 level. However, Russia's cumulative FDI inflow of 8.2 per cent is the lowest of any EME except Turkey and its FDI inflow per capita was only about one tenth of that of the EU-8.[210] Several countries, including Armenia, Azerbaijan and Georgia (averaging 30.3 per cent) and Kazakhstan (8.5 per cent) attracted large amounts of FDI relative to GDP during 2003QIII-2004QII. Azerbaijan's FDI inflow to GDP ratio of 50.4 per cent over the last year is one of the highest in the world by this measure. Except for Azerbaijan and Kazakhstan, all the other CIS members have cumulative per capita FDI inflows similar to or less than Russia.

As countries develop they initially receive inflows of FDI; only after reaching a relatively higher level of development do significant outflows begin. Except for Russia, this pattern appears to be holding for the ECE emerging market economies, all of which have very small FDI outflows. Russia is unique among the EME in that its FDI outflow has generally exceeded its inflow. According to UNCTAD, Russia's estimated stock of outward FDI of $52 billion at the end of 2003 was approximately equal to its inward stock of $53 billion.[211] Russian outflows of FDI are concentrated in the CIS and the EU as their firms attempt to establish a foothold in these markets. Since a significant amount of Russian outward FDI is undertaken by state-owned enterprises, some of this investment may be influenced by geopolitical rather than purely economic considerations. Recent empirical analysis suggests that FDI outflows can also be beneficial for the parent country.[212] Russia, Ukraine and Uzbekistan were net exporters of capital over the last year. Because of political uncertainty, they continue to have significant capital flight (see box 5.1.1).

More generally, the investment climate in the CIS could be improved with additional institutional reform. Extensive government regulation combined with weak public administration, barriers to entry, ineffective bankruptcy procedures and weak corporate governance continue to be cited as impediments to FDI.[213] An additional factor limiting investment in Russia and the other CIS oil exporters may be due to limited

opportunities as a result of the "Dutch Disease", whereby rouble appreciation due to booming oil exports has lowered the competitiveness of, and thus the desire for, investment by firms in other sectors. Russia's and to a lesser degree the other CIS oil exporters' need for FDI is not based upon the need for capital funds, for which they have sufficient amounts of their own, but on the need for foreign management and technology, and as a mechanism to increase domestic competition.

Although the poorer CIS countries were able to attract reasonable levels of FDI over the last year, they face a major challenge in continuing to attract FDI: they lack natural resources; they are far from the European market, which will always limit to some extent their trade with this market; and they are unlikely to become members of the EU in the foreseeable future. For them, faster institutional reform would be desirable. Regional cooperation to improve transport links among the CIS members is also needed. Regional trade integration with the other CIS members, as well as WTO membership could help to promote FDI and economic growth by creating larger markets where economies of scale can be exploited. However, even this option may only provide limited benefits for the smaller CIS nations since a number of theoretical analyses using core-periphery trade and investment models[214] often show that the benefits of integration generally go to the core area; in this case that would be Russia.

6.2 International trade of eastern Europe

Merchandise trade booms in the new EU member countries...

The continued buoyancy of global economic growth gave a strong impetus to the trade of the enlarged European Union, especially in the first half of 2004, both with third country partners and among the member states themselves.[215] The new EU members from central Europe and the Baltic region were important contributors to this growth (table 6.2.1, chart 6.2.1): the expansion of their aggregate exports and imports accelerated in the first eight months of 2004, growing in volume at annualized rates of 16-18 per cent, well above the EU-25 average.[216] In

---

[210] The low level of FDI inflows into Russia is discussed in detail in *OECD Investment Policy Reviews: Russian Federation* (Paris), 2004.

[211] UNCTAD, op. cit., annex tables B.1-B.4. However, the UNCTAD data do not reflect recent upward revisions in Russian FDI inflows, which if included, would give Russia a small net cumulative inflow.

[212] B. Lee, *FDI from Developing Countries: A Vector for Trade and Development* (Paris, OECD, 2002).

[213] C. Shiells, *FDI and the Investment Climate in the CIS Countries*, IMF Policy Discussion Paper PDP/03/5 (Washington, D.C.), November 2003. Standard & Poor's still characterizes Russia as needing significant structural reform, including judicial, administrative and financial sector reforms.

[214] This refers to a class of widely used trade models which include increasing returns, agglomeration effects and transportation costs; this model was initially developed by P. Krugman, "Increasing returns and economic geography", *Journal of Political Economy*, Vol. 99, 1991, pp. 483-499.

[215] An assessment of the overall impact of accession on the new EU members' trade within the EU in 2004, however, remains difficult due in part to changes in the trade reporting systems after May 2004 (box 6.2.1) and also because of the one-off effects of trade liberalization on "sensitive" goods.

[216] According to Eurostat data, total EU-25 exports to third countries increased more than 10 per cent in the first six months of 2004 (imports, above 6 per cent) in volume while intra-EU transactions grew by 6 per cent, year-on-year. Allowing for the strengthening of the euro and export price developments, year-on-

---

Box 6.2.1

Foreign trade statistics in the new EU member countries after accession

Foreign trade reporting practices have changed on several occasions in most of the new EU member countries during the last 10 to 15 years, particularly as regards the publication of official trade data according to the *general trade* or *special trade* reporting systems. The former system embraces all goods entering or leaving the economic territory of a country with the exception of simple transit trade; the latter system excludes goods from a foreign country, which are received into customs warehouses unless they subsequently go into free circulation. By 2004, almost all countries were using the *special trade* concept for their official foreign trade statistics. Lithuania's foreign trade, however, was reported as *general trade*, while Slovenia used an "extended" version of *special trade*. Until their accession to the EU, foreign trade statistics in the new member countries were collected by the customs authorities on the basis of customs declarations, and processed and published by the national statistical offices.

Upon accession to the EU internal customs borders were eliminated and customs data on trade between individual member countries of the EU ceased to be collected at the border. To continue recording this intra-union portion of foreign trade, a system (Intrastat) based on information collected from enterprises on their trade transactions with EU partners was adopted by the new EU members. Trade with non-EU countries is recorded on the basis of customs data according to the *special trade* concept and are uniformly reported by national statistical offices as so-called Extrastat data. Since May 2004, the national statistical offices have also published data for total foreign trade based on various adjustments to reconcile data from these two, not fully compatible systems. While work on compiling comparable data in historical time series is still in progress, Eurostat, in collaboration with national statistical offices, has already published estimates of intra-EU trade for the new EU member countries since 1999.

The major sources of incompatibility between recent and earlier foreign trade data

Intra-EU statistics are compiled according to the EU's own definitions and not on a *general* or *special trade* basis. Intrastat's coverage is closer to the wider concept of *general trade*; thus, currently reported values for trade with the EU-25 may well be higher, in some cases notably so (Estonia), than those based on the previous methodology.

In turn, the coverage of intra-EU trade obtained through enterprise surveys is not as complete since data are not collected from a large number of small businesses (non-VAT-payers). In Hungary, for instance, some two thirds of registered enterprises (representing, however, less than 2 per cent of trade value) do not report on their trade with partners in the EU. Further, with the introduction of Intrastat, almost none of the border trade with the neighbouring regions is captured. National statistical offices, however, make some adjustments for this "missing trade", as well as for enterprises' late responses to the surveys.

Another difference between the earlier and current systems is in the partner country allocation. For exports (Extrastat) and dispatches (Intrastat), the trading partner continues to be the country of final destination (as far as it is known at the time of dispatch). For imports, the trading partner is supposed to be the country of origin in the case of extra-EU partners, and the country of consignment in the case of intra-EU trade. Under the previous system all imports were allocated uniformly to the country of origin (the practice of most of the new EU members) or according to the country of consignment. After May 2004, some of the new EU member countries started reporting imports on a country of consignment basis for extra-EU trade, which has made the comparability of the geographical structure of trade over time more problematic. The difference between imports recorded by country of origin or country of consignment can be quite considerable: for example, in the first quarter of 2004, the share of Lithuania's imports from the EU-15 accounted for 41.4 per cent of the total according to the country of origin method, and for 46.5 per cent according to the country of consignment method; similarly, its share of imports from Russia varied between 24.4 per cent and 20.3 per cent under the two procedures (this could imply the re-export of Russian goods by EU countries). Thus, since the Intrastat rules are applied henceforth to intra-EU imports, in the case of Lithuania these are relatively inflated if compared with those from Russia.

Most of these trade data problems will eventually be resolved, but at present they point to the need for caution in assessing the foreign trade performance of the new EU member countries.

---

addition to favourable external demand, certain one-off effects of the full trade liberalization that occurred at the date of accession to the EU supported this growth.

An increasing number of east European producers appear to have succeeded in reaping the benefits of the single EU market. At the same time the big exporters,

mainly firms with significant foreign participation, were able to take advantage of the well-established EU commercial ties with third countries.[217] Moreover, the

---

year increases of 8-9 per cent in euros in July-September suggest continued growth in trade volumes. Eurostat, *Euro-indicators,* News Release STAT/04/137, 22 November 2004 and UNECE secretariat computations, based on short-term indicators of external trade available at [europa.eu.int/comm/eurostat/newcronos/].

---

[217] The extension to the new members of Mutual Recognition Agreements (MRAs) between the EU and the third countries is a case in point. Prior to the enlargement, the EU undertook measures to ensure that all its trade partners would grant the same treatment to the new members from 1 May 2004. However, there were some delays: for instance, the Russian Federation, after intense negotiations, agreed to the extension of the Russia-EU "Partnership and Cooperation Agreement" to the 10 new EU member countries

TABLE 6.2.1

International trade of European emerging market economies, 2003-2004

(Rates of change and shares, per cent)

	Merchandise exports (growth rates)		Merchandise imports (growth rates)		Trade balance (per cent of GDP)	
	2003	2004 Jan.-Sep.ᵃ	2003	2004 Jan.-Sep.ᵃ	2003	2004 Jan.-Jun.
New EU members	29.1	30.6	26.1	28.5	-7.0	-7.1
Cyprus	9.3	9.5	9.8	29.2	-27.8	-31.6
Czech Republic	26.6	33.8	25.9	30.7	-2.9	-1.5
Estonia	31.6	31.7	35.4	35.3	-21.6	-24.9
Hungary	23.7	27.0	26.4	27.0	-6.1	-6.7
Latvia	26.2	18.4	28.9	17.2	-21.1	-21.9
Lithuania	30.7	30.3	27.3	28.7	-14.1	-14.7
Malta	11.1	10.2	19.8	15.1	-18.3	-20.7
Poland	30.6	35.7	23.4	29.6	-6.9	-6.8
Slovakia	51.7	28.0	35.9	29.9	-2.0	-1.5
Slovenia	23.3	21.7	26.7	23.4	-3.9	-4.8
South-east Europe	28.4	31.3	31.8	36.4	-13.1	-16.4
Albania ᵇ	35.2	12.4	24.1	0.2	-23.1	-16.5
Bosnia and Herzegovina	35.4	30.8	22.1	21.1	-46.6	-42.0
Bulgaria	30.7	28.0	35.9	30.6	-16.6	-19.8
Croatia	25.7	29.9	32.4	18.1	-27.9	-26.3
Romania	27.0	33.2	34.4	35.5	-11.2	-13.2
Serbia and Montenegro	11.5	21.1	18.8	40.9	-25.4	-30.2
The former Yugoslav Republic of Macedonia	22.2	20.2	15.3	22.1	-20.1	-22.8
Turkey	30.0	32.3	33.3	42.4	-9.2	-13.4
Memorandum items:						
EU-25 (extra-EU trade)	17.4	20.6	17.9	19.2	-0.4	-0.6
Baltic states	30.0	28.1	30.0	27.4	-18.1	-19.3
Central Europe	29.5	31.2	26.2	28.9	-5.4	-5.1
South-east Europe without Turkey	26.5	30.1	30.3	29.8	-19.8	-21.4

Source: UNECE secretariat calculations, based on national statistics and Eurostat data.

Note: Foreign trade growth is measured in current dollar values. Trade balances are related to GDP at current prices.

ᵃ Over same period of the previous year.

ᵇ January-June instead of January-September.

effects of accession to the EU were accentuated by enlarged export capacities (Estonia)[218] or the improved cost competitiveness of exporters. The depreciation of the dollar against the euro, as well as the currencies of the

---

on 27 April 2004, but the accord only came into effect after its final ratification on 6 November 2004. As of 1 May 2004, the 10 new EU member states started to apply the EU's Common Commercial Policy in its entirety, including the EU's bilateral trade agreements, its multilateral commitments, its trade safeguards and, especially, its common external tariff. The external tariffs in the new member states were expected to fall from an average of 9 per cent to 4 per cent. European Commission: Press Releases, *Trade Implications of EU Enlargement: Facts and Figures,* MEMO/04/23 (Brussels), 4 February 2004 [europa.eu.int/rapid/].

[218] See chap 3.2. In 2003, there was also a very large increase in FDI-financed productive capacities in the automotive sector of Slovakia, which helps to account for the large increases in export volume in the second half of 2003 and in the beginning of 2004 (chart 6.2.1).

new EU members, boosted dollar-denominated imports earlier in the year. The fall of the dollar also mitigated the impact of rising dollar prices for fuels and further dampened the prices of intermediate goods from China and other Asian countries linked to the dollar. This helped to raise or at least to safeguard the profit margins of the EU-8 exporters, particularly in countries where their exchange rates appreciated in real effective terms (chart 6.2.2).

Aggregate exports of the new EU member countries to partners outside the EU soared by some 25 per cent in volume in the first eight months of 2004, compared with the same period of 2003, while their dollar value increased by more than one third (for individual countries, see chart 6.2.1). The CIS (largely Russia) and south-east European markets, followed by the developed economies outside the EU, absorbed most of this export growth. This reflects the strong growth of demand in these markets, coupled in some cases with lower trade barriers after 1 May 2004. In the Czech Republic, Hungary, Slovakia and Slovenia exports of capital goods to non-EU partners rose by 35 to 55 per cent in volume (in Estonia, they doubled) in the first eight month of 2004. Foreign owned firms generated the bulk of this increase. In Lithuania and Poland, firms with foreign participation were mainly important in increasing exports of consumption goods.[219]

Merchandise exports to countries within the enlarged EU also rose at two-digit rates in volume, taking the EU-8 producers' market share of the EU-25 to 8.5 per cent in May-August 2004. This was a 1 percentage point gain over the same period of 2003. In this trade, a notable development was a strong pick-up in exporting by small- and medium-size enterprises.[220] The removal of customs barriers (including quotas) and other restrictions has especially boosted exports of agricultural products, food and beverages and some other "sensitive" goods. In Poland, for example, reported food exports to the EU grew by more than 50 per cent in dollar value in May-August

---

[219] According to the Eurostat methodology, the broad economic category "consumption goods" refers to the BEC's "consumer goods" grouped together with passenger cars.

[220] In Hungary, for instance, exports from small enterprises (5-49 employees) grew by 38 per cent in real terms, year-on-year, during the first half of 2004 (Kopint-Datorg, *Economic Trends in Eastern Europe,* No. 3 (Budapest), Autumn 2004, p. 45.) The much more active participation of firms at the various international fairs is also a good indication of this development: for example, at the biggest food industry fair in eastern Europe, *Polagra – Food 2004,* held in October in Poland, the number of exhibitors from eastern Europe was 30 per cent higher than in 2003 (Ministry of Agriculture and Rural Development of Poland, *Food and Polagra International Fairs 2004,* 10 October 2004 [www.minrol.gov.pl]). A similar experience is attested by SME development agencies in many other east European countries.

CHART 6.2.1

Merchandise trade in the new EU member states, 2001-2004QII

(Trade balance in million euros, percentage changes of export and import volumes over the same quarter of the previous year)

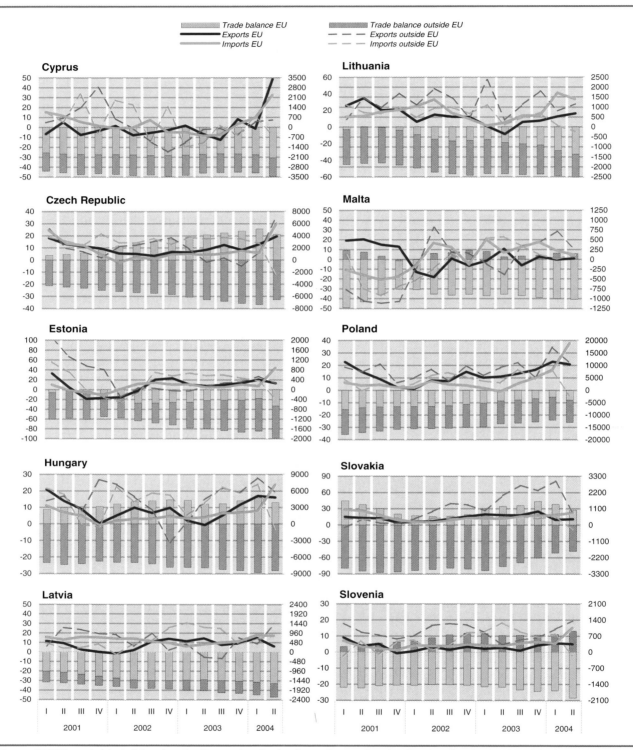

Source: UNECE secretariat calculations, based on Eurostat data of trade values and seasonally and working day adjusted trade volume index (2000=100).

Note: Merchandise trade balances in the final month of the quarter cumulated over 12 months.

CHART 6.2.2

Real effective exchange rates in the ECE emerging market economies, 2001-2004QIII
(Indices, 2001QI=100)

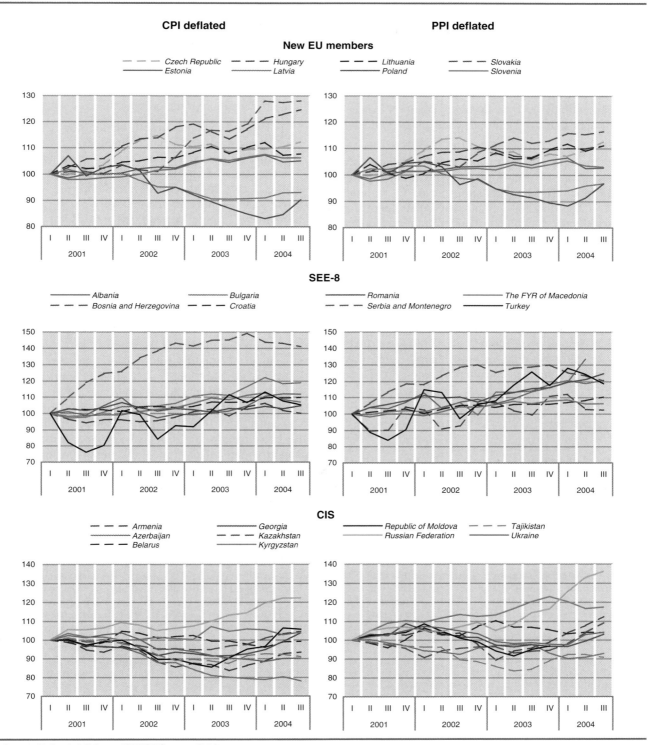

Source: National statistics and UNECE Common Database.

Note: The real effective exchange rates were computed from the nominal exchange rates against the euro and the dollar, deflated by the domestic and European Union or United States consumer and producer price indices. In the case of the CIS, changes against the Russian rouble and Russia's consumer and producer price indices were also taken into account. The shares of the EU and rest of the world (and Russia for the CIS) in total exports of individual ECE emerging market economies were used to determine the euro, the dollar and the rouble trade weights, respectively. An increase in the index denotes real appreciation and vice versa.

2004, year-on-year.[221] Accession to the EU has also given a strong stimulus to border trade.[222] Aided by a perceptible price advantage, comparable quality and, in some cases, consumers' desire for novelty, the presence of food and agricultural products from central Europe and the Baltic countries has increased not only in the neighbouring Austrian, German, Italian and Scandinavian markets, but also in the more distant markets of France, Ireland, Portugal and Spain. Other, generally labour-intensive consumer goods, in particular clothing and footwear, continue to face strong competition in the EU from cheaper south-east European and Asian products.[223]

The boom in the new EU member countries' imports in 2004 was driven not only by the growth of domestic demand but also by the needs of an expanding export sector. These trends are expected to continue in 2005. In the first four months of 2004 imports also increased due to stockpiling in anticipation of changes in administrative rules and customs duties upon accession.[224] Although the boom in imports has abated somewhat since then, their volume in the first eight months of 2004 was still some 19 per cent higher than in the same period of 2003. While lagging behind exports in volume, the dollar value of imports increased more or less in line with exports as the rise in world commodity prices began to inflate import expenditures in the second quarter. Moreover, intra-EU imports rose sharply after 1 May 2004,[225] with capital and consumption goods accelerating

in the Czech Republic, Estonia, Hungary, Poland and Slovakia. The terms of trade deteriorated for the region as a whole, and the aggregate merchandise trade deficit increased both in dollars and euros, and in relation to GDP (table 6.2.1, chart 6.2.1). By the end of August, the cumulative 12 months of deficits were substantially higher than in 2003 in Hungary, Slovenia and the three Baltic countries; in Poland the deficit increased slightly in dollar terms but fell in terms of euros, while in the Czech Republic and Slovakia the deficits shrank because of a sharp deceleration of import growth.

The merchandise exports of the new EU member countries are expected to continue to grow rapidly in 2005, partly because of the increased opportunities for a broader range of businesses to trade on the internal EU market. This could mitigate the dampening effect of a possible weakening in the recovery in the major EU economies. Some setback for east European textile (including clothing) exporters, however, can be anticipated due to the expiration of the international textile quota system on 31 December 2004.[226] In contrast, access to the EU subsidy system for east European EU exporters of agricultural products, and additional financing from structural funds, could boost this sector's exports in both the short and medium term.

Immediately after accession there was a sharp slowdown of imports from non-EU partners, but this is unlikely to last long, as demand, particularly for intermediate goods from the export sector, is expected to continue to grow rapidly in 2005.[227] With housing and consumer credit more readily available, a rising demand for consumption goods is also expected to further boost imports, particularly since all import restrictions on purchases from other EU countries were abolished on accession,[228] and protection against imports from third

---

[221] The meat industry, which is the biggest sector of the food industry in Poland, nearly doubled its average monthly export sales in May-August 2004. According to Eurostat, food is Europe's second largest manufacturing sector: for most new EU member states food industries account for more than 20 per cent of total manufacturing value added, while the average for the EU-25 is 11.5 per cent. Eurostat, "The food industry in Europe", *Statistics in Focus: Industry, Trade and Services,* 39/2004 [epp.eurostat.cec.eu.int].

[222] According to some estimates, trade turnover on the open air markets on Poland's western border is currently some 40 per cent higher than before May 2004. *Rzeczpospolita,* 25 October 2004.

[223] In fact, clothing and footwear exports to the EU from Poland, Slovenia and a few other EU-8 countries stagnated or even declined in May-August 2004, year-on-year. Most affected were exports to the eastern EU partners since, after accession, access to these markets became free or less protected vis-à-vis south-east European and Asian producers (see the subsection below on south-east European trade).

[224] These increases were clearly reflected in a surge in the volume of imports of consumer and capital goods originating from non-EU markets: in some cases, the EU import regime was seen as less favourable than that applied by central European and Baltic countries under bilateral trade agreements, which were to be cancelled upon accession to the EU, hence importers opted for an increase of inventories. In aggregate, seasonally adjusted imports from non-EU-25 partners in March and April 2004 were 28 per cent above the average monthly levels in 2003 for consumer goods and 32 per cent up for capital goods; Czech, Estonian, Latvian and Slovak importers were most active in stockpiling consumer goods, while imports of capital goods by Polish and Slovene businesses saw rises of some 50-80 per cent and those of Latvia more than doubled.

[225] The change in the recording of imports from "country of origin" to "'country of consignment" may have brought some loss of

comparability of the statistical data (box 6.2.1), and so some of these changes may eventually have to be revised.

[226] The European Commission has prepared a plan, including a proposal for the creation of a special reserve fund within the structural funds that could be used to alleviate the impact of quota-free trade and help the textile industry to restructure and modernize. European Commission: *Trade Issues,* Textile sector: legislation, reports and texts (Brussels), 12 and 26 October 2004 [trade-info.cec.eu.int].

[227] Intermediate goods account for over 60 per cent of total non-EU imports in the eastern EU countries. In July-September these imports were some 30-40 per cent higher, year-on-year, in dollar value, in the three Baltic countries, and 10-15 per cent in Poland and Slovenia.

[228] In Poland, for instance, new regulations (regarding technical requirements and an obligatory verification system) are to be introduced early in 2005 in order to curtail imports of used cars that inundated the Polish market after its previous import restrictions ended on 1 May 2004: nearly 500,000 used cars were imported from the EU in May-September, 30 times the number of the previous four months. (Since May, more than half a billion zlotys in excise duty has been levied on imports of used cars.) These imports badly affected locally-produced new car sales, which according to some estimates could be about 20 per cent down in 2004, year-on-year. *Gazeta Wyborcza,* 16 October 2004, and "Poland this week", *Reuters News Service,* 18 October 2004.

countries was generally reduced by adoption of the common EU commercial policy.

Thus, if oil and other major commodity prices stay at recent levels, the merchandise trade balances of many EU-8 countries are likely to deteriorate further, raising problems for policy makers. Debates about how to improve export competitiveness and provide assistance in penetrating foreign markets remain high on the agenda in all of the new EU countries. However, the instruments available to the authorities in the short run are rather limited: freezes on public sector wages have a limited impact, are highly unpopular and may lead to a drain of qualified labour from public services;[229] and interventions on the exchange rate market are often counterproductive, given the export sector's reliance on imported inputs.[230]

Trade of south-east European countries expands rapidly

In south-east Europe, the rapid acceleration of export and import growth in the first six months of 2004 (chart 6.2.3) seems to have abated slightly in the months that followed in some countries but gained further momentum in Bulgaria, Croatia, Serbia and Montenegro, and The former Yugoslav Republic of Macedonia. The rapid growth of exports mainly reflected strong foreign demand, but for Turkey and some of the western Balkan countries, the enlargement of the EU also provided better access to the markets of the new EU member countries.[231]

Relatively low labour costs in general, coupled with a degree of success in keeping wage increases below those of productivity in Bulgaria and Croatia, and more recently in Turkey (see chap. 4.2 above), have led to increased outsourcing orders by companies in the EU and other developed countries (traditionally in the clothing and footwear sectors and, more recently, in machinery and electronics). Low labour costs have also prompted foreign investors to increase productive and infrastructure capacities in the four EU candidate countries. Increased economic stability and the approach of EU accession (Bulgaria and Romania) may have also helped to increase trade and attract FDI. The exports of the four EU candidate countries to all major partner groups increased rapidly, but those to trading partners in south-east Europe

---

[229] However, large increases in public sector wages tend to have a strong spillover effect on the private sector in these countries. For instance, the escalation of wages in Hungarian industry in 2002-2003 (see sect. 3.2(ii) above) was prompted in part by increases in public sector wages.

[230] More details on the implications of fiscal and monetary policy on competitiveness in the medium to long term in the new EU member countries are presented in chap. 3.

[231] This improvement stems from the Turkey-EU agreement on Customs Union (in force since 1999) and from free EU market access extended to more than 80 per cent of exports from the western Balkan countries under the Stabilization and Association Process arrangements. Some of these countries did not have preferential trade arrangements with the countries that acceded to the EU on 1 May 2004, enjoying only MFN status until then.

CHART 6.2.3

Merchandise trade in south-east Europe, January 2001-September 2004

(Trade balance in billion euros, percentage changes of export and import values over same month of the previous year)

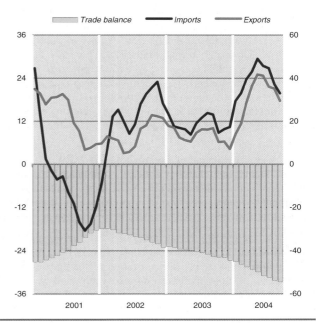

Source: National statistics and UNECE Common Database.

Note: Merchandise trade balances at the end of the month, cumulated over 12 months. Monthly year-on-year percentage changes for exports and imports based on the three-month moving average values in euros.

soared some 45 per cent in dollar value, thanks in part to improved regional cooperation.[232] The profit margins of exporters, however, continued to be rather tight in some of these countries, due in part to an appreciation of their domestic currencies (chart 6.2.2). This applied less to Turkey, where the terms of trade improved perceptibly in January-September 2004 as a result of higher export prices. Export prices also increased in Bulgaria, but were outpaced by the rise in import prices in the second and third quarters of 2004.[233]

Stronger regional cooperation (box 6.2.2) and improved access to the enlarged EU market under the EU-sponsored Stabilization and Association Process have supported the expansion of exports from the western Balkan countries. Their exports to other countries in the region and to the CIS grew most rapidly, while those to the EU and other developed market economies increased in dollar terms but stagnated or declined in euros (and probably in volume as well). The latter was mainly due to

---

[232] Several free trade agreements between Turkey and the south-east European countries as well as between the other three EU candidates and the western Balkan countries (box 6.2.2) came into force recently.

[233] Data on export and import price developments in 2004 in the other south-east European countries were not available at the time of writing this *Survey*.

Box 6.2.2

Towards a free trade area in south-east Europe

Since the Kosovo crisis in 1999 there have been several attempts to revive trade among the south-east European countries. With the active involvement of the international community, especially the EU, these attempts finally started to produce results under the auspices of the Stability Pact for South-eastern Europe. In June 2001, a Memorandum of Understanding (MoU) on Trade Liberalization and Facilitation was signed by Albania, Bosnia and Herzegovina, Bulgaria, Croatia, Romania, Serbia and Montenegro and The former Yugoslav Republic of Macedonia. In 2002, the Republic of Moldova joined these countries in the process of trade liberalization. Due mainly to political reasons, however, the south-east European countries did not adopt a multilateral approach to trade liberalization but resorted to negotiating a network of bilateral free trade agreements (FTAs) with the prospect of eventually creating a "virtual" free trade area in the region. In little more than three years a network of 28 bilateral free trade agreements was created (including five FTAs that had been signed prior to June 2001), and by September 2004, according to the Stability Pact Working Group on Trade Liberalization and Facilitation (WGT), 22 of these FTAs were in force. The MoU commitment to reach a 90 per cent threshold in terms of tariff lines and actual import value liberalization has been achieved in many of the FTAs that are in force and is within reach to the rest within the maximum six-year transitional period.[1]

Although the majority of the 28 FTAs were elaborated according to the same set of rules, they are not uniform in several important areas, including notably their coverage of agricultural goods, public procurement and services. Bilateral agreements have advantages in that they are easier to implement since only the two countries involved have to agree, but they do not lead to the same degree of integration that is likely to result from a free trade area or a customs union. It would therefore appear desirable to create some type of umbrella over all these FTAs with the aim of ensuring consistency and making the trade content rules less difficult to fulfil, a benefit desired by the domestic and international business community.

In 2004, recognizing the benefits of such a move and encouraged by the international community, the south-east European countries started to consider the next step in their regional integration process. Currently, three main alternatives are under discussion: (1) a simple harmonization of the existing FTAs under the auspices of the Stability Pact's WGT. This could be limited to a simple harmonization of the structure of the agreements (i.e. how the agreements are worded, chapters numbered, etc.) or could also involve harmonization of the provisions of the agreements; (2) an extension of CEFTA[2] towards the rest of the south-east European countries; and (3) creating a new South-east European Free Trade Area (SEEFTA).

The first alternative would be the least costly in terms of the managerial and administrative work involved, and would be the simplest and easiest to implement. It would also allow for at least a partial international supervision of its implementation. However, the economic benefits from such harmonization would be rather limited.

Expanding CEFTA would probably be less costly for the three existing members but would require the other five countries to incorporate their existing FTAs into a new Treaty (CEFTA), which, as it stands now, has in some cases a more restricted product coverage (e.g. agricultural products) and no provision concerning the new trade issues (services and public procurement) that are covered in many of the current FTAs. With the three current CEFTA member countries heading for EU accession, the elaboration of new provisions, however, is very unlikely. Admission to CEFTA, moreover, currently requires WTO membership, which is not an immediate prospect for Bosnia and Herzegovina or for Serbia and Montenegro.[3]

Creating a new free trade area, SEEFTA, would be a more difficult task but it might also provide more flexibility in fostering the regional integration process. If the process started with a simple harmonization of the existing FTAs, aligning them on the best available text, and moving on to the inclusion of provisions for other matters (services, public procurement, etc.), the result could be a larger and more attractive market for domestic and foreign businesses. If the existing CEFTA member countries (EU candidates) were uninterested in such an option, a SEEFTA could still be created among the remaining five countries as long as there appears to be a political will to cooperate on the issue.

The process of identifying the best ways to intensify regional integration is expected to continue under the auspices of the Stability Pact's Working Group. Until now, however, it has been difficult for the eight countries to agree on a common position on any of the above-mentioned alternatives. Their concerns appear to have been due more to political sensitivities rather than economic policy considerations. In any case, additional work is needed to ensure the actual implementation of the existing FTAs.

---

[1] Unless otherwise indicated, the factual information presented in this box has been obtained from materials available on the Stability Pact for South-eastern Europe website [www.stabilitypact.org/trade/].

[2] Since May 2004, CEFTA has consisted of three members (all EU candidates): Bulgaria, Croatia and Romania. The former Yugoslav Republic of Macedonia is currently negotiating accession to CEFTA.

[3] Both countries are actually loose unions of several autonomous entities with their separate markets, currencies, legislation and governing bodies, and have difficulty in presenting their common position in the WTO accession negotiations. (A two-track approach, allowing the separate entities to negotiate accession in parallel, was recently suggested by some WTO members in order to speed up the process.) Bosnia and Herzegovina loosely unites the Federation of Bosnia and Herzegovina (FBiH), Republika Srpska and the Brcko District; while the state union of Serbia and Montenegro, established in February 2003, actually represents two independent republics. In addition, Kosovo, which is part of Serbia, is at present under the authority of the United Nations Interim Administration (UNMIK). Since June 2004, UNMIK/Kosovo has been gradually integrated into the network of FTAs of south-east Europe.

supply-side constraints: recent setbacks to industrial output in Albania and The former Yugoslav Republic of Macedonia, under-investment in productive and infrastructure facilities, and the virtual absence of greenfield FDI in the region have held back the development of the export sector. However, there was an increase in outsourcing from EU firms that has mainly helped to boost textile and footwear exports from most of these countries.[234]

Rapid import growth in south-east Europe in 2004 reflected the strong growth of domestic demand, particularly in the four EU candidate countries. In the latter group, the exporting sectors' needs for capital and intermediate goods are being met by imports, but it was consumption goods that fuelled their growth in 2004, particularly in Turkey.[235] Imports of fuels and intermediate goods in the western Balkan countries have grown steadily in value (inflated in part by higher commodity prices on international markets). Imports of capital goods picked up most noticeably in Serbia and Montenegro due to inflows of FDI. However, the rise in imports of consumption goods – which account for at least one fifth of total merchandise imports in the western Balkans – have outpaced the other import categories.

Merchandise trade deficits, in dollars, increased across the region. In relation to GDP, the deficits were noticeably higher than a year earlier in five of the eight south-east European countries (table 6.2.1). Checking the rise of merchandise trade deficits is a difficult task, particularly in some of the west Balkan countries which are still recovering from the effects of armed conflict.

In the EU candidate countries, where the process of economic transformation is more advanced, the authorities have been able to deploy various monetary and fiscal policy instruments to curb the consumer demand for imports. This could include restrictions on credit, the abolition of certain incentives and tax breaks (already scheduled in Turkey), and so on. However, being closely tied to the EU commercial policies and parties to the WTO, they are less free to impose additional import

restrictions. Another important task facing policy makers in the region is to create an environment that will attract more FDI and enhance the competitiveness of domestic industries, thus helping them deal with a very difficult external environment. Textile producers and major exporters in several south-east European countries, especially Bulgaria, Romania and Turkey, could face such a challenge in early 2005 when the WTO Agreement on Textile and Clothing comes to the end.[236]

6.3 International trade of the CIS

In the first six months of 2004, year-on-year, the aggregate dollar value of international trade of the CIS region continued to expand significantly for the second year in a row (table 6.3.1).[237] The value of merchandise exports in the CIS increased by more than a quarter.[238] The improvement was largely the result of higher commodity prices as most CIS countries are highly dependent on foreign sales of crude oil, oil products, natural gas, base metals, cotton and gold.[239] The volume of Russian exports – indicative of the CIS as a whole – increased by 6 per cent, year-on-year, but average export prices increased by 15 per cent in the first half of 2004.[240]

The continuing high rate of economic growth in the CIS countries – driven by robust demand for consumer and investment goods – gave a strong impetus to merchandise imports.[241] Exchange rate appreciations in

_____

[234] Of the south-east European countries only Serbia and Montenegro does not yet have a preferential agreement with the EU on trade in textiles. The accord between Bosnia and Herzegovina and the EU came into force recently and has resulted in a considerable rise of clothing exports since the beginning of 2004 (particularly, from the Federation of Bosnia and Herzegovina where nearly 90 per cent of textile sector capacities are currently operating under outsourcing agreements). *South East European Newswire,* 17 June 2004. Note that the Federation of Bosnia and Herzegovina is one of the two entities (the other is Republika Srpska) that constitute the country under the Dayton Accord. The Federation covers 51 per cent of Bosnia's territory.

[235] In Turkey, passenger car imports boomed thanks in part to a generous $3,000 tax break for exchanging old vehicles for new ones. Although reduced by half in May 2004 the concession will remain in place until 2005. Relatively cheap consumer credit (about 10 per cent interest rate until August, 15 per cent since) has also helped. Oxford Analytica, *Turkey: Deficit Increases Lira Risks,* 11 October 2004.

[236] The WTO Agreement on Textiles and Clothing, which established a 10-year period for the elimination of the quotas, will expire on 31 December 2004, and trade in textile and clothing products will be subject to the general GATT rules. According to one estimate, Turkey may lose from 1 to 3 percentage points of market share for these goods in the EU and suffer a decline of some 2.2 per cent in its current export earnings. Fitch Ratings: Sovereigns, *Phasing Out the Multi-Fibre Agreement,* Special Report, 22 September 2004 [www.fitchratings.com].

[237] The aggregate dollar value of CIS exports continued to increase in the first three quarters of 2004 (at a faster rate than in the first half of 2004), mainly reflecting exports by crude oil producing countries. Azerbaijan, Kazakhstan and Russia all increased the value of their exports relative to the first half of 2004. Rates of growth in the value of imports were roughly unchanged both in aggregate and for individual countries.

[238] The CIS trade data are affected by the weaker dollar, which biases year-on-year comparisons measured in dollars.

[239] Prices of key CIS natural resource exportables increased considerably, year-on-year, in the first half of 2004. The dollar price of crude oil rose by 17 per cent and gasoline by 28 per cent, while prices for base metals such as aluminium, copper and nickel increased by 20, 67 and 63 per cent, respectively. Gold and cotton prices, which are important sources of export revenue in central Asia also increased significantly (15 and 21 per cent, respectively). The price of Russia's natural gas rose by 2 per cent.

[240] Russia is the only CIS country that publishes estimates of the volumes of aggregate trade.

[241] In the first half of 2004 compared with the corresponding period in 2003, retail sales increased in most CIS countries by at least 10 per cent while investment outlays continued to grow strongly (by between 12 and 61 per cent).

TABLE 6.3.1

CIS countries' trade with CIS and non-CIS countries, 2002-2004
(Value in million dollars, growth rates in per cent)

	Export growth		Import growth		Trade balances		
	2003	2004[a]	2003	2004[a]	2002	2003	2004[a]
Armenia	34.2	7.2	28.6	3.8	- 482	- 591	- 285
CIS	31.5	- 3.8	2.7	- 9.4	- 205	- 183	- 71
Non-CIS	34.9	9.8	40.0	7.9	- 277	- 408	-214
Azerbaijan	19.6	33.8	57.7	33.6	502	- 34	- 199
CIS	36.9	170.7	30.8	47.1	- 407	- 518	- 207
Non-CIS	17.4	13.2	74.9	26.9	909	484	8
Belarus	24.2	32.4	26.5	32.5	-1 071	-1 541	- 756
CIS	24.4	37.4	27.2	33.9	-1 911	-2 553	-1 700
Non-CIS	24.0	27.2	25.1	29.2	840	1 012	944
Georgia	27.7	66.7	44.6	57.1	- 384	- 614	- 467
CIS	27.0	96.5	23.5	59.0	- 121	- 143	- 106
Non-CIS	28.3	42.6	58.5	56.1	- 263	- 470	- 361
Kazakhstan	33.4	40.2	26.5	56.0	3 086	4 574	2 873
CIS	34.6	51.3	28.8	61.4	- 849	- 966	- 805
Non-CIS	33.0	37.1	24.5	51.2	3 935	5 539	3 678
Kyrgyzstan	19.8	44.9	22.1	43.6	- 101	- 135	- 83
CIS	19.4	49.4	27.1	57.9	- 154	- 209	- 140
Non-CIS	20.0	42.6	16.0	26.0	53	74	57
Republic of Moldova	22.7	33.3	35.1	34.0	- 395	- 612	- 313
CIS	20.9	26.9	45.1	35.9	- 59	- 170	- 104
Non-CIS	25.0	40.6	28.5	32.6	- 336	- 443	- 209
Tajikistan	8.3	25.9	22.3	63.1	17	- 83	- 170
CIS	- 26.3	12.6	9.5	61.0	- 359	- 461	- 365
Non-CIS	20.1	28.8	62.9	68.4	376	377	195
Turkmenistan	20.8	..	20.8	..	759	918	..
CIS	0.8	..	- 0.5	..	684	700	..
Non-CIS	45.2	..	35.3	..	75	218	..
Ukraine	28.5	50.8	35.6	33.0	980	59	2 411
CIS	38.2	56.8	28.3	33.8	-4 591	-5 460	-2 999
Non-CIS	25.4	48.9	43.8	32.1	5 571	5 520	5 410
Uzbekistan	26.9	..	9.8	..	89	527	..
CIS	23.3	..	15.2	..	- 314	- 315	..
Non-CIS	27.9	..	6.6	..	403	842	..
Total above	27.4	42.5	30.6	37.1	3 000	2 467	3 011
CIS	27.3	49.7	26.1	39.1	-8 285	-10 277	-6 497
Non-CIS	27.5	39.6	35.6	34.8	11 285	12 744	9 508
Russian Federation	25.9	22.0	24.2	30.9	60 001	76 312	42 805
CIS	31.3	35.8	28.5	40.9	5 376	7 343	4 427
Non-CIS	25.0	19.7	23.0	27.9	54 625	68 969	38 378
CIS total	26.4	27.7	27.3	33.8	63 001	78 779	45 815
CIS	29.4	41.7	26.8	39.7	-2 909	-2 933	-2 070
Non-CIS	25.6	24.4	27.5	30.3	65 910	81 713	47 885

Source: CIS Statistical Committee (Moscow); for Turkmenistan: Dow Jones Reuters estimates. For Uzbekistan: *Statistical Review of Uzbekistan 2003*, Taskhent 2004 (data adjusted for trade in services).

[a] January-June.

real terms against the dollar, ranging from 3 to 5 per cent in Azerbaijan, Kyrgyzstan and Ukraine to between 9 and 22 per cent elsewhere also supported increased imports.[242]

_____

[242] In some countries, however, domestic currencies depreciated in real terms against the euro (except in Georgia, Kazakhstan, the Republic of Moldova and Russia). This may have dampened their demand for goods traded in euros. Because of the divergent changes vis-à-vis the euro and the dollar, the value of aggregate CIS exports

In addition, the recovery of intra-CIS trade – up by 40 per cent in value – was also responsible for a large part of the increase in the value of total merchandise CIS trade.[243] Russia, which accounts for almost half of total intra-CIS trade, recorded increases ranging between 15 and 19 per cent in both volume and prices. Moreover, Russian imports from the CIS were supported by the real appreciation of the rouble.[244] While currency appreciation may have been important for stimulating Russia's bilateral trade with the smaller CIS economies, its trade with the largest CIS economies was primarily driven by high rates of GDP growth. Belarus, Kazakhstan, Russia and Ukraine – which account for about 90 per cent of Russia's CIS trade – grew at rates of between 7 and 13 per cent, year-on-year, in the first half of 2004. This growth continued to sustain increased trade in a variety of investment and consumer goods.[245] Since the first half of 2002, the value of CIS trade has risen by two thirds, driven by strong economic growth in the largest CIS economies.

The four largest CIS economies have also continued to develop their "common economic space". The plan includes the creation of a free trade zone by July 2005. Consistent with this goal, the VAT regime in Russia was changed from the origin principle to the destination principle (applicable to sales of crude oil and natural gas to CIS countries).[246] The Russian government is also promoting a similar initiative to integrate some other CIS economies into the Eurasian Economic Community (Belarus, Kazakhstan, Kyrgyzstan and Tajikistan).

Overall, the Commonwealth of Independent States is an organization that aims at providing a framework for economic coordination and trade relations for the former Soviet Union republics (except the Baltic states). The original agreement stipulated the creation of a CIS free trade zone, but this has not been realized. Instead, CIS members have opted for bilateral free trade agreements, some of which have never been implemented. Moreover, many of the arrangements that have been implemented provide, to varying degrees, for quotas and tariff exceptions. In addition to these formal impediments to trade, there are also other barriers that impede trade within the CIS region. State monopolies frequently control the production or transport of key exportables; transport infrastructure is

_____

and imports expressed in euros increased by 15 and 20 per cent, respectively.

[243] The intraregional contribution to the increase in total imports was about one half and about a quarter of the increase in exports.

[244] The Russian rouble appreciated in real terms by up to 14 per cent against all the CIS currencies except that of the Republic of Moldova against which it depreciated.

[245] In dollar value, Russian trade with Belarus, Kazakhstan and Ukraine grew between one third and about a half.

[246] Under the August 2004 agreement, Russian exports of energy products will be zero-rated (before the change they were taxed at 18 per cent). The loss in revenue to the Russian budget – more than $1 billion annually – will be offset by increased taxation of extractive activities in Russia.

generally of poor quality; and political instability in many regions and corrupt practices at border crossings often greatly inhibit trade by raising the official and unofficial costs of shipping goods. In sum, despite considerable geographical diversification outside the CIS region,[247] the CIS member countries have retained significant economic ties and their potential for trade is greater than at present, but it has remained largely unfulfilled due to the absence of effective pan-CIS cooperation.[248]

In the context of the objectives for the above-noted CIS subregional trade organizations – while not the most crucial in appearance – there have also been discussions about coordinating efforts to join the WTO. Despite its advantages, WTO membership continues to present a major challenge for the majority of the CIS countries.[249] Of the eight remaining non-WTO members from the CIS, only Turkmenistan has not applied for membership.[250] The others are at various stages of the accession process. Azerbaijan and Uzbekistan are at the early stages of document submission, while the others are typically negotiating goods and services schedules and market access issues.[251] In May 2004, the EU and Russia agreed on terms for Russia's accession to the WTO. As part of the agreement, Russia is to raise gradually the domestic price of natural gas above its cost of production, but will not match west European price levels as originally demanded by the EU. This agreement brings Russia a step closer to WTO membership, but it has yet to reach similar deals with its remaining key trade partners. Thus, Georgia – already a WTO member – has raised questions about a number of trade impediments in its bilateral negotiations with Russia.[252]

In general, international trade policies in the CIS area continue to be politically sensitive. Moreover, large variations in taxes and subsidies create profitable arbitrage opportunities for quasi-legal border trade.[253] For example, in September, a free trade agreement between the Republic of Moldova and Ukraine had not been ratified by the Ukrainian parliament whose members justified their refusal by the need to protect domestic producers. Also in September, the Moldovan government announced that it was planning to raise import duties on alcoholic drinks purchased from non-WTO members, in an effort to stem the flow of alcoholic beverages from Ukraine, which are cheaper due to lower excise taxes. In central Asia, where the high transit cost of shipping is already a major deterrent to merchandise trade, matters are often made worse by cumbersome customs and border regimes. Uzbekistan, for example, has introduced a new regulation that requires imported goods be sold by those who bring them into the country. The new requirement is reportedly aimed at regulating bazaar trade, but it undermines a system of shuttle trade, based on a division of labour between importers and bazaar sellers. In contrast, Kyrgyzstan's exports to Kazakhstan rose by over 80 per cent, helped by reductions in transit fees and the easing of various regulations that have made mutual trade more profitable.

High commodity prices continue to stimulate exports

As noted above, the aggregate dollar value of exports from the CIS increased considerably in the first half of 2004. In the European CIS economies, such as Russia and Ukraine, rising commodity prices – due to robust external demand – were generally accompanied by greater export volumes. However, Russian exports – mostly crude oil, natural gas and metals – increased more slowly than those of other three European CIS economies. Production constraints, transport bottlenecks and the duration of natural gas contracts, all impeded larger increases of exports.[254] As Russia's state-owned oil pipeline monopoly was reportedly operating at full capacity, the high prices of crude oil justified the use of alternative – albeit more costly – export routes such as railcars.[255] The volume of exports of oil products was

---

[247] The CIS countries also have more potential to trade with countries outside of the region. For example, after accounting for distance, by one estimate the CIS countries could have tripled their trade with the EU if they had made greater progress in transition from central planning to market. K. Elborgh-Woytek, *Of Openness and Distance: Trade Developments in the Commonwealth of Independent States, 1993-2002*, IMF Working Paper, WP/03/207 (Washington, D.C.), October 2003.

[248] The presidents of Kazakhstan, the Republic of Moldova and Russia have publicly criticized the organization and its ineffectiveness. "CIS: group functions as vehicle of Russian influence", *Oxford Analytica*, 22 September 2004.

[249] For example, Russia – by virtue of its not being a WTO member – could not claim compensation for the admission of new members to the EU in May 2004.

[250] The current WTO members from the CIS are Armenia, Georgia, Kyrgyzstan and the Republic of Moldova.

[251] Azerbaijan began a second round of talks on its accession in October 2004. The country's accession process is expected to receive technical assistance from other WTO members, the United States and the EU in particular.

[252] For example, "uncontrollable flows of smuggling from Russia", the operation of "illegal customs checkpoints", and the restriction of Georgian wine into Russia by railway only. TACIS, *Georgian Economic Trends*, No. 3, 2004, p. 33. The country is also trying to secure a formal certification of its wine and mineral water by the European Commission so it can export these goods (traditionally sent to Russia) to the EU.

[253] The average import tariff in the CIS is about 9 per cent and it has gradually declined over time. But the IMF's trade restrictiveness index for the CIS (which includes taxes and non-tariff barriers to trade) is twice the level of that for the central European countries.

[254] In Russia, crude oil and natural gas producers boosted their export revenues but only slightly increased the volumes of exports (up by over 4 per cent), which reflected higher extraction rates (up by 10 and 5 per cent, respectively).

[255] This trend has continued. For the January-September 2004 period, oil exports by rail rose by 5 per cent, year-on-year. Moreover, Russian oil producers re-routed oil deliveries from inland destinations such as central Europe (down by a quarter) and to seaports (up by almost 60 per cent), which are more profitable. "Exports by rail in January-September rose 5 per cent", *Reuters News Service*, 15 October 2004. Paradoxically, the Polotsk-Ventspils pipeline was greatly underutilized (by almost half of its capacity) in 2004, while crude oil shipments by rail to the Ventspils terminal increased by over 2 million tons. "Prospects and pitfalls of oil transit through Ventspils port", *The Baltic Times*, 11 November 2004 [www.baltictimes.com].

down, however, consistent with output in the Russian refining sector. Exports of steel products rose by a third in volume, making steel and other metals the fastest growing category of exports in the first half of 2004.[256] Similarly, the value of Russia's machinery and equipment exports surged by more than a fifth supported by high rates of economic growth in the region.[257]

Ukrainian exports grew very rapidly owing to the continued boom in the global steel and chemicals markets, particularly in Asia, which has become the principal destination for its ferrous metal exports. Steel and chemicals exports, accounting for almost half of the country's foreign exchange, rose by about a half in value terms compared with the first six months of 2003. The recent completion of new refining capacity is also bearing fruit: various oil products – which now account for about 15 per cent of total exports – benefited from increased prices. Exports of machinery and equipment (including transport vehicles) almost doubled in value on the strength of Russia's surging import demand.

The economies of Belarus and the Republic of Moldova are relatively less dependent on the global business cycle but, at the same time, are more closely dependent on Russian import demand, especially for machinery and equipment and agricultural products. In Belarus, where strong Russian demand continued to support agricultural and manufactured exports, the value of exports increased by a third. The expansion was broadly based on major export items such as machinery and equipment, transport equipment and food.[258] In the Republic of Moldova, the value of exports was driven primarily by increased sales of clothing products that originate in and are destined for the EU (after local processing) as well as more traditional products such as vegetables to other CIS markets.[259]

In the last few years, in the Caucasian region of the CIS, Armenian exports of jewellery to Belgium and Israel have usually dominated movements in its total exports.

In the first half of 2004, output in the diamond processing sector, which is the main source of both industrial output and exports, slumped 11 per cent. This slump was due to a slowdown after two years of rapid growth and disruptions in the supply of raw materials. As a result, Armenia's exports were the slowest growing in the CIS (up by 7 per cent). In contrast, Georgia's exports rose by two thirds in value, largely reflecting the delivery of military aircraft in the second quarter of 2004. Higher prices for ferrous scrap and waste, usually destined for Turkey, also contributed.[260] The value of Azerbaijan's exports – about 80 per cent dependent on oil – also rose by a third due to a one-off sale of oil extraction equipment to Turkmenistan. The more traditional sales of oil products to non-CIS markets increased in volume by about a quarter, but exports of crude oil were down by 11 per cent as a result of sluggish extraction rates.

In central Asia, Kazakhstan was one of many CIS natural resource producers taking advantage of higher commodity prices. The volume of oil exports rose by 16 per cent (year-on-year), various steel products rose by up to 10 per cent, and copper sales rose by 13 per cent in the first half of 2004.[261] In Kyrgyzstan, the growth of exports reflected higher gold prices and production from the Kumtor mine, strong external demand and improved access to regional markets.[262] In Tajikistan, higher prices for aluminium and textiles (including cotton fibre), which account for almost all of the country's exports, boosted their total value by a quarter.[263] In Turkmenistan, where the official data remain scant and their reliability questionable, the total value of exports reportedly increased by 13 per cent due to an increase in the volume of natural gas exports. (Natural gas is sold under a fixed price contract but the volume is believed to have increased by 5 per cent.) Exports of oil products were up by 20 per cent in volume – a reflection of the value adding strategy of processing domestic crude oil. Similarly in Uzbekistan, international trade data are often unavailable or provided in a format that is not easily comparable with other countries. Gold and cotton exports are believed to have increased in the first half of 2004.

---

[256] The composition of Russian exports did not change significantly. Exports to non-CIS countries continue to rely on sales of crude oil, oil products and metals (over 80 per cent of the total), while these same commodities account for slightly more than half of Russia's exports to the CIS. Since 2003, the share of steel and base metals in total exports has increased by about 5 percentage points; this was due to increases in both volume and price and was mostly at the expense of oil and oil products.

[257] Russian exports of machinery and equipment go mainly to other CIS countries ($2.5 billion or 86 per cent of total capital goods exports in the first half of 2004).

[258] As in the past, export growth was driven by Russian import demand, which accounts for about half of the value of Belarus' total exports. In the first half of 2004, exports of food to Russia rose by almost two thirds, consumer goods by a third and machinery by almost 40 per cent in value. Non-CIS sales – mostly crude oil, oil products and chemicals – increased by up to 15 per cent in volume.

[259] However, exports of food, beverages and tobacco – consisting mostly of sales of wine to Russia – expanded more slowly than total exports.

[260] The newly elected government has claimed some success in curbing smuggling, and this appears to have resulted in increases in recorded trade.

[261] The corresponding dollar values increased by much more: oil by 34 per cent, steel products by up to 72 per cent depending on the product, and copper by 73 per cent. Crude oil, natural gas and steel production increased by 10 per cent, 48 per cent and up to 18 per cent, respectively.

[262] Exports to the CIS markets rose mainly due to increased exports of sugar, fruit and vegetables, and building materials, but their share in total exports is relatively small.

[263] The volume of cotton shipments was flat while aluminium sales rose by 16 per cent. Tajikistan also generates electricity that is largely sold to Uzbekistan. The country is trying to diversify and will sell electricity to Russia through Kazakhstan and Uzbekistan after signing a contract with Russia in the first half of 2004.

Energy prices, investment and consumption drive imports

The dollar value of CIS imports increased by a third in the first half of 2004, year-on-year. The increases were very large in all the CIS countries (except Armenia) ranging from 31 per cent in Russia to 63 per cent in Tajikistan. Russian imports were driven by domestic investment and consumption. In the first six months of 2004, imports of machinery and equipment rose by almost a half, and capital goods are expected to continue to be the most important single category of Russian imports. The modernization of the existing capital stock and investment in new productive capacity has also been behind rising imports in most of the CIS.

In Azerbaijan, import growth continued to be related to the expansion of the pipeline system and further exploration and development of the country's oil and natural gas fields. Similarly, in Georgia pipeline construction made a large contribution to the 60 per cent rise in imports. As noted above, some of these increases may be exaggerated as changes in government policies as well as tighter border controls have led to more imports being captured in the official statistics. In Kazakhstan imports of machinery, equipment and transportation vehicles increased by more than a half and now account for over a quarter of total imports.

For the CIS energy importers and the major net energy exporters, both importing energy from neighbouring countries because of the legacy of the Soviet-designed transport system, the increased dollar value of imports was related to both higher volumes and prices for crude oil, natural gas and electricity. Azerbaijan's imports of natural gas and electricity increased by 14 and 23 per cent, respectively, in volume. The rise in Belarussian imports is partly due to higher import volumes for crude oil and natural gas (up by 4-6 per cent). Kazakhstan, a major crude oil producer, imported much larger volumes of natural gas and electricity (43 and 64 per cent, respectively), while its imports of oil products more than doubled. Similarly Kyrgyzstan imported significantly greater volumes of crude oil, oil products and natural gas. The Republic of Moldova and Tajikistan imported more electricity and oil products. In Ukraine, imports of fuels and mineral products were up by one third in value.

Some recent empirical research has examined the trade patterns of the CIS countries in order to determine the degree to which they differ from those of other countries in similar circumstances.[264] Factors included are the levels of development and the economic sizes of not only the CIS countries but their trading partners as well; in addition this analysis considers the distances

between trading partners and whether or not they use a similar language or are in a similar trading bloc. This study, based on 1996-2000 trade flows, analyses the value of trade, its geographical distribution and its commodity composition. Since 2000, there have only been minor changes in the CIS economies' structures of trade. Russia and Ukraine appear to have trade patterns in terms of value and geographical destinations that are generally consistent with expectations based upon world trade patterns. Sectorally, however their exports are overly concentrated in a few natural resource-based products. The poorer CIS countries, including the central Asian countries, Belarus and the Republic of Moldova, although trading normally within the CIS, appear to "under-trade" with the rest of the world. What is missing in their trade is mainly manufactures.

Thus, the clear pattern that emerges from this analysis is that trade in manufactures, especially with non-CIS countries, is much smaller than what would be expected based upon average world trade patterns. In many cases, the manufacturing sectors in the CIS simply have not adjusted to the movement from a planned to a market economy, and these countries find themselves partially excluded from global manufacturing chains. Limited access to foreign markets for their manufactures is a factor contributing to this problem, as is their non-membership to the WTO. This finding of "missing" manufactures trade has several important implications. Given that manufacturing is likely to be labour intensive in these countries, the lack of a manufacturing base contributes to low levels of employment. Globally, productivity growth in almost all countries tends to be driven by the manufacturing sector; thus the absence of a viable manufacturing base greatly weakens the economic dynamism of these countries and reduces their potential for long-term sustainable growth based upon technological advancement. Dependence on commodity trade subjects the CIS to the risks of instability in export earnings and possibly exposes them to a long-run deterioration in their terms of trade. Since the trade of these countries is primarily inter-industry trade, they have been unable to get the benefits associated with intra-industry trade in manufactures such as economies of scale and increases in product variety. Where there is an inter-industry trade pattern, changes in trade policy tend to produce painful adjustment costs; as a result there tends to be greater political opposition to trade liberalization than when trade patterns consist more of intra-industry trade.

Given these differences in the actual CIS trade pattern relative to the expected pattern, an obvious question is to what degree government policy should attempt to address them. While there has been considerable progress in achieving macroeconomic stability, the CIS countries need to put greater emphasis on the establishment of high quality institutions, a well-functioning infrastructure, market determined prices, liberalized trade, an openness towards FDI, and progress on WTO accession and regional trade integration.

---

[264] This analysis uses a gravity model, which is the standard analytical framework for examining these types of issues. L. Freinkman, E. Polyakov and C. Revenco, *Trade Performance and Regional Integration of the CIS Countries*, World Bank Working Paper, No. 38 (Washington, D.C.), August 2004.

Overall, however, there remains a question as to whether this should be the extent of policy to address this issue or whether more specific policy interventions are desirable to address the lack of manufacturing trade.[265] Although an industrial policy, an import substitution programme, or an export promotion programme as a means of fostering manufacturing industries have been out of favour for more than 20 years in the policy advice provided by the international financial institutions, the poor growth performance of many of the countries following their advice has given rise to significant criticism of their market oriented "hands off" policy recommendations. From a technical point of view, there are a number of valid arguments as to why more activist government policies might be desirable, but in practice they often lead to rent-seeking behaviour that can be more costly than the initial problem. Regardless of the possible economic rationale for some type of manufacturing promotion

programme, WTO policies (assuming accession) are likely to limit significantly the type of programme that could actually be implemented. The ability to conduct a successful industrial policy, however, requires a highly advanced and coordinated institutional structure (see chapter 1.2(iii)). Given the generally weak institutions in many of the CIS countries, the best advice for now may be to concentrate initially on the fundamentals including early WTO accession and improved governance, and only after more progress has been achieved in these directions, should the possibility of an "active" industrial policy be considered. An additional way to minimize the impact of export earnings volatility instead of altering the sectoral composition of output is to export the risks to foreigners. This can be accomplished in several ways such as encouraging more foreign ownership of the natural resource industries or encouraging domestic producers to hedge their risk by using futures and options markets.

---

[265] The proper role of government in addressing an export pattern concentrated on a few commodities has generated a long and controversial literature dating back to the seminal contributions of Raul Prebisch of the United Nations Economic Commission for Latin America. Gunnar Myrdal, the first Executive Secretary of the UNECE, also argued that specific government policies should be directed towards modifying an export structure concentrated on commodities.

CHAPTER 7

TOWARDS A NEW EUROPEAN MODEL OF A REFORMED WELFARE STATE: AN ALTERNATIVE TO THE UNITED STATES MODEL[266]

The better performance of the United States relative to western Europe in terms of output and productivity growth since the 1990s is now an accepted fact. This chapter views this from a longer-term perspective, and suggests that a more comprehensive comparison between the United States and western Europe, that includes social and environmental indicators, income distribution, social welfare and health care, may present a different picture than if per capita gross domestic product (GDP) alone is considered. Many analysts, in seeking to explain the differences in economic performance since the early 1990s, blame high welfare costs, rigid labour market rules and higher environmental standards for western Europe's poor performance. This would imply that western Europe has been trading off faster economic growth against the objective to achieve ambitious social and environmental goals. Surprisingly, however, the best performing European countries over the past 10 to 15 years in terms of overall economic performance have been three Nordic states (Denmark, Finland, Sweden) that have comprehensive welfare systems and a high degree of environmental awareness. All three suffered severe structural and cyclical crises in the 1980s and 1990s, but over the past 10 to 15 years they have been performing better than the larger European economies, and have been matching the United States in their dynamic performance. This chapter analyses whether the post-crisis reforms undertaken in these three countries have followed the United States model or whether they provide a new European model of a reformed welfare state.

7.1 Introduction

The better economic performance of the United States relative to western Europe since the early 1990s is an accepted fact. This chapter attempts to put this into perspective, first, by showing that while the United States forged ahead in terms of output and productivity, this was not the case in terms of per capita GDP; secondly, its better performance occurred following decades of catching up by western Europe in terms of productivity; and thirdly, a more comprehensive comparison than one of per capita income alone, covering welfare – that includes income distribution, environmental conservation, social and health coverage, and the comprehensive nature of its social welfare system in general – reveals a better performance by western Europe.

Many analysts blame precisely these higher welfare and environmental standards, along with inflexible labour markets, for western Europe's poorer performance.[267] If this were true, countries with lower social costs, unrestricted labour markets and lower environmental quality should have performed better. Surprisingly, the best performing European countries have been three Nordic welfare States, which have high taxes, a proactive innovation policy and comprehensive labour market

[266] Karl Aiginger is Deputy Director at the Austrian Institute of Economic Research (WIFO) and Professor of Economics at the University of Linz, Austria. This study is a revised version of his paper presented at the UNECE Spring Seminar on *Competitiveness and Economic Growth in the ECE Region*, held in Geneva on 23 February 2004 (for more details about the Seminar programme see www.unece.org/ead). The paper was written when the author was at the Graduate School of Business at Stanford University, United States. The author is particularly grateful for comments received from Kenneth Arrow, Jorgen Elmeskov, Alois Guger, Angela Köppel, Markus Marterbauer, Karl Pichelmann, Stephan Schulmeister, Gunter Tichy and Ewald Walterskirchen. Dagmar Guttmann provided valuable research assistance.

[267] This has been termed the "Paris consensus" by some authors (K. Aiginger, *Labour Market Reforms and Economic Growth – The European Experience in the Nineties*, WIFO Working Paper, No. 232 (Vienna), September 2004; A. Guger, M. Marterbauer and E. Walterskirchen, "Stagnation policy versus growth strategies", paper presented at the conference in honour of Josef Steindl (Vienna), 2003), as such analyses are often found in OECD (Paris) publications. The term "Paris consensus" draws on the term "Washington consensus" for developing countries, which described strategies promoted by the IMF and World Bank.

institutions. Earlier, all of them had suffered severe crises, which may have been partially the consequence of rigidities, overspending and wage increases that were higher than productivity. But more recently, these "top 3" countries have been performing better than the European average and quite similar to the United States. This chapter examines whether these countries changed their economic model to follow more closely that of the United States or whether they are on the verge of developing a new European model that combines comprehensive coverage of risks (high share of union members and high share of workers covered by collective wage agreements) with a high degree of efficiency and modern technology.

The chapter begins by comparing economic performance, followed in section 7.2 by extending the comparison to a broader set of goals. Section 7.3 analyses the economic dynamics of western Europe and the United States since the 1990s, and speculates as to whether the higher growth in output, productivity and employment in the United States will extend into the next decade. Section 7.4 investigates whether the differences in welfare costs and labour market regulations between the United States and western Europe, which are often used to explain the lower European dynamics, also determine which western European countries performed better and worse during the 1990s. Section 7.5 uses the structure and policy strategies of the three most successful European countries (termed the top 3) to sketch a new European model, in which social and environmental responsibility is combined with rapid innovation and a high degree of efficiency of production. Section 7.6 presents a summary.

7.2 Differences in performance between the United States and western Europe

(i) Growth of output and productivity

Economic growth, as measured by real GDP, grew somewhat faster in western Europe than in the United States over much of the post-Second World War period, including the 1980s. However, since 1990 the United States has been outperforming western Europe: it was less affected by the business downturn of 1993, achieved

higher growth during the second half of the decade, and proved more resistant to the most recent crisis of 2001-2003. For the period 1990 to 2003, the difference in economic growth between the EU-15 and the United States amounted to 1 per cent per annum and 14 per cent cumulative.

In the United States, GDP per capita has been some 40 per cent higher than the average level for the EU-15 in 2002, a gap that has remained broadly unchanged over the past decades (table 7.2.1). When comparing GDP per person employed, the gap between the United States and the EU-15 reduces to 30 per cent in 2002. The difference in levels of GDP per hour worked is much smaller, amounting to only 9 per cent. The large difference in levels of GDP per capita in 2002 reflects therefore in the main the combined effect of the higher United States employment rate, i.e. the larger proportion of persons aged 15-64 that are employed (some 80 per cent compared to 67 per cent in the EU-15 in 2002) and the larger number of hours worked per person per annum (shorter annual leave and longer weekly working hours).

In general, GDP per hour worked is considered to be the best measure of overall productivity in the economy, although reliable (and internationally comparable) time series on hours worked are difficult to obtain. GDP per person employed is used as an indicator of economic efficiency in case there are no reliable statistics on hours worked available. Per capita GDP is more relevant for measuring the average income of the population and, related to that, the potential to consume.

Looking at developments over time, Europe has been catching up with the United States in terms of GDP per person employed and per hour worked: in terms of GDP per person employed, the difference was 28 per cent in 1980, narrowing to 20 per cent in 1995, and in terms of GDP per hour worked it narrowed from 21 to 5 per cent over the same period. Since 1995, the differences have again become wider, by about 10 percentage points for GDP per person employed and 4 percentage points for GDP per hour worked (chart 7.2.1). The reason why United States productivity has been able to forge ahead after decades of European catching up has been widely discussed; there are at least three explanations: (i) the

TABLE 7.2.1

Differences in GDP per capita, GDP per person employed and GDP per hour worked between the EU-15 and the United States, 1980, 1990, 1995 and 2002

	GDP per capita			GDP per person employed			GDP per hour worked		
	EU-15	United States	United States/ EU-15	EU-15	United States	United States/ EU-15	EU-15	United States	United States/ EU-15
	(Thousand euros)			(Thousand euros)			(Euros)		
1980	16.30	22.31	1.37	39.84	51.16	1.28	23.00	27.93	1.21
1990	20.08	27.88	1.39	47.43	58.66	1.24	28.82	32.25	1.12
1995	21.30	29.81	1.40	52.52	62.79	1.20	32.53	34.13	1.05
2002	24.43	34.08	1.40	56.26	72.94	1.30	35.52	38.83	1.09

Source: WIFO calculations, based on data from the Groningen Growth and Development Centre.

CHART 7.2.1

European catching up in GDP per capita, GDP per person employed and GDP per hour worked (United States=100), 1979-2002

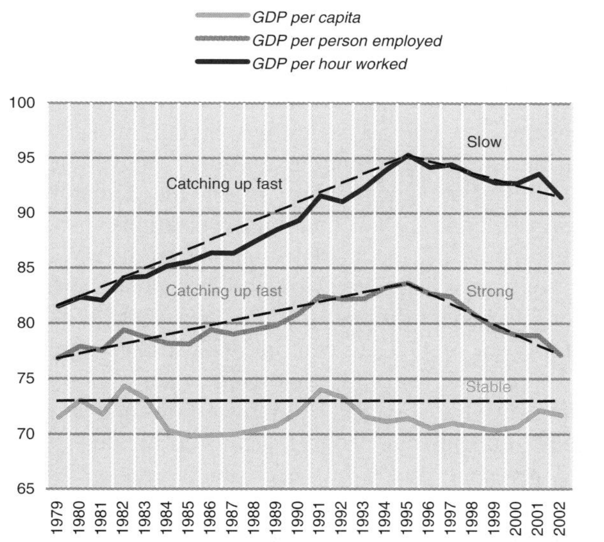

CHART 7.2.2

United States ahead of Europe on three indicators, 1995 and 2002

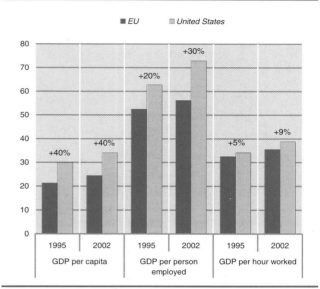

Source: WIFO calculations, based on data from Groningen Growth and Development Centre.

Source: WIFO calculations, based on data from Groningen Growth and Development Centre.

earlier adoption of information and communications technologies (ICT) by the United States;[268] (ii) insufficient European investment in R&D and human capital;[269] and (iii) rather restrictive monetary and fiscal policies in Europe.[270] In terms of GDP per capita the gap has not widened; the United States has been leading since the early twentieth century, and the difference increased only slightly between 1990 and 2002. Some researchers have considered this good news, but the difference of 40 per cent is still extremely large (chart 7.2.2).[271]

(ii)   Other welfare components

Broader comparisons of welfare include evaluations of: (i) employment and unemployment; (ii) income distribution, either investigating the spread between rich and poor or measuring poverty rates; (iii) the

comprehensiveness of social and health care coverage; and (iv) environmental conservation and prudent use of resources. This implies that a more broadly defined welfare concept embraces considerations of not only employment and income distribution, but also the comprehensiveness of the social safety net and environmental conservation.[272] Extended even farther, concepts of welfare could also include life expectancy, democracy, security, cultural goals, the rule of law and all aspects of human development (chart 7.2.3). The broader the set of goals to be evaluated, the more difficult it is to measure them, and the more difficult it is to determine the relative weights of the individual objectives and make a general assessment.

Until the mid-1970s, the employment rate for the working-age population was higher in western Europe than in the United States (e.g. in 1960 the employment rate was 70 per cent in western Europe, as compared to 66 per cent in the United States). However, by 1980 the employment rate in the United States had overtaken that

[268] R. Gordon, "Two centuries of economic growth: Europe chasing the American frontier", paper prepared for the Economic History Workshop, Northwestern University (Chicago), October 2002; D. Jorgenson and K. Stiroh, "U.S. economic growth in the new millennium", *Brookings Papers on Economic Activity*, 1 (Washington, D.C.), 2000; K. Aiginger and M. Landesmann, *Competitive Economic Performance: The European View*, WIFO Working Paper, No. 179 (Vienna), June 2002.

[269] K. Aiginger, "The three tier strategy followed by successful European countries in the 1990s", *International Review of Applied Economics*, Vol. 18, No. 4, 2004, pp. 399-422.

[270] S. Schulmeister, *Die unterschiedliche Wachstumsdynamik in den USA und Deutschland in den neunziger Jahren*, WIFO Working Paper, No. 134 (Vienna), 2000.

[271] The large difference in income per capita versus the relatively low difference in GDP per hour worked led Gordon to question how Europe could be so productive yet so poor. R. Gordon, "Two centuries of economic growth: …", op. cit., p. 2.

[272] This is not to overlook the fact that certain other economic variables are also closely monitored, such as inflation, budgetary stability and the trade balance. However, these are not goals, but rather instruments or constraints, which have the potential to become important obstacles for raising welfare if they are out of balance. If inflation is in the two-digit range, it will sooner or later dampen economic growth and endanger employment. However, a zero rate of inflation is not an economic end (and negative rates even less so). Trade deficits are unimportant if they are compensated by investment flows; they may signal the loss of competitiveness if they increase without these compensatory flows. Budget deficits may help stabilize income and employment in the short run (anti-cyclical spending) or in the long run (if they boost research and infrastructure), but they may endanger growth if they are the result of excessive spending on items that do not help improve the production potential.

CHART 7.2.3

Hierarchy of European economic and social goals

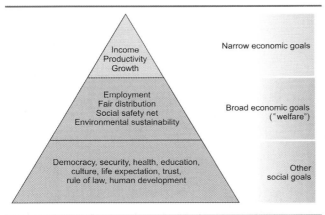

Source: K. Aiginger, "The economic agenda: a view from Europe", *Review of International Economics*, Vol. 12, Issue 2 (Special Issue: Economic Agenda for the 21ˢᵗ Century), May 2004.

of western Europe, and continued to increase at a faster rate, to reach almost 80 per cent in 2002 compared with western Europe where it was 67 per cent (table 7.2.2). A detailed analysis of the changes in these trends is beyond the scope of this paper. However, one reason is that faster growing economies need more employees. Another is that, at the lower end of the wage spectrum, United States labour became comparatively cheap, thereby increasing the rate of employment growth in the United States. The United States created 78 million new jobs between 1960 and 2000, while western Europe created 42 million. However, employment creation in more recent years has accelerated in western Europe: between 1995 and 2002, western Europe created 12 million jobs; and even during the last three years of slow growth (2001-2003) employment increased, in contrast to other periods of sluggish growth, although many of the jobs were part-time. In 2002, the unemployment rate was 5.8 per cent in the United States, broadly unchanged from 1995. In contrast, in western Europe, the unemployment rate fell from 10.1 per cent in 1995 to 7.6 per cent in 2002 (table 7.2.2).

The social safety net is considerably more generous in western Europe. Net public spending on welfare is about 16 per cent in the United States and 24 per cent in western Europe (table 7.2.3). Most Europeans have government-funded or obligatory health insurance, pensions are higher, retirement can be taken earlier and governments' contributions to pensions are higher. Unemployment payments are higher in relation to income (replacement rate), they are paid for a longer period of time and the fall-back payments (social assistance) are relatively high and practically unlimited in time.

Income is less evenly distributed in the United States. The top 20 per cent earn 45 per cent of total income and the bottom 20 per cent earn 4.8 per cent, which results in an inequality ratio of 9.4. In western Europe, the corresponding numbers (using an unweighted

average for the member countries) are 38.5 per cent for the top 20 per cent and 8.3 per cent for the bottom 20 per cent, resulting in a ratio of 4.7 (table 7.2.3). The lowest ratio in western Europe is 3.2 for Austria, followed closely by the Scandinavian countries and Belgium; Portugal is the only country where the inequality ratio is closer to that of the United States. As for poverty ratios, which can be calculated absolutely or relatively, by both measures the United States has higher rates. Income distribution is becoming increasingly uneven in many countries, but much more so in the United States. However, contrary to common expectations – suggested by the increasing inequality of incomes – the poverty rate has not been rising in the United States when viewed over a long period: it dropped from 22 per cent in 1960 to a historic low of 11.1 per cent in 1973; it later increased to 15.2 per cent in 1983, following a shift in economic policy by the Reagan Administration and a rise in unemployment, but declined again during the 1990s to 11.3 per cent, and it has been increasing only slightly since the most recent recession (12.5 per cent in 2003).[273] The reason for the relatively low level of poverty, despite increasing income inequality, is the relatively high employment rate.

There are social indicators that indicate a worse performance of the United States model (or greater downside risks in American society). For example, the number of homeless, the illiteracy rate, the proportion of the population in prison,[274] the homicide rate, the relative prevalence of drugs and guns, racial discrimination and the discrepancies in living standards between the slums and suburbs are higher in the United States. On the other hand, data on mobility reveal that expectations of upward mobility are greater in the United States, although the difference in actual mobility between the United States and western Europe is far lower than is commonly believed.[275] The number of immigrants in the United States is also larger than in the EU-15.

Western Europe is far ahead of the United States in terms of environmental performance. The ratio of energy consumption to GDP is 73 per cent higher in the United States than in western Europe (United States: 0.26 Mtoe/GDP; western Europe: 0.15 Mtoe/GDP) and that of carbon dioxide emissions is 84 per cent higher (table 7.2.3). With respect to the cutting down of emissions, western Europe is at least trying to fulfil the targets of reducing greenhouse gases set by the Kyoto Protocol of the United Nations Framework Convention on Climate Change, while the United States is not even a signatory to that Protocol.

[273] *Economic Report of the President,* 2004 (Washington, D.C.), transmitted to the United States Congress, February 2004.

[274] For every 100,000 people, 469 are in prison in the United States versus 65 in Europe.

[275] A. Alesina, E. Glaeser and B. Sacerdote, *Why Doesn't the US Have a European-style Welfare System?*, NBER Working Paper, No. w8524 (Cambridge, MA), October 2001.

TABLE 7.2.2

Employment and unemployment rates: EU-15 and the United States, 1980, 1990, 1995 and 2002

	Employment rate [a]			Employment (million persons)			Working hours (per year and per person)			Unemployment rate [b]		
	EU-15	United States	United States/EU-15	EU-15	United States	United States/EU-15	EU-15	United States	United States/EU-15	EU-15	United States	United States/EU-15
1980	64.5	71.0	1.10	145 160	99 303	0.68	1 732.5	1 831.4	1.06	5.6	7.1	1.27
1990	64.5	77.9	1.21	154 249	118 793	0.77	1 643.8	1 819.0	1.11	7.4	5.5	0.74
1995	62.7	78.6	1.25	150 721	124 900	0.83	1 612.0	1 839.9	1.14	10.1	5.6	0.55
2002	67.0	79.7	1.19	164 471	134 398	0.82	1 581.3	1 878.4	1.19	7.6	5.8	0.76

Source: WIFO calculations, based on data from the Groningen Growth and Development Centre.

[a] Persons employed in the 15-64 age group as a percentage of population in the same age group.

[b] As a per cent of the civil labour force.

TABLE 7.2.3

Broad indicators of economic welfare, 2002

	EU-15	United States	Top 3 European countries [a]	Big 3 European countries [b]
Employment rate (per cent)	67.00	79.70	73.30	64.30
Employment generation, 1990-2002 (millions)	10.30	19.60	-0.20	3.70
Unemployment rate (per cent).............	7.60	5.80	6.20	8.60
Net social expenditures, public and private (per cent of GDP)	25.80	23.40	26.40	21.20
Net social expenditures, public (per cent of GDP)	24.00	16.40	24.30	18.70
Income distribution				
Share of top 20 per cent	38.50	45.20	34.90	38.70
Share of bottom 20 per cent	8.30	4.80	9.70	7.90
Ratio of top 20 per cent/bottom 20 per cent	4.70	9.40	3.60	4.90
Energy consumption (Mtoe/GDP)	0.15	0.26	0.16	0.14
Carbon dioxide (t/GDP)	0.31	0.57	0.27	0.29
Self-assessment of happiness (on a scale of 1 to 10)	7.05 [c]	7.60	7.87	6.87
Self-assessment of life satisfaction (on a scale of 1 to 10)	6.81 [c]	7.46	7.75	6.68
Health adjusted life expectancy at birth (years)	70.14	67.60	70.67	70.83
Persons sentenced to imprisonment per 100 000	65	469	..	..

Source: W. Adema, "Net social expenditure", 2nd edition, *Labour Market and Social Occasional Paper*, No. 52, OECD (Paris), August 2001; OECD, *Society at a Glance* (Paris), 2003; IMD, *World Competitiveness Yearbook*, 1999; International Energy Agency, *Total Primary Energy Supply* (Paris) 2003; R. Veenhoven, "Advances in understanding happiness", *Revue Quebecoise de Psychologie*, Vol. 18, 1997, pp. 29-74.

Note: Mtoe/GDP = million tonnes of oil equivalent per GDP; t/GDP = tonnes per GDP.

[a] Denmark, Finland and Sweden.

[b] France, Germany and Italy.

[c] The four largest EU countries only (France, Germany, Italy, United Kingdom).

Western Europeans have more leisure time. More specifically, there are 16 per cent fewer working hours per year (more vacations and fewer working hours per week), although the share of the population in work is lower in Europe by 13 percentage points. It is difficult to assess the extent to which the fewer hours worked are voluntary, and to what extent they are the by-products of

the economic environment – such as the lack of full-time jobs, or jobs for middle-aged workers who have lost their jobs and have little chance of regaining employment. Gordon ventures the "wild guess that about one third of the difference represents voluntary chosen leisure and the remaining two thirds represent a lack of employment opportunities".[276]

How can we weigh these factors? There is no satisfactory method, and indeed there should be none, since an assessment of the success or failure of an economic and social system should be concerned with specific questions. One way of making an overall assessment by means of socio-economic research is to raise two internationally comparable questions: whether people are happy, and whether they are satisfied with their lives. This might seem somewhat primitive at first, but it is a serious line of research. It includes many tests for cultural bias, and displays careful sampling and wording. Results indicate that people are influenced by income, but the rankings ascribed to income and individuals' assessments of life satisfaction do not necessarily coincide. For both subjective indicators, Americans rank higher: the United States rating for "happiness" is 7.6 on a scale of 10 versus 7.1 for the four largest western European countries (France, Germany, Italy and the United Kingdom); for "life satisfaction", the United States rating is 7.5, while the corresponding value for the four largest western European countries is 6.8. Interestingly, differences within the United States are smaller than those within France and the United Kingdom.[277]

---

[276] R. Gordon, "Two centuries of economic growth: ...", op. cit., p. 10. Europeans worked longer hours than Americans during the 1945-1973 era of post-war reconstruction. "So passion for long vacations and short weekly hours of work is a recently acquired taste", while "Americans seem happy to be bribed to work long hours for premium overtime pay ... everyone wants his fair share of compulsory overtime". R. Gordon, ibid., p. 9.

[277] The research is based at Erasmus University in the Netherlands (see its website on this subject at: www.eur.nl/fsw/research/happiness, directed by R. Veenhoven). See also, R. Veenhoven, "Advances in understanding happiness", *Revue Quebecoise de Psychologie*, Vol. 18, 1997, pp. 29-74; G .Tichy, "Die Unzufriedenheit der Bürger mit den

TABLE 7.3.1

Growth dynamics of the EU-15 and the United States in the 1990s
(Average annual growth rates)

	Real GDP		GDP per person employed		Employment		GDP per hour worked	
	EU-15	United States	EU-15	United States	EU-15	United States	EU-15	United States
1991-1995	1.59	2.39	2.06	1.37	-0.46	1.01	2.45	1.14
1996-2000	2.65	4.04	1.22	2.40	1.41	1.60	1.42	1.97
2001-2002	1.29	1.27	0.41	1.58	0.87	-0.30	0.88	1.59
1996-2002	2.26	3.24	0.99	2.16	1.26	1.05	1.26	1.86
1991-2002	2.16	3.15	1.56	2.00	0.59	1.13	1.92	1.70

Source: WIFO calculations, based on data from the Groningen Growth and Development Centre.

7.3 Differences in dynamics between the EU-15 and the United States in the 1990s

This section examines the differences in growth of output, productivity and employment between the United States and western Europe. Between 1991 and 2002, output growth in western Europe was 2.2 per cent per annum – 1 percentage point less than in the United States, labour productivity expanded by 1.6 per cent in western Europe, compared to 2 per cent in the United States, and employment increased by 0.6 per cent in western Europe compared with 1.1 per cent in the United States (table 7.3.1). The amounts might seem small in per annum figures but cumulative growth of GDP was 26.5 per cent for western Europe and 40.7 per cent for the United States over this period. We summarize the main reasons for the differences,[278] and then attempt to assess what can be expected over the next decade.

Most international studies, and specifically those by the Organisation for Economic Co-operation and Development (OECD), the International Monetary Fund (IMF) and the European Commission, explicitly or implicitly blame high welfare costs and low labour market flexibility for western Europe's poor performance. While it is true that welfare costs are higher and west European labour as well as product markets are more regulated, there are some doubts as to whether these are the main reasons. First, differences in product markets and in labour market regulations narrowed considerably during the 1990s; secondly, there is a weak – if any – relationship between the degree of regulatory change during the 1990s and economic performance.[279]

It has been argued that macroeconomic policy (e.g. growth-supporting monetary policy, and demand stabilization through fiscal policy during troughs) is at

least as important as regulatory changes.[280] The strongest and increasing difference between the United States and western Europe is, however, the dynamics of investment in future growth, such as in education, research and diffusion of new technologies (ICT and biotechnology). Aiginger uses 16 indicators to measure the investments of countries in these variables, including indicators of research input and output, education expenditures and educational attainment, as well as spending on ICT in both production and consumption (as a proxy for spending and the diffusion of new technologies). The astonishing result is that in 1990, the United States led in all 16 indicators, and by the end of the 1990s it was still leading in 14 of the 16 indicators. The EU-15 as a group is catching up in four of the indicators, and has surpassed the United States in two, while the difference is increasing for 11 indicators (and constant for one). In light of this evidence, it is therefore no surprise that growth rates have been higher in the United States since the 1990s.[281] Chart 7.3.1 allows comparing these drivers of future growth. Each value inside the unit circle indicates lower levels in western Europe relative to the United States

While stressing that investment in the future is the most important explanation for differences in growth performance, the importance of the other policy areas should not, however, be overlooked. There are several interactions, and causality runs in both directions: innovation supports growth and growth fosters innovation. Innovations are easier to implement if markets are less strictly regulated, and regulations can be abandoned if people who lose their jobs can find new ones easily.

Zielen der Wirtschaftspolitik, Zu den Erkenntnissen der, 'happiness-Forschung'", *Wirtschaft und Gesellschaft*, Vol. 30, No. 4, 2004 and "Die 'Neue Unsicherheit' als Ursache der europäischen Wachstumsschwäche", *Perspektiven der Wirtschaftspolitik*, Vol. 5, No. 4, 2004.

[278] K. Aiginger, "The three tier strategy …", op. cit.

[279] K. Aiginger, "Economic agenda for the 21st century", *Review of International Economics*, Vol. 12, Issue 2, May 2004, pp. 187-206.

[280] K. Aiginger, "The three tier strategy …", op. cit.

[281] Some of the advantages of investment into future components of growth were already evident in previous decades, when Europe grew faster than the United States. There are two explanations as to why insufficient investments in Europe did not hamper growth earlier: first of all, per capita GDP as well as productivity were initially much lower in Europe, so that the higher levels of European growth included an element of catching up; secondly, it is argued that the European system of innovation may have been particularly apt during periods of imitation and diffusion, while the United States system of innovation is better adapted to periods marked by the emergence of new general-purpose technologies such as ICT. K. Aiginger and M. Landesmann, "Competitive economic performance, …", op. cit.

CHART 7.3.1

Indicators of future growth potential: EU-15 versus the United States

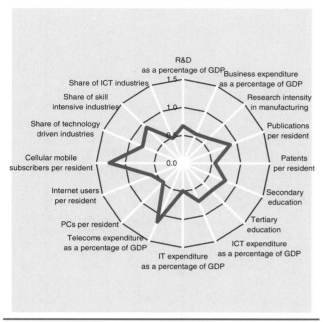

Source: WIFO calculations, based on Eurostat NewCronos Database; European Information Technology Observatory (EITO).

Note: Values inside the unit circle indicate that levels in the EU-15 are below the United States levels for the corresponding indicator. Data refer to last year available for the period 1999-2001.

Economists need to be cautious when judging whether the United States lead will be extended into the next decade, given that in 1990 neither the accelerated growth of the United States had been forecast nor the demise of the Japanese economy. If present trends were to continue, the following developments could reasonably be expected to occur:

- The differences in macroeconomic policy will probably become narrower, given that the deficit in the United States is now higher than in western Europe. Thus fiscal policy in the United States will have to become more restrictive. It is difficult to predict whether a more growth-oriented monetary policy will compensate for this;

- Western Europe is reforming its welfare systems and is increasingly cost conscious: several countries have started to tackle the pension problem, welfare costs have been reduced in most western European countries without dismantling the core elements of the welfare state , and unfavourable incentive structures are being changed;

- Western Europe still has an advantage in the technology diffusion phase: the European system of innovation, with its reliance on skilled labour and small-scale innovation, seems to be more competitive during the diffusion phase of a new technology, and step-by-step improvement in quality is one of western Europe's core capabilities;

- EU enlargement, the shaping of new institutions, liberalization and the consequences of the Single Market will favour growth and competitiveness in the long run. Some of these policies may have resulted in short-term costs associated with structural change and declining employment, but the growth effect of European integration should eventually become evident, and then accelerate as a result of rapid growth in the accession countries;

- Higher levels of research and a high degree of efficiency in the United States persist. Even if certain European countries are catching up and differences in some of the growth drivers are diminishing, there continue to be differences in the levels of most of these determinants, reflecting differences in quantitative inputs as well as efficiency;

- The industry structure should remain more favourable in the United States, where the share of technology-intensive and ICT industries is higher. The share of labour-intensive industries is declining, but is still higher in western Europe. However, western Europe is likely to maintain its advantage in medium-skilled industries and in upgrading the quality of existing structures;[282]

- Taxes, welfare and the regulatory burden are lower in the United States. The creation of new firms is easier, venture capital is more abundant, and more cheap labour is available, due to the open labour market as well as high rates of legal and illegal immigration;

- The long-term impact of increased expenditures on security will probably be a burden for the United States. Expenditure on war and security can initially boost demand and stabilize growth, but a long-standing preoccupation with security is likely to create a heavy financial burden and may divert financial resources from more profitable projects (and from areas higher in the priority of the more developed countries: health, education and equity).

Summing up, the difference between United States and western European rates of growth may decline, since the risk of a widening trade deficit and the costs of war and security could prove to be a burden for the United States. Nevertheless, a higher growth rate for the United States in the medium term is forecast.

7.4 Differences among western European countries

Differences in dynamics among western European countries have become larger in the 1990s. Cross-county comparisons of such differences can be used to learn about the determinants of growth in the 1990s.

---

[282] K. Aiginger, "Europe's position in quality competition", background report for *The European Competitiveness Report 2000*, European Commission (Brussels), 2000.

TABLE 7.4.1

Performance of top 3 and big 3 European countries relative to the EU-15 and the United States

	Top 3 European countries [a]	Big 3 European countries [b]	EU-15	United States
Real growth of GDP				
Growth, 1993-2002	2.9	1.6	2.1	3.2
Acceleration [c]	1.2	-1.0	-0.5	-0.2
Macro productivity growth				
Growth, 1993-2002	2.4	1.2	1.4	1.6
Acceleration [c]	0.5	-0.8	-0.6	–
Employment rate				
Average, 1993-2002	70.8	61.9	64.4	79.7
Absolute change, 1993-2002	1.2	2.0	3.0	3.7
Unemployment rate				
Average, 1993-2002	8.7	9.9	9.2	5.2
Absolute change, 1993-2002	-2.5	0.3	-1.0	-1.6
Inflation rate				
Average, 1993-2002	1.8	2.2	2.4	2.5
Absolute change, 1993-2002	-0.3	-1.9	-2.1	-1.4
Budget deficit as a per cent of GDP [d]				
2002	-2.3	3.0	2.0	3.2
Absolute change, 1993-2002	-5.0	-3.7	-3.9	-2.7
Public debt as a per cent of GDP				
2002	46.8	75.7	62.7	61.0
Absolute change, 1993-2002	-9.9	12.3	3.7	-13.8
Taxes as a per cent of GDP				
2002	56.6	47.0	45.5	31.6
Absolute change, 1993-2002	-4.5	1.0	-0.1	0.6
GDP per capita at PPP 2002				
Thousand euros	25.3	24.5	23.9	33.5

Source: WIFO calculations, based on the annual macroeconomic database of the European Commission's Directorate General for Economic and Financial Affairs (AMECO) (DG ECFIN).

[a] Denmark, Finland and Sweden.

[b] France, Germany and Italy.

[c] Growth per annum 1993-2002 minus growth per annum 1983-1992.

[d] Negative value = surplus.

Specifically, if the high welfare costs were at the heart of the European problem of low dynamics, it could be expected that the worst performers should be countries with the most comprehensive welfare programmes and high taxes.

Denmark, Finland and Sweden can be ranked[283] as the three best performers in western Europe using indicators on growth of output, productivity and employment to measure "overall economic performance". The same conclusions have been reached in assessments of the competitiveness of western European countries by the International Institute of Management Development (IMD) and the World

CHART 7.4.1

Indicators of future growth potential: top 3 European countries [a] versus 3 large European economies [b]

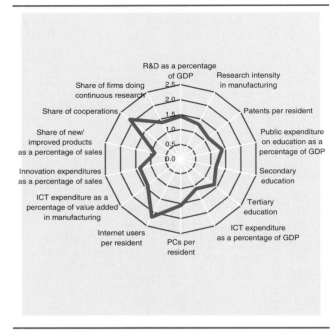

Source: WIFO calculations, based on Eurostat NewCronos Database; European Information Technology Observatory (EITO).

Note: Values inside the unit circle indicate that levels in the top 3 countries are below the levels of the corresponding indicator in the 3 large economies. Data refer to last year available for the period 1999-2001.

[a] Denmark, Finland and Sweden.

[b] France, Germany and Italy.

Economic Forum (WEF), and in studies by the OECD on countries' growth differences. These three countries are also welfare states of the Nordic type, which means they are characterized by ambitious social goals and a high degree of government involvement.

The strategy pursued by these successful countries has been called the three tier strategy.[284] First, they contained private and public costs in order to restore profitability and fiscal prudence. Second, they improved incentives by fine-tuning their welfare systems and liberalizing part-time work as well as product markets. And third, they significantly increased investment in future growth, surpassing that of the larger western European economies in research input and output, in education expenditures and quality, and in information technology. In contrast, the larger continental economies (France, Germany and Italy) underperformed in terms of investments in growth drivers (chart 7.4.1).

7.5 Towards a new European model: a tentative sketch of its features

The structures and policies of the most successful European countries are very different from those of the

---

[283] K. Aiginger, "The three tier strategy ...", op. cit. Ranking the countries according to the indicators in table 7.4.1 reveals Ireland as the top performing country, followed by Sweden, Denmark and Finland. While Ireland's is a remarkable story of catching up and finally forging ahead (in terms of a subset of indicators, but not in terms of income per head or wages per worker), we consider the other three as important examples of how mature and rich countries can continue to grow, and call them the "top 3 countries".

[284] K. Aiginger, "The three tier strategy ...", op. cit.

TABLE 7.5.1

Old model versus new European model of a reformed welfare state

Old model of European welfare	New model of the leading three countries [a]
Welfare pillar	
Security in existing jobs	Assistance in finding a new job
High replacement ratios	Incentives to accept new jobs (return to labour force)
Structural change in existing firms (often large firms)	Job creation in new firms, service, self-employment
Comprehensive health coverage, pensions, education	Coverage dependent on personal obligations
Regulation of labour and product markets	Flexibility as a strategy for firms and as a right for employees
Focus on stable, full-time jobs	Part-time work as individual choice (softened by some rules)
Early retirement	Encouraging employment of the elderly
Policy pillar	
Focus on price stability	Focus on growth and new technologies
Asymmetric fiscal policy (deficits)	Fiscal prudence (but flexible in crisis)
Incentives for physical investment	Incentives for research, education and new technologies
Subsidies for ailing firms (public ownership)	Industrial areas, university nexus
Industrial policy for large firms	Start-ups, venture capital, services
Local champions, permissive competition policy	Exploit current strengths (cluster and regional policy) and competition

Source: K. Aiginger, "The economic agenda: a view from Europe", *Review of International Economics*, Vol. 12, Issue 2 (Special Issue: Economic Agenda for the 21st Century), May 2004.

[a] Denmark, Finland, Sweden.

United States system as far as welfare and government involvement are concerned, as well as in their commitments to training and redistribution as goals of labour market policy. Their labour market policies offer a high degree of flexibility for firms (e.g. easy dismissals and low corporate taxes), but also provide security to individuals in helping them to find new jobs and upgrade their qualifications. This system could therefore be called "flexicurity", and it builds on the broader concept of "active labour market policies". These countries accord high priority to new technologies, efficiency of production and the competitiveness of firms (table 7.5.1). In contrast to the United States, they rely on proactive industrial policies, with government support for information technology, for agencies promoting research, for regional policies and for clusters. Although these countries suffered severe financial crises when many of the problems suspected of dampening growth in a highly developed welfare state surfaced (e.g. costs increased faster than productivity and government expenditures increased faster than taxes), they changed their course without, however, abandoning the principles of the welfare state and without giving up their environmental goals. We believe that the specific elements of the political reforms in the northern European countries suggest that there may be a new kind of reformed European model, which combines welfare and sustainability on the one hand with efficiency and economic incentives on the other.[285]

The new welfare state, as represented by the policy strategy in these leading European countries, is different from the old welfare state in the following ways:

- The social system remains inclusive and tight, but the social benefits may depend on the individual's inputs; they may be conditional on certain obligations; replacement rates are lower than they used to be (but still high by international standards) to provide better incentives to work;

- Taxes are relatively high, but in line with expenditures, and aim at positive balances to take care of future pensions or to repay current debt;

- Wages are high, but the individual's position is not guaranteed, as business conditions vary. However, assistance and training opportunities that are personalized, less bureaucratic and less centralized are offered to people who lose their jobs;

- Welfare-to-work elements have been introduced, usually on a decentralized – sometimes even private – basis; conditions differ according to the size and kind of problem, the background philosophy being one of giving help but without encouraging laziness;

- Part-time work and adaptation of work to life cycles is encouraged – not prevented – and social benefits are pro rata extended to part-time work, which becomes an individual right and a measure voluntarily taken to enforce, rather than prevent, gender equality;

- Technology policy and adoption of new technologies, rather than subsidizing old industries, are a

---

[285] For earlier suggestions along this line, see K. Aiginger, *The New European Model of the Reformed Welfare State*, European Forum Working Paper 2/2002, Stanford University, December 2002;

K. Aiginger and M. Landesmann, op. cit.; K. Aiginger, "Economic agenda …, op. cit.

precondition for the survival of the welfare state, and lead to more challenging and interesting work.[286]

The new European model differs from the United States model in the following ways:

- Even where welfare costs are streamlined and incentives improved, the welfare system offers comprehensive insurance against economic and social risks and a broad coverage of health risks;

- Environmental and social goals as well as equity of income distribution and prevention of poverty are high on the political agenda;

- Government and public institutions play a proactive role in promoting innovation, efficiency, structural change, higher qualifications and lifelong learning. Public institutions also provide the largest share of education and health care;

- Social partners (institutions comprising representatives of firms and employees) determine many elements of wage formation, and together they develop labour laws and institutions specifically and economic policy in general;

- Government is large and taxes are high, even if there are mechanisms to limit increases in spending and goals for achieving a sound fiscal policy in periods of increasing demand.

7.6 Summary

Income per capita in the United States is 40 per cent higher than in Europe and is unlikely to converge. Productivity is 30 per cent higher, although Europe had been catching up in GDP per person employed over a long period in the post-war years. However, in the past 10 years the United States has once again increased its lead. GDP per hour worked is the most favourable indicator of European performance, revealing a gap of less than 10 per cent, but again the difference has been increasing recently. Employment indicators show that the United States created 78 million jobs between 1990 and 2003, while Europe created 42 million. The employment rate in Europe, which up to the 1970s was higher, is now 13 percentage points lower than that of the United States (although the gap has recently narrowed slightly). Unemployment is higher in Europe, even excluding the significant number of people on disability or in early retirement schemes, which decreases open unemployment. There are fewer hours worked in Europe, partly voluntarily and partly due to the lack of full-time jobs. Leisure takes a higher priority in Europe.

International organizations (e.g. OECD and the EU Commission) often blame the higher welfare costs and stricter regulations of labour and product markets for the low dynamics in the European economies ("Paris consensus"). However, assessing performance differences in Europe reveals that the best performing countries (besides Ireland, which experienced a remarkable catching up) are three Nordic European welfare states: Denmark, Finland and Sweden. All three countries had suffered structural and cyclical crises, which appeared to confirm some of the bleak predictions for welfare states, but over the past 10 years they have been performing better than the other European countries, with a growth performance similar to that of the United States. At the same time, they are successfully trying to combine welfare with higher efficiency. This chapter has highlighted the main characteristics of these countries and their reforms, enabling the definition of a new European model of a reformed welfare state. It provides an alternative model to that of the United States in that it aims at achieving economic efficiency while maintaining the traditional European concerns for social welfare and environmental quality. The model thus combines security for citizens with efficiency and flexibility for firms, and may be considered as being in the tradition of Josef Steindl and Michal Kalecki.[287]

The fact that the three Nordic states performed well in the 1990s does not imply that welfare costs are irrelevant for performance. After suffering severe crises, these countries realized that costs needed to be cut and the fiscal balance stabilized, that incentives had to be implemented and institutions reformed. But, most importantly, they realized also that cost-cutting represents a short-term strategy which needs to be complemented by proactive policies to promote research, education and the diffusion of new technologies. This chapter has attempted to present the tentative hypothesis that a new European model is in the offing, with an emphasis on cost balancing, institutional flexibility and technology orientation. Even in the trough period, from 2001 to 2004, the budgets in all three countries have been balanced. The firms are more flexible with regard to the use of labour, and workers who are laid off are efficiently assisted in finding new jobs. Replacement ratios have been reduced and benefits are conditional upon job searches and training efforts. Thus the new European model of the reformed welfare state has three major elements: social and environmental responsibility, openness and technology promotion.

---

[286] Surprisingly, the policies pursued by the leading countries have many similarities with the economic policy recommendations of the Steindl-Kalecki tradition, as described in A. Guger, M. Marterbauer and E. Walterskirchen, op. cit.

[287] J. Steindl, *Maturity and Stagnation in American Capitalism* (Oxford, Blackwell, 1952); M. Kalecki, *Studies in the Theory of Business Cycles, 1933-1939* (New York, Augustus M. Kelley, 1966).

STATISTICAL APPENDIX

For the user's convenience, as well as to lighten the text, the *Economic Survey of Europe* includes a set of appendix tables showing time series for main economic indicators over a longer period. The data are presented in two sections: *Appendix A* provides macroeconomic indicators for the market economies in western Europe and the 10 new EU member states, which joined the European Union at the beginning of May 2004, as well as North America and Japan. *Appendix B* provides comparative macroeconomic indicators for the south-east European countries and the Commonwealth of Independent States. For all countries, national accounts data for more recent years may be subject to revision as more comprehensive benchmark figures become available.

Data were compiled from international and national statistical sources. Regional aggregates are UNECE secretariat calculations using PPPs. Greece, which became a member of the euro area at the beginning of 2001, has been included in the euro area aggregates for all years shown in the appendix tables in order to ensure continuity of time series.

The figures for 2004 are based on data available in mid-December 2004.

APPENDIX TABLE A.1

Real GDP in Europe, North America and Japan, 1989-2003
(Percentage change over the preceding year)

	1989	1990	1991	1992	1993	1994	1995	1996	1997	1998	1999	2000	2001	2002	2003
France	4.2	2.6	1.0	1.5	-0.9	2.1	1.7	1.1	1.9	3.4	3.2	3.8	2.1	1.2	0.5
Germany [a]	3.9	5.7	5.1	2.2	-1.1	2.3	1.7	0.8	1.4	2.0	2.0	2.9	0.8	0.1	-0.1
Italy	2.9	2.0	1.4	0.8	-0.9	2.2	2.9	1.1	2.0	1.8	1.7	3.0	1.8	0.4	0.3
Austria	3.5	4.6	3.6	2.4	0.3	2.7	1.9	2.6	1.8	3.6	3.3	3.4	0.7	1.2	0.8
Belgium	3.5	3.1	1.8	1.5	-1.0	3.2	2.4	1.2	3.5	2.0	3.2	3.9	0.7	0.9	1.3
Finland	4.8	-0.3	-6.4	-3.8	-1.2	3.9	3.4	3.9	6.3	5.0	3.4	5.1	1.1	2.3	1.9
Greece	3.8	–	3.1	0.7	-1.6	2.0	2.1	2.4	3.6	3.4	3.4	4.5	4.3	3.6	4.5
Ireland	5.8	8.5	1.9	3.3	2.7	5.8	9.8	8.1	10.8	8.9	11.1	9.9	6.0	6.1	3.7
Luxembourg	9.8	5.3	8.6	1.8	4.2	3.8	1.4	3.3	8.3	6.9	7.8	9.0	1.5	2.5	2.9
Netherlands	4.8	4.1	2.4	1.5	0.7	2.9	3.0	3.0	3.8	4.3	4.0	3.5	1.4	0.6	-0.9
Portugal	6.4	4.0	4.4	1.1	-2.0	1.0	4.3	3.5	4.0	4.6	3.8	3.4	1.7	0.4	-1.2
Spain	4.8	3.8	2.5	0.9	-1.0	2.4	2.8	2.4	4.0	4.3	4.2	4.4	2.8	2.2	2.5
Euro area	4.0	3.6	2.6	1.4	-0.8	2.4	2.3	1.5	2.4	2.9	2.9	3.5	1.7	0.9	0.6
United Kingdom	2.2	0.8	-1.4	0.2	2.3	4.4	2.9	2.8	3.3	3.1	2.9	3.9	2.3	1.8	2.2
Denmark	0.2	1.0	1.1	0.6	–	5.5	2.8	2.5	3.0	2.5	2.6	2.8	1.6	1.0	0.5
Sweden	2.7	1.0	-1.1	-1.2	-2.0	4.2	4.1	1.3	2.4	3.6	4.6	4.3	1.0	2.0	1.5
EU-15	3.6	3.0	1.9	1.2	-0.4	2.8	2.5	1.7	2.6	2.9	2.9	3.6	1.8	1.1	0.9
Cyprus	7.9	7.4	0.6	9.8	0.7	5.9	6.1	1.8	2.3	5.0	4.8	5.0	4.1	2.1	1.9
Czech Republic	..	..	-11.6	-0.5	0.1	2.2	5.9	4.2	-0.7	-1.1	1.2	3.9	2.6	1.5	3.7
Estonia	..	..	-10.0	-14.1	-8.5	-1.6	4.5	4.5	10.5	5.2	-0.1	7.8	6.4	7.2	5.1
Hungary	..	..	-11.9	-3.1	-0.6	2.9	1.5	1.3	4.6	4.9	4.2	5.2	3.8	3.5	3.0
Latvia	..	..	-12.6	-32.1	-11.4	2.2	-0.9	3.8	8.3	4.7	3.3	6.9	8.0	6.4	7.5
Lithuania	..	..	-5.7	-21.3	-16.2	-9.8	5.2	4.7	7.0	7.3	-1.7	3.9	6.4	6.8	9.7
Malta	8.2	6.3	6.3	4.7	4.5	5.7	6.2	3.9	4.9	3.4	4.0	6.4	-2.4	2.6	-0.3
Poland	..	..	-7.0	2.6	3.8	5.2	7.0	6.0	6.8	4.8	4.1	4.0	1.0	1.4	3.8
Slovakia	..	..	-14.6	-6.4	-3.7	6.2	5.8	6.1	4.6	4.2	1.5	2.0	3.8	4.6	4.5
Slovenia	..	..	-8.9	-5.5	2.8	5.3	4.1	3.6	4.8	3.6	5.6	3.9	2.7	3.3	2.5
New EU members-10	..	..	-9.6	-2.8	0.2	3.6	5.5	4.7	4.7	3.6	3.1	4.1	2.4	2.4	4.0
EU-25	..	..	0.9	0.9	-0.3	2.8	2.7	2.0	2.8	3.0	2.9	3.6	1.8	1.2	1.2
Iceland	0.3	1.2	0.1	-3.3	0.8	4.0	0.1	5.2	4.7	5.6	4.2	5.6	2.7	-0.5	4.0
Israel	1.4	6.6	6.1	7.2	3.8	7.0	6.5	5.3	3.0	3.3	2.6	7.5	-0.3	-0.7	1.3
Norway	1.2	2.0	3.6	3.3	2.7	5.3	4.4	5.3	5.2	2.6	2.1	2.8	2.7	1.4	0.4
Switzerland	4.3	3.7	-0.8	–	-0.2	1.1	0.4	0.5	1.9	2.8	1.3	3.6	1.0	0.3	-0.4
WECEE	..	..	0.9	0.9	-0.3	2.8	2.7	2.0	2.8	3.0	2.9	3.6	1.8	1.2	1.1
Canada	2.6	0.2	-2.1	0.9	2.3	4.8	2.8	1.6	4.2	4.1	5.5	5.2	1.8	3.4	2.0
United States	3.5	1.8	-0.2	3.3	2.7	4.0	2.5	3.7	4.5	4.2	4.4	3.7	0.8	1.9	3.0
North America	3.4	1.6	-0.3	3.1	2.6	4.1	2.5	3.5	4.5	4.2	4.5	3.8	0.8	2.0	3.0
Japan	5.3	5.2	3.4	1.0	0.2	1.1	2.0	3.4	1.8	-1.0	-0.1	2.4	0.2	-0.3	1.3
Europe, North America and Japan	..	..	0.7	1.8	1.0	3.1	2.5	2.8	3.3	2.9	3.2	3.5	1.2	1.3	1.9
Memorandum items:															
EU-8 [b]	..	..	-9.7	-2.9	0.2	3.5	5.5	4.7	4.7	3.6	3.1	4.1	2.4	2.4	4.0
Western Europe	3.6	3.0	1.8	1.2	-0.3	2.8	2.4	1.8	2.6	2.9	2.9	3.6	1.8	1.1	0.9
Western Europe and North America	3.5	2.3	0.7	2.1	1.2	3.4	2.5	2.7	3.6	3.6	3.7	3.7	1.3	1.6	2.0

Source: Eurostat, NewCronos Database; OECD, *National Accounts* (Paris), various issues; national statistics.

Note: Excluding south-east Europe and the European CIS countries. The same proviso applies through appendix table A.11. Statistical data for south-east Europe and the CIS are provided in the second part of this appendix. All aggregates exclude Israel. Growth rates of regional aggregates have been calculated from national data at constant prices of 2000 converted into dollars using purchasing power parities.

[a] West Germany, 1989-1991.

[b] Czech Republic, Estonia, Hungary, Latvia, Lithuania, Poland, Slovakia and Slovenia.

APPENDIX TABLE A.2

Real private consumption expenditure in Europe, North America and Japan, 1989-2003
(Percentage change over the preceding year)

	1989	1990	1991	1992	1993	1994	1995	1996	1997	1998	1999	2000	2001	2002	2003
France	2.8	2.5	0.7	0.9	-0.4	1.2	1.2	1.3	0.2	3.4	3.2	2.6	2.7	1.5	1.5
Germany [a]	3.2	4.1	4.6	2.7	0.1	1.1	2.1	1.0	0.6	1.8	3.7	2.0	1.7	-0.7	–
Italy	3.7	2.1	2.9	1.9	-3.7	1.5	1.7	1.2	3.2	3.2	2.6	2.7	0.8	0.5	1.3
Austria	3.9	4.6	3.6	3.6	-0.3	3.3	0.4	3.4	–	1.6	2.0	3.9	1.0	-0.1	0.6
Belgium	3.3	3.2	3.0	1.9	-0.4	2.4	1.6	1.1	2.0	3.1	2.3	3.5	0.6	0.3	2.2
Finland	5.3	-1.1	-3.8	-4.0	-3.8	2.5	4.1	3.7	3.4	4.3	3.5	3.1	1.8	1.5	4.3
Greece	6.3	2.6	2.9	2.3	-0.8	1.9	2.5	2.4	2.7	3.5	2.5	2.0	3.0	3.0	4.4
Ireland	6.5	1.4	1.8	2.9	2.9	4.4	3.4	6.4	7.2	7.2	8.8	9.0	5.2	2.6	2.6
Luxembourg	4.8	3.8	7.0	-2.3	2.1	4.0	1.9	4.3	3.9	6.6	2.6	4.6	5.1	3.2	1.6
Netherlands	3.0	3.8	2.7	0.5	0.3	1.4	2.9	4.0	3.0	4.8	4.7	3.5	1.4	0.8	-2.6
Portugal	2.9	6.4	4.2	4.7	1.1	1.0	0.6	3.0	3.3	5.0	5.1	2.9	1.2	1.1	-0.5
Spain	5.4	3.5	2.9	2.2	-1.9	1.1	1.7	2.2	3.2	4.4	4.7	4.1	2.8	2.9	2.9
Euro area	3.6	3.2	2.9	2.0	-1.1	1.4	1.8	1.6	1.7	3.1	3.5	2.8	1.9	0.7	1.1
United Kingdom	3.4	1.0	-1.5	0.5	3.0	3.1	1.7	3.6	3.6	3.9	4.4	4.6	2.9	3.3	2.3
Denmark	-0.1	0.1	1.6	1.9	0.5	6.5	1.2	2.5	2.9	2.3	0.7	-0.7	-0.2	0.6	0.8
Sweden	1.2	-0.4	1.1	-1.3	-3.5	1.9	1.0	1.6	2.7	3.0	3.8	5.0	0.4	1.4	1.5
EU-15	3.5	2.7	2.1	1.6	-0.4	1.8	1.7	2.0	2.1	3.2	3.6	3.1	2.0	1.2	1.3
Cyprus	6.9	9.0	9.9	3.2	-4.8	5.0	10.3	3.5	3.9	8.6	2.8	8.2	4.6	2.5	2.4
Czech Republic	..	..	-21.4	8.8	1.2	6.9	5.9	8.8	1.3	-1.5	2.1	2.9	2.6	2.8	4.9
Estonia	..	..	..	..	..	0.6	5.0	10.1	10.5	5.2	-2.5	8.6	6.2	10.3	5.7
Hungary	..	..	..	1.3	3.1	0.1	-6.9	-3.6	1.9	4.8	5.6	5.5	5.7	10.2	8.0
Latvia	..	..	-26.0	-43.4	-7.4	3.2	-1.7	10.6	5.0	0.7	4.3	6.3	7.3	7.4	8.6
Lithuania	..	..	..	..	..	..	..	6.5	5.3	4.8	4.1	6.1	3.6	6.1	11.0
Malta	9.2	3.8	3.8	4.3	0.8	2.3	10.5	7.1	1.6	2.5	6.1	7.4	-0.8	-0.4	1.6
Poland	..	..	6.6	2.5	5.4	3.9	3.2	8.5	6.9	4.8	5.2	2.8	2.0	3.4	3.0
Slovakia	..	..	..	..	1.3	1.0	5.4	7.9	5.5	6.5	3.2	-0.8	4.7	5.5	-0.6
Slovenia	..	..	-10.9	-3.6	13.8	4.0	9.2	2.6	2.5	3.0	5.9	0.4	2.3	0.4	2.9
New EU members-10	..	..	..	..	..	..	..	6.5	4.9	3.7	4.4	3.1	3.1	4.5	4.2
EU-25	..	..	..	..	..	..	..	2.3	2.3	3.3	3.7	3.1	2.1	1.5	1.6
Iceland	-4.2	0.5	2.8	-3.1	-4.6	3.0	2.2	5.3	5.1	10.1	7.3	3.8	-3.0	-1.0	6.4
Israel	0.5	6.0	7.2	7.6	7.2	9.6	7.8	5.6	2.9	4.2	4.2	7.6	2.1	1.1	1.3
Norway	-0.6	0.7	2.3	2.2	2.4	3.3	3.7	6.5	3.2	2.7	3.3	3.9	1.8	3.6	3.7
Switzerland	2.7	1.0	1.7	0.4	-0.6	1.0	0.7	1.0	1.5	2.4	2.3	2.3	2.0	0.3	0.5
WECEE	..	..	..	..	..	..	..	2.4	2.3	3.3	3.7	3.1	2.1	1.5	1.6
Canada	3.4	1.2	-1.6	1.5	1.8	3.0	2.1	2.6	4.6	2.8	3.8	4.0	2.7	3.4	3.1
United States	2.7	1.8	0.2	3.3	3.3	3.7	2.7	3.4	3.8	5.0	5.1	4.7	2.5	3.1	3.3
North America	2.7	1.8	–	3.1	3.2	3.7	2.7	3.4	3.8	4.9	5.0	4.6	2.5	3.1	3.3
Japan	4.8	4.6	2.9	2.6	1.4	2.7	1.9	2.5	0.7	-0.2	–	0.5	1.1	0.5	0.2
Europe, North America and Japan	..	..	..	..	..	..	..	2.8	2.8	3.5	3.8	3.5	2.2	2.2	2.2
Memorandum items:															
EU-8	..	..	..	..	..	..	..	6.6	4.9	3.6	4.4	3.1	3.1	4.5	4.3
Western Europe	3.4	2.6	2.1	1.6	-0.4	1.8	1.7	2.0	2.1	3.2	3.6	3.1	2.0	1.2	1.3
Western Europe and North America	3.0	2.2	1.0	2.4	1.5	2.8	2.2	2.8	3.0	4.1	4.4	4.0	2.3	2.3	2.4

Source: Eurostat, NewCronos Database; OECD, *National Accounts* (Paris), various issues; national statistics.

Note: See appendix table A.1.

[a] West Germany, 1989-1991.

APPENDIX TABLE A.3

Real general government consumption expenditure in Europe, North America and Japan, 1989-2003
(Percentage change over the preceding year)

	1989	1990	1991	1992	1993	1994	1995	1996	1997	1998	1999	2000	2001	2002	2003
France	1.6	2.5	2.7	3.8	4.6	0.7	-0.1	2.3	2.1	-0.1	1.5	2.8	2.9	4.6	2.4
Germany [a]	-1.1	3.1	1.9	5.0	0.1	2.4	1.5	1.8	0.3	1.9	0.8	1.1	1.0	1.9	0.1
Italy	0.2	2.5	1.7	0.6	-0.2	-0.9	-2.2	1.0	0.2	0.2	1.3	1.7	3.9	1.9	2.2
Austria	1.9	2.2	2.6	2.8	3.2	2.6	3.0	1.5	3.0	2.3	3.0	0.2	-1.4	1.1	0.4
Belgium	1.2	-0.4	3.6	1.5	-0.2	1.4	1.5	2.4	0.2	1.1	3.6	2.3	2.8	2.3	2.7
Finland	2.3	4.2	1.9	-2.5	-4.2	0.8	2.0	2.6	2.9	2.0	1.4	–	2.4	3.8	0.7
Greece	5.4	0.6	-1.5	-3.0	2.6	-1.1	5.6	0.9	3.0	1.7	2.1	14.8	-3.1	5.3	-2.5
Ireland	-1.3	5.4	2.7	3.0	0.1	4.1	3.9	3.4	5.1	5.8	7.4	8.1	11.3	8.4	2.6
Luxembourg	8.2	6.7	4.0	3.2	5.2	1.0	4.7	5.6	3.0	1.3	7.3	4.8	6.5	3.2	5.0
Netherlands	1.9	2.2	2.9	2.9	1.6	1.5	1.5	-0.4	3.2	3.6	2.5	2.0	4.2	3.8	2.7
Portugal	6.4	4.2	9.6	-0.9	-0.2	4.3	1.0	3.4	2.2	4.1	5.6	4.1	3.3	2.3	-0.4
Spain	8.3	6.3	6.0	3.5	2.7	0.5	2.4	1.3	2.9	3.7	4.2	5.6	3.5	4.1	3.9
Euro area	1.3	2.9	2.6	2.9	1.5	1.0	0.6	1.6	1.4	1.4	1.9	2.5	2.6	3.1	1.7
United Kingdom	1.0	2.2	3.0	0.7	-0.7	1.0	1.4	1.3	-0.4	1.2	3.5	2.3	2.6	3.8	3.5
Denmark	-0.8	-0.2	0.6	0.8	4.1	3.0	2.1	3.4	0.8	3.1	2.0	0.9	2.7	2.1	1.0
Sweden	3.0	2.5	3.4	2.1	0.1	-0.8	-0.4	0.6	-0.9	3.4	1.7	-1.2	0.9	2.3	0.8
EU-15	1.2	2.7	2.7	2.5	1.1	1.0	0.7	1.6	1.1	1.5	2.1	2.3	2.5	3.2	1.9
Cyprus	1.9	17.4	3.9	13.8	-14.3	4.1	2.9	12.6	4.0	7.3	-7.7	-0.1	10.4	8.5	1.7
Czech Republic	..	..	-12.3	-6.7	3.6	0.2	-4.3	1.5	1.4	-1.0	5.4	0.2	3.8	4.5	4.2
Estonia	..	..	..	..	..	4.0	13.5	-3.1	-1.3	1.7	2.9	1.1	1.8	5.9	5.8
Hungary	..	..	..	-1.1	9.8	-7.4	-5.7	-2.3	3.1	1.8	1.5	1.9	6.2	5.0	5.4
Latvia	..	..	-3.3	8.0	-0.1	-1.2	1.3	-7.3	3.2	13.2	-0.4	-4.0	2.8	2.2	1.9
Lithuania	..	..	..	..	..	..	..	2.5	6.3	6.0	-8.1	3.9	0.3	1.9	5.7
Malta	12.7	5.7	10.9	8.9	6.0	6.4	8.5	8.5	-1.2	-4.0	-0.6	5.4	0.3	3.8	1.6
Poland	..	..	9.6	5.9	3.2	1.2	3.7	2.3	3.3	2.0	1.9	1.3	0.6	0.4	0.1
Slovakia	..	..	-17.8	8.5	-4.3	-10.7	3.6	17.2	-5.4	12.5	-7.1	1.6	4.6	4.9	2.7
Slovenia	..	..	-0.3	-1.7	5.3	2.1	2.5	3.4	2.4	5.4	2.9	2.3	3.9	2.5	1.9
New EU members-10	..	..	..	..	..	..	..	2.3	2.2	2.7	1.3	1.2	2.7	2.7	2.5
EU-25	..	..	..	..	..	..	..	1.7	1.1	1.6	2.1	2.2	2.5	3.1	2.0
Iceland	3.0	4.4	3.1	-0.7	2.3	4.0	1.8	1.2	2.5	3.4	4.9	4.4	3.1	3.9	3.0
Israel	-9.2	7.6	4.6	1.6	4.2	-0.3	-1.0	5.4	1.9	2.2	2.9	2.2	5.6	5.0	-2.0
Norway	2.1	5.3	5.4	5.6	2.7	1.5	1.5	3.1	2.5	3.3	3.2	1.3	5.8	3.1	1.4
Switzerland	5.4	5.4	4.3	1.7	-0.7	2.0	1.0	0.9	-0.1	-0.9	0.3	2.6	4.2	3.2	1.4
WECEE	..	..	..	..	..	..	..	1.7	1.2	1.6	2.1	2.2	2.6	3.1	2.0
Canada	2.8	3.5	2.9	1.0	–	-1.2	-0.6	-1.2	-1.0	3.2	2.1	3.1	3.7	2.8	3.8
United States	2.5	2.5	1.3	0.4	-0.3	0.3	0.2	0.4	1.8	1.6	3.1	1.7	3.1	4.0	2.9
North America	2.5	2.6	1.5	0.5	-0.3	0.1	0.1	0.2	1.5	1.8	3.0	1.9	3.2	3.9	3.0
Japan	2.9	3.2	4.1	2.5	3.0	3.2	4.4	3.0	1.1	2.2	4.7	4.9	3.0	2.6	1.1
Europe, North America and Japan	..	..	..	..	..	..	..	1.3	1.3	1.7	2.7	2.4	2.9	3.3	2.3
Memorandum items:															
EU-8	..	..	..	..	..	..	..	2.2	2.2	2.7	1.4	1.2	2.7	2.6	2.5
Western Europe	1.3	2.8	2.8	2.5	1.1	1.0	0.7	1.6	1.1	1.5	2.1	2.3	2.6	3.2	1.9
Western Europe and North America	1.9	2.7	2.1	1.6	0.5	0.6	0.5	1.0	1.3	1.6	2.5	2.1	2.9	3.5	2.4

Source: Eurostat, NewCronos Database; OECD, *National Accounts* (Paris), various issues; national statistics.

Note: See appendix table A.1.

[a] West Germany, 1989-1991.

APPENDIX TABLE A.4

Real gross domestic fixed capital formation in Europe, North America and Japan, 1989-2003
(Percentage change over the preceding year)

	1989	1990	1991	1992	1993	1994	1995	1996	1997	1998	1999	2000	2001	2002	2003
France	7.3	3.3	-1.5	-1.6	-6.4	1.5	2.0	–	-0.1	7.0	8.3	7.8	1.9	-1.6	-0.2
Germany [a]	6.7	7.7	5.2	4.5	-4.4	4.0	-0.6	-0.8	0.6	3.0	4.1	2.7	-4.2	-6.4	-2.2
Italy	4.2	4.0	1.0	-1.4	-10.9	0.1	6.0	3.6	2.1	4.0	5.0	6.9	1.9	1.2	-2.1
Austria	4.2	5.2	8.1	0.2	-1.2	5.2	-1.0	2.6	1.4	3.5	2.3	6.5	-2.1	-3.4	6.2
Belgium	11.8	8.6	-4.1	1.1	-2.5	0.4	3.4	0.9	7.1	3.3	4.4	4.4	0.3	-3.7	-0.9
Finland	12.5	-4.6	-18.5	-16.4	-15.2	-3.6	11.2	6.7	13.8	8.4	2.5	4.1	3.9	-3.1	-2.3
Greece	6.1	4.5	4.2	-3.5	-4.0	-3.1	4.1	8.4	6.8	10.6	11.0	8.0	6.5	5.7	13.7
Ireland	10.1	13.4	-7.0	–	-5.1	11.8	15.8	17.4	18.0	15.5	15.1	7.6	-1.5	2.8	3.6
Luxembourg	6.9	3.4	15.8	-15.1	20.6	–	-1.5	3.8	12.7	11.8	14.6	-3.5	10.0	-1.1	-6.3
Netherlands	5.2	2.6	0.3	0.7	-3.2	2.1	4.1	6.3	6.6	4.2	7.8	1.4	-0.1	-4.5	-3.2
Portugal	3.7	7.6	3.3	4.5	-5.5	2.7	6.6	5.7	13.9	11.5	6.4	3.8	0.8	-5.1	-9.8
Spain	12.0	6.5	1.7	-4.1	-8.9	1.9	7.7	2.1	5.0	10.0	8.8	5.7	3.0	1.7	3.2
Euro area	7.0	5.3	1.4	–	-6.4	2.1	2.9	1.7	2.8	5.6	6.2	5.1	0.1	-2.1	-0.4
United Kingdom	6.0	-2.6	-8.2	-0.9	0.3	4.7	3.1	5.7	6.8	12.7	1.6	3.6	2.6	2.7	2.2
Denmark	-0.6	-2.2	-3.4	-2.1	-3.8	7.7	11.6	3.9	10.9	10.0	1.4	7.1	4.9	4.5	0.1
Sweden	12.1	0.2	-8.5	-11.3	-14.6	6.6	9.9	4.5	-0.3	7.8	8.2	5.7	-1.0	-2.6	-1.5
EU-15	6.9	4.0	-0.1	-0.4	-5.8	2.6	3.2	2.3	3.3	6.6	5.6	5.0	0.5	-1.4	-0.1
Cyprus	20.0	-2.8	-1.6	16.2	-12.8	-2.5	-1.7	7.2	-4.1	7.9	-1.0	3.8	3.2	8.0	-3.4
Czech Republic	..	..	-27.3	16.5	0.2	9.1	19.8	7.6	-3.4	-1.1	-3.5	4.9	5.4	3.4	4.8
Estonia	..	..	..	..	..	9.2	5.6	9.6	19.9	14.0	-15.6	14.3	13.0	17.2	5.4
Hungary	..	..	-10.5	-2.6	2.0	12.5	-4.3	6.7	9.2	13.2	5.9	7.7	5.0	8.0	3.4
Latvia	..	..	-63.9	-28.7	-15.8	0.8	8.7	22.3	20.7	61.4	-6.8	10.2	11.4	13.0	10.9
Lithuania	..	..	..	..	..	..	..	15.2	24.5	21.8	-6.1	-9.0	13.5	11.1	11.4
Malta	1.0	17.9	–	-0.2	11.1	8.5	17.8	-8.4	-4.5	-3.4	4.0	17.5	-8.5	-29.6	41.4
Poland	..	..	-4.4	2.3	2.9	9.2	16.5	19.7	21.7	14.2	6.8	2.7	-8.8	-5.8	-0.5
Slovakia	..	..	-25.2	-4.4	-4.2	-2.5	0.6	29.1	15.0	11.0	-19.6	-7.2	13.9	-0.6	-1.5
Slovenia	..	..	-11.5	-12.9	10.7	14.1	16.8	11.3	13.5	9.9	21.0	0.6	4.1	2.6	5.4
New EU members-10	..	..	..	..	..	..	..	14.3	11.7	10.7	0.9	2.9	–	0.5	2.4
EU-25	..	..	..	..	..	..	..	3.3	4.1	7.0	5.1	4.8	0.4	-1.2	0.2
Iceland	-7.9	3.0	3.3	-11.1	-10.7	0.6	-1.1	25.7	10.0	32.8	-3.0	14.8	-7.6	-15.1	19.0
Israel	-2.2	25.3	41.9	5.2	5.3	8.4	6.6	9.1	-1.0	-3.8	0.1	1.7	-3.1	-7.0	-4.9
Norway	-6.9	-10.8	-3.0	-1.1	6.5	5.3	3.9	10.3	15.5	13.1	-5.6	-3.6	-0.7	-3.4	-3.7
Switzerland	5.3	3.8	-2.2	-8.0	-2.9	6.5	4.4	-1.7	2.0	6.5	1.2	4.3	-3.1	0.3	-0.3
WECEE	..	..	..	..	..	..	..	3.3	4.2	7.1	4.8	4.7	0.3	-1.2	0.1
Canada	5.6	-4.0	-5.5	-2.7	-2.0	7.5	-2.1	4.4	15.2	2.4	7.3	4.7	4.1	2.4	4.9
United States	2.9	-0.2	-5.1	4.8	6.0	7.3	5.7	8.1	8.0	9.1	8.2	6.1	-1.7	-3.1	4.5
North America	3.2	-0.6	-5.1	4.1	5.2	7.3	5.0	7.8	8.6	8.5	8.1	5.9	-1.3	-2.7	4.6
Japan	8.5	7.9	2.3	-2.4	-2.8	-1.5	0.8	6.5	0.5	-3.8	-1.1	1.9	-1.4	-5.8	0.8
Europe, North America and Japan	..	..	..	..	..	..	..	5.6	5.1	5.5	5.0	4.7	-0.6	-2.6	2.0
Memorandum items:															
EU-8	..	..	..	..	..	..	..	14.6	11.9	10.7	0.9	2.9	–	0.6	2.5
Western Europe	6.6	3.8	-0.2	-0.6	-5.6	2.7	3.2	2.3	3.5	6.7	5.2	4.8	0.4	-1.4	-0.1
Western Europe and North America	5.1	1.8	-2.4	1.4	-0.9	4.9	4.1	4.9	6.0	7.6	6.7	5.4	-0.5	-2.0	2.3

Source: Eurostat, NewCronos Database; OECD, *National Accounts* (Paris), various issues; national statistics.

Note: See appendix table A.1.

[a] West Germany, 1989-1991.

APPENDIX TABLE A.5

Real total domestic expenditures in Europe, North America and Japan, 1989-2003
(Percentage change over the preceding year)

	1989	1990	1991	1992	1993	1994	1995	1996	1997	1998	1999	2000	2001	2002	2003
France	3.9	2.8	0.5	0.8	-1.6	2.1	1.6	0.7	0.7	4.0	3.6	4.1	2.0	1.5	1.2
Germany [a]	3.2	4.7	4.4	2.8	-1.1	2.3	1.7	0.3	0.6	2.4	2.8	1.9	-0.8	-1.9	0.5
Italy	3.1	2.7	2.1	0.9	-5.1	1.7	2.0	0.9	2.7	3.1	3.2	2.3	1.4	1.3	1.2
Austria	3.3	4.4	4.2	2.4	-0.4	4.1	1.8	2.7	0.6	2.3	3.0	3.0	-0.3	-0.8	2.3
Belgium	4.1	3.3	1.7	1.7	-0.9	2.4	2.1	0.9	2.7	2.7	2.5	3.7	0.4	0.5	1.7
Finland	6.3	-0.8	-7.8	-6.1	-5.4	3.0	2.7	3.8	4.8	4.2	2.0	2.5	1.8	0.6	1.8
Greece	5.3	2.2	3.5	-0.5	-1.0	1.1	3.5	3.3	3.5	4.6	3.8	5.6	2.4	4.2	5.3
Ireland	6.9	6.3	0.2	-0.1	1.0	5.1	6.5	7.8	9.4	10.3	7.6	9.0	3.7	3.6	3.0
Luxembourg	6.4	4.7	8.6	-4.1	4.6	2.4	0.7	5.0	6.5	7.3	6.6	5.2	4.3	-0.1	2.8
Netherlands	4.8	3.2	2.0	1.3	-1.6	2.3	3.5	2.8	3.9	4.8	4.3	2.5	1.8	0.5	-0.5
Portugal	4.9	5.3	6.1	3.4	-2.1	1.5	4.1	3.0	5.1	6.7	5.9	2.9	1.6	-0.3	-2.7
Spain	7.3	4.6	3.0	1.0	-3.3	1.5	3.1	1.9	3.5	5.7	5.6	4.6	2.9	2.8	3.2
Euro area	4.0	3.6	2.5	1.4	-2.3	2.1	2.1	1.2	1.9	3.7	3.6	3.1	1.1	0.5	1.2
United Kingdom	3.0	-0.3	-2.5	0.9	2.1	3.6	1.9	3.2	3.7	5.2	4.1	4.0	3.1	3.1	2.5
Denmark	-0.1	-0.7	-0.1	0.9	-0.3	7.0	4.2	2.2	4.9	4.0	0.1	2.4	1.0	1.9	0.3
Sweden	4.0	0.7	-2.0	-1.4	-5.2	3.2	2.2	0.9	1.1	4.3	3.3	3.6	-0.3	0.7	0.9
EU-15	3.8	2.8	1.5	1.3	-1.7	2.4	2.1	1.5	2.2	3.9	3.6	3.2	1.4	1.0	1.4
Cyprus	9.7	6.3	5.1	9.3	-9.5	7.4	7.8	4.1	1.1	5.6	2.1	6.1	3.2	4.7	2.3
Czech Republic	..	..	-21.1	4.6	2.2	8.4	8.2	7.7	-1.0	-1.7	1.0	3.9	3.9	3.4	4.2
Estonia	..	..	..	..	..	2.0	7.3	7.0	11.8	4.5	-5.1	10.5	7.1	12.2	5.3
Hungary	..	..	..	-2.8	9.0	1.3	-3.8	0.3	4.9	8.2	5.1	4.8	1.9	5.4	5.4
Latvia	..	..	-21.6	-33.1	-22.5	3.9	-1.7	7.6	5.7	11.4	2.9	3.5	11.2	6.0	11.0
Lithuania	..	..	..	..	..	..	..	6.5	10.3	8.0	-0.3	2.0	5.5	6.5	10.4
Malta	8.1	8.2	4.8	-0.7	5.3	6.4	9.5	2.9	-0.5	-0.2	4.5	9.4	-6.1	-5.3	9.9
Poland	..	..	0.3	0.5	6.0	4.6	6.8	9.4	9.1	6.3	4.8	2.8	-1.6	0.8	2.5
Slovakia	..	..	-24.6	-4.5	-3.8	-4.5	9.9	18.2	3.7	7.2	-6.3	0.1	7.4	4.6	-2.5
Slovenia	..	..	-9.5	-3.2	12.9	5.5	10.2	3.3	4.7	5.1	8.7	1.3	0.9	2.3	4.2
New EU members-10	..	..	..	..	..	..	..	7.9	5.6	5.1	3.0	3.2	1.4	2.8	3.5
EU-25	..	..	..	..	..	..	..	2.0	2.5	4.0	3.6	3.2	1.4	1.2	1.6
Iceland	-4.2	1.5	3.8	-4.4	-3.7	2.2	2.2	6.9	5.4	13.2	4.4	6.6	-3.6	-2.7	7.9
Israel	-3.3	9.4	12.3	5.5	6.2	6.4	5.6	6.1	1.6	1.8	4.4	3.9	2.4	-0.7	-1.7
Norway	-1.4	–	1.7	2.2	3.2	4.2	4.6	4.4	6.7	5.7	0.3	2.3	1.1	2.3	0.7
Switzerland	4.3	3.8	-1.1	-2.3	-0.8	2.8	1.6	0.2	0.5	4.0	0.3	2.1	2.3	-0.8	0.2
WECEE	..	..	..	..	..	..	..	2.0	2.5	4.1	3.5	3.2	1.4	1.1	1.6
Canada	4.1	-0.3	-1.9	0.5	1.5	3.3	1.8	1.3	6.1	2.5	4.2	4.7	1.3	3.7	4.6
United States	2.8	1.4	-0.7	3.3	3.2	4.3	2.4	3.7	4.7	5.3	5.3	4.4	0.9	2.5	3.3
North America	2.9	1.3	-0.8	3.0	3.1	4.2	2.3	3.5	4.8	5.0	5.2	4.4	0.9	2.6	3.4
Japan	5.7	5.3	3.0	0.6	0.2	1.3	2.6	3.9	0.7	-1.5	–	1.9	0.8	-0.9	0.7
Europe, North America and Japan	..	..	..	..	..	..	..	2.9	3.2	3.7	3.8	3.6	1.1	1.5	2.3
Memorandum items:															
EU-8	..	..	..	..	..	..	..	7.9	5.7	5.1	3.0	3.1	1.4	2.9	3.5
Western Europe	3.7	2.8	1.5	1.2	-1.6	2.5	2.2	1.5	2.3	4.0	3.5	3.2	1.4	1.0	1.4
Western Europe and North America	3.3	2.0	0.3	2.1	0.7	3.4	2.2	2.5	3.6	4.5	4.4	3.9	1.2	1.8	2.5

Source: Eurostat, NewCronos Database; OECD, *National Accounts* (Paris), various issues; national statistics.

Note: See appendix table A.1.

[a] West Germany, 1989-1991.

APPENDIX TABLE A.6

Real exports of goods and services in Europe, North America and Japan, 1989-2003
(Percentage change over the preceding year)

	1989	1990	1991	1992	1993	1994	1995	1996	1997	1998	1999	2000	2001	2002	2003
France	10.0	4.8	5.9	5.4	–	7.7	7.7	3.5	11.8	8.3	4.3	12.6	1.6	1.9	-2.5
Germany [a]	10.3	13.2	12.9	-0.8	-5.5	7.6	5.7	5.1	11.2	7.0	5.5	13.5	5.7	4.1	1.8
Italy	7.8	7.5	-1.4	7.3	9.0	9.8	12.6	0.6	6.4	3.4	0.1	9.7	1.6	-3.4	-3.9
Austria	10.1	8.2	3.0	1.5	-2.6	5.5	6.3	4.8	11.4	8.6	5.7	10.5	6.8	3.8	1.4
Belgium	8.2	4.6	3.1	3.7	-0.4	8.3	5.0	3.0	5.9	6.0	5.1	8.4	1.3	1.5	1.7
Finland	3.0	1.5	-7.4	10.1	16.3	13.6	8.5	5.7	13.7	9.2	6.5	19.3	-0.8	5.1	1.3
Greece	1.9	-3.5	4.1	10.0	-2.6	7.4	3.0	3.5	20.0	5.3	18.1	14.1	-1.1	-7.7	1.0
Ireland	10.3	8.7	5.7	13.9	9.7	15.1	20.0	12.2	17.4	22.0	15.2	20.4	8.4	5.7	-0.8
Luxembourg	12.6	5.6	9.2	2.7	4.8	7.7	4.6	5.8	14.7	14.1	14.8	17.3	1.8	-0.6	1.8
Netherlands	7.5	5.6	5.6	1.8	4.8	9.7	8.8	4.6	8.8	7.4	5.1	11.3	1.6	0.8	–
Portugal	12.2	9.5	1.2	3.2	-3.3	8.4	8.8	7.1	7.1	9.1	2.9	7.8	1.4	2.0	4.0
Spain	1.4	4.7	8.2	7.5	7.8	16.7	9.4	10.4	15.3	8.2	7.7	10.1	3.6	1.2	2.6
Euro area	8.4	7.6	6.0	3.5	1.2	9.2	8.2	4.4	10.4	7.3	5.1	11.9	3.2	1.6	0.1
United Kingdom	4.5	5.5	-0.1	4.3	4.4	9.2	9.3	8.6	8.4	2.8	4.3	9.4	2.9	0.1	0.1
Denmark	4.2	6.2	6.1	-0.9	-1.5	7.0	2.7	4.3	4.2	4.3	12.3	13.5	4.4	4.7	–
Sweden	3.2	1.8	-1.9	2.2	8.3	14.1	11.5	3.7	13.8	8.6	7.4	11.5	0.5	1.2	5.0
EU-15	7.6	7.1	4.9	3.5	1.7	9.3	8.3	4.9	10.1	6.7	5.2	11.6	3.1	1.5	0.3
Cyprus	16.8	7.9	-8.4	18.7	-1.3	7.9	4.6	3.5	3.1	1.0	8.5	10.6	6.3	-5.2	-1.4
Czech Republic	..	..	-6.0	9.5	15.8	1.7	16.7	5.5	8.4	10.5	5.5	16.5	11.5	2.1	7.3
Estonia	..	..	..	..	..	3.5	5.3	2.8	28.9	12.0	0.7	28.3	-0.2	0.9	5.7
Hungary	..	..	..	2.1	-10.1	13.7	13.4	12.1	22.3	17.6	12.2	21.0	7.8	3.7	7.6
Latvia	..	..	-32.2	14.9	-22.4	-8.4	4.3	20.2	13.1	4.9	-6.4	11.4	7.5	5.2	5.0
Lithuania	..	..	..	..	..	..	..	19.3	18.7	4.6	-16.8	9.8	21.2	19.5	6.0
Malta	10.7	13.3	7.5	9.7	5.3	7.1	5.4	-6.0	4.0	8.2	8.2	5.6	-4.9	6.6	-3.8
Poland	..	..	-1.7	10.8	3.2	13.1	22.8	12.0	12.2	14.3	-2.6	23.2	3.1	4.8	14.7
Slovakia	..	..	33.4	47.5	-0.2	14.8	4.5	-1.1	17.6	12.8	5.0	13.7	6.3	5.6	22.5
Slovenia	..	..	-20.1	-23.5	0.6	12.3	1.1	2.8	11.3	7.4	1.6	13.0	6.3	6.8	3.1
New EU members-10	..	..	..	..	..	..	..	8.0	14.0	12.5	3.1	18.5	7.2	4.4	10.4
EU-25	..	..	..	..	..	..	..	5.2	10.5	7.3	5.0	12.3	3.5	1.8	1.4
Iceland	2.9	–	-5.9	-2.0	6.5	9.5	-2.3	9.9	5.3	2.2	4.0	5.0	7.7	3.6	-0.7
Israel	4.1	2.0	-2.8	13.9	–	12.9	10.0	5.7	8.6	6.4	12.0	24.0	-12.3	-2.4	6.2
Norway	11.0	8.6	6.1	4.7	3.2	8.4	4.9	10.2	7.7	0.6	2.8	4.0	5.0	0.1	1.2
Switzerland	6.9	2.6	-1.3	3.1	1.3	1.9	0.5	3.6	11.1	3.9	6.5	12.2	0.2	-0.2	–
WECEE	..	..	..	..	..	..	..	5.3	10.4	7.0	5.0	12.2	3.5	1.7	1.4
Canada	1.0	4.7	1.8	7.2	10.8	12.7	8.5	5.6	8.3	9.1	10.7	8.9	-2.8	1.1	-2.4
United States	11.8	8.7	6.6	6.9	3.2	8.7	10.1	8.4	11.9	2.4	4.3	8.7	-5.4	-2.4	1.9
North America	8.8	7.7	5.4	7.0	5.1	9.7	9.7	7.7	11.0	4.1	6.0	8.8	-4.7	-1.4	0.7
Japan	9.3	6.7	4.1	3.9	-0.1	3.6	4.3	6.2	11.3	-2.4	1.5	12.1	-6.0	7.3	9.1
Europe, North America and Japan	..	..	..	..	..	..	..	6.0	10.6	5.6	5.0	11.3	0.7	1.3	1.7
Memorandum items:															
EU-8	..	..	..	..	..	..	..	8.2	14.3	12.7	3.0	18.8	7.4	4.5	10.7
Western Europe	7.7	7.0	4.7	3.5	1.8	9.0	8.0	5.0	10.0	6.4	5.2	11.5	3.0	1.4	0.3
Western Europe and North America	8.0	7.2	4.9	4.5	2.7	9.2	8.5	5.8	10.3	5.7	5.4	10.6	0.7	0.6	0.4

Source: Eurostat, NewCronos Database; OECD, *National Accounts* (Paris), various issues; national statistics.

Note: See appendix table A.1.

[a] West Germany, 1989-1991.

APPENDIX TABLE A.7

Real imports of goods and services in Europe, North America and Japan, 1989-2003

(Percentage change over the preceding year)

	1989	1990	1991	1992	1993	1994	1995	1996	1997	1998	1999	2000	2001	2002	2003
France	8.0	5.5	3.1	1.8	-3.7	8.2	8.0	1.6	6.9	11.6	6.2	14.6	1.3	2.9	-0.1
Germany [a]	8.5	10.7	12.2	1.5	-5.5	7.4	5.6	3.1	8.3	9.1	8.4	10.6	1.0	-1.6	4.0
Italy	8.9	11.5	2.3	7.4	-10.9	8.1	9.7	-0.3	10.1	8.9	5.6	7.1	0.5	-0.2	-0.6
Austria	9.6	7.6	4.6	1.6	-4.8	10.2	6.0	5.0	7.8	5.6	5.0	10.1	5.0	-0.2	4.8
Belgium	9.7	4.9	2.9	4.1	-0.4	7.3	4.7	2.6	5.1	7.3	4.2	8.5	1.0	1.0	2.3
Finland	9.1	-0.6	-12.9	0.5	1.5	12.4	7.4	5.9	11.2	7.9	3.5	16.9	0.2	1.9	0.9
Greece	10.5	8.4	5.8	1.1	0.6	1.5	8.9	7.0	14.2	9.2	15.0	15.1	-5.2	-2.9	4.8
Ireland	13.5	5.1	2.4	8.2	7.5	15.5	16.4	12.5	16.7	26.0	12.1	21.3	6.7	3.3	-2.3
Luxembourg	9.1	5.0	9.1	-3.1	5.2	6.7	4.2	7.6	13.9	15.3	14.6	15.4	3.7	-2.6	1.6
Netherlands	7.7	3.8	4.9	1.5	0.3	9.4	10.5	4.4	9.5	8.5	5.8	10.5	2.2	0.8	0.6
Portugal	5.9	14.5	7.2	10.7	-3.3	8.8	7.4	4.9	10.0	14.2	8.5	5.5	1.1	-0.2	-0.9
Spain	17.7	9.6	10.3	6.8	-5.2	11.4	11.1	8.0	13.2	13.2	12.6	10.5	3.9	3.1	4.8
Euro area	9.3	8.1	6.0	3.5	-4.5	8.4	7.8	3.3	9.1	10.1	7.5	10.9	1.6	0.5	1.9
United Kingdom	7.4	0.5	-4.5	6.8	3.3	5.8	5.6	9.7	9.8	9.3	7.9	9.1	4.9	4.1	1.3
Denmark	4.1	1.2	3.0	-0.4	-2.7	12.3	7.2	3.6	10.0	8.9	5.5	13.5	3.5	7.3	-0.6
Sweden	7.7	0.7	-4.9	1.5	-2.2	12.2	7.2	3.0	12.5	11.3	4.9	11.3	-2.6	-1.9	4.9
EU-15	8.9	6.7	4.2	3.8	-3.4	8.2	7.5	4.2	9.3	10.0	7.4	10.7	2.0	1.1	1.8
Cyprus	20.4	5.8	2.2	18.2	-18.1	8.2	11.5	8.0	0.8	2.3	2.9	12.9	4.7	-0.5	-0.4
Czech Republic	..	..	-32.8	29.7	23.7	14.7	21.2	12.1	6.9	8.4	5.0	16.3	13.0	4.9	7.9
Estonia	..	..	..	..	..	11.1	6.4	7.5	29.3	12.3	-5.2	28.3	2.1	3.7	11.0
Hungary	..	..	..	0.2	20.2	8.8	-0.7	9.4	23.1	23.8	13.3	19.4	5.1	6.2	10.4
Latvia	..	..	-43.9	8.0	-39.8	-0.7	1.4	28.5	6.8	19.0	-5.2	3.1	14.5	4.6	13.0
Lithuania	..	..	..	..	..	..	..	23.3	25.0	6.2	-12.4	4.7	17.7	17.6	8.8
Malta	11.1	15.7	5.4	3.0	5.9	7.5	10.0	-5.9	-1.6	2.5	10.2	10.4	-8.6	-2.4	7.1
Poland	..	..	29.6	1.7	13.2	11.3	24.3	28.0	21.4	18.5	1.0	15.6	-5.3	2.6	9.3
Slovakia	..	..	-14.7	47.1	-0.7	-4.7	11.6	19.7	14.2	16.5	-6.7	10.5	11.0	5.5	13.6
Slovenia	..	..	-22.4	-22.9	17.6	13.1	11.3	2.3	11.5	10.3	8.0	7.6	3.0	4.8	6.4
New EU members-10	..	..	..	..	..	..	..	16.4	15.9	15.3	2.9	15.2	4.7	4.9	9.5
EU-25	..	..	..	..	..	..	..	5.4	10.0	10.6	6.9	11.2	2.3	1.6	2.8
Iceland	-10.3	1.0	5.3	-6.0	-7.8	4.1	3.9	16.5	7.7	23.4	4.2	8.0	-9.0	-2.6	9.7
Israel	-5.1	9.5	15.8	8.4	14.1	10.8	7.7	7.7	3.3	1.7	14.9	12.2	-4.6	-2.1	-1.8
Norway	2.2	2.5	0.5	1.6	4.9	5.8	5.7	8.8	12.4	8.5	-1.8	2.7	0.9	2.3	2.2
Switzerland	6.6	2.8	-1.9	-3.8	-0.1	7.7	4.3	3.2	8.3	7.5	4.3	9.6	3.2	-2.8	1.4
WECEE	..	..	..	..	..	..	..	5.4	10.0	10.5	6.7	11.1	2.3	1.5	2.8
Canada	5.9	2.0	2.5	4.7	7.4	8.0	5.7	5.1	14.2	5.1	7.8	8.1	-5.0	1.4	3.8
United States	3.9	3.8	-0.6	6.9	8.8	11.9	8.0	8.7	13.6	11.6	11.5	13.1	-2.7	3.4	4.4
North America	4.4	3.4	0.1	6.4	8.4	11.0	7.5	7.9	13.7	10.2	10.7	12.1	-3.2	3.0	4.3
Japan	16.9	7.8	-1.1	-0.7	-1.4	7.9	13.3	12.9	0.7	-6.7	3.7	8.5	-0.7	1.3	3.9
Europe, North America and Japan	..	..	..	..	..	..	..	6.6	10.4	9.3	7.7	11.3	0.5	1.9	3.3
Memorandum items:															
EU-8	..	..	..	..	..	..	..	16.9	16.3	15.6	2.8	15.2	4.8	5.0	9.6
Western Europe	8.7	6.5	3.9	3.5	-3.2	8.2	7.4	4.2	9.3	9.9	7.2	10.6	2.0	1.0	1.8
Western Europe and North America	7.3	5.5	2.8	4.3	0.2	9.1	7.4	5.4	10.7	10.0	8.4	11.1	0.2	1.7	2.7

Source: Eurostat, NewCronos Database; OECD, *National Accounts* (Paris), various issues; national statistics.

Note: See appendix table A.1.

[a] West Germany, 1989-1991.

APPENDIX TABLE A.8

Industrial output in Europe, North America and Japan, 1989-2003

(Percentage change over the preceding year)

	1989	1990	1991	1992	1993	1994	1995	1996	1997	1998	1999	2000	2001	2002	2003
France	3.5	1.4	-0.5	-1.5	-3.9	3.8	1.9	-0.1	4.1	3.6	2.4	3.8	1.1	-1.6	-0.2
Germany [a]	4.9	5.2	2.9	-2.3	-7.5	2.9	0.6	0.2	3.2	3.7	1.1	5.6	0.2	-1.0	0.4
Italy	3.9	-0.6	-0.9	-1.0	-2.2	5.9	5.8	-1.7	3.8	1.2	-0.1	4.1	-1.0	-1.6	-0.6
Austria	6.0	7.1	1.7	-1.2	-1.6	4.0	5.1	1.0	6.4	8.2	6.0	9.0	2.8	0.8	2.0
Belgium	3.4	3.8	-1.9	-0.4	-5.1	2.1	6.5	0.5	4.7	3.4	0.9	5.4	-1.0	1.3	0.7
Finland	2.4	0.4	-8.7	0.8	5.6	11.3	6.2	2.9	8.6	9.3	5.7	11.8	0.1	2.1	0.8
Greece	1.8	-2.4	-1.0	-1.1	-2.9	1.3	1.8	1.2	1.3	7.1	3.9	0.5	1.4	0.4	1.3
Ireland	11.6	4.7	3.3	9.1	5.6	11.9	20.5	8.1	17.5	19.8	14.8	15.4	10.2	7.5	5.0
Luxembourg	7.8	-0.5	0.3	-0.8	-4.3	5.9	1.4	0.1	5.8	-0.1	11.5	4.3	1.8	1.0	2.6
Netherlands	5.3	2.4	1.7	-0.2	-1.1	4.9	2.9	2.4	0.2	2.2	1.4	3.5	0.4	-0.3	-2.4
Portugal	6.7	9.0	–	-2.3	-4.8	-0.2	4.7	5.3	2.6	5.7	3.0	0.5	3.1	-0.5	-0.1
Spain	5.1	-0.4	-0.6	-3.1	-4.7	7.8	4.9	-1.2	7.0	5.4	2.7	4.4	-1.4	0.1	1.4
Euro area	4.7	4.0	1.4	-1.7	-4.7	4.4	3.3	0.1	4.1	3.8	1.8	5.2	0.4	-0.5	0.4
United Kingdom	2.1	-0.3	-3.4	0.3	2.2	5.4	1.8	1.4	1.4	1.0	1.2	1.9	-1.6	-2.5	-0.1
Denmark	0.4	0.8	0.3	3.0	-3.7	10.3	4.0	1.4	4.9	2.9	0.2	5.4	1.6	1.4	0.2
Sweden	3.7	6.9	-5.2	-2.3	-1.0	11.8	9.5	–	4.9	4.0	2.6	6.4	-1.3	0.1	1.7
EU-15	4.1	2.4	0.3	-1.3	-3.3	4.9	3.2	0.3	3.7	3.3	1.6	4.7	–	-0.8	0.3
Cyprus	..	..	..	..	..	..	..	..	..	..	..	4.5	1.9	4.3	2.3
Czech Republic	..	..	-21.9	-8.0	-5.3	2.1	8.7	2.0	4.5	1.6	-3.2	5.4	6.5	9.5	5.8
Estonia	..	..	..	..	..	..	..	..	..	..	-3.9	15.0	8.5	8.5	10.3
Hungary	-5.1	-9.3	-18.3	-9.8	4.0	9.7	4.6	3.4	11.1	12.5	10.3	18.2	3.6	2.7	6.4
Latvia	..	..	..	..	..	..	..	..	6.1	1.8	-9.0	3.9	6.9	6.4	6.9
Lithuania	..	..	..	..	..	..	..	..	..	..	-9.9	2.2	16.0	3.1	16.1
Malta	..	..	..	..	..	..	..	..	..	..	..	..	..	..	..
Poland	-2.8	-25.4	-16.0	4.0	4.8	13.1	10.3	9.4	11.3	4.7	4.8	7.5	0.4	1.4	8.8
Slovakia	..	-4.5	-19.3	-9.7	-3.7	4.9	8.3	2.4	1.4	5.4	-2.0	8.5	7.4	6.7	5.4
Slovenia	..	..	..	..	..	..	..	..	..	..	-0.8	8.7	2.0	2.1	-1.9
New EU members-10 [b]	..	..	..	..	..	..	..	..	..	..	..	8.4	3.6	4.2	7.1
EU-25	..	..	0.3	-1.3	-3.3	4.9	3.2	0.5	3.9	3.3	1.7	4.8	0.2	-0.6	0.7
Iceland	..	..	..	..	..	..	..	..	..	..	..	..	..	..	..
Israel	-1.6	8.0	6.8	8.2	6.9	7.4	8.4	5.4	1.8	2.8	1.4	10.1	-5.5	-1.5	-0.5
Norway	9.1	3.4	1.7	5.6	3.9	7.0	5.8	5.2	3.6	-1.2	-0.2	2.9	-1.3	1.0	-4.1
Switzerland	1.5	2.6	0.5	-1.0	-1.8	4.3	2.0	–	4.7	3.6	3.5	8.4	-0.7	-5.1	–
WECEE [c]	..	..	..	..	..	..	..	..	..	..	..	5.0	0.3	-0.4	0.9
Canada	-0.3	-2.8	-3.6	1.3	4.8	6.3	4.6	1.2	5.6	3.5	5.9	8.6	-3.9	1.5	0.8
United States	0.9	0.9	-1.5	2.8	3.3	5.4	4.8	4.3	7.4	5.9	4.4	4.4	-3.4	-0.6	0.3
North America	0.7	0.4	-1.8	2.7	3.5	5.5	4.8	4.0	7.2	5.7	4.6	4.9	-3.5	-0.3	0.4
Japan	5.8	4.2	1.9	-5.7	-3.5	1.3	3.3	2.3	3.5	-6.6	0.3	5.4	-6.3	-1.1	3.0
Europe, North America and Japan [c]	..	..	..	..	..	..	..	..	..	..	..	5.0	-2.3	-0.5	1.0
Memorandum items:															
EU-8	..	..	..	..	..	..	..	..	..	..	1.8	8.5	3.6	4.2	7.1
Western Europe	4.2	2.5	0.3	-1.2	-3.0	4.9	3.3	0.4	3.7	3.1	1.6	4.7	–	-0.9	0.2
Western Europe and North America	2.6	1.6	-0.6	0.5	-0.1	5.2	4.0	2.1	5.4	4.4	3.1	4.8	-1.7	-0.6	0.3

Source: National statistics; Eurostat; OECD, *Main Economic Indicators* (Paris), latest issues.

Note: All aggregates exclude Israel. Except for the European Union member countries, industrial output indices for regional aggregates have been calculated as weighted averages of the indices of the constituent countries; the European Union member countries' aggregates are provided by Eurostat. Weights were derived from 2000 value added originating in industry converted from national currency units into dollars using 2000 GDP purchasing power parities.

[a] West Germany, 1989-1991.

[b] Computed as a weighted average, excluding Malta.

[c] Excluding Malta and Iceland.

APPENDIX TABLE A.9

Total employment in Europe, North America and Japan, 1989-2003
(Percentage change over the preceding year)

	1989	1990	1991	1992	1993	1994	1995	1996	1997	1998	1999	2000	2001	2002	2003
France	1.7	0.8	0.1	-0.6	-1.3	0.1	0.9	0.4	0.4	1.5	2.0	2.7	1.7	0.7	0.2
Germany [a]	1.8	3.1	2.5	-1.5	-1.4	-0.2	0.2	-0.3	-0.2	1.1	1.2	1.8	0.4	-0.6	-1.0
Italy	0.7	1.6	1.9	-0.5	-2.5	-1.5	-0.1	0.6	0.4	1.0	1.1	1.9	2.0	1.8	1.2
Austria	1.1	1.8	1.3	0.5	-0.5	0.1	-0.2	0.3	0.9	1.3	1.8	1.0	0.6	-0.1	0.1
Belgium	1.2	0.9	0.1	-0.5	-0.8	-0.4	4.1	0.3	0.9	1.8	1.4	1.9	1.5	-0.3	–
Finland	0.9	-0.4	-5.6	-7.0	-6.0	-1.4	1.8	1.4	3.4	2.0	2.5	2.3	1.5	0.9	–
Greece	0.4	1.3	-1.7	1.4	0.8	1.9	0.9	-0.5	-2.2	7.5	0.1	0.3	-0.3	0.1	1.4
Ireland	–	4.4	-0.3	0.3	1.4	3.2	4.4	3.6	5.6	8.6	6.0	4.7	3.0	1.3	2.0
Luxembourg	3.4	3.9	4.3	2.6	2.0	2.4	2.9	2.3	3.2	4.8	5.0	5.6	5.7	2.9	1.7
Netherlands	2.6	3.0	1.9	1.3	0.3	0.6	2.3	2.3	3.2	2.6	2.6	2.2	2.1	0.4	-0.4
Portugal	2.3	2.2	2.8	-1.6	-2.0	-1.0	-0.2	-5.9	1.7	2.7	1.8	2.3	1.5	0.3	-0.4
Spain	3.6	3.8	1.2	-1.4	-2.8	-0.5	1.9	1.3	2.9	3.9	3.5	3.5	2.4	1.5	1.8
Euro area	1.7	2.2	1.4	-0.9	-1.6	-0.3	0.8	0.2	0.8	2.0	1.8	2.2	1.4	0.5	0.2
United Kingdom	2.8	0.5	-2.9	-2.2	-0.7	0.8	1.2	0.9	1.8	1.0	1.3	1.1	0.8	0.7	0.9
Denmark	-0.6	-0.7	-0.6	-0.8	-1.7	2.0	0.9	0.4	0.8	1.6	2.1	0.3	0.3	-0.4	-0.9
Sweden	1.5	0.9	-1.5	-4.4	-5.2	-0.9	1.5	-0.9	-1.3	1.5	2.1	2.4	1.9	0.2	-0.3
EU-15	1.9	1.8	0.5	-1.2	-1.5	-0.1	0.9	0.3	0.9	1.8	1.7	2.0	1.3	0.5	0.3
Cyprus	3.9	2.7	0.3	4.5	-0.1	2.8	4.3	0.4	0.2	1.4	1.8	2.3	2.0	1.3	1.0
Czech Republic	0.6	-0.9	-5.5	-2.6	-1.6	0.8	2.6	0.7	-1.9	-1.3	-2.5	-0.2	0.3	-0.4	-0.7
Estonia	2.4	-1.4	-2.3	-5.6	-8.2	-3.4	-6.2	-2.2	-0.3	-1.7	-4.5	-1.2	0.9	1.4	1.5
Hungary	-0.7	-3.3	-10.3	-10.0	-6.3	-2.0	-1.9	-0.8	–	1.4	3.1	1.0	0.5	0.1	1.3
Latvia	-0.5	0.1	-0.8	-7.3	-6.9	-10.1	-3.5	-2.6	4.3	-0.4	-1.8	-2.8	2.2	2.8	1.8
Lithuania	0.2	-2.7	2.4	-2.2	-4.2	-5.8	-1.9	0.9	0.6	-0.8	-2.2	-4.0	-3.3	4.0	2.3
Malta	0.9	0.8	1.8	1.5	-0.4	1.8	3.4	0.9	-0.5	0.5	0.8	1.9	2.1	-0.7	-0.7
Poland	-0.1	-4.2	-5.9	-4.2	-2.4	1.0	1.8	1.9	2.8	2.3	-2.7	-2.3	-0.6	-2.2	-0.7
Slovakia	0.2	-1.8	-12.5	1.1	-2.6	-4.2	2.1	3.3	-0.5	-0.3	-3.0	-1.4	1.0	0.2	1.8
Slovenia	-1.3	-3.9	-7.8	-5.5	-2.9	-2.5	-0.2	-0.5	-0.2	0.2	1.8	1.3	1.4	0.6	-0.8
New EU members-10	–	-3.0	-6.2	-4.4	-3.2	-0.8	0.9	1.1	1.2	1.1	-1.8	-1.4	-0.1	-0.8	–
EU-25	1.5	0.9	-0.7	-1.7	-1.8	-0.2	0.9	0.4	0.9	1.7	1.2	1.5	1.1	0.3	0.3
Iceland	-1.6	0.1	–	-1.6	-0.8	0.8	0.8	2.4	1.6	3.1	2.3	2.2	2.2	-1.4	1.4
Israel	0.5	2.1	6.1	4.2	6.1	6.9	5.2	2.4	1.4	1.6	3.1	4.0	2.0	0.9	2.0
Norway	-2.8	-0.8	-0.9	-0.2	0.5	1.4	2.1	2.0	3.0	2.5	0.8	0.4	0.3	0.3	-0.6
Switzerland	2.7	3.2	1.9	-1.5	-0.8	-0.7	–	–	0.1	1.4	0.8	1.0	1.6	0.6	-0.1
WECEE	1.5	0.9	-0.6	-1.7	-1.8	-0.2	0.9	0.4	1.0	1.7	1.1	1.4	1.1	0.3	0.2
Canada	2.4	0.6	-1.8	-0.7	1.1	1.8	1.7	0.9	2.1	2.4	2.8	2.4	0.8	2.3	1.9
United States	2.3	1.3	-1.0	0.1	2.0	2.3	2.2	1.7	2.3	1.7	2.0	2.0	-0.2	-0.9	–
North America	2.3	1.2	-1.1	–	1.9	2.3	2.1	1.7	2.3	1.7	2.1	2.0	-0.1	-0.6	0.2
Japan	1.5	1.7	2.0	1.1	0.4	0.1	0.1	0.4	1.0	-0.7	-0.8	-0.1	-0.6	-1.4	-0.2
Europe, North America and Japan	1.8	1.1	-0.4	-0.6	-0.1	0.7	1.2	0.9	1.5	1.3	1.2	1.4	0.4	-0.3	0.2
Memorandum items:															
EU-8	–	-3.1	-6.3	-4.5	-3.2	-0.8	0.9	1.1	1.2	1.1	-1.9	-1.5	-0.2	-0.9	–
Western Europe	1.8	1.8	0.5	-1.2	-1.5	-0.1	0.9	0.3	0.9	1.8	1.7	1.9	1.3	0.5	0.3
Western Europe and North America	2.0	1.5	-0.2	-0.6	0.1	1.0	1.5	1.0	1.6	1.8	1.9	2.0	0.6	_	0.2

Source: Eurostat, NewCronos Database; OECD, *National Accounts* and *Economic Outlook*, latest issues; national statistics; UNECE secretariat estimates.

Note: All aggregates exclude Israel. Total employment is defined as the number of persons engaged in some productive activity within resident production units (national accounts concept). The labour force survey concept (based on resident household surveys) is used for Iceland, Malta and the United Kingdom (up to 1989), Germany (up to 1990).

[a] West Germany, 1989-1991.

APPENDIX TABLE A.10

Standardized unemployment rates [a] in Europe, North America and Japan, 1989-2003
(Per cent of civilian labour force)

	1989	1990	1991	1992	1993	1994	1995	1996	1997	1998	1999	2000	2001	2002	2003
France	8.9	8.5	9.0	9.9	11.1	11.7	11.1	11.6	11.5	11.1	10.5	9.1	8.4	8.9	9.4
Germany [b]	5.6	4.8	4.2	6.4	7.7	8.2	8.0	8.7	9.7	9.1	8.4	7.8	7.8	8.7	9.6
Italy	9.7	8.9	8.5	8.7	10.1	11.0	11.5	11.5	11.6	11.7	11.3	10.4	9.4	9.0	8.6
Austria	3.1	3.2	3.5	3.6	4.0	3.8	3.9	4.4	4.4	4.5	3.9	3.7	3.6	4.2	4.3
Belgium	7.4	6.6	6.4	7.1	8.6	9.8	9.7	9.5	9.2	9.3	8.6	6.9	6.7	7.3	8.0
Finland	3.1	3.2	6.6	11.7	16.3	16.6	15.4	14.6	12.7	11.4	10.2	9.8	9.1	9.1	9.0
Greece	6.7	6.4	7.1	7.9	8.6	8.9	9.2	9.6	9.8	10.9	11.8	11.0	10.4	10.0	9.3
Ireland	14.7	13.4	14.7	15.4	15.6	14.3	12.3	11.7	9.9	7.5	5.6	4.3	3.9	4.3	4.6
Luxembourg	1.8	1.7	1.6	2.1	2.6	3.2	2.9	2.9	2.7	2.7	2.4	2.3	2.1	2.8	3.7
Netherlands	6.6	5.8	5.5	5.3	6.2	6.8	6.6	6.0	4.9	3.8	3.2	2.9	2.5	2.7	3.8
Portugal	5.2	4.8	4.2	4.3	5.6	6.9	7.3	7.3	6.8	5.1	4.5	4.1	4.0	5.0	6.3
Spain	13.9	13.1	13.2	14.9	18.6	19.8	18.8	18.1	17.0	15.2	12.8	11.3	10.6	11.3	11.3
Euro area	8.2	7.6	7.3	8.5	10.1	10.8	10.5	10.7	10.8	10.2	9.4	8.5	8.0	8.4	8.8
United Kingdom	7.1	6.9	8.6	9.8	10.0	9.3	8.5	8.0	6.9	6.2	5.9	5.4	5.0	5.1	4.9
Denmark	6.8	7.2	7.9	8.6	9.6	7.7	6.7	6.3	5.2	4.9	4.8	4.4	4.3	4.6	5.6
Sweden	1.6	1.7	3.1	5.6	9.1	9.4	8.8	9.6	9.9	8.2	6.7	5.6	4.9	4.9	5.6
EU-15	7.8	7.3	7.4	8.7	10.0	10.4	10.1	10.2	10.0	9.4	8.7	7.8	7.4	7.7	8.1
Cyprus	2.3	1.8	3.0	1.8	2.6	4.1	4.0	4.7	5.2	5.2	5.5	5.2	4.4	3.9	4.5
Czech Republic	..	..	..	..	4.4	4.4	4.1	3.9	4.8	6.3	8.6	8.6	8.0	7.3	7.8
Estonia	..	..	..	..	..	..	..	..	9.6	9.2	11.3	12.5	11.8	9.5	10.2
Hungary	5.3	5.5	6.7	7.4	6.8	6.1	5.6	9.6	9.0	8.4	6.9	6.3	5.6	5.6	5.8
Latvia	..	..	..	..	..	..	..	..	..	14.3	14.0	13.7	12.9	12.6	10.4
Lithuania	..	..	..	..	..	..	..	..	..	13.2	13.7	16.4	16.4	13.5	12.7
Malta	5.6	5.8	5.6	6.1	7.1	6.5	5.7	6.8	7.5	7.6	7.9	6.8	7.7	7.7	8.0
Poland	..	..	..	..	14.0	14.4	13.3	12.3	10.9	10.2	13.4	16.4	18.5	19.8	19.2
Slovakia	..	..	..	..	..	13.7	13.1	11.3	11.9	12.6	16.7	18.7	19.4	18.7	17.5
Slovenia	..	..	..	..	..	..	..	6.9	6.9	7.4	7.2	6.6	5.8	6.1	6.5
New EU members-10	..	..	..	..	..	..	..	..	..	9.7	11.8	13.6	14.5	14.7	14.3
EU-25	..	..	..	..	..	..	..	..	..	9.4	9.2	8.7	8.5	8.8	9.0
Iceland	1.6	1.8	2.6	4.3	5.3	5.4	4.9	3.8	3.9	2.7	2.1	2.3	2.3	3.2	3.4
Israel [c]	8.9	9.6	10.6	11.2	10.0	7.8	6.9	6.7	7.7	8.5	8.9	8.8	9.4	10.3	10.7
Norway	4.9	5.2	5.5	5.9	6.0	5.4	4.9	4.7	4.0	3.2	3.2	3.4	3.6	3.9	4.5
Switzerland	0.5	0.5	1.9	3.0	3.9	3.9	3.5	3.9	4.2	3.6	3.0	2.7	2.6	3.2	4.2
WECEE	..	..	..	..	..	..	..	..	..	9.3	9.0	8.6	8.3	8.7	8.9
Canada	7.6	8.1	10.3	11.2	11.4	10.4	9.4	9.6	9.1	8.3	7.6	6.8	7.2	7.7	7.6
United States	5.3	5.5	6.7	7.4	6.8	6.1	5.6	5.4	4.9	4.5	4.2	4.0	4.8	5.8	6.0
North America	5.5	5.8	7.1	7.8	7.3	6.5	6.0	5.8	5.3	4.9	4.5	4.3	5.0	6.0	6.2
Japan	2.3	2.1	2.1	2.2	2.5	2.9	3.1	3.4	3.4	4.1	4.7	4.7	5.0	5.4	5.3
Europe, North America and Japan	..	..	..	..	..	..	..	..	..	6.9	6.8	6.5	6.7	7.2	7.4
Memorandum items:															
EU-8	..	..	..	..	..	..	..	..	..	9.7	11.9	13.7	14.6	14.9	14.4
Western Europe	7.6	7.1	7.2	8.5	9.8	10.2	9.9	10.0	9.8	9.2	8.5	7.6	7.2	7.6	7.9
Western Europe and North America	6.7	6.5	7.2	8.2	8.7	8.6	8.1	8.1	7.8	7.2	6.7	6.1	6.2	6.9	7.1

Source: OECD, *Main Economic Indicators* and *Quarterly Labour Force Statistics* (Paris), latest issues; Eurostat, NewCronos Database; national statistics.

Note: All aggregates exclude Israel. Comparisons with previous years are limited by changes in methodology in Austria (1993), Cyprus (2000), Iceland (1991), Israel (1995), Malta (2000), Norway (1989), and Switzerland (1991).

[a] Eurostat-OECD definition except for Iceland and Switzerland (1989-1990), Austria (1989-1992), Israel (1989-1995), Cyprus and Malta (1989-1999).

[b] West Germany, 1989-1991.

[c] Definitions comply with ILO guidelines but do not follow the Eurostat-OECD standards.

APPENDIX TABLE A.11

Consumer prices in Europe, North America and Japan, 1989-2003
(Percentage change over the preceding year)

	1989	1990	1991	1992	1993	1994	1995	1996	1997	1998	1999	2000	2001	2002	2003
France	3.5	3.2	3.2	2.4	2.1	1.7	1.8	2.0	1.2	0.6	0.5	1.7	1.6	1.9	2.1
Germany [a]	2.8	2.7	4.1	5.1	4.4	2.7	1.7	1.4	1.9	0.9	0.6	1.5	2.0	1.4	1.0
Italy	6.3	6.4	6.3	5.3	4.6	4.1	5.2	4.0	2.0	2.0	1.7	2.5	2.8	2.5	2.7
Austria	2.6	3.3	3.3	4.0	3.6	2.9	2.2	1.9	1.3	0.9	0.6	2.3	2.7	1.8	1.4
Belgium	3.1	3.4	3.2	2.4	2.8	2.4	1.5	2.1	1.6	1.0	1.1	2.5	2.5	1.6	1.6
Finland	6.6	6.2	4.3	2.9	2.2	1.1	0.8	0.6	1.2	1.4	1.2	3.0	2.6	1.6	0.9
Greece	13.7	20.4	19.5	15.9	14.4	10.9	8.9	8.2	5.5	4.8	2.6	3.1	3.4	3.6	3.6
Ireland	4.1	3.3	3.2	3.1	1.4	2.3	2.5	1.7	1.6	2.4	1.6	5.6	4.9	4.7	3.5
Luxembourg	3.4	3.3	3.1	3.2	3.6	2.2	1.9	1.3	1.4	1.0	1.0	3.1	2.7	2.1	2.1
Netherlands	1.1	2.5	3.2	3.2	2.6	2.8	1.9	2.0	2.2	2.0	2.2	2.4	4.2	3.3	2.1
Portugal	12.6	13.4	10.5	9.4	6.7	5.4	4.2	3.1	2.3	2.8	2.3	2.9	4.3	3.6	3.3
Spain	6.8	6.7	5.9	5.9	4.6	4.7	4.7	3.6	2.0	1.8	2.3	3.4	3.6	3.1	3.0
Euro area	4.3	4.5	4.8	4.6	4.0	3.2	3.0	2.6	1.9	1.4	1.2	2.2	2.6	2.2	2.1
United Kingdom	7.8	9.5	5.9	3.7	1.6	2.5	3.4	2.5	3.1	3.4	1.6	2.9	1.8	1.6	2.9
Denmark	4.8	2.6	2.4	2.1	1.3	2.0	2.1	2.1	2.2	1.8	2.5	2.9	2.3	2.4	2.1
Sweden	6.6	10.4	9.7	2.6	4.7	2.4	2.9	0.8	0.9	0.4	0.3	1.3	2.6	2.4	2.1
EU-15	4.9	5.4	5.0	4.4	3.5	3.0	3.0	2.5	2.1	1.7	1.3	2.3	2.4	2.1	2.2
Cyprus	3.8	4.5	5.0	6.5	4.9	4.7	2.6	2.9	3.6	2.2	1.7	4.3	2.0	2.8	4.1
Czech Republic	..	9.9	56.7	11.1	20.8	10.0	9.1	8.8	8.5	10.7	2.1	3.9	4.7	1.8	0.2
Estonia	..	18.0	202.0	1 076.0	89.8	47.7	29.0	23.1	11.2	8.2	3.3	4.0	5.8	3.6	1.1
Hungary	..	28.9	35.0	23.0	22.5	18.8	28.2	23.6	18.3	14.3	10.0	9.8	9.2	5.3	4.9
Latvia	..	10.9	172.2	951.2	109.2	35.9	25.0	17.6	8.4	4.7	2.4	2.6	2.5	1.9	3.0
Lithuania	..	9.1	216.4	1 020.8	410.2	72.2	39.6	24.6	8.9	5.1	0.8	1.0	1.3	0.3	-1.2
Malta	0.9	3.0	2.5	1.6	4.1	4.1	4.0	2.0	3.3	2.2	2.1	2.4	2.9	2.2	0.7
Poland	..	585.8	70.3	43.0	35.3	32.2	27.8	19.9	14.9	11.8	7.3	10.1	5.5	1.8	0.7
Slovakia	..	10.4	61.2	10.0	23.2	13.4	9.9	5.8	6.1	6.7	10.6	12.0	7.1	3.3	8.5
Slovenia	..	551.6	115.0	207.3	32.9	21.0	13.5	9.9	8.4	7.9	6.1	8.9	8.4	7.5	5.7
New EU members-10	..	..	..	..	31.9	23.8	21.2	16.3	12.5	10.6	6.4	8.4	5.8	2.7	2.0
EU-25	..	..	..	..	4.5	3.9	3.9	3.3	2.7	2.4	1.7	2.8	2.7	2.1	2.2
Iceland	20.8	15.5	6.8	4.0	4.0	1.6	1.6	2.3	1.8	1.7	3.2	5.1	6.4	5.2	2.1
Israel	20.2	17.2	19.0	12.0	11.0	12.3	10.1	11.3	9.0	5.4	5.2	1.1	1.1	5.7	0.7
Norway	4.5	4.1	3.4	2.4	2.3	1.4	2.4	1.2	2.6	2.3	2.3	3.1	3.0	1.3	2.5
Switzerland	3.1	5.4	5.9	4.0	3.3	0.9	1.8	0.8	0.5	–	0.8	1.6	1.0	0.6	0.6
WECEE	..	..	..	..	4.4	3.8	3.9	3.2	2.7	2.3	1.6	2.8	2.7	2.1	2.2
Canada	5.0	4.8	5.6	1.5	1.9	0.2	2.2	1.6	1.6	1.0	1.7	2.7	2.5	2.3	2.8
United States	4.8	5.4	4.2	3.0	2.9	2.6	2.8	2.9	2.3	1.6	2.1	3.4	2.8	1.7	2.2
North America	4.8	5.4	4.3	2.9	2.9	2.4	2.7	2.8	2.3	1.6	2.1	3.4	2.8	1.7	2.2
Japan	2.3	3.1	3.2	1.7	1.3	0.7	-0.1	0.1	1.7	0.7	-0.3	-0.7	-0.7	-0.9	-0.3
Europe, North America and Japan	..	..	..	..	3.2	2.7	2.8	2.6	2.4	1.8	1.6	2.6	2.3	1.6	1.9
Memorandum items:															
EU-8	..	66.6	60.2	32.9	32.6	24.0	21.8	16.6	12.7	10.8	6.5	8.5	5.9	2.7	2.0
Western Europe	4.9	5.4	5.0	4.3	3.5	2.9	3.0	2.4	2.0	1.7	1.3	2.3	2.4	2.1	2.2
Western Europe and North America	4.8	5.4	4.6	3.5	3.1	2.7	2.9	2.7	2.2	1.6	1.7	2.9	2.6	1.9	2.2

Source: National statistics.

Note: All aggregates exclude Israel. Consumer price indexes for regional aggregates have been calculated as weighted averages of constituent country indices. Weights were derived from 2000 private final consumption expenditure converted from national currency units into dollars using 2000 purchasing power parities.

[a] West Germany, 1989-1991.

APPENDIX TABLE B.1

Real GDP in south-east Europe and the CIS, 1990-2003
(Percentage change over the preceding year)

	1990	1991	1992	1993	1994	1995	1996	1997	1998	1999	2000	2001	2002	2003	2003 over 1989 [a]
South-east Europe [b]	-0.1	-6.5	-3.1	2.1	-1.7	7.4	5.2	3.4	1.7	-3.6	5.9	-2.6	6.5	5.1	20.1
Albania	-10.0	-28.0	-7.2	9.6	8.3	13.3	9.1	-10.2	12.7	10.1	7.3	7.2	3.4	6.0	24.0
Bosnia and Herzegovina	..	..	..	..	..	..	54.2	36.6	16.6	9.5	5.4	4.5	3.7	3.2	217.2[c]
Bulgaria	-9.1	-8.4	-7.3	-1.5	1.8	2.9	-9.4	-5.6	4.0	2.3	5.4	4.1	4.9	4.3	-13.0
Croatia	-7.1	-21.1	-11.7	-8.0	5.9	6.8	5.9	6.8	2.5	-0.9	2.9	4.4	5.2	4.3	-8.8
Romania	-5.6	-12.9	-8.8	1.5	3.9	7.1	3.9	-6.1	-4.8	-1.2	2.1	5.7	5.0	4.9	-7.4
Serbia and Montenegro [d]	-7.9	-11.6	-27.9	-30.8	2.5	6.1	5.9	7.4	2.5	-17.7	6.4	5.5	3.8	1.5	-49.9
The former Yugoslav Republic of Macedonia	-10.2	-6.2	-6.6	-7.5	-1.8	-1.1	1.2	1.4	3.4	4.3	4.5	-4.5	0.9	3.4	-18.4
Turkey	9.3	0.9	6.0	8.0	-5.5	7.2	7.0	7.5	3.1	-4.7	7.4	-7.5	7.9	5.8	64.0
CIS	-3.1	-6.1	-14.0	-9.8	-14.4	-5.7	-3.5	1.4	-3.2	5.1	8.9	6.1	5.2	7.7	-25.8
Armenia	-5.5	-11.7	-41.8	-8.8	5.4	6.9	5.9	3.3	7.3	3.3	5.9	9.6	15.1	13.9	-7.9
Azerbaijan	-11.7	-0.7	-22.6	-23.1	-19.7	-11.8	1.3	5.8	10.0	7.4	11.1	9.9	10.6	11.2	-29.8
Belarus	-1.9	-1.4	-9.6	-7.6	-11.7	-10.4	2.8	11.4	8.4	3.4	5.8	4.7	5.0	6.8	2.0
Georgia	-15.1	-21.1	-44.9	-29.3	-10.4	2.6	11.2	10.5	3.1	2.9	1.8	4.8	5.5	11.1	-60.9
Kazakhstan	-1.0	-11.0	-5.3	-9.2	-12.6	-8.2	0.5	1.7	-1.9	2.7	9.8	13.5	9.8	9.3	-6.3
Kyrgyzstan	4.8	-7.9	-13.8	-15.5	-20.1	-5.4	7.1	9.9	2.1	3.7	5.4	5.3	0.0	6.7	-21.6
Republic of Moldova [e]	-2.4	-17.5	-29.0	-1.2	-30.9	-1.4	-5.9	1.6	-6.5	-3.4	2.1	6.1	7.8	6.3	-58.7
Russian Federation	-3.0	-5.0	-14.5	-8.7	-12.7	-4.1	-3.6	1.4	-5.3	6.4	10.0	5.1	4.7	7.3	-23.0
Tajikistan	0.2	-8.5	-32.3	-16.3	-21.3	-12.4	-16.7	1.7	5.3	3.7	8.3	10.2	9.5	10.2	-52.3
Turkmenistan	1.8	-4.7	-15.0	1.5	-17.3	-7.2	6.7	-11.4	7.1	16.5	6.1	4.1	1.8	6.8	-9.1
Ukraine	-3.6	-8.7	-9.9	-14.2	-22.9	-12.2	-10.0	-3.0	-1.9	-0.2	5.9	9.2	5.2	9.4	-47.6
Uzbekistan	-0.8	-0.5	-11.1	-2.3	-5.2	-0.9	1.7	5.2	4.4	4.4	4.0	4.5	4.2	4.4	11.0
Total above [b]	-2.5	-6.2	-11.7	-7.0	-11.1	-2.0	-0.8	2.1	-1.5	2.1	7.9	3.3	5.6	6.9	-16.2
Memorandum items:															
South-east Europe without															
Turkey [b]	-7.1	-13.1	-12.5	-5.4	3.5	7.6	2.9	-2.1	-0.3	-1.9	3.7	5.0	4.6	4.2	-12.9
CIS without Russian Federation	-3.4	-8.1	-12.9	-11.8	-17.7	-9.1	-3.3	1.5	1.5	2.6	6.4	8.3	6.2	8.5	-30.9
Low-income CIS	-5.7	-8.3	-24.6	-12.2	-12.9	-3.0	1.6	5.7	4.3	4.0	5.2	6.2	6.3	7.7	-28.0
Caucasian CIS	-12.3	-11.4	-34.3	-23.1	-12.7	-3.7	5.5	6.9	7.0	4.9	6.9	8.2	9.9	11.7	-40.7
Central Asian CIS	-0.2	-7.4	-10.6	-7.2	-12.1	-6.0	1.2	1.8	1.5	4.8	7.2	8.9	6.6	7.5	-7.1
European CIS	-3.3	-7.9	-10.6	-12.6	-21.1	-11.5	-7.2	0.6	0.6	0.8	5.7	7.8	5.3	8.6	-40.0
EU-8	-6.3	-9.7	-2.9	0.2	3.5	5.5	4.7	4.7	3.6	3.1	4.1	2.4	2.4	4.0	19.6

Source: UNECE Common Database; national statistics; CIS Statistical Committee.

Note: Regional aggregates: *low-income CIS* – Armenia, Azerbaijan, Georgia, Kyrgyzstan, Republic of Moldova, Tajikistan, Uzbekistan; *Caucasian CIS* – Armenia, Azerbaijan, Georgia; *central Asian CIS* – Kazakhstan, Kyrgyzstan, Tajikistan, Turkmenistan, Uzbekistan; *European CIS* – Belarus, Republic of Moldova, Ukraine; *EU-8* – Czech Republic, Estonia, Hungary, Latvia, Lithuania, Poland, Slovakia, Slovenia. Aggregation is performed using weights based on purchasing power parities.

[a] Cumulative change for the period.

[b] Excluding Bosnia and Herzegovina for 1990-1995.

[c] 1995=100.

[d] Excluding Kosovo and Metohia since 1999.

[e] Excluding Transdniestria since 1993.

APPENDIX TABLE B.2

Real total consumption expenditure in south-east Europe and the CIS, 1990-2003
(Percentage change over the preceding year)

	1990	1991	1992	1993	1994	1995	1996	1997	1998	1999	2000	2001	2002	2003
South-east Europe [a]	..	..	-0.8	5.2	-2.4	6.2	6.1	3.5	1.4	-1.1	5.0	-4.3	2.7	..
Bulgaria	0.6	-7.7	-3.1	-3.6	-4.5	-1.9	-8.2	-9.6	4.0	8.8	5.7	4.4	3.6	6.6
Croatia	..	..	-12.8	-2.2	7.9	15.9	-0.1	10.0	0.2	-1.1	2.3	1.2	4.9	3.0
Romania	8.9	-11.8	-5.6	1.2	3.8	10.8	7.0	-4.3	1.1	-2.5	1.5	6.3	2.4	6.9
The former Yugoslav Republic of Macedonia	..	-6.1	-10.3	6.5	6.9	-1.7	2.4	2.0	3.4	3.7	8.0	-3.5	6.3	..
Turkey	12.6	2.8	3.3	8.6	-5.4	5.0	8.5	8.0	1.3	-1.7	6.3	-9.1	2.5	5.6
CIS [b]	..	..	..	..	-6.4	-4.3	-3.1	2.4	-0.8	-0.8	5.1	7.7	7.2	8.4
Armenia	..	-2.6	-12.8	-21.8	3.8	8.0	3.2	6.3	4.6	1.4	7.7	7.1	8.2	9.0
Azerbaijan	..	..	..	-22.6	-19.7	-2.8	8.1	10.5	11.4	9.6	8.6	8.6	9.2	11.7
Belarus	..	-6.5	-10.0	-6.3	-11.2	-9.4	3.7	10.0	11.8	8.4	7.4	13.7	8.1	5.3
Kazakhstan	..	-3.2	-0.7	-11.7	-20.2	-18.8	-6.7	1.0	-2.8	1.4	3.1	9.6	9.1	19.8
Kyrgyzstan	..	-16.5	-12.8	-11.6	-19.6	-16.1	6.3	-8.1	15.1	0.9	-2.9	1.4	3.7	8.5
Republic of Moldova	..	..	..	..	-17.4	9.4	10.4	11.8	-2.0	-15.8	17.2	4.4	9.7	13.4
Russian Federation	..	-6.1	-5.2	-1.0	-3.1	-2.7	-2.6	2.8	-2.1	-1.2	5.6	6.8	7.3	6.6
Ukraine	..	-5.3	-6.3	-18.7	-9.7	-3.6	-8.4	-1.8	-0.1	-3.7	2.0	9.3	5.0	12.8
Memorandum items:														
South-east Europe without Turkey [a]	..	..	-6.4	–	2.4	7.8	2.7	-3.2	1.6	–	2.7	4.7	3.1	..
CIS without Russian Federation [b]	..	..	..	..	-13.0	-7.8	-4.2	1.7	2.5	0.3	4.0	9.7	6.8	12.5
European CIS	..	..	..	..	-10.2	-4.6	-5.0	1.5	2.8	-0.9	4.1	10.4	6.0	10.6
EU-8	..	..	..	..	..	..	5.4	4.2	3.4	3.6	2.6	3.0	4.0	3.8

Source: UNECE Common Database; national statistics; CIS Statistical Committee.

[a] Excluding Albania, Bosnia and Herzegovina, and Serbia and Montenegro.

[b] Excluding Georgia, Tajikistan, Turkmenistan and Uzbekistan.

APPENDIX TABLE B.3

Real gross domestic fixed capital formation in south-east Europe and the CIS, 1990-2003
(Percentage change over the preceding year)

	1990	1991	1992	1993	1994	1995	1996	1997	1998	1999	2000	2001	2002	2003
South-east Europe [a]	..	..	5.0	18.4	-7.8	9.2	10.7	10.5	-2.8	-11.6	13.2	-18.7	3.0	10.5
Bulgaria	..	-20.0	-7.3	-17.5	1.1	16.1	-21.2	-20.9	35.2	20.8	15.4	23.3	8.5	13.8
Croatia	..	..	-11.5	6.8	-1.0	15.6	37.6	26.4	2.5	-3.9	-3.8	7.1	12.0	16.8
Romania	-35.6	-31.6	11.0	8.3	20.7	6.9	5.7	1.7	-5.7	-4.8	5.5	10.1	8.2	9.2
The former Yugoslav Republic of Macedonia	..	-4.2	-16.6	-7.9	-8.6	10.2	6.5	-4.3	-2.6	-1.4	-3.2	-8.6	17.6	10.0
Turkey	15.9	0.4	6.4	26.4	-16.0	9.1	14.1	14.8	-3.9	-15.7	16.9	-31.5	-1.1	10.0
CIS [b]	..	..	..	..	-25.6	-14.7	-19.7	-4.7	-7.4	5.0	14.2	10.2	5.7	14.2
Armenia	..	-33.0	-87.2	-7.8	45.0	-17.3	10.3	2.1	12.0	0.6	16.2	5.3	33.1	33.7
Azerbaijan	..	..	..	-39.0	89.0	-18.0	111.4	67.0	23.0	-2.0	2.6	20.6	84.0	61.5
Belarus	..	4.2	-18.7	-7.6	-13.7	-29.6	-3.1	21.7	10.1	-4.0	2.3	-2.3	6.7	17.7
Kazakhstan	..	-25.8	-16.6	-28.5	-11.4	-37.9	-23.9	3.3	-7.2	0.5	16.1	25.3	10.2	8.9
Kyrgyzstan	..	-10.6	-29.3	-21.8	-28.9	60.7	-13.0	-29.6	-1.6	28.1	26.9	-1.9	-7.4	-1.4
Republic of Moldova	..	..	..	..	-43.5	-10.0	25.6	-5.3	9.2	-23.1	-8.7	17.3	5.7	13.3
Russian Federation	..	-15.5	-41.5	-25.8	-26.0	-7.5	-21.9	-9.6	-12.4	8.1	16.6	10.9	3.5	12.2
Ukraine	..	-20.9	-14.9	-30.5	-41.0	-30.8	-22.7	2.1	2.6	0.1	12.4	6.2	3.4	15.8
Memorandum items:														
South-east Europe without Turkey [a]	..	..	2.4	2.3	13.8	9.3	4.4	1.9	-0.1	-0.9	5.1	11.1	9.2	11.3
CIS without Russian Federation [b]	..	..	..	..	-24.9	-29.9	-14.5	8.5	4.5	-1.0	9.8	8.5	10.9	18.4
European CIS	..	..	..	..	-34.3	-30.0	-17.2	6.6	5.2	-2.1	8.2	3.5	4.5	16.3
EU-8	..	..	..	..	..	..	14.6	11.9	10.7	0.9	2.9	–	0.6	2.5

Source: UNECE Common Database; national statistics; CIS Statistical Committee.

[a] Excluding Albania, Bosnia and Herzegovina, and Serbia and Montenegro.

[b] Excluding Georgia, Tajikistan, Turkmenistan and Uzbekistan.

APPENDIX TABLE B.4

Real gross industrial output in south-east Europe and the CIS, 1990-2003

(Percentage change over the preceding year)

	1990	1991	1992	1993	1994	1995	1996	1997	1998	1999	2000	2001	2002	2003	2003 over 1989 [a]
South-east Europe	-9.3	-14.1	-14.9	-4.2	-2.3	7.5	5.9	3.3	-2.7	-5.3	6.1	-3.1	7.5	6.3	-20.9
Albania [b]	-13.3	-41.9	-30.1	-10.0	-18.6	-7.2	-24.4	2.8	21.8	15.2	12.0	-20.0	11.0	8.0	-72.0
Bosnia and Herzegovina [c]	1.8	-24.5	-66.8	-92.2	-12.6	59.1	87.6	35.7	23.8	10.6	8.8	12.2	9.2	4.8	-86.5
Bulgaria	-16.8	-20.2	-18.4	-9.8	10.6	4.5	5.1	-18.4	-8.5	-8.0	8.3	1.6	6.5	8.3	-48.3
Croatia	-11.3	-28.5	-14.6	-5.9	-2.7	0.3	3.1	6.8	3.7	-1.4	1.7	6.0	5.4	4.1	-33.8
Romania	-23.7	-23.0	-25.3	0.7	3.1	9.4	6.3	-7.2	-13.8	-2.4	7.1	8.4	6.0	3.2	-47.4
Serbia and Montenegro	-12.0	-17.6	-21.4	-37.3	1.3	3.8	7.5	9.5	3.6	-23.1	11.2	–	1.7	-2.7	-61.2
The former Yugoslav Republic of Macedonia	-10.6	-17.2	-15.8	-13.9	-10.5	-10.7	3.2	1.6	4.5	-2.6	3.5	-3.1	-5.3	4.7	-54.5
Turkey	10.0	3.1	5.2	5.9	-6.3	8.5	5.9	10.7	0.9	-5.0	5.4	-8.8	9.2	8.5	64.4
CIS	-0.4	-7.0	-17.0	-13.1	-22.2	-5.7	-3.2	2.2	-3.2	9.1	12.0	6.8	4.7	8.4	-30.6
Armenia	-7.5	-7.7	-48.2	-10.7	5.3	1.5	1.4	1.0	-2.1	5.3	6.4	5.3	14.6	14.9	-34.3
Azerbaijan	-6.3	-8.9	-30.4	-19.7	-24.7	-21.4	-6.7	0.3	2.2	3.6	6.9	5.1	3.6	6.1	-65.4
Belarus	2.1	-1.0	-9.2	-9.4	-14.6	-11.7	3.5	18.8	12.4	10.3	7.8	5.9	4.5	7.1	22.1
Georgia	-5.7	-22.6	-45.8	-36.7	-39.1	-13.5	6.8	8.2	-1.5	4.8	6.1	-1.1	4.9	10.6	-80.8
Kazakhstan	-0.8	-0.9	-13.8	-14.8	-28.1	-8.2	0.3	4.0	-2.4	2.7	15.5	13.8	10.5	8.8	-21.3
Kyrgyzstan	-0.6	-0.3	-25.8	-23.5	-36.9	-24.7	3.9	39.7	5.3	-4.3	6.0	5.4	-10.9	17.0	-54.5
Republic of Moldova [d]	3.2	-11.1	-27.1	0.3	-27.7	-3.9	-6.5	–	-15.0	-11.6	7.7	13.7	10.6	13.6	-49.6
Russian Federation	-0.1	-8.0	-18.0	-14.1	-20.9	-3.3	-4.0	2.0	-5.2	11.0	11.9	4.9	3.7	7.0	-33.5
Tajikistan	1.2	-3.6	-24.3	-7.8	-25.4	-13.6	-23.9	-2.0	8.2	5.6	9.9	14.8	8.2	10.2	-43.7
Turkmenistan	3.2	4.8	-14.9	4.0	-24.7	-6.4	20.0	-22.0	2.0	15.0	26.0	9.0	5.0	8.0	15.4
Ukraine	-0.1	-4.8	-6.4	-8.0	-27.3	-12.0	-5.1	-0.3	-1.0	4.0	13.2	14.2	7.0	15.8	-18.2
Uzbekistan	1.8	1.5	-6.7	3.6	1.6	0.1	2.6	4.1	3.6	5.7	5.9	7.6	8.5	6.2	56.0
Total above	-2.6	-8.6	-16.6	-11.2	-17.5	-2.0	-0.4	2.6	-3.1	4.3	10.2	3.9	5.5	7.8	-28.2
Memorandum items:															
South-east Europe without															
Turkey	-16.8	-22.9	-28.6	-14.4	2.5	6.4	6.0	-5.2	-7.5	-5.7	7.2	5.3	5.3	3.5	-53.8
CIS without Russian Federation	-1.0	-4.6	-14.9	-11.0	-25.0	-11.0	-1.3	2.8	1.2	4.9	12.1	11.0	6.9	11.4	-23.8
Low-income CIS	-3.9	-9.6	-30.7	-16.7	-21.6	-12.4	-2.7	5.7	1.5	2.7	6.6	6.3	5.1	9.1	-52.0
Caucasian CIS	-6.2	-13.4	-36.9	-23.4	-24.9	-16.9	-2.9	2.0	0.7	4.1	6.6	3.9	5.7	8.6	-67.6
Central Asian CIS	–	-0.1	-15.0	-11.2	-24.9	-8.0	2.6	1.3	0.1	4.4	14.5	11.5	8.0	8.7	-15.3
European CIS	0.4	-4.3	-7.5	-8.1	-25.1	-11.7	-3.4	3.9	2.0	5.4	11.6	11.9	6.4	13.5	-12.2
EU-8	-11.3	-14.1	-9.1	-3.1	5.5	7.8	4.9	7.9	4.4	1.4	7.0	4.7	3.0	7.1	12.9

Source: UNECE Common Database; national statistics; CIS Statistical Committee.

Note: Aggregation was performed using PPP-based value added weights.

[a] Cumulative change for the period.

[b] Public sector only.

[c] Excluding Republika Srpska.

[d] Excluding Transdniestria since 1993.

APPENDIX TABLE B.5

Total employment in south-east Europe and the CIS, 1990-2003
(Percentage change over the preceding year)

	1990	1991	1992	1993	1994	1995	1996	1997	1998	1999	2000	2001	2002	2003	2003 over 1989 [a]
South-east Europe [b]	-0.6	-0.3	-3.5	-4.7	3.4	–	0.6	-1.1	0.6	–	-1.0	-1.4	-1.6	-0.5	-8.5
Albania	-0.8	-1.7	-22.0	-4.4	11.0	-0.3	-3.6	-0.7	-2.0	-1.8	0.3	-13.8	–	0.7	-35.7
Bosnia and Herzegovina [c]	..	..	-62.0	-55.4	-7.5	10.8	123.0	52.7	5.9	3.1	0.7	-0.9	-3.2	-1.7	-38.6
Bulgaria	-6.1	-13.0	-8.1	-1.6	0.6	1.3	0.1	-3.9	-0.2	-2.1	-3.5	-0.4	0.4	1.4	-30.8
Croatia	-2.9	-8.2	-11.2	-3.4	-2.3	-1.2	-0.1	-0.7	-1.0	-1.1	-1.7	0.5	0.8	2.5	-26.7
Romania [d]	-1.0	-0.5	-3.0	-4.7	-1.5	-6.3	-2.3	–	-3.1	-1.8	-1.3	-1.9	-4.2	-0.1	-27.7
Serbia and Montenegro	-3.0	-3.0	-3.4	-2.8	-2.1	-1.6	-0.4	6.0	-0.1	-8.2	-2.6	0.2	-1.6	-1.3	-21.9
The former Yugoslav Republic of Macedonia	-1.8	-7.7	-4.8	-5.6	-6.0	-9.9	-4.7	-6.0	-2.9	1.8	-1.3	-4.5	-6.0	-4.4	-48.2
Turkey	1.7	3.9	0.9	-4.8	7.9	3.7	2.1	-2.5	2.8	2.1	-0.4	-1.0	-0.8	-1.0	15.0
CIS	0.2	-1.4	-2.3	-2.5	-3.0	-1.3	-0.8	-1.4	-1.2	-0.4	0.1	0.8	1.1	0.3	-11.2
Armenia [e]	1.6	1.7	-6.5	-3.1	-4.6	-1.7	-3.9	-5.7	-3.8	-4.3	-2.9	-2.3	–	0.1	-30.4
Azerbaijan	0.9	0.8	-0.3	-0.2	-2.2	-0.5	2.0	0.2	0.2	–	–	0.3	0.3	0.6	2.1
Belarus	-0.9	-2.5	-2.6	-1.3	-2.6	-6.2	-1.0	0.1	1.1	0.6	–	-0.5	-0.8	-0.9	-16.5
Georgia	2.3	-8.9	-21.2	-9.6	-2.4	-1.2	2.7	0.2	-6.3	0.1	6.2	2.1	-2.1	-1.3	-35.3
Kazakhstan	1.3	-1.1	-1.9	-8.5	-5.0	-0.5	-0.5	-0.7	-5.3	-0.4	1.6	8.0	0.2	4.1	-9.4
Kyrgyzstan	0.5	-1.0	6.0	-8.5	-2.1	-0.2	0.6	2.3	0.9	3.5	0.2	1.1	1.2	0.9	4.9
Republic of Moldova [f]	-0.9	-0.1	-1.0	-0.8	-0.4	-0.5	-0.8	-0.8	-0.2	-9.0	1.3	-1.1	0.4	-9.9	-35.1
Russian Federation	-0.4	-2.0	-2.4	-1.7	-3.3	-3.0	-0.7	-1.9	-1.4	0.2	0.6	0.6	1.0	-0.2	-13.7
Tajikistan	3.2	1.7	-3.2	-2.8	–	-0.1	-6.6	3.5	0.3	-3.3	0.5	4.8	1.5	1.5	0.3
Turkmenistan	3.4	3.5	3.3	3.2	3.9	3.4	1.8	2.0	1.3	0.7	3.0	2.0	2.5	2.2	42.8
Ukraine	–	-1.7	-2.0	-2.3	-3.8	3.0	-2.1	-2.7	-1.1	-2.3	-2.5	-1.2	1.7	0.3	-15.6
Uzbekistan	4.2	4.0	0.2	-0.1	1.4	0.8	1.3	1.4	1.4	1.0	1.1	1.7	2.1	2.8	25.8
Total above [b]	–	-1.2	-2.6	-3.0	-1.5	-1.0	-0.4	-1.3	-0.7	-0.3	-0.1	0.2	0.4	0.1	-10.6
Memorandum items:															
South-east Europe without Turkey [b]	-2.3	-3.8	-7.3	-4.5	-0.8	-3.8	-0.9	0.5	-1.8	-2.5	-1.7	-1.9	-2.6	0.1	-26.8
CIS without Russian Federation	1.0	-0.7	-2.2	-3.4	-2.5	0.8	-0.9	-0.9	-1.0	-1.1	-0.4	1.0	1.1	0.9	-8.2
Low-income CIS	2.3	0.6	-2.9	-3.9	-0.6	–	0.3	0.7	-0.1	-0.5	1.0	1.3	1.1	0.7	-0.4
Caucasian CIS	1.5	-2.4	-8.4	-3.5	-2.8	-0.9	1.0	-1.0	-2.3	-0.7	1.1	0.3	-0.4	–	-17.3
Central Asian CIS	2.6	1.4	-0.2	-3.9	-1.0	0.5	–	1.0	-0.9	0.4	1.3	3.8	1.4	2.9	9.6
European CIS	-0.2	-1.7	-2.0	-3.1	-3.5	1.4	-1.9	-2.2	-0.7	-2.3	-1.9	-1.1	1.2	-0.4	-17.0
EU-8	-3.1	-6.3	-4.5	-3.2	-0.8	0.9	1.1	1.2	1.1	-1.9	-1.5	-0.2	-0.9	–	-16.9

Source: UNECE Common Database; national statistics; CIS Statistical Committee.

Note: Establishment-based data for all countries except Romania and Turkey, for which labour force survey (LFS) data have been used.

[a] Cumulative change for the period.

[b] Excluding Bosnia and Herzegovina through 1991.

[c] Excluding Republika Srpska.

[d] Original LFS data are available from 1996 onwards. For earlier years the LFS data have been retropolated using the movement in the reported establishments-based data. The whole time series has then been benchmarked to the 1992 and 2002 census results.

[e] Data have been benchmarked to the 1989 and 2001 census results.

[f] Excluding Transdniestria since 1993.

APPENDIX TABLE B.6

Employment in industry in south-east Europe and the CIS, 1990-2003

(Percentage change over the preceding year)

	1990	1991	1992	1993	1994	1995	1996	1997	1998	1999	2000	2001	2002	2003	2003 over 1989[a]
South-east Europe[b]	-2.8	-5.8	-8.2	-7.4	0.9	-4.5	2.1	0.6	-1.9	-7.4	2.3	-1.4	2.6	-1.7	-26.5
Albania	..	..	..	..	..	-14.4	-10.1	3.8	-4.9	-2.3	-28.7	20.2	-0.5	-4.0	-39.2
Bosnia and Herzegovina[c]	..	..	-61.3	-64.6	11.0	104.2	17.4	21.9	7.6	0.2	–	-4.8	-2.2	-4.5	-57.4
Bulgaria	-9.0	-17.9	-13.2	-8.3	-3.7	-2.2	-1.2	-4.4	-4.0	-9.2	-5.7	-1.4	0.3	0.4	-56.8
Croatia	2.4	-17.2	-17.1	0.2	-4.5	-11.6	-0.9	-4.0	5.9	-2.8	-2.2	-0.6	-1.0	1.3	-43.2
Romania[d]	-3.5	-5.0	-13.2	-8.7	-5.5	-6.5	0.4	-3.2	-6.1	-7.4	-7.4	-2.6	4.8	0.6	-48.5
Serbia and Montenegro	0.9	-8.7	-5.3	-2.5	-2.7	-3.5	-1.8	-3.3	2.6	-9.4	-4.9	-2.8	-7.8	-6.3	-43.7
The former Yugoslav Republic of Macedonia	-4.7	-8.4	-6.5	-5.1	-5.9	-13.4	-6.6	-7.8	-3.4	5.5	-4.5	7.1	-9.5	-3.8	-50.7
Turkey	-0.3	2.8	6.2	-6.3	11.7	-3.3	6.3	6.3	-0.2	-7.8	14.4	-0.9	4.8	-2.8	32.3
CIS	–	-1.7	-5.0	-4.2	-10.0	-7.7	-5.1	-8.0	-3.7	-1.5	-0.4	-0.3	-1.1	-1.8	-40.7
Armenia[e]	2.2	-7.8	-12.1	-11.1	-2.6	-15.6	-17.0	-11.5	-9.9	-8.3	-9.7	-7.4	-3.4	-3.0	-71.2
Azerbaijan	-2.9	-2.3	-6.3	-8.8	-4.6	-5.8	-19.7	-14.5	3.8	3.1	-3.7	-1.0	1.9	0.2	-47.8
Belarus	-1.4	-1.7	-4.9	-3.9	-4.6	-10.9	-1.2	0.2	1.4	0.8	-0.3	-1.2	-3.4	-1.0	-28.3
Georgia	4.2	-11.2	-28.7	-14.4	-8.6	-9.4	-1.0	-0.5	-9.3	-8.3	5.9	-5.2	-3.3	-2.7	-63.8
Kazakhstan	-1.5	1.4	-3.7	-13.1	-8.0	-9.4	-3.9	-11.8	-2.0	0.1	-5.5	-2.9	-0.8	3.8	-45.3
Kyrgyzstan	-0.1	-4.7	-6.0	-10.0	-10.5	-15.0	-10.8	-6.1	-2.2	-7.6	-10.6	-0.4	-0.8	1.4	-58.5
Republic of Moldova[f]	2.4	-7.1	-2.1	-28.9	-5.3	-14.2	-2.0	-2.1	-4.7	-12.1	4.4	-1.2	3.6	-4.1	-63.2
Russian Federation	0.7	-1.8	-4.8	-2.4	-10.7	-7.6	-4.6	-8.9	-5.0	1.0	1.7	1.0	-1.1	-2.7	-37.6
Tajikistan	2.5	-1.6	-2.6	-12.3	-4.9	-12.1	-1.1	-12.2	-3.8	-13.3	-8.6	1.2	-0.7	-5.9	-54.9
Turkmenistan	4.2	-3.3	0.2	9.5	-0.1	4.4	3.9	10.9	13.0	1.8	5.9	5.7	5.0	2.4	84.1
Ukraine	-1.9	-0.8	-4.7	-5.2	-11.0	-7.8	-7.4	-8.5	-3.1	-8.3	-5.6	-3.9	-2.2	-1.8	-52.6
Uzbekistan	1.5	-1.9	-2.7	1.7	-8.6	2.5	1.3	0.2	0.5	0.9	1.9	1.3	2.2	2.8	2.9
Total above[b]	-0.6	-2.6	-5.7	-4.9	-7.8	-7.0	-3.4	-5.9	-3.2	-3.1	0.3	-0.6	-0.2	-1.8	-37.4
Memorandum items:															
South-east Europe without															
Turkey[b]	-3.6	-9.1	-14.0	-8.0	-4.6	-5.1	-0.4	-3.0	-3.1	-7.2	-6.4	-1.8	0.7	-0.8	-46.8
CIS without Russian Federation	-1.0	-1.6	-5.1	-6.8	-9.0	-7.8	-5.8	-6.6	-1.8	-5.0	-3.6	-2.3	-1.2	-0.4	-45.1
Low-income CIS	1.3	-4.6	-7.2	-10.3	-6.9	-6.1	-5.4	-4.5	-1.8	-3.0	-0.9	-0.4	1.1	0.6	-39.2
Caucasian CIS	0.9	-6.8	-14.4	-10.9	-4.7	-10.3	-14.8	-10.1	-4.4	-3.5	-3.3	-3.9	-1.0	-1.4	-60.7
Central Asian CIS	0.2	-0.7	-3.3	-6.7	-7.8	-4.9	-1.7	-5.0	0.1	-0.7	-1.7	0.2	1.2	2.6	-25.3
European CIS	-1.7	-1.2	-4.7	-6.4	-9.9	-8.5	-6.3	-6.9	-2.3	-6.7	-4.4	-3.2	-2.3	-1.7	-49.5
EU-8	-4.9	-7.1	-9.5	-6.3	-4.1	0.4	-1.0	-0.2	-0.7	-4.8	-3.7	-1.3	-2.5	-1.2	-38.4

Source: UNECE Common Database; national statistics; CIS Statistical Committee.

Note: Establishment-based data for all countries except Romania and Turkey, for which labour force survey (LFS) data have been used.

[a] Cumulative change for the period.

[b] Excluding Albania through 1994 and Bosnia and Herzegovina through 1991.

[c] Excluding Republika Srpska.

[d] Original LFS data are available from 1996 onwards. For earlier years the LFS data have been retropolated using the movement in the reported establishments-based data. The whole time series has then been benchmarked to the 1992 and 2002 census results.

[e] Data have been benchmarked to the 1989 and 2001 census results.

[f] Excluding Transdniestria since 1993.

APPENDIX TABLE B.7

Registered unemployment in south-east Europe and the CIS, 1990-2003
(Per cent of labour force, end of period)

	1990	1991	1992	1993	1994	1995	1996	1997	1998	1999	2000	2001	2002	2003
South-east Europe [a]	..	8.4	11.0	11.4	11.3	10.1	9.3	10.5	11.1	12.3	11.8	12.4	13.4	13.0
Albania	9.5	9.2	27.0	22.0	18.0	13.1	12.4	14.9	17.7	18.4	16.8	16.4	15.8	15.0
Bosnia and Herzegovina	..	..	..	..	..	..	..	39.0	38.7	39.0	39.4	39.9	42.7	44.0
Bulgaria	1.8	11.1	15.3	16.4	12.8	11.1	12.5	13.7	12.2	16.0	17.9	17.9	16.3	13.5
Croatia	..	14.1	17.8	16.6	17.3	17.6	15.9	17.6	18.1	20.4	22.3	22.8	21.3	18.7
Romania	1.3	3.0	8.2	10.4	10.9	9.5	6.6	8.8	10.3	11.5	10.5	8.8	8.4	7.2
Serbia and Montenegro [b]	..	21.0	24.6	24.0	23.9	24.7	26.1	25.6	27.2	27.4	26.6	28*	26*	28*
The former Yugoslav Republic of Macedonia	..	24.5	26.2	27.7	30.0	36.6	38.8	41.7	32.3	44.0	45.1	41.8	45.3	45.3
Turkey [c]	8.2	7.9	7.9	7.6	8.1	6.9	6.1	6.4	6.8	7.6	6.5	8.3	10.3	10.5
CIS	..	..	0.6	1.0	1.5	2.5	2.9	2.8	2.9	2.4	2.3	2.2	2.3	2.4
Armenia	..	..	3.5	6.3	6.0	8.1	9.7	11.0	8.9	11.5	10.9	9.8	9.1	9.8
Azerbaijan	..	..	0.2	0.7	0.9	1.1	1.1	1.3	1.4	1.2	1.2	1.3	1.3	1.4
Belarus	..	..	0.5	1.3	2.1	2.7	4.0	2.8	2.3	2.0	2.1	2.3	3.0	3.1
Georgia	..	..	0.3	2.0	3.8	3.4	3.2	8.0	4.2	5.6	6.0	5.0	4.0	2.5*
Kazakhstan	..	..	0.4	0.6	1.0	2.1	4.1	3.9	3.7	3.9	3.7	2.8	2.6	1.8
Kyrgyzstan	..	..	0.1	0.2	0.8	3.0	4.5	3.1	3.1	3.0	3.1	3.1	3.1	3.0
Republic of Moldova	..	..	0.7	0.7	1.0	1.4	1.5	1.7	1.9	2.1	1.8	1.7	1.5	1.2
Russian Federation	..	..	0.8	1.1	2.1	3.2	3.4	2.8	2.7	1.7	1.4	1.6	1.8	2.3
Tajikistan	..	..	0.4	1.1	1.8	1.8	2.4	2.8	2.9	3.1	3.0	2.6	2.7	2.4
Turkmenistan	..	..	..	..	..	..	..	..	..	..	..	..	..	..
Ukraine	..	..	0.3	0.4	0.3	0.6	1.5	2.8	4.3	4.3	4.2	3.7	3.8	3.6
Uzbekistan	..	..	0.1	0.2	0.3	0.3	0.3	0.3	0.4	0.4	0.4	0.4	0.4	0.3
Total above	..	..	3.3	3.7	4.1	4.4	4.5	4.8	5.1	4.9	4.7	4.8	5.2	5.1
Memorandum items:														
South-east Europe without Turkey [a]	..	..	14.2	15.0	14.6	13.6	12.8	15.0	15.9	17.8	17.8	17.3	17.0	15.9
CIS without Russian Federation	..	..	0.4	0.8	0.9	1.4	2.2	2.8	3.3	3.3	3.3	2.9	3.0	2.6
Low-income CIS	..	..	0.5	1.2	1.5	1.8	2.0	2.4	2.2	2.3	2.3	2.1	2.0	1.6
Caucasian CIS	..	..	1.0	2.5	3.1	3.7	3.9	5.6	4.0	4.5	4.5	4.0	3.5	3.2
Central Asian CIS	..	..	0.2	0.5	0.8	1.3	2.2	2.0	2.1	2.0	2.0	1.7	1.7	1.2
European CIS	..	..	0.4	0.6	0.6	1.0	1.9	2.7	3.9	3.9	3.8	3.4	3.6	3.4
Russian Federation [d]	..	..	5.2	6.1	7.8	9.0	10.0	11.2	13.3	12.2	9.8	8.7	8.8	8.2

Source: UNECE Common Database; national statistics; CIS Statistical Committee.

[a] Excluding Bosnia and Herzegovina through 1996.

[b] Since 1999, excluding Kosovo and Metohia.

[c] Annual average, labour force survey data.

[d] Based on Rosstat's monthly estimates according to the ILO definition, i.e. including all persons not having employment but actively seeking work.

APPENDIX TABLE B.8

Consumer prices in south-east Europe and the CIS, 1990-2003
(Percentage change over preceding year)

	1990	1991	1992	1993	1994	1995	1996	1997	1998	1999	2000	2001	2002	2003
South-east Europe	..	69.2	143.4	251.9	120.3	25.3	34.1	82.5	50.3	43.1	44.6	45.0	35.0	21.0
Albania	..	35.5	226.0	85.0	22.5	8.0	12.7	33.1	20.3	-0.1	–	3.1	5.3	2.5
Bosnia and Herzegovina	594.0	116.2	83 327.6	32 662.0	581.6	-12.1	-21.2	11.8	4.9	-0.6	1.7	1.8	0.9	0.2
Bulgaria	23.8	338.5	79.4	56.1	87.1	62.1	121.6	1 058.4	18.7	2.6	10.3	7.4	5.8	2.3
Croatia	597.1	124.2	634.0	1 486.3	107.2	2.0	3.6	3.7	5.2	3.5	5.4	4.7	1.8	2.2
Romania	5.1	170.2	210.4	256.1	136.7	32.2	38.8	154.9	59.3	45.9	45.7	34.5	22.5	15.4
Serbia and Montenegro	580.0	122.0	8 926.0	2.2E+14	3.3	71.8	90.5	23.2	30.4	44.1	77.5	90.4	19.3	9.6
The former Yugoslav Republic of Macedonia	596.6	110.8	1 511.3	362.0	128.3	16.4	2.5	0.9	-1.4	-1.3	6.6	5.2	2.3	1.1
Turkey	60.3	66.0	70.1	66.1	105.2	92.3	82.7	85.4	84.6	65.0	55.2	54.3	44.9	25.4
CIS	5.3	148.9	2 237.2	897.1	341.5	215.2	48.6	16.8	19.3	57.6	24.3	20.9	15.0	13.3
Armenia	6.9	174.1	728.7	3 731.8	4 962.3	175.5	18.7	13.8	8.7	0.7	-0.8	3.2	1.0	4.7
Azerbaijan	6.1	106.6	912.3	1 129.1	1 663.5	411.5	19.8	3.6	-0.8	-8.6	1.8	1.5	2.8	2.1
Belarus	4.7	94.1	970.8	1 190.2	2 221.0	709.3	52.7	63.9	73.2	293.7	168.9	61.4	42.8	28.5
Georgia	4.2	78.7	1 176.9	4 084.9	22 470.0	261.4	39.4	7.1	3.5	19.3	4.2	4.6	5.7	4.9
Kazakhstan	5.6	114.5	1 514.8	1 658.4	1 877.4	176.3	39.2	17.5	7.3	8.4	13.4	8.5	6.0	6.6
Kyrgyzstan	5.5	113.9	854.6	1 208.7	278.1	43.5	32.0	23.4	10.5	35.9	18.7	6.9	2.1	3.1
Republic of Moldova	5.7	101.1	1 108.7	1 183.7	486.8	29.9	23.5	11.8	7.7	39.3	31.3	9.8	5.3	11.7
Russian Federation	5.2	160.0	2 510.0	840.0	220.0	197.4	47.8	14.7	27.8	85.7	20.8	21.6	16.0	13.6
Tajikistan	5.9	112.9	906.8	2 136.1	239.4	682.1	422.4	85.4	43.1	27.5	32.9	38.6	12.2	16.3
Turkmenistan	..	..	..	..	..	..	..	..	..	..	..	..	..	..
Ukraine	5.4	94.0	1 527.0	4 734.9	891.2	376.7	80.2	15.9	10.6	22.7	28.2	12.0	0.8	5.2
Uzbekistan	5.8	97.3	414.5	1 231.8	1 550.0	76.5	54.0	58.8	17.7	29.0	24.9	..	..	..
Memorandum items:														
South-east Europe without														
Turkey	..	75.3	274.9	402.9	124.4	9.5	14.0	80.7	26.9	21.4	30.4	30.2	16.2	10.7
CIS without Russian														
Federation	5.7	105.6	886.7	1 644.3	1 199.3	237.7	49.5	19.2	10.3	23.2	30.7	19.8	13.1	12.6
Low-income CIS	5.7	105.3	753.7	1 245.7	1 098.5	211.3	33.5	22.4	9.6	16.7	15.0	..	..	..
Caucasian CIS	6.1	112.1	895.7	1 447.2	3 728.4	285.1	24.9	7.1	2.9	2.5	2.0	3.1	3.4	3.8
Central Asian CIS	5.6	106.9	785.6	1 361.6	1 143.5	176.4	44.2	29.1	11.6	17.3	18.6	..	..	..
European CIS	5.6	99.1	1 216.7	2 335.8	756.8	298.3	74.9	16.9	12.8	39.0	51.1	26.1	16.4	16.0
EU-8	66.6	60.2	32.9	32.6	24.0	21.8	16.6	12.7	10.8	6.5	8.5	5.9	2.7	2.0

Source: UNECE Common Database; national statistics; CIS Statistical Committee.

Note: Based on annual data reported by national statistical offices for 1990-1994 and monthly statistics from 1995 onwards. All CIS aggregates exclude Turkmenistan. Data for regional aggregates, in some cases, are estimated from partial regional totals.

APPENDIX TABLE B.9

Producer prices in industry [a] **in south-east Europe and the CIS, 1990-2003**

(Percentage change over preceding year)

	1990	1991	1992	1993	1994	1995	1996	1997	1998	1999	2000	2001	2002	2003
South-east Europe [b]	..	..	..	..	..	37.2	40.7	84.1	42.2	38.7	46.9	50.5	37.9	22.2
Albania	..	..	..	..	..	..	..	..	..	..	4.9	-5.4	6.4	6.2
Bosnia and Herzegovina	..	129.5	68 034.0	9 254.5	1 203.3	68.7	-4.8	3.2	3.6	4.3	0.9	2.3	0.7	2.6
Bulgaria	14.7	296.4	56.1	28.3	75.7	50.7	132.7	971.0	16.6	3.3	17.0	3.6	1.3	4.9
Croatia	455.3	146.3	825.2	1 512.4	77.6	0.8	1.3	3.7	-1.5	2.5	9.6	3.4	-0.5	1.9
Romania	26.9	220.1	184.8	165.0	140.5	35.3	50.0	144.0	33.2	41.2	53.4	41.0	24.6	21.1
Serbia and Montenegro	468.0	124.0	8 993.0	1.4E+13	7.6	75.7	88.8	20.6	25.9	43.3	105.4	84.4	10.9	5.8
The former Yugoslav														
Republic of Macedonia	394.0	112.0	2 198.2	258.3	88.9	4.7	–	4.0	3.5	–	9.1	2.7	-0.6	–
Turkey [c]	..	..	..	..	..	86.0	75.9	81.8	71.8	53.1	51.4	61.6	50.1	25.6
CIS	3.8	229.1	3 182.5	989.4	333.0	250.5	49.0	14.6	7.7	49.7	44.0	18.8	12.1	16.2
Armenia	2.0	120.0	947.0	892.0	4 714.0	187.8	36.3	21.7	6.0	4.1	-0.4	1.1	3.6	3.7
Azerbaijan	..	179.5	7 453.6	1 974.0	3 779.0	1 340.1	70.6	11.4	-5.5	-1.3	9.4	-2.6	3.3	18.6
Belarus	2.1	151.1	1 939.2	1 536.3	2 171.0	538.6	35.7	89.4	72.8	355.7	185.6	71.7	40.6	37.4
Georgia	..	..	..	..	..	..	..	..	2.2	15.5	5.8	3.6	6.0	2.6
Kazakhstan	..	193.0	2 465.1	1 042.8	2 920.4	139.7	23.8	15.6	0.8	19.0	38.0	0.4	0.3	9.5
Kyrgyzstan	..	160.0	1 664.0	831.0	228.0	15.8	28.4	23.4	8.9	51.1	29.6	9.6	5.5	7.5
Republic of Moldova	..	130.0	1 210.9	1 078.5	893.7	52.2	30.2	14.9	9.7	47.1	33.6	12.6	8.0	8.3
Russian Federation	3.9	240.0	3 280.0	900.0	230.0	237.6	50.8	15.0	7.0	59.1	46.5	19.1	11.8	15.6
Tajikistan	..	163.0	1 316.5	1 080.0	327.8	351.7	340.7	103.7	28.4	45.6	39.0	25.1	9.1	15.3
Turkmenistan	..	..	..	..	..	..	..	..	..	..	..	..	..	..
Ukraine	..	163.4	4 128.5	9 667.5	774.0	488.9	52.1	7.8	13.2	31.1	20.8	8.6	3.1	7.8
Uzbekistan	..	147.0	1 296.0	1 119.0	1 066.0	792.5	128.5	53.9	40.0	38.0	61.1	..	..	..
Memorandum items:														
South-east Europe without														
Turkey [c]	46.1	217.4	316.9	543.7	102.7	19.9	21.4	85.9	19.1	22.7	40.8	34.1	16.3	14.7
CIS without Russian														
Federation	..	154.3	2 109.1	2 700.1	1 036.0	277.6	45.6	13.8	9.1	32.1	38.6	18.2	13.0	18.0
Low-income CIS	..	153.3	1 613.0	916.3	762.2	296.5	66.1	21.9	6.8	17.7	25.2	..	..	..
Caucasian CIS	..	117.0	2 088.7	1 547.7	3 998.5	658.7	62.9	13.3	-2.2	2.8	6.9	-0.7	4.0	12.5
Central Asian CIS	..	167.6	1 904.3	927.4	1 491.1	132.6	31.3	21.1	6.8	25.1	41.3	9.1	4.3	9.6
European CIS	..	113.5	3 043.5	7 999.6	781.2	456.4	51.3	9.3	14.9	45.9	44.1	26.2	17.3	21.2
EU-8	52.6	55.4	24.3	22.2	15.7	18.2	11.0	10.1	6.4	3.8	7.9	3.2	0.5	1.7

Source: UNECE Common Database; national statistics; CIS Statistical Committee.

Note: Based on annual data reported by national statistical offices for 1990-1994 and monthly statistics from 1995 onwards. All CIS aggregates exclude Turkmenistan. Data for regional aggregates, in some cases, are estimated from partial regional totals.

[a] Industry = mining + manufacturing + utilities.

[b] Excluding Albania.

[c] Wholesale price index.

APPENDIX TABLE B.10

Nominal gross wages per employee in industry [a] **in south-east Europe and the CIS, 1990-2003**

(Percentage change over preceding year)

	1990	1991	1992	1993	1994	1995	1996	1997	1998	1999	2000	2001	2002	2003
South-east Europe [b]	58.6	104.1	156.9	100.4	92.0	32.1	43.4	84.9	51.1	48.8	48.7	37.5	28.8	..
Albania	..	..	..	..	..	..	..	..	..	..	..	..	..	..
Bosnia and Herzegovina	..	..	..	..	..	..	247.3	30.6	34.9	10.5	12.1	..	..	..
Bulgaria	20.8	175.5	132.8	55.1	53.9	57.7	90.4	882.9	34.5	5.8	12.4	0.2	4.1	7.2
Croatia	..	..	..	..	..	31.7	14.2	10.7	10.0	5.8	6.0	7.9	6.7	5.3
Romania	6.4	138.6	178.3	210.7	139.4	55.3	56.7	99.5	49.3	40.7	48.9	48.2	23.2	..
Serbia and Montenegro [c]	400.0	100.6	4 886.4	-62.5	229.6	74.1	74.5	41.7	39.6	24.6	115.2	110.5	..	..
The former Yugoslav Republic of Macedonia [c]	433.6	79.2	1 083.7	454.0	105.8	11.1	3.6	2.3	3.1	1.5	7.0	0.5	4.4	2.0
Turkey [d]	83.2	93.1	58.8	82.6	53.1	65.2	73.6	100.9	77.5	78.5	56.8	37.5	37.4	21.2
CIS	12.6	91.4	1 039.8	793.4	310.2	138.0	58.4	22.4	14.9	51.2	52.3	48.4	31.8	20.9
Armenia	5.9	31.8	352.3	739.1	3 640.2	210.9	62.3	41.7	20.5	15.2	19.5	22.3	12.6	31.8
Azerbaijan	4.4	82.9	870.4	700.8	575.7	354.8	53.0	58.2	19.8	18.1	33.3	14.6	13.6	20.2
Belarus	14.1	112.1	910.9	1 073.8	69.6	618.7	58.5	96.8	109.4	323.9	197.1	101.8	48.5	35.8
Georgia	6.0	33.9	457.3	2 117.2	23 300.5	112.6	145.4	12.7	26.8	23.2	33.8	19.6	14.2	..
Kazakhstan	11.0	80.5	1 053.1	993.1	1 542.5	178.2	30.9	22.5	7.8	21.6	26.1	15.3	10.4	12.6
Kyrgyzstan	0.5	62.1	773.1	615.1	176.3	54.8	29.1	60.3	20.0	43.2	0.9	18.1	20.7	12.1
Republic of Moldova	14.2	90.1	815.0	773.0	284.4	43.8	32.2	24.9	16.6	22.5	31.8	20.9	21.2	26.8
Russian Federation	13.0	94.9	1 065.7	798.2	260.2	131.4	64.3	21.6	14.3	52.2	48.8	46.8	27.7	29.2
Tajikistan	8.0	76.2	550.2	917.5	142.2	145.2	425.3	71.9	96.4	26.4	31.5	51.1	29.7	..
Turkmenistan	..	83.8	1 010.1	1 467.7	622.2	686.2	915.3	121.5	27.1	28.6	75.7	53.0	..	..
Ukraine	39.0	107.9	1 419.0	2 286.1	737.8	408.5	71.5	13.5	7.1	18.3	37.3	34.4	19.5	21.9
Uzbekistan	..	82.3	706.1	1 159.3	806.8	278.4	99.8	76.3	60.3	50.0	..	..	..	..
Memorandum items:														
South-east Europe without														
Turkey [b]	19.1	117.7	383.7	118.9	113.9	23.1	32.2	78.6	34.9	23.9	37.5	39.6	15.4	..
CIS without Russian														
Federation	..	71.9	867.1	689.9	778.4	164.4	39.1	25.1	16.5	48.3	67.1	55.3	33.8	28.9
Low-income CIS	4.7	73.8	841.2	623.2	355.3	119.1	58.5	43.1	24.2	24.5	22.9	21.4	18.7	..
Caucasian CIS	2.8	67.7	787.6	736.7	1 587.0	229.6	73.9	40.8	22.6	19.2	29.3	18.1	15.1	24.0
Central Asian CIS	4.0	63.5	854.8	786.6	873.6	164.2	32.4	25.4	10.5	24.0	23.3	16.7	12.3	16.0
European CIS	..	82.2	836.7	491.5	305.8	83.4	39.4	48.0	56.2	206.5	174.4	95.9	46.4	35.8
EU-8	..	..	..	26.2	30.6	24.6	22.0	17.0	12.8	9.0	9.3	8.2	2.8	5.2

Source: UNECE Common Database; national statistics; CIS Statistical Committee.

Note: The aggregates are calculated from average wage per employee in dollars, converted from national currencies at PPP for 2000. Data for regional aggregates, in some cases, are estimated from partial regional totals.

[a] Industry = mining + manufacturing + utilities.

[b] Excluding Albania.

[c] 1990-1998 – estimates on the basis of net wages in industry.

[d] Average compensation per employee in industry.

APPENDIX TABLE B.11

Merchandise exports of eastern Europe and the CIS, 1993-2003

(Billion dollars)

	1993	1994	1995	1996	1997	1998	1999	2000	2001	2002	2003
New EU members	55.549	64.224	86.419	89.460	96.741	108.773	108.156	121.682	134.764	152.923	197.458
Cyprus	0.868	0.967	1.229	1.393	1.246	1.064	1.000	0.951	0.978	0.843	0.921
Czech Republic	14.463	15.882	21.273	22.180	22.779	26.351	26.265	29.052	33.397	38.488	48.723
Estonia	0.802	1.305	1.838	2.079	2.934	3.236	2.938	3.174	3.309	3.428	4.511
Hungary	8.921	10.701	12.867	15.704	19.100	23.005	25.012	28.092	30.498	34.337	42.480
Latvia	1.401	0.988	1.304	1.443	1.673	1.812	1.723	1.865	2.001	2.279	2.877
Lithuania	1.994	2.031	2.705	3.355	3.860	3.711	3.004	3.809	4.583	5.519	7.212
Malta	1.357	1.567	5.416	1.734	1.385	1.540	1.983	2.447	1.957	2.215	2.461
Poland	14.202	17.240	22.887	24.440	25.756	28.229	27.407	31.651	36.085	41.010	53.577
Slovakia	5.458	6.714	8.585	8.822	9.640	10.775	10.277	11.908	12.704	14.478	21.960
Slovenia	6.083	6.828	8.316	8.310	8.369	9.050	8.546	8.732	9.252	10.326	12.737
South-east Europe	..	..	42.485	43.975	48.046	48.738	47.173	51.770	57.055	65.245	83.800
Albania	0.123	0.139	0.202	0.213	0.137	0.207	0.352	0.261	0.305	0.330	0.446
Bosnia and Herzegovina	..	..	0.024	0.058	0.193	0.352	0.750	1.069	1.027	1.001	1.355
Bulgaria	3.769	3.935	5.345	4.890	4.940	4.194	4.006	4.825	5.113	5.692	7.439
Croatia	3.709	4.260	4.633	4.512	4.171	4.541	4.302	4.432	4.666	4.904	6.164
Romania	4.892	6.151	7.910	8.085	8.431	8.302	8.487	10.367	11.385	13.869	17.618
Serbia and Montenegro	..	..	1.531	1.846	2.677	2.858	1.498	1.723	1.903	2.275	2.537
The former Yugoslav Republic of Macedonia	1.055	1.086	1.204	1.147	1.237	1.311	1.191	1.319	1.323	1.116	1.363
Turkey	15.345	18.106	21.637	23.224	26.261	26.974	26.587	27.775	31.334	36.059	46.878
CIS total	..	90.929	113.172	125.647	123.181	106.160	106.030	145.928	144.248	152.864	193.016
of which: **non-CIS**	52.547	61.751	79.800	88.922	86.539	76.657	83.146	116.681	113.768	122.470	154.126
Armenia	0.156	0.216	0.271	0.290	0.233	0.221	0.232	0.301	0.342	0.505	0.678
Non-CIS	0.029	0.058	0.101	0.162	0.138	0.140	0.175	0.227	0.253	0.409	0.551
Azerbaijan	0.725	0.653	0.637	0.631	0.781	0.606	0.929	1.745	2.314	2.168	2.592
Non-CIS	0.351	0.378	0.352	0.341	0.403	0.374	0.718	1.510	2.091	1.924	2.258
Belarus	..	2.510	4.707	5.652	7.301	7.070	5.909	7.331	7.448	8.021	9.964
Non-CIS	0.789	1.031	1.777	1.888	1.922	1.910	2.287	2.927	2.957	3.637	4.511
Georgia	..	0.156	0.154	0.199	0.240	0.193	0.238	0.330	0.320	0.348	0.482
Non-CIS	0.069	0.039	0.057	0.070	0.102	0.085	0.131	0.198	0.176	0.179	0.242
Kazakhstan	..	3.231	5.250	5.911	6.497	5.436	5.592	9.126	8.639	9.670	12.900
Non-CIS	1.501	1.357	2.366	2.732	3.515	3.266	4.100	6.750	5.995	7.476	9.946
Kyrgyzstan	0.396	0.340	0.409	0.505	0.604	0.514	0.454	0.505	0.476	0.486	0.582
Non-CIS	0.112	0.117	0.140	0.112	0.285	0.283	0.271	0.297	0.308	0.317	0.380
Republic of Moldova	0.483	0.565	0.746	0.795	0.875	0.632	0.464	0.472	0.568	0.644	0.790
Non-CIS	0.178	0.159	0.279	0.252	0.267	0.203	0.211	0.196	0.222	0.293	0.367
Russian Federation [a]	..	67.800	82.419	90.600	86.895	74.444	75.551	105.033	101.900	107.200	134.800
Non-CIS	44.297	52.100	65.400	72.000	67.800	58.700	63.600	90.800	86.600	91.000	114.000
Tajikistan	0.350	0.492	0.749	0.770	0.746	0.597	0.689	0.784	0.652	0.737	0.798
Non-CIS	0.227	0.399	0.497	0.439	0.473	0.394	0.374	0.411	0.440	0.549	0.659
Turkmenistan	..	2.145	1.881	1.682	0.751	0.594	1.190	2.500	2.620	2.616	3.160
Non-CIS	1.049	0.494	0.951	0.610	0.300	0.442	0.700	1.200	1.170	1.178	1.710
Ukraine	7.817	10.272	13.128	14.401	14.232	12.637	11.582	14.573	16.265	17.957	23.080
Non-CIS	3.223	4.653	6.168	6.996	8.646	8.435	8.329	10.075	11.589	13.580	17.032
Uzbekistan [b]	..	2.549	2.821	4.211	4.026	3.218	3.200	3.230	2.704	2.513	3.189
Non-CIS	0.721	0.966	1.712	3.321	2.689	2.425	2.250	2.090	1.968	1.930	2.469
Total above	..	..	242.076	259.081	267.968	263.671	261.359	319.380	336.067	371.031	474.273
Memorandum items:											
Baltic states	4.197	4.324	5.846	6.877	8.467	8.759	7.665	8.848	9.893	11.226	14.599
Central Europe	49.127	57.365	73.928	79.456	85.644	97.410	97.508	109.436	121.937	138.638	179.476
South-east Europe without Turkey	..	..	20.848	20.751	21.785	21.764	20.586	23.995	25.721	29.186	36.922
CIS without Russian Federation	..	23.129	30.753	35.047	36.286	31.716	30.479	40.895	42.348	45.664	58.216
Caucasian CIS	..	1.025	1.062	1.120	1.253	1.019	1.399	2.376	2.976	3.021	3.752
Central Asian CIS	..	8.757	11.110	13.079	12.625	10.358	11.125	16.145	15.091	16.022	20.629
European CIS	..	13.347	18.581	20.848	22.408	20.339	17.955	22.375	24.281	26.622	33.835

Source: UNECE secretariat calculations, based on national statistics and direct communications from national statistical offices.

Note: Changes in the method of recording trade are reflected from 1993 in data for the Czech Republic (inclusion of OPT transactions, etc.), from 1995 in Latvia (imports registered c.i.f.) and Lithuania (change from special to general system), from 1996 in Hungary (inclusion of trade flows of free trade zones), from 1997 in Slovakia (inclusion of OPT transactions, etc.) and from 2000 in Estonia (change from general to special trade system). All trade values are expressed in dollars at prevailing market exchange rates.

[a] Russian Federal State Statistics Service (Rosstat) data including trade flows not crossing the Russian borders such as off-board fish sales and estimates of value of goods exported or imported by individuals within an approved duty-free quota.

[b] National data adjusted for trade in services: from 2001 by UNECE secretariat, for previous years by the CIS Statistical Committee.

APPENDIX TABLE B.12

Merchandise imports of eastern Europe and the CIS, 1993-2003

(Billion dollars)

	1993	1994	1995	1996	1997	1998	1999	2000	2001	2002	2003
New EU members	67.780	78.180	102.684	120.628	131.154	144.766	141.759	155.908	166.086	184.484	232.689
Cyprus	2.648	3.013	3.696	3.986	3.695	3.677	3.630	3.627	3.944	4.072	4.472
Czech Republic	14.617	17.427	25.265	27.919	27.563	28.789	28.126	32.183	36.472	40.736	51.306
Estonia	0.896	1.659	2.540	3.231	4.441	4.786	4.108	4.252	4.294	4.780	6.471
Hungary	12.648	14.554	15.466	18.144	21.234	25.706	28.008	32.080	33.682	37.612	47.526
Latvia	0.961	1.240	1.818	2.320	2.724	3.189	2.946	3.189	3.507	4.040	5.210
Lithuania	2.244	2.352	3.649	4.559	5.644	5.794	4.834	5.457	6.353	7.769	9.894
Malta	2.175	2.431	2.940	2.799	2.550	2.667	2.847	3.405	2.722	2.831	3.391
Poland	18.758	21.566	29.043	37.137	42.314	47.054	45.911	48.940	50.275	55.113	68.004
Slovakia	6.332	6.634	8.777	11.112	11.622	13.006	11.265	12.660	14.689	16.629	22.604
Slovenia	6.501	7.304	9.492	9.421	9.367	10.098	10.083	10.116	10.148	10.902	13.811
South-east Europe	..	..	64.693	75.780	82.654	80.759	73.813	91.923	84.846	101.580	133.904
Albania	0.421	0.549	0.650	0.913	0.620	0.795	0.903	1.070	1.317	1.488	1.848
Bosnia and Herzegovina	..	..	0.524	1.204	1.555	2.120	3.297	3.106	3.240	3.741	4.568
Bulgaria	5.120	4.272	5.638	5.074	4.932	4.957	5.515	6.507	7.261	7.903	10.742
Croatia	4.166	5.229	7.510	7.788	9.104	8.383	7.799	7.887	9.147	10.722	14.199
Romania	6.522	7.109	10.278	11.435	11.280	11.838	10.557	13.055	15.552	17.857	24.003
Serbia and Montenegro	..	..	2.665	4.113	4.826	4.830	3.296	3.711	4.837	6.320	7.510
The former Yugoslav Republic of Macedonia	1.199	1.484	1.719	1.627	1.779	1.915	1.776	2.085	2.094	1.995	2.300
Turkey	29.428	23.270	35.709	43.627	48.559	45.921	40.671	54.503	41.399	51.554	68.734
CIS: total	..	74.976	95.470	107.587	112.731	95.162	70.542	81.786	94.365	103.664	131.497
of which: **non-CIS**	33.696	44.899	56.861	63.607	71.815	61.760	44.571	47.881	59.443	68.985	87.449
Armenia	0.255	0.394	0.674	0.856	0.892	0.902	0.811	0.885	0.877	0.987	1.269
Non-CIS	0.087	0.188	0.340	0.578	0.593	0.672	0.624	0.711	0.659	0.685	0.960
Azerbaijan	0.629	0.778	0.668	0.961	0.794	1.077	1.036	1.172	1.431	1.666	2.626
Non-CIS	0.241	0.292	0.440	0.621	0.443	0.673	0.711	0.797	0.986	1.015	1.775
Belarus	..	3.066	5.564	6.939	8.689	8.549	6.674	8.574	8.178	9.092	11.505
Non-CIS	1.119	0.974	1.887	2.369	2.872	2.995	2.385	2.551	2.512	2.797	3.499
Georgia	..	0.338	0.385	0.687	0.944	0.884	0.602	0.651	0.685	0.731	1.144
Non-CIS	0.167	0.066	0.231	0.417	0.603	0.617	0.377	0.423	0.428	0.441	0.778
Kazakhstan	..	3.561	3.807	4.241	4.301	4.350	3.687	5.051	6.446	6.584	8.327
Non-CIS	0.494	1.384	1.154	1.295	1.969	2.290	2.089	2.295	3.137	3.541	4.407
Kyrgyzstan	0.448	0.317	0.522	0.838	0.709	0.842	0.600	0.554	0.467	0.587	0.717
Non-CIS	0.112	0.107	0.168	0.351	0.273	0.401	0.341	0.256	0.210	0.264	0.307
Republic of Moldova	0.628	0.659	0.841	1.072	1.172	1.024	0.587	0.776	0.893	1.039	1.403
Non-CIS	0.184	0.183	0.272	0.420	0.567	0.584	0.345	0.517	0.552	0.630	0.809
Russian Federation [a]	..	50.500	62.603	68.000	71.983	58.015	39.537	44.862	53.764	61.000	75.700
Non-CIS	26.807	36.500	44.300	47.200	53.400	43.700	29.200	31.400	40.700	48.800	60.000
Tajikistan	0.630	0.547	0.810	0.668	0.750	0.711	0.663	0.675	0.688	0.721	0.881
Non-CIS	0.374	0.314	0.332	0.285	0.268	0.265	0.148	0.115	0.150	0.173	0.282
Turkmenistan	..	1.468	1.364	1.011	1.183	1.008	1.500	1.780	2.349	1.857	2.242
Non-CIS	0.501	0.782	0.619	0.450	0.531	0.530	1.000	1.100	1.146	1.103	1.492
Ukraine	9.533	10.745	15.484	17.603	17.128	14.676	11.846	13.956	15.775	16.977	23.021
Non-CIS	2.652	2.907	5.488	6.427	7.249	6.779	5.103	5.916	6.943	8.009	11.512
Uzbekistan [b]	..	2.603	2.748	4.712	4.186	3.125	3.000	2.850	2.812	2.425	2.662
Non-CIS	0.958	1.202	1.630	3.195	3.047	2.256	2.250	1.800	2.021	1.527	1.628
Total above	..	..	262.847	303.996	326.538	320.686	286.114	329.618	345.297	389.728	498.090
Memorandum items:											
Baltic states	4.101	5.251	8.006	10.110	12.809	13.768	11.888	12.897	14.154	16.590	21.575
Central Europe	58.856	67.485	88.043	103.733	112.100	124.653	123.393	135.979	145.266	160.991	203.251
South-east Europe without Turkey	..	..	28.984	32.154	34.095	34.838	33.142	37.420	43.447	50.026	65.170
CIS without Russian Federation	..	24.476	32.867	39.587	40.748	37.147	31.005	36.924	40.601	42.664	55.797
Caucasian CIS	..	1.510	1.727	2.503	2.630	2.864	2.449	2.708	2.994	3.384	5.040
Central Asian CIS	..	8.496	9.251	11.470	11.129	10.034	9.449	10.910	12.762	12.172	14.829
European CIS	..	14.470	21.889	25.614	26.989	24.249	19.107	23.307	24.846	27.108	35.928

Source: UNECE secretariat calculations, based on national statistics and direct communications from national statistical offices.

Note: See appendix table B.11.

[a] Rosstat data including trade flows not crossing the Russian borders such as off-board fish sales and estimates of value of goods exported or imported by individuals within an approved duty-free quota.

[b] National data adjusted for trade in services: from 2001 by UNECE secretariat, for previous years by the CIS Statistical Committee .

APPENDIX TABLE B.13

Balance of merchandise trade of eastern Europe and the CIS, 1993-2003

(Billion dollars)

	1993	1994	1995	1996	1997	1998	1999	2000	2001	2002	2003
New EU members	-12.231	-13.955	-16.266	-31.168	-34.413	-35.993	-33.603	-34.226	-31.322	-31.561	-35.232
Cyprus	-1.780	-2.045	-2.467	-2.593	-2.450	-2.613	-2.630	-2.676	-2.967	-3.229	-3.551
Czech Republic	-0.154	-1.545	-3.992	-5.739	-4.784	-2.438	-1.861	-3.131	-3.075	-2.248	-2.583
Estonia	-0.094	-0.353	-0.702	-1.152	-1.507	-1.550	-1.170	-1.078	-0.985	-1.352	-1.960
Hungary	-3.727	-3.853	-2.599	-2.440	-2.134	-2.701	-2.996	-3.988	-3.184	-3.275	-5.047
Latvia	0.440	-0.252	-0.515	-0.877	-1.051	-1.377	-1.223	-1.323	-1.506	-1.761	-2.333
Lithuania	-0.250	-0.322	-0.944	-1.204	-1.784	-2.083	-1.831	-1.647	-1.770	-2.250	-2.682
Malta	-0.818	-0.863	2.476	-1.066	-1.165	-1.128	-0.864	-0.958	-0.765	-0.615	-0.930
Poland	-4.555	-4.326	-6.156	-12.697	-16.558	-18.825	-18.504	-17.289	-14.190	-14.103	-14.427
Slovakia	-0.874	0.080	-0.192	-2.290	-1.983	-2.231	-0.988	-0.752	-1.985	-2.151	-0.644
Slovenia	-0.418	-0.476	-1.176	-1.111	-0.998	-1.048	-1.537	-1.384	-0.895	-0.576	-1.074
South-east Europe	..	..	-22.208	-31.806	-34.609	-32.021	-26.640	-40.153	-27.791	-36.335	-50.104
Albania	-0.298	-0.410	-0.448	-0.701	-0.483	-0.589	-0.551	-0.809	-1.012	-1.158	-1.402
Bosnia and Herzegovina	..	..	-0.500	-1.146	-1.362	-1.768	-2.547	-2.038	-2.213	-2.740	-3.213
Bulgaria	-1.352	-0.336	-0.294	-0.184	0.008	-0.763	-1.509	-1.683	-2.148	-2.211	-3.304
Croatia	-0.457	-0.969	-2.877	-3.276	-4.933	-3.842	-3.496	-3.455	-4.481	-5.818	-8.035
Romania	-1.630	-0.958	-2.368	-3.351	-2.849	-3.536	-2.070	-2.688	-4.167	-3.988	-6.385
Serbia and Montenegro	..	..	-1.134	-2.267	-2.149	-1.972	-1.798	-1.988	-2.934	-4.045	-4.973
The former Yugoslav Republic of											
Macedonia	-0.144	-0.398	-0.515	-0.480	-0.542	-0.604	-0.585	-0.766	-0.771	-0.880	-0.937
Turkey	-14.083	-5.164	-14.072	-20.403	-22.298	-18.947	-14.084	-26.728	-10.065	-15.495	-21.856
CIS: total	..	15.953	17.702	18.059	10.450	10.999	35.488	64.142	49.882	49.200	61.519
of which: non-CIS	18.851	16.852	22.939	25.315	14.725	14.897	38.575	68.800	54.325	53.485	66.677
Armenia	-0.099	-0.178	-0.403	-0.566	-0.660	-0.682	-0.580	-0.584	-0.536	-0.482	-0.591
Non-CIS	-0.058	-0.130	-0.239	-0.416	-0.455	-0.532	-0.449	-0.484	-0.406	-0.277	-0.408
Azerbaijan	0.096	-0.125	-0.031	-0.330	-0.013	-0.471	-0.107	0.573	0.883	0.502	-0.034
Non-CIS	0.110	0.086	-0.088	-0.280	-0.040	-0.299	0.007	0.713	1.106	0.909	0.483
Belarus	..	-0.556	-0.857	-1.287	-1.388	-1.480	-0.765	-1.244	-0.730	-1.071	-1.541
Non-CIS	-0.330	0.057	-0.110	-0.481	-0.950	-1.085	-0.098	0.376	0.445	0.839	1.012
Georgia	..	-0.182	-0.231	-0.488	-0.704	-0.692	-0.364	-0.321	-0.365	-0.384	-0.662
Non-CIS	-0.098	-0.027	-0.174	-0.347	-0.501	-0.532	-0.246	-0.226	-0.252	-0.263	-0.537
Kazakhstan	..	-0.330	1.443	1.670	2.196	1.086	1.906	4.075	2.193	3.086	4.574
Non-CIS	1.007	-0.027	1.212	1.437	1.547	0.976	2.011	4.456	2.858	3.935	5.539
Kyrgyzstan	-0.052	0.023	-0.113	-0.333	-0.105	-0.328	-0.146	-0.050	0.009	-0.101	-0.135
Non-CIS	0.000	0.010	-0.028	-0.239	0.012	-0.118	-0.070	0.041	0.097	0.053	0.074
Republic of Moldova	-0.145	-0.094	-0.095	-0.277	-0.297	-0.392	-0.123	-0.305	-0.325	-0.395	-0.612
Non-CIS	-0.006	-0.024	0.007	-0.168	-0.300	-0.381	-0.134	-0.321	-0.331	-0.336	-0.443
Russian Federation [a]	..	17.300	19.816	22.600	14.912	16.429	36.014	60.171	48.136	46.200	59.100
Non-CIS	17.490	15.600	21.100	24.800	14.400	15.000	34.400	59.400	45.900	42.200	54.000
Tajikistan	-0.280	-0.055	-0.061	0.102	-0.004	-0.114	0.026	0.109	-0.036	0.017	-0.083
Non-CIS	-0.147	0.085	0.165	0.154	0.205	0.129	0.225	0.295	0.290	0.376	0.377
Turkmenistan	..	0.677	0.517	0.670	-0.432	-0.414	-0.310	0.720	0.271	0.759	0.918
Non-CIS	0.548	-0.288	0.332	0.160	-0.231	-0.088	-0.300	0.100	0.024	0.075	0.218
Ukraine	-1.716	-0.473	-2.356	-3.202	-2.896	-2.038	-0.265	0.617	0.490	0.980	0.059
Non-CIS	0.571	1.746	0.680	0.569	1.397	1.657	3.227	4.159	4.646	5.571	5.519
Uzbekistan [b]	..	-0.054	0.073	-0.501	-0.159	0.093	0.200	0.380	-0.108	0.089	0.527
Non-CIS	-0.237	-0.236	0.082	0.126	-0.358	0.169	–	0.290	-0.053	0.403	0.842
Total above	..	..	-20.771	-44.914	-58.571	-57.015	-24.755	-10.238	-9.230	-18.696	-23.817
Memorandum items:											
Baltic states	0.096	-0.927	-2.160	-3.232	-4.343	-5.009	-4.224	-4.049	-4.261	-5.363	-6.976
Central Europe	-9.729	-10.120	-14.115	-24.277	-26.456	-27.243	-25.885	-26.543	-23.329	-22.354	-23.775
South-east Europe without Turkey	..	..	-8.136	-11.403	-12.311	-13.074	-12.556	-13.426	-17.726	-20.840	-28.248
CIS without Russian Federation	..	-1.347	-2.114	-4.541	-4.462	-5.430	-0.526	3.971	1.746	3.000	2.419
Caucasian CIS	..	-0.485	-0.665	-1.383	-1.377	-1.845	-1.050	-0.332	-0.017	-0.364	-1.287
Central Asian CIS	..	0.261	1.859	1.608	1.496	0.324	1.675	5.235	2.329	3.849	5.800
European CIS	..	-1.123	-3.308	-4.766	-4.581	-3.909	-1.152	-0.932	-0.565	-0.486	-2.094

Source: UNECE secretariat calculations, based on national statistics and direct communications from national statistical offices.

Note: See appendix table B.11.

[a] Rosstat data including trade flows not crossing the Russian borders such as off-board fish sales and estimates of value of goods exported or imported by individuals within an approved duty-free quota.

[b] National data adjusted for trade in services: from 2001 by UNECE secretariat, for previous years by the CIS Statistical Committee .

APPENDIX TABLE B.14

Merchandise trade of eastern Europe and the Russian Federation, by direction, 1980, 1990, 1992-2003
(Shares in total trade, per cent)

	1980	1990	1992	1993	1994	1995	1996	1997	1998	1999	2000	2001	2002	2003
Eastern Europe, *to and from:*														
Exports														
World	100.0	100.0	100.0	100.0	100.0	100.0	100.0	100.0	100.0	100.0	100.0	100.0	100.0	100.0
Eastern Europe and the CIS	48.5	38.1	23.0	30.7	28.5	28.6	28.5	28.6	24.7	20.8	20.7	21.4	21.2	21.6
CIS	27.1	22.3	12.4	11.4	10.0	9.8	10.0	10.6	7.4	4.2	4.1	4.7	4.5	4.4
Eastern Europe	21.4	15.8	10.7	19.3	18.5	18.7	18.5	18.0	17.3	16.6	16.6	16.7	16.7	17.2
Developed market economies	35.7	49.5	63.0	57.5	61.9	62.6	63.5	63.6	68.3	73.4	73.1	72.9	72.7	72.8
Developing economies	15.8	12.4	14.0	11.8	9.6	8.8	8.0	7.8	7.0	5.8	6.2	5.7	6.1	5.6
Imports														
World	100.0	100.0	100.0	100.0	100.0	100.0	100.0	100.0	100.0	100.0	100.0	100.0	100.0	100.0
Eastern Europe and the CIS	42.0	26.6	24.7	29.9	26.2	25.8	24.7	23.1	20.0	20.6	23.6	23.2	22.5	22.8
CIS	26.8	18.3	17.9	16.5	14.0	13.0	12.0	11.0	8.6	8.5	11.4	10.8	9.9	9.7
Eastern Europe	18.8	14.3	6.8	13.4	12.2	12.9	12.7	12.1	11.4	12.1	12.2	12.4	12.6	13.1
Developed market economies	38.7	53.3	64.4	61.2	65.2	65.6	66.2	66.7	70.2	69.7	66.7	66.2	65.3	64.4
Developing economies	19.3	20.1	10.9	8.9	8.6	8.5	9.1	10.2	9.8	9.7	9.7	10.6	12.2	12.8
Former Soviet Union/Russian Federation, *to and from:*														
Exports														
World	100.0	100.0	100.0	100.0	100.0	100.0	100.0	100.0	100.0	100.0	100.0	100.0	100.0	100.0
Eastern Europe	34.5	21.8	22.3	18.1	15.1	16.8	18.2	19.5	18.1	17.8	20.0	19.3	17.5	17.0
Developed market economies	42.2	49.5	57.9	59.7	66.6	60.6	58.1	58.6	60.0	57.8	55.6	55.0	55.6	53.3
Developing economies	23.3	28.7	19.8	22.2	18.3	22.6	23.7	21.9	21.9	24.4	24.4	25.7	26.9	29.7
Imports														
World	100.0	100.0	100.0	100.0	100.0	100.0	100.0	100.0	100.0	100.0	100.0	100.0	100.0	100.0
Eastern Europe	31.5	24.7	15.9	10.6	14.1	15.5	12.6	13.7	12.0	9.6	10.9	10.1	10.3	10.9
Developed market economies	46.4	52.9	62.4	60.6	70.3	69.5	67.8	68.3	68.2	68.3	69.3	67.8	65.7	64.8
Developing economies	22.1	22.4	21.7	28.8	15.6	15.0	19.6	18.0	19.8	22.1	19.8	22.1	24.0	24.3

Source: UNECE Common Database, derived from national statistics.

Note: Data for 1980-1990 refer to the east European CMEA countries (Bulgaria, Czechoslovakia, German Democratic Republic, Hungary, Poland and Romania) and to the former Soviet Union. Trade data in national currencies were revalued at consistent rouble/dollar cross-rates (see the note to appendix table B.11). As from 1991, the second panel reflects non-CIS trade of the Russian Federation only. In the first panel, reporting group "eastern Europe" covers Bulgaria, former Czechoslovakia, Hungary, Poland and Romania in 1992; in 1993-1995 it covers Albania, Bulgaria, Croatia, the Czech Republic, Estonia, Hungary, Latvia, Lithuania, Poland, Romania, Slovakia, Slovenia and The Former Yugoslav Republic of Macedonia while Bosnia and Herzegovina and Serbia and Montenegro are included only from 1996.

APPENDIX TABLE B.15

Exchange rates of eastern Europe and the CIS, 1990, 1993-2004
(Annual averages, national currency units per dollar)

	Unit [a]	1990	1993	1994	1995	1996	1997	1998	1999	2000	2001	2002	2003	2004
Albania	lek	8.90	102.06	94.62	92.70	104.50	148.93	150.63	137.69	143.71	143.48	139.93	121.87	102.77
Bosnia and Herzegovina	con. marka [b]	..	..	..	1.43	1.50	1.73	1.76	1.84	2.12	2.19	2.08	1.73	1.58
Bulgaria	leva [c]	2.36	27.85	54.13	67.08	177.88	1 681.87	1 760.37	1.84	2.12	2.18	2.08	1.73	1.58
Croatia	kuna [d]	11.00	3 577.42	6.03	5.23	5.43	6.10	6.36	7.11	8.28	8.34	7.87	6.70	6.05
Czech Republic	koruna	18.56	29.15	28.79	26.54	27.14	31.70	32.28	34.57	38.60	38.04	32.74	28.21	25.70
Estonia	kroon [e]	..	13.22	12.99	11.46	12.03	13.88	14.07	14.69	16.98	17.49	16.63	13.86	12.60
Hungary	forint	63.21	91.93	105.16	125.68	152.65	186.79	214.40	237.15	282.18	286.49	257.89	225.14	202.75
Latvia	lats [f]	..	0.67	0.56	0.53	0.55	0.58	0.59	0.59	0.61	0.63	0.62	0.57	0.54
Lithuania	litas [g]	..	4.34	3.98	4.00	4.00	4.00	4.00	4.00	4.00	4.00	3.68	3.06	2.78
Poland	zloty [h]	9 500	18 136	22 723	2.42	2.70	3.28	3.49	3.96	4.35	4.09	4.08	3.89	3.66
Romania	leu	22.43	760.05	1 655	2 033	3 084	7 168	8 876	15 333	21 709	29 061	33 055	33 200	32 637
Serbia and Montenegro	dinar [i]	10.65	..	1.55	4.74	4.96	5.70	11.07	22.84	54.74	67.67	64.19	57.41	58.69
Slovakia	koruna	18.56	30.77	32.05	29.72	30.66	33.62	35.23	41.36	46.04	48.35	45.33	36.77	32.26
Slovenia	tolar	11.32	113.24	128.81	118.52	135.37	159.69	166.13	181.77	222.66	242.75	240.25	207.11	192.83
The former Yugoslav Republic of Macedonia	denar [j]	11.32	23.26	43.26	37.88	39.98	50.00	54.46	56.90	65.90	68.04	64.82	54.32	49.43
Armenia	dram	..	9.11	288.65	405.91	414.04	490.77	504.92	535.06	539.53	555.08	573.35	578.76	534.82
Azerbaijan	manat	..	102.33	1 739	4 414	4 301	3 985	3 869	4 120	4 474	4 657	4 861	4 911	4 914
Belarus	rouble [k]	..	3 160	4 652	11 538	13 472	26 729	58 971	274 512	882	1 390	1 785	2 054	2 160
Georgia	lari [l]	..	..	1.66	1.29	1.26	1.30	1.39	2.03	1.98	2.07	2.20	2.14	1.92
Kazakhstan	tenge	..	..	35.54	60.95	67.30	75.44	78.30	119.52	142.13	146.74	153.30	149.71	136.10
Kyrgyzstan	som	..	..	10.86	10.82	12.81	17.36	20.84	39.01	47.70	48.38	46.94	43.61	42.67
Republic of Moldova	leu	..	1.58	4.08	4.50	4.60	4.62	5.37	10.52	12.43	12.87	13.57	13.95	12.33
Russian Federation	rouble [m]	0.59	993.00	2 204	4 559	5 121	5 785	9.71	24.62	28.13	29.17	31.35	30.69	28.87
Tajikistan	samoni [n]	..	..	..	107.59	293.82	560.64	778.30	1 225.96	1.83	2.39	2.76	3.06	2.97
Turkmenistan	manat	..	..	14.08	116.67	3 595	4 143	4 592	5 200	5 200	5 200	5 200	5 202	5 220
Ukraine	hryvnia [o]	..	4 796	3 170	14 728	1.83	1.86	2.45	4.13	5.44	5.37	5.33	5.33	5.32
Uzbekistan	sum [p]	..	..	10.69	30.12	40.66	66.02	94.79	124.64	236.58	423.08	771.42	971.35	1 019.94

Source: UNECE Common Database, derived from national, IMF and CIS statistics. Annual averages are unweighted arithmetic averages of monthly values. Change or redenomination of currency is indicated by a vertical bar.

[a] Currency unit of the last period shown. For prior periods, see footnotes.

[b] BAM (convertible marka), the official rate is pegged to the euro. Prior to January 1999, the official rate was pegged to the deutsche mark at a 1:1 rate.

[c] The leva was redenominated at 1:1,000 from 5 July 1999.

[d] The kuna replaced the Croat dinar on 3 May 1994 at 1:1,000; the 1994 average is shown in kuna terms.

[e] The kroon replaced the Soviet rouble in June 1992 with a peg to the deutsche mark (8:1); the average shown for 1992 refers to June-December.

[f] The lats replaced an earlier Latvian rouble at 1:200 on 18 October 1993; the 1993 average is shown in lats terms.

[g] The litas replaced the earlier talonas at 1:100 on 1 June 1993; the 1993 average is shown in litas terms.

[h] The zloty was redenominated at 1:10,000 from 1 January 1995.

[i] The dinar was further redenominated on 1 July 1992 (1:10), 1 October 1993 (1:1 million), 1 January 1994 (1:1 billion) and 24 January 1994 (1:13 million). Average annual exchange rates not available for 1993. Estimated market exchange rates for 1998-2000.

[j] The denar (which had replaced the Yugoslav dinar 1:1 on 26 April 1992) was redenominated 1:100 on 1 May 1993; the 1993 average is shown in terms of that unit.

[k] The Belarus rouble was redenominated 1:10 on 10 August 1994; the 1994 average here assumes this applied to the entire year. The Belarus rouble was further redenominated at 1:1,000 since January 2000. Annual averages were calculated from end-of-period monthly rates, and the period average since January 1999.

[l] The lari replaced the lari-kupon on 25 September 1995; the annual average for 1994 is shown in million lari-kupon, and the average for 1995 in lari.

[m] 1980-1991: Soviet rouble/dollar rate used in the conversion of foreign trade data for statistical purposes. The rouble was redenominated at 1:1,000 from 1 January 1998.

[n] A new currency, the samoni, was put into circulation on 30 October 2000 replacing the Tajik rouble at 1:1,000. The average for 2000 is shown in samoni terms.

[o] The hryvnia replaced the former karbovanets on 2 September 1996 at 1:100,000; the average for 1996 is shown in hryvnia terms.

[p] The sum replaced the sum-kupon in June 1994 (1:1,000).

APPENDIX TABLE B.16

Current account balances of eastern Europe and the CIS, 1990-2003
(Million dollars)

	1990	1991	1992	1993	1994	1995	1996	1997	1998	1999	2000	2001	2002	2003
Eastern Europe	..	..	..	..	-3 027	-7 377	-18 284	-21 499	-22 312	-26 984	-23 462	-21 376	-26 096	-33 012
Albania	-118	-168	-51	19	31	37	-62	-254	-65	-133	-163	-218	-421	-407
Bosnia and Herzegovina	..	..	..	..	-177	-193	-748	-1 060	-813	-1 122	-1 033	-1 202	-1 693	-2 038
Bulgaria	-1 710	-77	-360	-1 098	-32	-198	164	1 046	-61	-652	-704	-984	-827	-1 676
Croatia [a]	-621	-589	329	637	711	-1 407	-956	-2 512	-1 453	-1 397	-461	-725	-1 918	-2 085
Czech Republic	-122	1 708	-456	456	-787	-1 369	-4 121	-3 564	-1 255	-1 462	-2 718	-3 273	-4 166	-5 570
Estonia	..	..	36	22	-167	-158	-398	-563	-478	-247	-294	-339	-716	-1 199
Hungary [b]	123	267	325	-3 455	-3 911	-1 638	-1 764	-2 076	-3 390	-3 773	-4 034	-3 237	-4 745	-7 446
Latvia	..	..	191	417	201	-16	-279	-345	-650	-654	-355	-626	-621	-917
Lithuania	..	..	321	-86	-94	-614	-723	-981	-1 298	-1 194	-675	-574	-734	-1 218
Poland [c]	3 067	-2 146	-3 104	-5 788	954	854	-3 264	-5 744	-6 901	-12 487	-9 980	-5 372	-5 007	-4 603
Romania	-3 337	-1 012	-1 564	-1 174	-428	-1 774	-2 571	-2 104	-2 917	-1 437	-1 374	-2 228	-1 535	-3 254
Serbia and Montenegro [d]	..	..	..	..	-400	-1 037	-1 317	-1 279	-660	-716	-350	-648	-1 731	-1 928
Slovakia	-767	-786	173	-532	759	511	-1 960	-1 827	-1 982	-980	-702	-1 746	-1 939	-280
Slovenia [a]	518	129	926	192	575	-75	56	51	-118	-698	-548	37	314	-114
The former Yugoslav Republic of Macedonia [a]	-409	-259	-19	-83	-263	-299	-340	-286	-270	-32	-72	-244	-358	-279
CIS [e]	..	..	-538	10 266	4 696	3 741	4 934	-6 448	-7 229	23 460	48 177	32 931	30 377	36 989
Armenia	..	..	-50	-67	-104	-218	-291	-307	-403	-307	-278	-200	-148	-191
Azerbaijan	..	153	488	-160	-121	-401	-931	-916	-1 365	-600	-168	-52	-768	-2 021
Belarus	..	..	131	-435	-444	-458	-516	-859	-1 017	-194	-338	-394	-311	-527
Georgia	..	..	-248	-354	-277	-363	-570	-514	-276	-200	-269	-211	-231	-398
Kazakhstan	..	-1 300	-1 900	-641	-905	-213	-751	-799	-1 236	-236	563	-1 203	-843	-39
Kyrgyzstan	..	..	-61	-88	-84	-235	-425	-138	-364	-184	-78	-17	-25	-24
Republic of Moldova	..	..	-152	-155	-82	-95	-192	-275	-335	-68	-116	-68	-52	-142
Russian Federation [f]	-6 300	2 500	1 142	12 792	7 844	6 963	10 847	-80	219	24 616	46 839	33 935	29 116	35 845
Tajikistan	..	..	-53	-208	-170	-89	-75	-61	-120	-36	-62	-74	-15	-5
Turkmenistan	-308	447	926	776	84	24	2	-580	-935	..	..	..	..	..
Ukraine	..	..	-526	-765	-1 163	-1 152	-1 185	-1 335	-1 296	1 658	1 481	1 402	3 173	2 891
Uzbekistan	..	..	-236	-429	118	-21	-980	-584	-103	-126	216	-113	..	..
Total above [e]	..	..	..	..	1 669	-3 636	-13 350	-27 946	-29 540	-3 524	24 715	11 555	4 281	3 977
Memorandum items:														
Central Europe	2 820	-828	-2 137	-9 127	-2 410	-1 717	-11 053	-13 160	-13 646	-19 400	-17 981	-13 590	-15 543	-18 013
South-east Europe without Turkey	..	..	..	..	-557	-4 871	-5 830	-6 449	-6 239	-5 489	-4 157	-6 248	-8 482	-11 666
Baltic states	..	..	548	353	-59	-788	-1 400	-1 890	-2 426	-2 095	-1 324	-1 538	-2 072	-3 333
EU-8	..	..	-1 589	-8 774	-2 469	-2 506	-12 454	-15 050	-16 072	-21 495	-19 305	-15 128	-17 614	-21 346
CIS without Russian Federation [e]	..	..	-1 680	-2 526	-3 148	-3 222	-5 913	-6 368	-7 448	-1 156	1 338	-1 005	1 262	1 145
European CIS	..	..	-547	-1 355	-1 689	-1 705	-1 893	-2 469	-2 647	1 396	1 027	939	2 810	2 222
Caucasian CIS	..	..	190	-581	-502	-983	-1 791	-1 736	-2 043	-1 106	-715	-464	-1 147	-2 609
Central Asian CIS [e]	..	..	-1 324	-590	-957	-534	-2 229	-2 162	-2 757	-1 446	1 025	-1 481	-402	1 532
Caucasian and central Asian CIS [e]	..	..	-1 133	-1 170	-1 459	-1 517	-4 020	-3 899	-4 800	-2 552	311	-1 944	-1 549	-1 077
Low-income CIS [e]	..	..	-312	-1 461	-720	-1 422	-3 463	-2 794	-2 965	-1 520	-754	-736	-1 017	-1 980

Source: National balance of payments statistics; IMF, *Balance of Payments Statistics* (Washington, D.C.) and IMF country studies; UNECE secretariat estimates.

[a] Excludes transactions with the republics of the former SFR of Yugoslavia: Croatia (1990-1992), Slovenia (1990-1991) and The former Yugoslav Republic of Macedonia (1990-1992).

[b] Methodological changes (mainly regarding treatment of reinvested earnings) were introduced in 2003 and 2004; 1995-2003 results have been revised accordingly. For 1990-1994, balance of payments data in convertible currencies only.

[c] National Bank of Poland started publishing balance of payments results on a transaction basis in 2004; the data have been revised accordingly back to 1990. Balance of payments data published in previous issues of this *Survey* until 2004 No. 1 were reported on a cash basis.

[d] Excludes Kosovo from 1999; 2003 data for Serbia only.

[e] Totals include estimates for Turkmenistan and Uzbekistan.

[f] 1990-1992 exclude transactions with the Baltic and CIS countries.

APPENDIX TABLE B.17

Inflows of foreign direct investment[a] in eastern Europe and the CIS, 1990-2003

(Million dollars)

	1990	1991	1992	1993	1994	1995	1996	1997	1998	1999	2000	2001	2002	2003
Eastern Europe	..	..	..	..	..	..	11 413	15 142	20 043	22 231	23 987	22 835	26 692	18 600
Albania[b]	–	–	20	68	53	70	90	48	45	41	143	207	135	178
Bosnia and Herzegovina[b]	..	..	..	..	–	–	–	–	67	177	146	119	268	382
Bulgaria[b]	4	56	41	40	105	90	109	505	537	819	1 002	813	905	1 419
Croatia	–	–	16	120	117	114	511	533	932	1 467	1 089	1 559	1 124	1 998
Czech Republic[c]	132	513	1 004	654	869	2 562	1 428	1 300	3 718	6 324	4 986	5 641	8 483	2 583
Estonia	..	..	82	162	215	202	151	267	581	305	387	542	284	891
Hungary[d]	311	1 459	1 471	2 339	1 146	4 741	3 291	4 166	3 344	3 311	2 777	3 949	3 021	2 340
Latvia	..	..	29	45	214	180	382	521	357	347	413	132	254	300
Lithuania	..	..	8	30	31	73	152	355	926	486	379	446	732	179
Poland	89	291	678	1 715	1 875	3 659	4 498	4 908	6 365	7 270	9 343	5 714	4 131	4 124
Romania	–	40	77	94	341	419	263	1 215	2 031	1 041	1 037	1 157	1 146	1 840
Serbia and Montenegro[be]	..	..	..	..	..	..	–	740	113	112	50	165	475	1 360
Slovakia	18	82	100	195	269	308	353	220	684	390	1 925	1 579	4 012	571
Slovenia	4	65	111	113	117	151	174	334	216	107	136	370	1 645	339
The former Yugoslav Republic of Macedonia[b]	–	–	–	–	24	9	11	30	128	33	175	442	78	95
CIS[f]	..	..	1 777	1 876	1 770	4 064	5 313	9 035	6 780	6 749	5 439	7 290	8 982	15 712
Armenia[b]	..	..	–	1	8	25	18	52	221	122	104	70	111	121
Azerbaijan[b]	..	..	–	60	22	330	627	1 125	1 023	510	130	227	1 392	3 285
Belarus[b]	..	..	7	18	11	15	105	352	203	444	119	96	247	172
Georgia[b]	..	..	–	–	8	6	40	243	265	82	131	110	165	338
Kazakhstan[b]	..	..	100	228	635	964	1 137	1 321	1 152	1 472	1 283	2 835	2 590	2 088
Kyrgyzstan[b]	..	..	–	10	38	96	47	83	109	44	-2	5	5	46
Republic of Moldova[b]	..	25	17	14	12	67	24	79	76	38	136	146	117	58
Russian Federation	–	100	1 454	1 211	690	2 065	2 579	4 865	2 761	3 309	2 714	2 748	3 461	7 958
Tajikistan[b]	..	..	9	9	12	20	18	18	25	21	24	9	36	32
Turkmenistan[b]	–	–	11	79	103	233	108	108	62	..	..	..	..	..
Ukraine[b]	..	..	170	198	159	267	521	623	743	496	595	792	693	1 424
Uzbekistan[b]	..	..	9	48	73	-24	90	167	140	121	75	83	..	..
Total above[f]	..	..	..	..	..	..	16 726	24 176	26 823	28 979	29 426	30 125	35 674	34 311
Memorandum items:														
Central Europe	555	2 410	3 364	5 015	4 275	11 420	9 744	10 929	14 327	17 402	19 167	17 254	21 292	9 957
South-east Europe without Turkey	..	..	..	..	..	..	984	3 070	3 853	3 690	3 642	4 461	4 130	7 272
Baltic states	..	..	119	238	460	454	685	1 142	1 863	1 139	1 178	1 120	1 270	1 370
EU-8	..	..	3 483	5 253	4 736	11 874	10 429	12 071	16 190	18 541	20 346	18 374	22 562	11 327
CIS without Russian Federation[f]	..	..	323	665	1 080	1 999	2 734	4 170	4 019	3 439	2 725	4 542	5 521	7 754
European CIS	..	..	194	229	181	349	649	1 053	1 022	978	850	1 034	1 057	1 654
Caucasian CIS	..	..	–	61	38	361	685	1 419	1 509	715	365	406	1 669	3 744
Central Asian CIS[f]	..	..	129	374	861	1 289	1 400	1 697	1 488	1 747	1 510	3 102	2 796	2 356
Caucasian and central Asian CIS[f]	..	..	129	435	899	1 651	2 085	3 116	2 997	2 461	1 875	3 508	4 464	6 099
Low-income CIS[f]	..	..	35	142	173	520	863	1 766	1 859	939	598	649	1 891	3 990

Source: National balance of payments statistics; IMF, *Balance of Payments Statistics* (Washington, D.C.) and IMF country studies; UNECE secretariat estimates.

[a] Inflows into the reporting country.

[b] Net of residents' investments abroad. Bulgaria, 1990-1994; The former Yugoslav Republic of Macedonia, 1994-1996; Armenia, 1993-2002; Azerbaijan, 1993-1999; Belarus, 1992-1996; Georgia, 1994-1998; Kazakhstan, 1992-1996; Kyrgyzstan, 1993-1997; Republic of Moldova, 1991-1994; Ukraine, 1992-1993.

[c] Excludes re-invested earnings and inter-company loans 1990-1997.

[d] Excludes re-invested earnings 1990-1994.

[e] Excludes Kosovo from 1999; 2003 data for Serbia only.

[f] Totals include estimates for Turkmenistan and Uzbekistan.

OTHER RECENT ISSUES OF THE ECONOMIC SURVEY OF EUROPE AND OCCASIONAL PAPERS PUBLISHED BY THE UNITED NATIONS ECONOMIC COMMISSION FOR EUROPE

- *Economic Survey of Europe, 2004 No. 2*, Sales No. E.04.II.E.21 (October)

  In addition to an assessment of the economic situation in the ECE region in the summer 2004, this issue contains a paper by Jan Fagerberg, Mark Knell and Martin Srholec on "The competitiveness of nations: economic growth in the ECE region". This paper was presented to the UNECE Spring Seminar in February 2004, which was devoted to Competitiveness and Growth in the ECE Region.

- *Economic Survey of Europe, 2004 No. 1*, Sales No. E.04.II.E.7 (May)

  This issue provides a review of macroeconomic developments in the whole of Europe, the CIS and North America in 2003 and discusses the outlook for 2004. In addition, there are special studies dealing with tax reforms in the EU acceding countries, benefits from product differentiation, and poverty in eastern Europe and the CIS.

- *Economic Survey of Europe, 2003 No. 2*, Sales No. E.03.II.E.27 (December)

  In addition to an assessment of the economic situation in the ECE region in the autumn 2003, this issue contains the two papers presented at the UNECE Spring Seminar of March 2003, which focused on *Sustainable Development in the ECE Region*. Theodore Panayotou analyses the relationship between economic growth and the environment and David Newbery examines sectoral dimensions of sustainable development.

- *Economic Survey of Europe, 2003 No. 1*, Sales No. E.03.II.E.26 (April)

  This issue contains the secretariat's review of recent macroeconomic developments in the ECE region and an assessment of the outlook for 2003. Special studies deal, *inter alia*, with corporate governance in the ECE region; progress in systemic reforms in the CIS; the impact of EU enlargement on non-candidate countries in eastern Europe and the CIS; and international trade of the CIS.

The Occasional Paper series is intended to make available to a wider audience papers on matters of topical interest that have been prepared by the staff of the UNECE secretariat or commissioned by the secretariat from external experts

- Occasional Paper No. 3, *The Process of European Integration and the Future of Europe*, Gunnar Myrdal Lecture 2004, Joseph E. Stiglitz, Sales No. E.05.II.E.5

- Occasional Paper No. 2, *The Accession of Central European Countries to the European Union: The Trade and Investment Effects on Belarus, The Russian Federation and Ukraine*, Elżbieta Kawecka-Wyrzykowska and Dariusz K. Rosati, Sales No. E.03.II.E.54

- Occasional Paper No. 1, *The Role of Institutions in Economic Development*, Gunnar Myrdal Lecture 2003, Douglass C. North, Sales No. E.03.II.E.50

* * * * *

More details about other publications and activities of the United Nations Economic Commission for Europe, which pay special attention to issues concerning the transition economies, can be found at the secretariat's website: http://www.unece.org

* * * * *

To obtain copies of publications contact:

Publications des Nations Unies
Section de Vente et Marketing
Organisation des Nations Unies
CH-1211 Genève 10
Suisse
Tel: (4122) 917 2612 / 917 2606 / 917 2613
Fax: (4122) 917 0027
E-mail: unpubli@unog.ch

United Nations Publications
2 United Nations Plaza
Room DC2-853
New York, NY 10017
USA
Tel: (1212) 963 8302 / (1800) 253 9646
Fax: (1212) 963 3489
E-mail: publications@un.org